# SYRIA-PALESTINE IN THE LATE BRONZE AGE

*Syria-Palestine in the Late Bronze Age* presents an explicitly anthropological perspective on politics and social relationships. An anthropological reading of the textual and epigraphic remains of the time allows us to see how power was constructed and political subordination was practised and expressed. *Syria-Palestine in the Late Bronze Age* identifies a particular political ontology, native to ancient Syro-Palestinian societies, which informs and constitutes their social worlds. This political ontology, based on patronage relationships, provides a way of understanding the political culture and the social dynamics of ancient Levantine peoples. It also illuminates the historical processes taking place in the region, processes based on patrimonial social structures and articulated through patron-client bonds.

**Emanuel Pfoh** is a Researcher at the National Research Council (CONICET) and teaches in the Department of History of the National University of La Plata, Argentina. He is the author of *The Emergence of Israel in Ancient Palestine: Historical and Anthropological Perspectives* (2009) and *The Politics of Israel's Past: The Bible, Archaeology and Nation-Building* (co-edited with K.W. Whitelam, 2013), among other studies.

COPENHAGEN INTERNATIONAL SEMINAR



**Available:**

JAPHETH BEN ALI'S BOOK OF JEREMIAH
*Joshua A. Sabih*

THE EMERGENCE OF ISRAEL IN ANCIENT PALESTINE
*Emanuel Pfoh*

ORIGIN MYTHS AND HOLY PLACES IN THE OLD TESTAMENT
*Lukasz Niesiowski-Spanò*

CHANGING PERSPECTIVES I
*John Van Seters*

ARGONAUTS OF THE DESERT
*Philippe Wajdenbaum*

THE EXPRESSION 'SON OF MAN' AND THE DEVELOPMENT OF CHRISTOLOGY
*Mogens Müller*

BIBLICAL STUDIES AND THE FAILURE OF HISTORY
*Niels Peter Lemche*

BIBLICAL NARRATIVE AND PALESTINE'S HISTORY
*Thomas L. Thompson*

'IS THIS NOT THE CARPENTER?'
*Edited by Thomas L. Thompson and Thomas S. Verenna*

THE BIBLE AND HELLENISM
*Edited by Thomas L. Thompson and Philippe Wajdenbaum*

RETHINKING BIBLICAL SCHOLARSHIP
*Philip R. Davies*

REPRESENTING ZION
*Frederik Poulsen*

BIBLICAL INTERPRETATION BEYOND HISTORICITY
*Edited by Thomas L. Thompson and Ingrid Hjelm*

**Forthcoming:**
HISTORY, ARCHAEOLOGY AND THE BIBLE FORTY YEARS AFTER "HISTORICITY"
*Edited by Ingrid Hjelm and Thomas L. Thompson*

THE JUDAEOKARAITE RECEPTION OF THE HEBREW BIBLE
*Joshua A. Sabih*

# SYRIA-PALESTINE IN THE LATE BRONZE AGE

## An anthropology of politics and power

*Emanuel Pfoh*

Routledge
Taylor & Francis Group
LONDON AND NEW YORK

First published 2016
by Routledge
2 Park Square, Milton Park, Abingdon, Oxon OX14 4RN

and by Routledge
711 Third Avenue, New York, NY 10017

*Routledge is an imprint of the Taylor & Francis Group, an informa business*



*British Library Cataloguing-in-Publication Data*
A catalogue record for this book is available from the British Library

*Library of Congress Cataloging-in-Publication Data*
A catalog record for this book has been requested

ISBN: 978-1-844-65784-1 (hbk)
ISBN: 978-1-315-67881-8 (ebk)

Typeset in Times New Roman
by Swales & Willis Ltd, Exeter, Devon, UK

FSC www.fsc.org MIX Paper from responsible sources FSC® C013604

Printed and bound by CPI Group (UK) Ltd, Croydon, CR0 4YY

PARA EVA

# CONTENTS

*List of illustrations* x
*Acknowledgements* xi
*List of abbreviations* xiii

Introduction 1

**PART I**
**Syria-Palestine during the Late Bronze Age** **11**

1 An overview of political history (*c.* 1550–1150 BCE) 13
2 'International' diplomacy during the Late Bronze Age 30
3 Alliances and exchanges 63

**PART II**
**Political systems in Syria-Palestine** **89**

4 Socio-politics of Syria-Palestine (I): analytical concepts 91
5 Socio-politics of Syria-Palestine (II): interpretative models 108

**PART III**
**Patrons and clients in the Levant** **121**

6 Patronage relationships: a theoretical overview 123
7 Patrimonialism in the Late Bronze Age 138
8 Political relations in Late Bronze Age Syria-Palestine 150

*Conclusions* 168
*Bibliography* 172
*Index of textual references* 212
*Index of authors* 218
*Index of subjects* 226

# ILLUSTRATIONS


| | | |
|---|---|---|
| Map 1 | Egyptian administrative rule over Syria-Palestine during the Amarna period | 26 |
| Figure 5.1 | The internal social structure of Ugarit | 117 |
| Figure 8.1 | The divine and human hierarchy according to the texts from Ugarit | 164 |

# ACKNOWLEDGEMENTS

This study is based on a PhD dissertation in History, written in Spanish and defended in 2011 at the University of Buenos Aires. My former PhD advisor, Marcelo Campagno, is to be thanked for his criticism and orientation while I was working on the dissertation and also for his advice during my years as a PhD student.

To Ingrid Hjelm, general editor of the Copenhagen International Seminar, I offer my thanks for her patience and support during the intermittent process of converting a PhD thesis into a book manuscript and also for her comments and suggestions. I also acknowledge here the support and advice of my 'Copenhagen godfathers' Thomas L. Thompson and Niels Peter Lemche over the years, and Jim West's revision of the language of the manuscript. I must also thank Tristan Palmer from Acumen Publishing, where this project started, for his patience and kindness, as well as the staff at Routledge, especially Lizzi Thomasson, and my copy-editor, Jeanne Brady. I am also grateful to Eisenbrauns and Harrassowitz for letting me adapt and reproduce a chart and a map from two of their books.

Any monographic composition of a considerable size accumulates many personal and academic debts throughout the years. Several scholars (stripped here of their academic titles and in alphabetical order) must be mentioned: Giorgio Buccellati, Francisco Céntola, Birgit Christiansen, Romina Della Casa, Elena Devecchi, Roxana Flammini, Julián Gallego, Augusto Gayubas, Graciela Gestoso Singer, Anne Katrine Gudme, Douglas A. Knight, Gunnar Lehmann, Mario Liverani, Alejandro Mizzoni, Luciano Monti, Jana Mynářová, Adelheid Otto, Diego Paiaro, Luca Peyronel, Gisèle Seimandi and Nicolas Wyatt. They all suggested many useful bibliographic sources, or provided advice or questions to my understanding of the topics discussed, for which I am very grateful. A special mention goes to Philippe Guillaume who provided me *literally* with dozens of articles in a most patient manner. Needless to say, I am solely responsible for the arguments (and limitations, possible omissions and/or errors) presented in the following pages.

The bibliographic research for this study was completed while beginning work on a different project, during a three-month research stay at the University of Tübingen, funded by the Faculty of Humanities, National University of La Plata, and the National Research Council (CONICET). To my host, Professor Herbert Niehr, I remain grateful for his hospitality and assistance.

Finally, I must acknowledge the greatest debt of gratitude to my wife Eva for putting up with my moods and fancies while producing the manuscript, but especially for being always such a beautiful person. The book is rightly dedicated to her, with love.

### *Technical note on translations*

All translations into English are mine, unless otherwise indicated. When quoting epigraphic-textual sources, the reproduction of transliterated texts in ancient languages will be done only when a direct interpretation of the text in its original language is of relevance for the argumentation.

For the Amarna letters, I have mainly followed the translation in Moran's *The Amarna Letters* but reference to Knudtzon's *Die el-Amarna Tafeln*, Liverani's *Le lettere di el-Amarna*, and Rainey's *The El-Amarna Correspondence* is also given in each quote. When Liverani's translation is preferred over Moran's, it is duly noted and rendered in English.

# ABBREVIATIONS

| | |
|---|---|
| ABRL | Anchor Bible Reference Library |
| *AHw* | W. von Soden (ed.), *Akkadisches Handwörterbuch*, 3 vols. Wiesbaden: Harrassowitz, 1959–81 |
| Akk. | Akkadian |
| AnBib | Analecta Biblica |
| *ANET*[3] | J.B. Pritchard (ed.), *Ancient Near Eastern Texts Relating to the Old Testament*. Princeton, NJ: Princeton University Pres, 3rd edn 1969 |
| AOAT | Alter Orient und Altes Testament |
| AOS | American Oriental Series |
| Ar. | Arabic |
| *ARE* | J.H. Breasted (ed. and trans.), *Ancient Records of Egypt: Historical Documents from Earliest Times to the Persian Conquest,* 5 vols. Chicago, IL: Chicago University Press, 1906 |
| *ARM* | A. Parrot and G. Dossin (dir.), *Archives Royales de Mari*. Paris: Imprimerie Nationale, 1950– |
| *ARMT* | *Archives Royales de Mari, Textes* |
| *AT* | Alalakh Tablet |
| AULAOS | Aula Orientalis Supplementa |
| *AuOr* | *Aula Orientalis* |
| *BA* | *The Biblical Archaeologist* |
| *BASOR* | *Bulletin of the American Schools of Oriental Research* |
| BISNELC | Bar-Ilan Studies in Near Eastern Languages and Culture |
| *BN* | *Biblische Notizen* |
| BTAVO | Beihefte zum Tübingen Atlas des Vorderer Orients |
| BZAW | Beihefte zur Zeitschrift für die Alttestamentliche Wissenschaft |
| *CA* | *Current Anthropology* |
| *CAD* | *The Assyrian Dictionary of the Oriental Institute of the University of Chicago*. Chicago, IL: Chicago University Press, 21 vols, 1956–2010. |
| *CAH*[3] | I.E.S. Edwards et al. (eds), *The Cambridge Ancient History*. Cambridge: Cambridge University Press, 3rd edn 1975 |
| *CBQ* | *Catholic Biblical Quarterly* |

| | |
|---|---|
| CHANE | Culture and History of the Ancient Near East |
| CIS | Copenhagen International Seminar |
| CMAO | Contributi e Materiali di Archeologia Orientale |
| *CSSH* | *Comparative Studies in Society and History* |
| *CTH* | E. Laroche, *Catalogue des texts hittites*. Paris: Klincksieck, 1971 |
| *DdA* | *Dialoghi di Archeologia* |
| EA | El Amarna letter |
| Eg. | Egyptian |
| ESHM | European Seminar in Historical Methodology |
| FBE | Forum for Bibelsk Eksegese |
| *GM* | *Göttinger Miszellen* |
| HBM | Hebrew Bible Monographs |
| HdO | Handbuch der Orientalistik |
| Hit. | Hittite |
| HSM | Harvard Semitic Monographs |
| HSS | Harvard Semitic Studies |
| *IEJ* | *Israel Exploration Journal* |
| *JAOS* | *Journal of the American Oriental Society* |
| *JARCE* | *Journal of the American Research Center in Egypt* |
| *JEA* | *Journal of Egyptian Archaeology* |
| *JESHO* | *Journal of the Economic and Social History of the Orient* |
| *JNES* | *Journal of Near Eastern Studies* |
| *JSOT* | *Journal for the Study of the Old Testament* |
| JSOTSup | *Journal for the Study of the Old Testament Supplement Series* |
| *JSSEA* | *Journal of the Society for the Study of Egyptian Antiquities* |
| *KBo* | *Keilschrifttexte aus Boghazköi*, Leipzig: J.C. Hinrichs, 1916–23; Berlin, 1954– |
| K*RI* | K.A. Kitchen, *Ramesside Inscriptions, I–VIII*. Oxford: Blackwell, 1969–90 |
| *KS* | A. Alt, *Kleine Schriften zur Geschichte des Volkes Israel*, 3 vols. München: C.H. Beck, 1953–59 |
| *KTU* | M. Dietrich, O. Loretz and J. Sanmartín. *The Cuneiform Alphabetic Texts from Ugarit, Ras Ibn Hani and Other Places* (ALASP, 8). Münster: Ugarit-Verlag, 2nd edn 1995 |
| *KUB* | *Keilschrifturkunde aus Boghazköi*. Berlin: Staatliche Museen, 1921– |
| LAPO | Littératures Anciennes du Proche-Orient |
| LHB/OTS | Library of Old Testament/Hebrew Bible Studies |
| MANE | Monographs on the Ancient Near East |
| NRSV | New Revised Standard Version of the Bible |
| *OA* | *Oriens Antiquus* |
| OAC | Orientis Antiqvi Collectio |
| OBO | Orbis Biblicus et Orientalis |
| *OJA* | *Oxford Journal of Archaeology* |
| OLA | Orientalia Lovaniensia Analecta |

| | |
|---|---|
| *Or* | *Orientalia* |
| *OxEncANE* | E.M. Meyers (ed.), *The Oxford Encyclopedia of Archaeology in the Ancient Near East*, 5 vols. New York and Oxford: Oxford University Press, 1997 |
| PEFSCEA | Programa de Estudios sobre las Formas de Sociedad y las Configuraciones Estatales de la Antigüedad |
| *PEQ* | *Palestine Exploration Quarterly* |
| PIOL | Publications de l'Institut Orientaliste de Louvain |
| *PRU* | J. Nougayrol and C. Virolleaud, *Le palais royal d'Ugarit*, vols II–VI (Mission de Ras Shamra, Tomes VI–VII, IX–XIII), Paris: Imprimerie Nationale, 1955–70 |
| *RA* | *Revue d'assyriologie et archéologie orientale* |
| *RIHAO* | *Revista del Instituto de Historia Antigua Oriental* |
| RS | Text from Ras Šamra/Ugarit |
| SAHL | Studies in the Archaeology and History of the Levant |
| *SAK* | Studien zur Altägyptischen Kultur |
| SAOC | Studies in Ancient Oriental Civilization |
| *SEL* | *Studi epigrafici e linguistici sul Vicino Oriente Antico* |
| SHANE | Studies in the History of the Ancient Near East |
| *SMEA* | *Studi micenei ed egeo-anatolici* |
| Sum. | Sumerian |
| SWBAS | Social World of Biblical Antiquity Series |
| *TA* | *Tel Aviv* |
| TVOA | Testi del Vicino Oriente antico |
| *Ug* | *Ugaritica*, vols V–VI. Paris: Imprimerie Nationale, 1968–69 |
| Ug. | Ugaritic |
| *Urk.* | *Urkunden der 18. Dinastie: Übersetzungen zu den Heften 1–4* (ed. K. Sethe), Leipzig: J.C. Hinrichs; *Urkunden der 18. Dinastie: Übersetzungen zu den Heften 5–16* (ed. A. Burkhardt), Berlin: Akademie-Verlag; *Urkunden der 18. Dinastie: Übersetzungen zu den Heften 17–22* (ed. W. Helck), Berlin: Akademie-Verlag, 1961 |
| *VO* | *Vicino Oriente* |
| *VT* | *Vetus Testamentum* |
| VTSup | Supplements to Vetus Testamentum |
| WAWSBL | Writings from the Ancient World – Society of Biblical Literature |
| *ZABR* | *Zeitschrift für Altorientalische und Biblische Rechtsgeschichte* |
| *ZAW* | *Zeitschrift für die Alttestamentliche Wissenschaft* |
| *ZDPV* | *Zeitschrift des Deutschen Palästina-Vereins* |

# INTRODUCTION

Traditional ancient Near Eastern and Egyptological historiography conceive of the region of Syria-Palestine[1] during the so-called Amarna period (*c.* 1353–20 BCE), at the peak of the Late Bronze Age (*c.* 1550–1150), as an 'abnormal' and critical phase in the socio-political history of Egyptian rule in Western Asia. The reasons for understanding this period as critical relate to the internal political crisis in Egypt, after Pharaoh Aḫenaten's religious 'revolution'. Aiming at replacing the cult of the god Amun with the supreme worship of the solar disc (Aten), Aḫenaten would have neglected the maintenance of the West Asiatic territories. According to this view, Egypt's weakness over Syria-Palestine was reflected in the Amarnian correspondence from the petty kings of the region and was related, as well, to the growing menace from the Hittite empire, slowly advancing into Syria after having set the kingdom of Mittani aside from the political game in the region of the Levant.[2]

This historical reconstruction depended heavily on a direct interpretation of the dozens of letters written in the Levant addressing the Egyptian Pharaohs. These letters were discovered at Tell el-Amarna in Egypt in 1887, at a location that provided the name for this particular period of Syro-Palestinian history (see further in Chapter 1). Already in 1898, W.M. Flinders Petrie, in his *Syria and Egypt from the Tell el Amarna Letters*, would observe:

> the more usual case seems to have been that the Egyptians had lost interest in Syria, lost the power of sparing troops to manage the country and to keep order, and lost heart in foreign matters since they were absorbed in the home politics of religious revolutions . . . all the petty chiefs and sheks [*sic*; sheikhs] whose ancestors had been cutting each other's throats for generations, and who, doubtless, had venerable blood-feuds unavenged, soon began to attack one another when not vigorously kept in hand by Egypt. Also any strong and capable man like Abdashirta and his son Aziru, soon found that he could safely bully his neighbours, and gradually acquire power over them . . . Hence the weakening of Egypt threw Syria into a state of internal discord unrepressed. The immediate effect of this was that various parties, without caring particularly about being for or against the Egyptians, began to fight with one another. Each

> tried to draw the power of Egypt to his own side by representing that he was loyally acting in the interest of his suzerain; and the weaker party was sure to place his trust most fully upon Egypt. It was only when a man had played his own hand for a long time, had strengthened himself by absorbing much of his neighbour's goods and lands, and had safely neglected the orders of the Egyptians on several occasions – it was only then that he cared to throw off the mask and act openly in his own interest, and allow himself to be classed as an enemy. Hence we often find very different views of people, and might put them as being on the Egyptian side according to their own account long after they were on the enemies' side according to other accounts. (Petrie 1898: 9–10)[3]

Almost a century later, in the third edition of the *Cambridge Ancient History* from 1975, we find that the socio-political picture had not changed that much. In the chapter on the Amarna letters by W.F. Albright, we read as well about the generalised anarchy and political competition between petty rulers:

> The native chieftains, in spite of their excessive grovelling before Pharaoh, which sometimes occupies over half their letters, were patricians, proud of their ancestry . . . The Canaanite chieftains are also spoken of more than once as 'kings' in the plural. The later use of the same expression in the Book of Joshua to designate local princes was, therefore, quite normal. The extent of the territory over which these chieftains held sway varied greatly . . . Though details are generally lacking, there seems to be no doubt that certain princes exercised acknowledged feudal rights over the weaker chieftains . . . The Amarna letters exhibit very frequently the unhappy results of this organization. The princes were continually at war with one another; each accused his neighbour of being a traitor to the crown. (Albright 1975: 104)

However, by the late 1960s scholars had already started to re-examine the character of the Egyptian rule over the southern Levant. It was then clear that, 'apart from the loss of Amurru and Kadesh, Egypt did *not* give up any part of its empire during the Amarna period', and that Egypt was still a powerful state in control of its Levantine subjects (Redford 1992: 179; emphasis original).[4] But, perhaps most relevant, the nature of Syro-Palestinian local politics has been revisited and reinterpreted. What used to be considered an anarchistic and chaotic situation should now be seen under new light. In fact, the glimpse we obtain from the Amarna letters of a short period of time (some twenty years) regarding the political configuration and the political relations between the rulers and the ruled, seems to reflect normality in socio-political terms during all of the Late Bronze Age. And this is precisely due to the particularity of Syro-Palestinian sociopolitics, as we will see in the following chapters, which included skirmishes and competition between the petty rulers and also the introduction in the local scene of disruptive elements of the 'order', that is, the native rules of political engagement: the *ḫabiru*, referred to many times in the Amarna letters and in other Near Eastern sources of the second millennium BCE (Bottéro 1954; Greenberg 1955; Liverani 1965, 1979a; Rowton 1965; 1976; 1977; Loretz 1984; Fleming 2012). It can also be argued, as W. Murnane indicates, that 'the Egyptians tolerated a good deal of independent action (including warfare and subversion) among their vassals in Asia, always providing that the overlord's interests suffered no damage in consequence' (Murnane 2000: 104).[5]

The basic structure of domination over Syria-Palestine in this period (see further in Chapter 1) was the following: Egypt's Asiatic subjects – namely, the leaders of the Levantine petty kingdoms, referred to in Akkadian as *ḫazannu*, 'mayor' or 'commissar', a term equivalent to the *ḥ3tyʿ* of Egypt's local administration[6] – would deal with their domestic affairs locally, under the supervision of an Egyptian commissioner (Akk. *rābiṣu*) posted in the region. Callings to the distant Pharaoh by these petty kings or princes for assistance or help seem to illustrate better the political ideology of the region than a concrete situation of crisis.[7] In effect, Egypt would maintain tight control of its possessions in the southern Levant by securing an effective presence in the region as well as an updated intelligence of the geopolitical situation, no less through local kinglets under Egyptian subordination (Cohen 2000).

Hittite rule over the northern Levant (Syria and south-west Anatolia) differed in structure and political dynamics from Egyptian rule. We have at our disposal a considerable amount of textual evidence about Hittite rule over this region during this period, evidence that suffices to construct a clear picture of the socio-political features of that rule, especially in relation to the 'vassal' polities, and the nature of the exerted political practices (Beckman 1996; Hoffner 2009). The identification of these 'vassal' polities has led some scholars to postulate the existence of some kind of 'Hittite feudalism' in ancient Anatolia, both within the kingdom and towards the exterior.[8] It should be noted from the very start, however, that the term 'vassalage' possesses an implied meaning for some of its concrete attested features, which rather belong to the political and juridical realm of the Middle Ages in Western Europe than to the pre-Hellenistic Near Eastern world. As noted by G. Beckman, a structured political order through an authority scheme, in which each individual at a particular political level is in the service of his lord, who at the same time swears loyalty to an even greater lord, such as the one regulating the inner socio-political behaviour of the medieval kingdoms, 'might be seen only in the organization of the empire, where each vassal swore an oath to the Great King, while his own population remained his "personal" servants, with no direct ties to the overlord' in Ḫattuša, the capital of the empire.[9] This means that vassal ties did not characterise the internal organisation of the kingdom of Ḫatti but they regulated instead a foreign domain to Hittite society, which cannot be rendered as 'feudal'. The use of a terminology such as 'vassalage' and 'feudalism' in a Near Eastern context, therefore, may be inappropriate in order to grasp the socio-political structure that linked Ḫatti to foreign subjects. This study, precisely, aims to offer a different analytical view on the dynamics of the socio-political relations in the Levant, especially through the interpretation of some of the 'diplomatic' treaties produced during the Late Bronze Age. One may ask, why did the Hittites impose loyalty oaths and treaties on their subjects when they could have exerted direct rule over Anatolian and Syrian territories without such symbolic brokerage? Instead of resorting to medieval analogies and the difficulty of avoiding connotations, this study is intended to offer some interpretive clues on ancient historical questions and situations from the field of political anthropology.

The Late Bronze Age, and in particular the Amarna period, is not an isolated phase in the history of the region, a special moment of crisis and upheaval due to Egypt's lack of interest or intervention, but instead an age that should be understood within greater temporal and spatial frames, concerning socio-political practices.[10] Inter-regional relations between the great powers of the ancient Near East during the second half of the second millennium BCE, as they appear in the epigraphic record, allow for a heuristic and analytical distinction on two levels. First, the relations between Great Kings (sing. *šarru rabû*, in the Akkadian terminology directed to the Egyptian court[11]), namely rulers of similar status and prestige, engaging in 'friendship', 'brotherhood' and reciprocity relations. Such mutual relations may reflect concrete events and actions, but their relevance lies in the ideological terms through which these relations are carried out. The second level is the relations between a Great King and a Small King (*šarru ṣihru*), as exemplified in the relation between the Pharaoh and the subjects from Palestine, or between the Hittite king and his 'vassals' in northern Syria. The status and prestige inequality it is notably evident and the mutual relation follows accordingly. Any kind of assistance or reciprocity between the parties was determined, in greater or lesser degree, by the will of the great king to whom the small king must remain loyal and obedient, under the penalty of retaliation (Liverani 1967; 2001).

From the history of research of ancient Levantine societies, it is evident that the aforementioned socio-political dynamic in so-called 'international' relations during the Late Bronze Age has not been properly analysed in regard to the societal structure of local communities, such as those attested in the ethnohistorical and ethnographic record of this section of the Eastern Mediterranean basin. In other words, the contribution of social anthropology and ethnography to the historical study of the political practices and structures referred to above has been neglected to a certain extent, or engaged only secondarily. It is, however, true that since the mid-1960s the Assyriologist Mario Liverani has made use of anthropological insights by noting in a number of studies the connotations of the ideological clash in the epistolary communication between Egypt and its Asiatic subjects (Liverani 1967; 1979a; 1979b; 1983a). Yet, after these contributions, Assyriology as a discipline has been slow to incorporate concepts and insights drawn from the social sciences in general.[12] It is therefore pertinent to address and pay attention to studies relating to 'traditional' societies from the Eastern Mediterranean and the Middle East in order to widen our analytical scope for interpreting ancient politics.

Questions on the nature of traditional socio-political practices in the Eastern Mediterranean have been addressed many times by historians and anthropologists (see now Horden and Purcell 2000). In particular, and concerning the present discussion, there exists a vast amount of specialised literature, from social histories of the Mediterranean to ethnographic reports of the Middle East, dealing with the relations between kinship and non-kinship realms of politics, namely 'tribe and state', and the by-products of such articulation through history.[13] These erudite studies, however, have relegated in some way, in their bipolar interpretation, the incidence of a third factor, arising from the articulation between tribal and state politics, but also affecting them: patron–client relations (an exception is Lemche 1985: 172, 184).

Patron–client relations – also known as patronage, or clientelism – play an important role in the socio-political life of traditional societies of the Eastern Mediterranean and the Middle East. However, it must be noted that the economic and political developments since the First World War in the region have restricted the practice of patronage mostly to rural and semi-rural environments and small communities. This situation has led some scholars (i.e. Gellner 1977), to propose the origins of patron–client relations in circumstances in which formal institutions such as the state are weak or peripheral, which ignores the long history and the persistence of patronage and sees it as a by-product of a malfunction of modern state structures.

Especially between the 1950s and the 1970s, a number of ethnographic fieldwork studies dealing with patronage and other features, such as honour and shame, vengeance, etc., considered as culturally bound in the region, were carried out in the Mediterranean basin and the Middle East (cf. Pitt-Rivers 1954; 1977; Peristiany 1965; 1968; 1976; Gellner and Waterbury 1977; Boissevain 1979; Davis 1983; Peristiany and Pitt-Rivers 1992; Roque 2000; 2005; Cassar 2004; Albera, Blok and Bromberger 2001; Albera and Tozy 2006a). However, the study of contemporary Mediterranean patronage as a means to investigate the socio-politics of ancient Near Eastern societies was simply non-existent until some twenty to thirty years ago. It is also important to pay attention to other foundational works of social anthropology, such as M. Mauss's essay on the gift and B. Malinowski's study on goods exchanges in Melanesia as pertinent to address the political relationships established between the Late Bronze Age's powers, especially in its economic level (Mauss 1990 [1950]; Malinowski 1922).

After the Second World War, a certain scholarly treatment of Mediterranean societies was based in a loosely argued comparative division between 'traditional, conservative and corporative societies' belonging to the Mediterranean coast and the Middle East, and 'modern, bureaucratic and individualist societies', belonging to Northern Europe. Also, this view considered Mediterranean societies as mostly homogeneous and basically unaffected by historical change (the anthropologist's savage in Europe's backyard; cf. Davis 1977; Marques 1999; Pitt-Rivers 2000; Harris 2005; Roque 2005: 11–26; Albera and Tozy 2006b).[14] Such analytical prejudices, of course, must be challenged. It is not casual that most of the classical

Mediterranean ethnographies were produced in small rural towns or communities, generalising some ethnographic conclusions to the rest of the Mediterranean and the Middle East and marking strong, almost opposite distinctions between rural village and urban town, or in political terms, between family/tribe and state, or community and society – F. Tönnies's classical distinction between *Gemeinschaft* and *Gesellschaft* (Tönnies 1887) or É. Durkheim's *solidarité mécanique* and *solidarité organique* respectively (Durkheim 1893). This analytical distinction is hardly found operating in Mediterranean and Middle Eastern societies as ethnographic reality shows, in general, a blurring of the lines between kinship, patronage and state politics (see, for instance, Salzman 1978; also Lemche 1985: 84–244). Further, the modernist view of Mediterranean societies sees patronage relations as backward and corrupting and essentially anti-modern and anti-legal, in regard to modern political systems, which often ill-conditions a critical use of the concept of patron–client relations as an interpretative tool for analysing ancient socio-politics.

Taking into account the historical and ethnographic record, we advance the working hypothesis, which this study will attempt to show, that the societies of the ancient Levant seem to have been internally organised, at the smallest level, through kinship bonds, which also constituted the basis for ideological, economic and political practices *outside* the local community, establishing a basic social differentiation between kin and not-kin. Such distinction affected the level of reciprocity exerted among people – from 'generalised reciprocity' for kinsmen to 'negative reciprocity' for foreigners (Gouldner 1960; Sahlins 1972: 185–230). Thus, when we detect a language proper of kinship relations in the Late Bronze Age's diplomatic exchanges, we might also be finding a particular expression of politics and power display at work in ancient Syria-Palestine, built on the principles of kinship (and patronage), even when this terminology may be deemed 'fictitious' or 'ideological'.

It may also be suggested that aspects of such socio-political practices, based on the inner dynamics of a community expressed to the outside, can be found clearly in the textual and epigraphic records of the Levant during the Late Bronze Age. The Amarna correspondence is especially relevant as it provides clues regarding instances of political reciprocity – the expectation of it and the consequences of its lack from the point of view of local Levantine kinglets. This study attempts to explain and understand (in an ethnographic sense) the nature of these socio-political relations, from the Levantine perspective (including here the Hittite king and the petty Syrian kings) but also from the Egyptian perspective.

Instead of building an interpretation from more traditional historiographic currents in Assyriology and Near Eastern studies – based essentially on philological and archaeological insights – the perspective favoured here is a historical-anthropological one. History and anthropology here are seen not only as complementary in their results, but fundamentally as epistemologically relevant in order to understand historical structures and processes and the cultural otherness of ancient societies. This was already noted by anthropologists of different traditions, such as the British E.E. Evans-Pritchard (1950; 1961) and the French C. Lévi-Strauss (1963: 24), the latter observing:

> It would be inaccurate, therefore, to say that on the road toward the understanding of man, which goes from the study of conscious content to that of unconscious forms, the historian and the anthropologist travel in opposite directions. On the contrary, they both go the same way. The fact that their journey together appears to each of them in a different light – to the historian, transition from the explicit to the implicit; to the anthropologist, transition from the particular to the universal – does not in the least alter the identical character of their fundamental approach. They have undertaken the same journey on the same road in the same direction; only their orientation is different. The anthropologist goes forward, seeking to attain, through the conscious, of which he is always aware, more and more of the unconscious; whereas the historian advances, so to speak, backward, keeping his eyes fixed on concrete and specific activities from which he withdraws only to consider them from a more complete and richer perspective. A true two-faced Janus, it is the solidarity of the two disciplines that makes it possible to keep the whole road in sight.

We do not get to know about ancient societies unless we accept the fact that we must go beyond what we find in the textual sources. Language translation is, of course, necessary and even essential to deal with past societies; but *culture translation* is also paramount. Further, as F.G. Bailey (1972: 22) wrote for contemporary ethnographic situations:

> Certainly we fail at the outset if we do not realize that, at some levels, the political actors of the Middle East are speaking, literally and metaphorically, languages that differ from our own. To a degree these languages and these political cultures are unique. But we only understand them to the extent that we generalize by showing that they are variations upon themes found in other cultures.

Ancient languages must be culturally decoded. And given that we are dealing with societies that do not exist anymore, the ethnographic record may offer some interpretive clues to analyse the textual data from ancient sources – especially when it comes to textual information about socio-political practices and relationships.

We may now offer some definitions about what is considered *political* in this study. Having in mind the explicitly anthropological outlook for interpretation, it is necessary to define and characterise each analytical concept used for explaining a particular social practice, detected in a non-Western and non-modern cultural context. *Politics* in this sense does not assume the necessary existence of formal institutions or impersonal structures of political relations. It does not necessarily depend either on legal or juridical statements comprising the whole of society.

*Politics* in this study refers to concrete social relationships, between two individuals or collectively, expressing a flow of prestige, authority and/or power, which are socially constructed values affecting particular realities and peoples and are also culturally and symbolically encoded. *Politics* relates therefore not only to particular relations within a state realm, or state interventions within a community, or relations between two or more states; *politics* are found also among kinship articulations, tribal realms and patron–client relations. The related term *socio-politics* refers here in a strict sense to political practices dependent on a particular social organisation or structure (which at the same time is reproduced by such political practice). As to *polity*, it is used in this study regarding any particular cohesive socio-political organisation, i.e. a kingdom, a chiefdom, a tribe, a state, an empire, etc., without implying any particular political evolutionary stage. It can also be said that *polity* 'denotes the political infrastructure of a social group or system: both the social group as such, in its political aspect, and also the authority structure within that group' (Rowton 1973a: 247 n. 1).[15]

* * *

Part I of the present work has an essentially descriptive and informative character, placing in historical context the discussion of the politics during the Late Bronze Age and in particular the Amarna period in Syria-Palestine. Textual and epigraphic sources are presented and discussed, especially the letters found in Tell el-Amarna (Egypt) and other relevant textual *corpora*. In this part, the relation of alliances between two polities is analysed having in mind the old but still heuristically valuable assertion, more theoretical than empirical, of C. Lévi-Strauss (1963: 83) regarding the nature of exchanges in pre-capitalist societies, who proposed:

> interpreting society as a whole in terms of a theory of communication. This endeavor is possible on three levels, since the rules of kinship and marriage serve to insure the circulation of women between groups, just as economic rules serve to insure the circulation of goods and services, and linguistic rules the circulation of messages. These three forms of communication are also forms of exchange which are obviously interrelated (because marriage relations are associated with economic prestations, and language comes into play at all levels).

According to this notable French anthropologist, what is exchanged can be conceptualised in three spheres: the exchange of goods; the exchange of women, namely the practice of marriage, and the exchange of messages, in our particular historical case, the exchange messengers and specialists, as bearers of a *symbolic capital* (Bourdieu 1992a: 112–21) transmitted between two or more communities. This understanding allows for attempting an economic anthropology of exchanges during the Late Bronze Age.

Part II offers a general theoretical characterisation regarding the structural organisation of ancient Near Eastern societies and their socio-political dynamics, analysing also the concepts and models traditional Near Eastern historiography has employed to give its account. In particular, notions of 'state/state society' and 'city-state' usually used to explain the material (i.e. archaeological) evidence from Syria-Palestine express a particular way of describing the internal social organisation of local communities. Such notions can be challenged and criticised in order to better interpret archaeological and textual remains through an anthropologically informed perspective. The same strategy applies to dealing with the model of feudalism and the concept of Asiatic Mode of Production, which impose a certain sociological image in the historical construction of Levantine societies that might go beyond what the extant evidence supports. This criticism is carried out having in mind a general *historical anthropological* perspective, which allows not only for creating a sound historical narrative of the past but also for recognizing the native worldviews expressed in the textual sources as key elements in understanding ancient politics.

Part III is essentially analytical and it discusses comprehensively the basic settings of patron–client relations in the Mediterranean and the Middle East as a key practice articulating a considerable portion of ancient Syro-Palestinian politics. Relevant in this regard is also the concept of *patrimonial society*, as proposed by J.D. Schloen (2001). Schloen applies this concept especially for the kingdom of Ugarit, and if we also use the concept of patronage in this connection, we may then reach a sound interpretation of textual evidence referring to political conceptions and practice, notions of alliance, friendship and subordination, and also the religious imagination of the Late Bronze Age Levant. We may also achieve a total social configuration[16] of the Late Bronze Age socities, expressed through the aforementioned concepts and reflecting what may be called a *native ontology*, proper of Levantine societies and anchored in the socio-political relation between a patron and a client.

## Notes

1 'Syria-Palestine' refers henceforth to the region occupied by the modern states of Syria, Israel, Lebanon and Palestine; together with the southern part of Turkey, Cyprus and Jordan, they all constitute what is usually called the 'Levant' and also 'Eastern Mediterranean'. Further, the term and concept 'Middle East' possesses its obvious Western bias (cf. Scheffler 2003); however, it is used in this study as a synonym of Southwest Asia.

2 Cf. Wilson 1951: Chapters 9–10; Abdul-Kader 1959: 137; Aldred 1975: 52; also Helck 1962: 174–80. On Aḫenaten's reign and his 'revolution', see the now-dated account in Wilson 1951: 206–35; and especially the more recent treatment in Redford 1984; Aldred 1988; Vandersleyen 1995: 461–5; van Dijk 2003.

3 Such an anarchistic depiction survived as late as the 1980s: see Chaney 1983: 61–5, 74–85; and compare, for instance, with Ahlström 1993: 240–51.

4 Even more, Liverani (1998: 32) indicates that 'the picture reflected on the letters is not one of collapse, not even one of progressive deterioration [of the situation], but rather

one of a stable equilibrium in the long term, notwithstanding some little occasional disruptions, variably warned and variably reabsorbed.' See further Campbell 1960; Helck 1962; Schulman 1964; Liverani 1967; Several 1972; Weinstein 1981; Gestoso 1992: 38–63; Gestoso Singer 2007: 66–83; Redford 1992: 192–213; Ahlström 1993: 217–81, esp. 239–77; Murnane 2000.

5 See also James 2000. On the Egyptian interest in the southern Levant, see Aḥituv 1978; Na'aman 1981, 1988. In general, on the Egyptian military presence in the region, see Hasel 1998.

6 Cf. Faulkner 1962: 162: 'local prince, nomarch, mayor'; Hannig 2006: 1596: 'Graf, Reichsgraf, Gaufürst'.

7 On the social structure in Syria-Palestine under Egyptian rule, see in general Helck 1962: 515–35; and Redford 1992: 193–213. Further on this, see Parts I and III of this study.

8 Cf., for instance, Korošec 1931; Goetze 1974: 95–109; Archi 1977. The question of 'vassalage' in the Levant will be treated in more detail in Chapter 5.

9 Beckman 1995: 541–2. Cf. also Alt 1959a: 99–102; for a synthesis on the organisation of the Hittite *Grossreich*, see Imparati 1999; Bryce 2005: 121–325; Starke 2005–6. For a description of the military organisation and also legal and social institutions in Ḫatti, see Beal 1995 and Hoffner 1995 respectively.

10 This hypothesis will be demonstrated especially in Part III.

11 See Chapters 1 and 2 for a thorough analysis of this terminology.

12 An exception would be the so-called 'Rome school' of scholars *autour de* Liverani (C. Zaccagnini, F.M. Fales, etc.).

13 Cf., among others, Lemche 1985: 164–201, who has treated the question very critically, especially when applying general, abstract socio-anthropological models for dealing with ancient Israelite (and Near Eastern) society. See also further studies by Khoury and Kostiner 1990a; Khazanov 1992: 228–302; Bonte, Conte and Dresch 2001; Jabar and Dawod 2003; Dawod 2004; van der Steen 2013.

14 Of course, this 'mediterraneanist' view can be scrutinised by the same criticism Edward Said offered to 'orientalist' visions of the Orient by modern Europe; cf. Said 1978.

15 Cf. in general the discussions in Smith 1968; Cohen 1969; Balandier 1972; Julliard 1974; Clastres 1989 [1974]; Gledhill 2000. For the ancient Near East, see the treatments in Schemeil 1999 and Buccellati 2013, which are unfortunately not as informed by political anthropology – especially the latter volume – as one would wish.

16 The reference here is to the terminology used by M. Mauss when addressing what he calls 'total social phenomena': 'In these "total" social phenomena, as we propose calling them, all kinds of institutions are given expression at one and the same time – religious, juridical, and moral, which relate to both politics and the family; likewise economic ones, which suppose special forms of production and consumption, or rather, of performing total services and of distribution. This is not to take into account the aesthetic phenomena to which these facts lead, and the contours of the phenomena that these institutions manifest' (1990 [1950]: 3–4); also Lévi-Strauss: 'The total social fact presents itself then with a tri-dimensional character. The proper sociological dimension with its multiple synchronic aspects, the historical dimension, or diachronic, and lastly the psycho-biological dimension coincide' (1950: xxv). See also Gofman 1998. For a related approach in ancient Near Eastern studies, see the marvellous anthology edited by Moscati 1976a.

# Part I

# SYRIA-PALESTINE DURING THE LATE BRONZE AGE

# 1

# AN OVERVIEW OF POLITICAL HISTORY (*c.* 1550–1150 BCE)

During the whole period of the Late Bronze Age, the historical processes in the region of Syria-Palestine were inextricably related to – and often caused by – the intervention of foreign powers, which established a deep interconnection between commercial, political and ideological factors as well. Such interconnection represented the general background for the attested socio-political relations, especially documented in the Amarna correspondence during the second half of the fourteenth century BCE (see Liverani 1983b). This particular period and the nature of its socio-political relations are not unique to the history of Syria-Palestine and we may actually refer to a kind of permanent structuration of socio-politics, which will be detailed in the forthcoming chapters. Moreover, in this regard, the notion of long-term history, coined by F. Braudel (1958) as *longue durée* in his discussions about historical time, together especially with the notion of *structure*, of an arrangement of social relations permanent through long periods of time, may be useful in order to conceptualise the kind of historical processes referred to in the present study; and this in spite of the series of events appearing in the epigraphic evidence. Precisely, as T. Bryce indicates:

> The Late Bronze Age Near East presents us with a complex and ever-changing picture – one of constantly shifting balances of power amongst the major kingdoms, of expanding and contracting spheres of influence, of rapidly changing allegiances and alliances as the Great Kings vied with one another, and sometimes co-operated with one another, to secure their share of power in the region. (Bryce 2003: 8; see also Cohen and Westbrook 2000b)

The Amarna period, in fact, constitutes a period of 'internationalism' *par excellence* in the ancient Near East, with five main players, the so-called 'club of the great powers', including Egypt, Ḫatti, Babylon, Mittani and, after the political eclipse of the latter, Assyria (Liverani 2000; Bryce 2003: 11–53).[1] These Great Powers interacted with each other, but they also engaged in a variety of relations with territorially minor powers, albeit independent (Arzawa, Alašiya/Cyprus), and with other polities subject to them (notably, the petty kingdoms and principalities of Syria-Palestine). The following sections (1.1–1.6) present a general overview of ancient Near Eastern political history between the sixteenth to twelfth centuries BCE. Other sociological aspects of ancient Syria-Palestine will be treated in the following chapters.[2]

## 1.1. Egypt

In the beginnings of the sixteenth century, Egypt was in the last stage of a situation of inner fragmentation and conflict, extending for two centuries, and called by modern historiographers the Second Intermediate Period. The decisive event at the beginning of the Egyptian conquest and expansion to Southwest Asia was the expulsion of the Hyksos (Eg. *ḥkꜣ ḫꜣswt*, lit. 'foreign rulers') by the pharaohs of the Eighteenth Dynasty, thus (re-)inaugurating an imperial phase in the history of Egypt, known as the New Kingdom.[3] Initially, pharaoh Amenḥotep I (1514–1493) had expanded the Egyptian domain to Nubia, and his successor Thutmose I (1493–83) in his campaign to Southwest Asia had had a first encounter with the kingdom of Mittani, disputing the zone of influence in Syria; yet the Asiatic campaigns of Thutmose III (1479–25) established in fact a permanent Egyptian rule over the southern Levant (Eg. *Rṯnw*).[4] Campaigns to Asia by his son and successor to the throne, Amenḥotep II (1425–1400), followed, as a means of reassuring the Egyptian presence, especially as Egypt faced the potential expansion into Syrian territory by Mittani (*ARE* II §§ 780–90; *ANET*³, 245–8). The following pharaohs of the dynasty, Thutmose IV (1400–1390), Amenḥotep III (1390–53), Amenḥotep IV/Aḫenaten (1353–36), Tuthanḫamun (1332–22) and Ay (1322–19), carried out a foreign policy of effective control over the region, although in general without the need of major military or punitive expeditions. Later on, the pharaohs of the Nineteenth Dynasty, especially Seti I (1290–79) and Ramesses II (1279–13), re-established military intervention in the Levant through successive conquest campaigns (Murnane 1990; Van de Mieroop 2007: 100–33), a situation in which the clash between Egypt and Ḫatti can be singled out, in the famous Battle of Qadeš (1275), as a measuring of imperial forces in Levantine territory (cf. the textual record in *ARE* III §§ 305–51; also *ANET*³, 253–8). After the reign of Ramesses III (1187–56), Egypt diminished its effective presence in the Levant, withdrawing to its historical and geographical frontier in the Sinai Peninsula.

## 1.2. Ḫatti

The main textual records about the Hittite kingdom come from the fourteenth century, namely the imperial age properly (for a recent historical synthesis, see Macqueen 1995 and especially Freu and Mazoyer 2007; see also von Schuler 1969; Klengel 1999: 135–308; Bryce 2005: Chapters 6–9; Starke 2005–6). During this period, Ḫatti had diplomatic relations with other contemporary powers of the Near East (Egypt, Babylonia) and held political bonds – mostly through loyalty and alliance treaties – with other minor polities, conquered as the kingdom expanded south-eastwards (see the translations of texts in Beckman 1996; Hoffner 2009; also *ANET*[3], 201–6; Briend, Lebrun and Puech 1994: 15–55; Starke 2005–6: 233–6). In fact, this period marks a resurgence of Hittite power in the region under Tudḫaliya I (*c*. 1420–1400),[5] who averted the Mittanian presence to the east and removed Kizzuwatna from the Mittanian political sphere of influence. This ruler campaigned also to Syria, conquering the petty kingdom of Ḫalab (Aleppo), and to the west he defeated the kingdom of Arzawa. However, it was actually Šuppiluliuma I (*c*. 1355–1320) who consolidated Hittite rule over Anatolia and its periphery. Under his reign, campaigns were carried out against the kingdom of Azzi, against the territory of the *kaška* people in the north of the Anatolian peninsula, and against the kingdom of Arzawa. Many of the most important Syrian kingdoms (Aleppo/Ḫalab, Alalaḫ, Qadeš, Nuḫašše and Amurru; but not Karkemiš and Mira, which constituted subsidiary polities of the empire)[6] came under the Hittite sphere of political influence. This rule continued under Muršili II (*c*. 1318–1290), son and successor of Šuppiluliuma I. However, with the ascension to the throne of Ḫattušili III (*c*. 1268–40) both inner and external problems appeared, notably with the reappearance of Assyria in Upper Mesopotamia as a powerful player. Problems continued under the reigns of Tudḫaliya IV (*c*. 1240–15) and Šuppiluliuma II (*c*. 1190–85), leading to the end of Hittite rule over the Anatolian Peninsula and the northern Levant. The kingdom fell into a deep crisis, with internal rebellion and political fragmentation, as well as having to face the arrival of the Sea Peoples in the eastern Mediterranean during the critical years of the twelfth century.[7]

## 1.3. Mittani

The kingdom of Mittani – also known as Ḫurri or Ḫanigalbat – was situated to the south-east of the Anatolian Peninsula, with its centre between the Euphrates and Tigris rivers. Considering the linguistic data, its Hurrite origin may be dated to the sixteenth century, linked to the diffusion of the Indo-Iranian element in the Near East – although this explanation seem to be now dated. From various testimonies in Hittite, Egyptian and Upper Mesopotamia (i.e. Nuzi, Alalaḫ) archives and according to J. Freu,[8] it is possible to distinguish the following six phases in the history of Mittani and its successor kingdom, Ḫanigalbat:

1 A formative period between 1560 and 1500, of which we have evidence in the archives of Ḫatti and Alalaḫ.
2 A period from 1500 to 1450, in which a 'Hurrite confederation' is formed, comprising a number of principalities under Mittani's command through 'vassalage' – among other strategies for ruling – in Syria (Aleppo/Ḫalab, Alalaḫ, Niya, Tunip, Ugarit, Karkemiš, Emar, Nuḫašše, Qadeš, among the main polities), in Cilicia (Kizzuwatna) and in the Middle Euphrates (Ḫana), with the great Mittanian king in its capital, Waššukanni, ruling over Upper Mesopotamia (Von Dassow 2014: 15–22).

3 A critical period from 1450 to 1430, during which the combined attacks by the Hittite kings Tudḫaliya I and Ḫattušili II and the Egyptian pharaohs Thutmose III and Amenḥotep II forced Mittani to withdraw from Cilicia and from Syria.
4 A period of hegemony, from 1430 to 1340, in which rule over Syria and over the kingdoms of Aššur and Arrapḫa is re-established; further, a truce with Egypt is accorded (*c.* 1419) and an alliance is sealed (*c.* 1385),[9] and together with the fading of the Hittite rule over south-western Asia, these events guaranteed a sustained Mittanian dominance in the region.
5 Between 1340 and 1325, 'imperial' Mittani came to an end, caused mostly by the military expansion of the Hittite king Šuppiluliuma, but also due to the resurgence of Assyria in Upper Mesopotamia.
6 Between 1325 and 1260, the whole of the Mittanian country, now named Ḫanigalbat, entered first under Hittite protectorate and then Assyrian, thus losing political autonomy hereafter.

## 1.4. Babylonia

The kingdom of Babylonia during the Late Bronze Age was controlled by Kassite people, a socio-ethnic element probably originating from Iran, and arriving in Mesopotamia through the Zagros Mountains. A socio-ethnic differentiation with the previous population of Babylon is currently made on the basis of linguistic data since there is not much more that can be known about Kassite origins.[10] It is not known how the Kassites rose to power in Babylon, but it is agreed that around the middle of the sixteenth century a Kassite dynasty was ruling the middle course of the river Euphrates and Lower Mesopotamia.[11] King Kara-indaš (around late fifteenth century) is the first attested ruler having regular contact with Egypt, according to the testimony of the Amarna letters (EA 10:8–9). We also know from the letters that pharaoh Amenḥotep III married the daughter of king Kurigalzu I (around early fourteenth century; cf. EA 11:22–4). Further negotiations between Kadašman-Enlil I ([1364]–1350) and Amenḥotep III concerning a later marriage is to be found as well in the Amarna archive, negotiations extended to the reigns of Burnaburiaš (1349–23) and Amenḥotep IV, without reaching a reciprocal agreement about the exchange of gold and princesses (cf. EA 1–5, 11, 13, 14). During Burnaburiaš's reign, the Assyrian resurgence in the regional political scene took place and, as a means of preventing future confrontations, an Assyrian princess was married to Burnaburiaš's son. A posterior palace rebellion eliminated this princess's son, who had succeeded Burnaburiaš on the throne, which triggered an Assyrian intervention in Babylonia. Without going into further details, the confrontation with Assyria was latent during the rest of the period, as also was that with the kingdom of Elam.[12] Nonetheless, the Babylonian king maintained good relations, essentially commercial, with the distant kingdom of Ḫatti. Some years later (precise dates are lacking), the Kassite dynasty approached its end after the military intervention of the Elamite king

Šutruk-naḫunte (*c.* 1150), who attacked a kingdom already weakened by a previous Assyrian military incursion led by the king Aššur-dan (*c.* 1179–35). Kutir-naḫunte, son of the aforementioned Elamite king, struck the final blow to the Kassite dynasty when he conquered the city of Babylon.

## 1.5. Assyria

Activities by Assyrian merchants can be already found during the early second millennium BCE, especially their contact with Anatolia in the trading colony of Kaneš, where gold and silver were obtained in exchange for tin and textiles (Bryce 2005: 11–15; on the commercial links between Assyria and Anatolia, see Peyronel 2008: 113–34). Shortly after the destruction of Mittanian hegemony by the Hittite armies led by Šuppiluliuma I – who installed a pro-Hittite dynasty on the throne – Assyria re-emerged as an independent military power in northern Mesopotamia under Aššur-uballit (1353–18). He began to expand rapidly on the previously Mittanian territories.[13] The Assyrian king attempted to strengthen the country's prestige as a major power in the regional political scene by exchanging diplomatic letters with the Egyptian king Amenḥotep IV, introducing himself as 'great king' and addressing the Pharaoh as his 'brother' (EA 16:1–2). This political status was not recognised by other powers of the period, like Ḫatti and Babylonia, and Assyria struggled to maintain it, mostly through military actions. During this period, Assyria had to face the now pro-Hititte kingdom of Mittani in Upper Mesopotamia – which eventually conquered Kassite Babylonia to the south and Ḫatti to the west – in addition to incursions in its territory by semi-nomadic elements from the mountains (*gutti*, *lullubi*, *turukku* peoples). There were situations favoured by marriage alliances (for instance, the daughter of Aššur-uballit and a Kassite prince), but the general option for the Assyrian foreign policy was military, especially under Adad-nirari I (1307–1275) and Šalmanasar I (1274–45). With Tukulti-ninurta I (1244–08), the Middle Assyrian kingdom reached its zenith as a regional power in this period, expanding the borders of the kingdom to the Zagros Mountains to the north-west, the upper course of the Tigris and the Euphrates to the west, with a mobile frontier to the south with Babylonia. Finally, the descendants of Tukulti-ninurta I managed to maintain the kingdom but without any major achievements, until the crisis of the twelfth century reduced the territory controlled by Assyria to its historical core.

## 1.6. Syria-Palestine

As noted before, political events and processes in the region of Syria-Palestine are intimately linked to, and to a certain extent conditioned by, foreign incursions and effective dominance. In the beginnings of the sixteenth century, the military expansion of Mittani towards the west produced the expulsion of Hittite presence from northern Syria, establishing control over the more modest polities of the region. In this period, some political centres of relative importance, such as Aleppo/Ḫalab and Qadeš, ruled over a periphery of minor polities (i.e. Megiddo and Tunip). As M. Liverani has noted, this phase marked the transition from a system of local coalitions led by kingdoms such as Yamḫad, Qatna and (perhaps) Hazor, to a system of subjection to a sole and mighty king, foreign to Syria-Palestine.[14]

Early in the fifteenth century, incursions into Palestine and Syria were begun by the Thutmosid pharaohs, making a considerable penetration in the territory but without achieving a stable rule. Actually, the Egyptian control of the whole of Palestine and the southern part of Syria was achieved only under Thutmose III (1479–25). Military campaigns by this Pharaoh can be arranged in three phases. The first phase, comprising the campaign of the first year of his reign and ending in the battle of Megiddo (*c.* 1457), assured the control of Palestine for Egypt (*ARE* II §§ 412–43).[15] The second phase, comprising the campaigns of the fifth, sixth and seventh years, ended with the conquest of Qadeš and the south of Syria (*ARE* II §§ 455–75). The third phase, comprising the campaign of the eighth year and later ones, expanded Egyptian dominance to the river Euphrates, deep into Mittanian territory, and over the coast to Ugarit and the Orontes river valley, with Tunip and Nuḫašše (*ARE* II §§ 477–83, 491, 498–501, 509, 517–19, 525, 529–34). The campaigns carried out by pharaoh Amenḥotep II reassured Egyptian rule over the region. The Egyptian–Mittanian border divided the kingdoms of Aleppo/Ḫalab, Mukiš, Niya and Nuḫašše under Mittani's control and Ugarit, Tunip and Qadeš under Egyptian control. The whole of the Amarna period in the Levant must be seen, in effect, under such a situation of foreign rule in the region. The difference is marked by the later Hittite intervention in Syria under Šuppiluliuma I, leaving thus Mittani out of the regional political game and readjusting the group of Mittanian 'vassals' to the Hittite sphere – also with the consequent reduction of principalities under Egyptian subjection to Hittite subjects – and pushing the Egyptian border down from Ugarit to Byblos and from Qadeš to Beqa' (nowadays, Lebanese territory). The second half of the fourteenth and the whole of the thirteenth centuries were marked by territorial stability under Egyptian and Hittite rules, notwithstanding the Egyptian attempts to push its northern imperial border further into Asia, as evidenced for instance in the battle of Qadeš (*c.* 1274) between the pharaoh Ramesses II and the Hittite king Muwatalli.

In sum, the political life of the petty local kingdoms in Syria-Palestine was essentially marked by foreign intervention through different channels, but mostly military occupation and political subordination. Even relatively important centres and polities, like Karkemiš, Amurru and Ugarit in the north, maintained, each according to the geopolitical circumstances, an external political articulation signalled by the political and economic interests of Egypt and Ḫatti, until the general crisis of the twelfth century led to the disappearance – even for a couple of centuries – of foreign rule over the region, enabling some centuries later the emergence of local polities of the Iron Age II (*c.* 1000–600 BCE) (see the long-term perspective in Lemche 1996; Pfoh 2004; 2013; also from a different perspective, Zwickel 2012).

## 1.7. Egyptian Rule over Syria-Palestine[16]

The beginnings of the Eighteenth Dynasty were marked by wars of conquest and the establishment of rule over Egypt's periphery, both to the south, in Nubia, and to the north in Southwest Asia, namely Syria-Palestine (Spalinger 2005: 46–69; Burke 2010).[17] Especially with Thutmose III's reign, during a phase of Egyptian consolidation in Southwest Asia, the presence of the army led by the Pharaoh himself was a regular affair through annual campaigns, the collection of the annual tribute (*ỉnw*) and the settlement of military garrisons and administrative centres under Egypt's direct control (Liverani 1998: 33).[18] Regarding the Egyptian intervention in the country, R. Gonen (1984: 70) indicates an important decrease in urbanisation during the Late Bronze age and most of the sites being unwalled as a direct consequence of it:

> The almost total lack of town fortifications is a striking phenomenon in the history of the settlement in the region. Contemporary historical sources [Amarna letters; EP] clearly convey the impression of a restless period, lacking civil security. The Egyptian kings led frequent military campaigns into or through Canaan, the city-states often quarrelled with each other, and the situation deteriorated further because of the occasional raids of the Shusu [semi-nomadic elements; EP] and the meddling of the Habiru. In such a situation a city wall would seem to have been a natural and universal urban feature. Its absence should perhaps be explained as an outcome of the Egyptian policy in Canaan, intended to weaken the power of the semi-independent city-states and to prevent uprisings and revolts.[19]

Of course, it is possible to think that the information conveyed by the Amarna letters from Canaan is exaggerated by the local petty kings, involved in a game of political persuasion of the Pharaoh in order to gain his attention and favour, and that the effective Egyptian dominance over the territory would have rendered unnecessary the fortification of settlements (cf. Herzog 1992: 244 n 46; also Faust 2013: 205). The situation seems then to be as described by T.L. Thompson (1999: 146):

> During the Late Bronze period, small villages had been almost entirely abandoned and, apart from the coast, most of the population lived in towns. The towns, however, were for the most part unfortified. This absence of fortification worked because these towns were under the protection of an Egyptian imperial administration. It was the Egyptians who were most interested in preventing the building of fortifications during the Late Bronze Age, because these towns were in the hands of local chiefs and patrons, and could be used to support resistance to the interests of the Egyptian empire. Correspondence between these local patrons

> and Egypt shows that the towns were in constant competition with each other. At the same time, Egypt's imperial control was limited to areas around the towns. The countryside was unsafe, and could not support small, unprotected villages and hamlets.

During Amenḥotep II's reign, military campaigns to the region continued – at least two, according to the available sources – especially regarding the Egypto-Mittanian competition for the control of Syria (Ahlström 1993: 232–8; Freu 2003: 55–79). However, after peace was accorded with Mittani, through marriage alliances between Hurrite princesses and Egyptian monarchs – first Thutmose IV and then Amenḥotep III (EA 17; 19; 24; 29) – the Egyptian military presence in Syria-Palestine was considerably reduced as Egyptian administration of the territory involved the local petty kingdoms.

It may now be asked, what kind of rule did Egypt exert over Syria-Palestine? To what extent is it possible to speak of an *Egyptian empire* in Syria-Palestine? Addressing the question from an older research paradigm that considered the Amarna period as a period of crisis in the region, C. Aldred (1975: 82) would affirm:

> Within its Asiatic sphere of influence, Egypt hardly exercised any Roman *imperium*, despite some ambiguous indications of its exploitation of the region. The pharaoh as the traditional vanquisher of the Nine Nations was the divine overlord whom vassals in Palestine and Syria addressed as 'my sun', 'my god', 'my lord' and in similar terms of subservience. Apart from this spiritual leadership, however, it is doubtful whether anything like an empire existed and the scenes of foreigners bearing tribute to lay before the mercy-seat of the pharaoh are capable of other interpretations than the mercantile development of the region.

And regarding the native socio-political configuration:

> The many vassal states kept up interminable internecine squabbles, their main objective being to preserve their own autonomy, to extend their frontiers and power at the expense of their weaker neighbours and to enlist the military might and resources of their overlord, ostensibly to protect his interests, but actually to advance their own ambitions. They therefore set up a constant clamour for help to preserve the town or state they were so loyally defending, coupled with assurances of their own honesty and fidelity and the treachery and ruthlessness of their rivals. (Aldred 1975: 82)[20]

Apart from not considering Egyptian rule over Syria-Palestine an *empire*, Aldred would offer a negative (if not derogatory) characterisation of the nature of local socio-politics: in the region anarchy and deceit abound, together with competition for satisfying the Pharaoh (cf. David 2000: 58–62). We will see later how this understanding can be seriously challenged by providing an interpretation drawn from the Mediterranean ethnographic record. For now, it is possible to refine Aldred's assertions by examining the Egyptian system of ruling foreign lands more closely. Following P.J. Frandsen, some basic differences may be noted between the Egyptian rule of Nubia and the one exerted over Syria-Palestine, both regions conquered during the military expansion of the Eighteenth Dynasty.[21]

In Nubia, the Egyptians imposed a considerable Egyptianisation on the population, at least in the upper echelons of society: the local rulers' children were sent to Egypt where they were re-educated in the Pharaoh's court as a means to guarantee a loyal conduct towards the Egyptian state (cf. Frandsen 1979: 169; in general, on the acculturation process, see Wachtel 1974). At a political and administrative level, Nubia was organised through the general Egyptian model: the territory was divided into two regions, Wawat (Lower Nubia) and Kuš (Upper Nubia), and at the head of the administration there was a viceroy, responsible only to the king and on the same level as a vizier in their functions. As in Lower and Upper Egypt, Wawat and Kuš were administrated respectively by two deputies and both regions were subdivided in administrative districts, each under the control of a 'mayor' (*ḥ3tyʿ*). In synthesis, Nubian bureaucracy was analogous to that of Lower and Upper Egypt because Nubia was now conceptually part of Egypt.

Apart from a military presence, Egyptianisation was carried out and reinforced through a policy of Egyptian settlements in the region, especially in Lower Nubia, according to a settlement pattern similar to the Egyptian one (Frandsen 1979: 170). Furthermore, even the Nubian economy was structurally integrated into the redistributive Egyptian economy, something that may well be inferred because of the presence of temples in Lower Nubia. Temples were a key engine of the Egyptian redistributive economy (Frandsen 1979: 171–3; on the nature of the Egyptian economy, see Janssen 1975; Bleiberg 1995). All these elements, following Frandsen, indicate an effort by Egypt to expand the ideological border of the kingdom to the south to the Fourth Cataract (cf. Frandsen 1979: 174; also Smith 2003).

Egyptian presence in Syria-Palestine dates back to Thutmose III's campaigns, as already indicated, and it was structured in a different manner.[22] Three urban sites functioned as Egyptian administrative centres for three large territorial zones: Gaza, on the southern Palestinian coast, was the centre of the zone of Canaan (e.g. *P3 k3nʿn3*), namely Cisjordan;[23] Kumidi, in the valley of Beqa', was the centre of the zone of Ube/Upe, namely inner Syria; and Ṣumur(a), on the Syrian coast, was the centre for the zone of Amurru, namely coastal Syria.[24] In each of these centres, a 'commissioner' (Akk. *rābiṣu*) resided, in a small palace and a military garrison.[25] According to the analysis by W. Helck over half a century ago, three formal provinces could thus be identified (Helck 1962: 257–61). However, it is nowadays usual to conceive of an Egyptian administrative system as much more 'informal', since these three districts were part of Egypt's political domain in Asia. They would not have constituted provinces of the land of Egypt in a strict sense, even though, from an Egyptian ideological perspective:

> Foreign lands belong to the king by right of divine ancestry and bequest. To this is added an existential argument: foreigners do not know how to live or how to use their resources. Therefore, lands, inhabitants, and resources must voluntarily be given up to Pharaoh. If not, he has every right to take them by force. For those who submit there are rewards, for the recalcitrant only destruction. (Redford 2006: 328–9)[26]

As it was the policy with Nubia, acculturation (Egyptianisation) practices were also carried out over young Levantine rulers and some family members in order to establish political loyalty and as a ruling strategy, as noted for instance in EA 296:23–9: 'May the king, my lord, inquire of Yanḫamu, his commissioner. When I was young, he brought me into Egypt. I served the king, my lord, and I stood at the city gate of King, my lord.'[27]

At other centres of lower rank – meaning, without local rulers – there were Egyptian garrisons, for instance, in Jaffa, on the Palestinian coast, in Beth-šean, in the northern Palestinian inland, in Ullasa, on the Syrian coast. The Egyptian troops stationed in the land (*ṣabe maṣarti* or *maṣ(ṣ)artu* in the Amarna correspondence; EA 114:31; 117:79 [*ma-ṣa-ar-ra*]) were rather modest, and their number might have had a more politico-symbolic importance rather than a concrete military role. In normal conditions, the Egyptian troops would number 200–300 permanent soldiers in a garrison (Pintore 1973; also Liverani 1998: 38). In the thirteenth century, during the Nineteenth and Twentieth Dynasties, the Egyptian presence in the southern Levant was intensified through a network of forts and administrative residencies, and also temples dedicated to Egyptian divinities, notably in the north of the Sinai Peninsula, north of the Negev, the coastal plain and the Beth-šean valley (Weinstein 1981: 17–23; Oren 1984; Mazar 1990: 279–87; Hasel 1998; Morris 2005: 343–611, 691–773). M. Müller (2011: 238) has argued that Egypt's 'grand strategy' of ruling Syria-Palestine consisted, on one hand, of a direct ruling of the three provinces in Canaan mentioned above with their administrative apparatus. On the other hand, it consisted of an indirect ruling of 'vassal principalities' through 'an abrasive net of dependency which is laid over the politically and economically most important settlements'. This mode of ruling over the Levant characterises Egypt more as a 'hegemonial rather than territorial' empire, according to Müller (2011: 239) since Egypt's intervention in the land was limited to periodic incursions, yet its rule over the land was effectively maintained.

There were also zones devoted to direct economic exploitation by Egypt. In the Amarna letters, Yarimuta is mentioned, a cereal production zone thought to be near Megiddo (cf. Halpern 2011). S. Aḥituv (1978: 104) has relativised the Egyptian economic interest in the Levant:

> It is indeed probable that there was no economic interest in the Egyptian conquest of Canaan, and if such an interest existed it was very limited. Canaan itself had very little to offer . . . Egypt, for it was not worthwhile

> to transport agricultural products of great bulk, since Egypt itself was rich and self-sufficient.

However, as N. Na'aman (1981: 184) has suggested, the 'existence of a network of supply for the Egyptian army embarking on military campaigns to the north, both along inland roads and along the coast, was an important military and economic factor of the Egyptian occupation of the land.'[28]

Nonetheless, we should bear in mind that the economy of Syria-Palestine was certainly not structurally integrated into the Egyptian economy, as the Nubian economy was.[29] But, why did Egypt not rule over Syria-Palestine as it did over Nubia? The answers may be several, not necessarily mutually excluding. It might have been due to the high cost of resources required for introducing and maintaining the Egyptian bureaucratic system in the Levant (Drower 1975: 468). Or it might that be Syria-Palestine was also under the sphere of influence of other powers, and Egypt's main interest was to keep the Levantine trade routes safe and protected.[30] B.J. Kemp (1978: 20 and 43–4) noted:

> At a very general level it might be said that Nubia was an administrative creation, whilst Western Asia provided the main scope for military shows . . . From the point of view of the history of imperialism, the western Asiatic side of the Egyptian empire is of less interest than Nubia, in that it was merely a variation on the common theme of vassalage and tribute.

Ahlström (1993: 237) offered another explanation, although questionable, as he seems to downplay Egypt's military control of the region:

> The reason why the Asiatic territory was not incorporated as a province, unlike Nubia, may be that Egypt was not militarily strong enough, and therefore needed the support of city princes. This can be supported by the fact that the Egyptians had to carry out so many campaigns in Syria-Palestine during the Eighteenth and Nineteenth dynasties in order to put down rebellions. The conflicts with Mitanni and later the Hittite empire also indicate that Egypt was not able to impose fully its hegemony in Syria. In fact, after Tuthmosis III the Egyptian sphere of dominion slowly receded, and during the reign of Tutankhamon (1334–25 BCE) the borderline was just north of Byblos and south of Qadesh. It is possible that the campaigns of Tuthmosis resulted in Egypt seeing the economic advantage of controlling these Asiatic countries and therefore being more inclined to have the princes acknowledge Egyptian supremacy than militarily subduing the city states. By the oath to the pharaoh the princes were made responsible for law and order, but the Egyptian supremacy was established by some garrisons and store cities with their administrative personnel, as well as by placing 'supervisors' at key positions. During the time of Amenhotep III (1386–49 BCE) the Egyptian military

> presence was very small, which indicates that the relationship between Egypt and the Asiatic princes functioned without too much friction.

Yet, independently of the reasons offered to explain the divergence in the rule of Nubia and Syria-Palestine, it has to be considered that in both situations Egypt possessed the political hegemony in the territory. If the economic factor is added to the equation (even after acknowledging that the Syro-Palestinian economy was not integrated into the Egyptian one), it would be thus reasonable to characterise Egypt's rule over the Levant as imperial; an 'hegemonial empire' as proposed by Müller above, although the specific conditions of such imperial rule must always be explicit.[31]

And moreover, we should also have in mind that, at an ideological level, Asia (but also Nubia) was always perceived by pharaonic Egypt as a place of chaos and threat from barbaric forces, as illustrated in the Instruction for King Merikara:

> Lo, the wretched Asiatic – it goes ill with the place where he is, afflicted with water, difficult from many trees, the ways thereof painful because of the mountains. He does not dwell in a single place, (but) his legs *are made to go astray.* He has been fighting (ever) since the time of Horus, (but) he does not conquer, nor yet can he be conquered. He does not announce a day in fighting, like *a thief* who . . . for a gang . . . Do not trouble thyself about him: he is (only) an Asiatic, *one despised* on his (own) coast. He may rob a single *person,* (but) he does not lead against a town of many citizens. (*ANET*$^{3}$, 416)[32]

Furthermore, the topographic difference of Syria-Palestine with the land of Egypt but also the considerable distance from the central government and the kind of interests (economic, political) in the region might have conditioned the Egyptian administrative presence in a particular way. S.T. Smith (1991: 91) concluded that 'the nature of exploitation created different imperial needs, requiring different levels of restructuring in indigenous systems and/or the creation of new systems'; further, that in the imperial policy for the Levant during the New Kingdom:

> there was no attempt at colonization. The Egyptian presence was never very large and always military and administrative (and also perhaps commercial). Each city state was left to govern its own territory, the only constraint being the regular collection of tribute for Egypt and the restriction of relations outside of the system. (1991: 84)

Also E.F. Morris (2005: 113) stated the following:

> It is interesting that the practice of erecting fortress-towns on foreign soil during the early Eighteenth Dynasty appears to have been limited

> to the southern frontier. While Upper Nubia and Syria-Palestine represented equally virgin territory, Egypt's long occupation of Lower Nubia and the comforting presence of the Nile almost certainly rendered the southern land less alien to potential settlers. If so, it may have been significantly easier to recruit Egyptians to inhabit a Nile Valley town than one in Syria-Palestine, where agricultural and cultural practices were far more foreign to the Egyptian tradition. Alternatively, it may have been that the pharaonic government had no intention of settling the Levant. Indeed, garrisons may well have been placed in southern Canaan predominantly as peacekeeping forces and as added protection for the Egyptian border but not as proto-settlements for an expanding Egyptian state. With regard to Syria-Palestine, archaeological and textual evidence suggests that Egypt may have preferred the role of absentee landlord to that of homeowner.

In any case, the articulation of power in the Levant, especially in the southern part, did not need large military or administrative structures to establish the domination of the many petty polities, which also acted as some sort of contention network before the potential penetration in the territory of important powers, such as Ḫatti or Mittani (cf. Sapin 1981; 1982). The socio-political order of Syro-Palestinian polities – characterised above by Aldred as anarchistic and in constant upheaval, and therefore *not* under imperial control or sovereignty of Egypt, otherwise there would be no notices of instability in the Amarna letters – seemed to work with normality under the apparent laxness of Egypt's rule. The reason for this is not the existence of a shared 'international' code,[33] nor that the local petty kings had been incorporated into the Egyptian administration of the region.[34] In effect, the apparent anarchy transmitted by the Amarna letters has to be in fact interpreted as socio-political normativity in the region, which only in its representation by the petty kings may be deemed chaotic. Therefore, an 'exaggeration' by the petty kings was always played out as a political tool in order to influence decisions at the Egyptian court, whether or not situations of imminent chaos, danger and menace by their neighbours had, in fact, occurred. Yet, such communication of constant distress is part of the local political game, aiming at getting the pharaoh's attention and assistance. All this does not represent any real alteration of Egypt's rule over the region. As A. Mazar (1990: 236) noted:

> The Egyptian conquests in the Levant were carried out in order to guard the main routes to Lebanon and Syria, and for the gains from the economic exploitation of the occupied country. Wood, oil, wine, wheat, cattle, copper, slaves, and concubines were brought from Canaan to Egypt. The Egyptians retained the structure of the Canaanite independent city-states established during the previous period; however, these city-states now became their vassals.

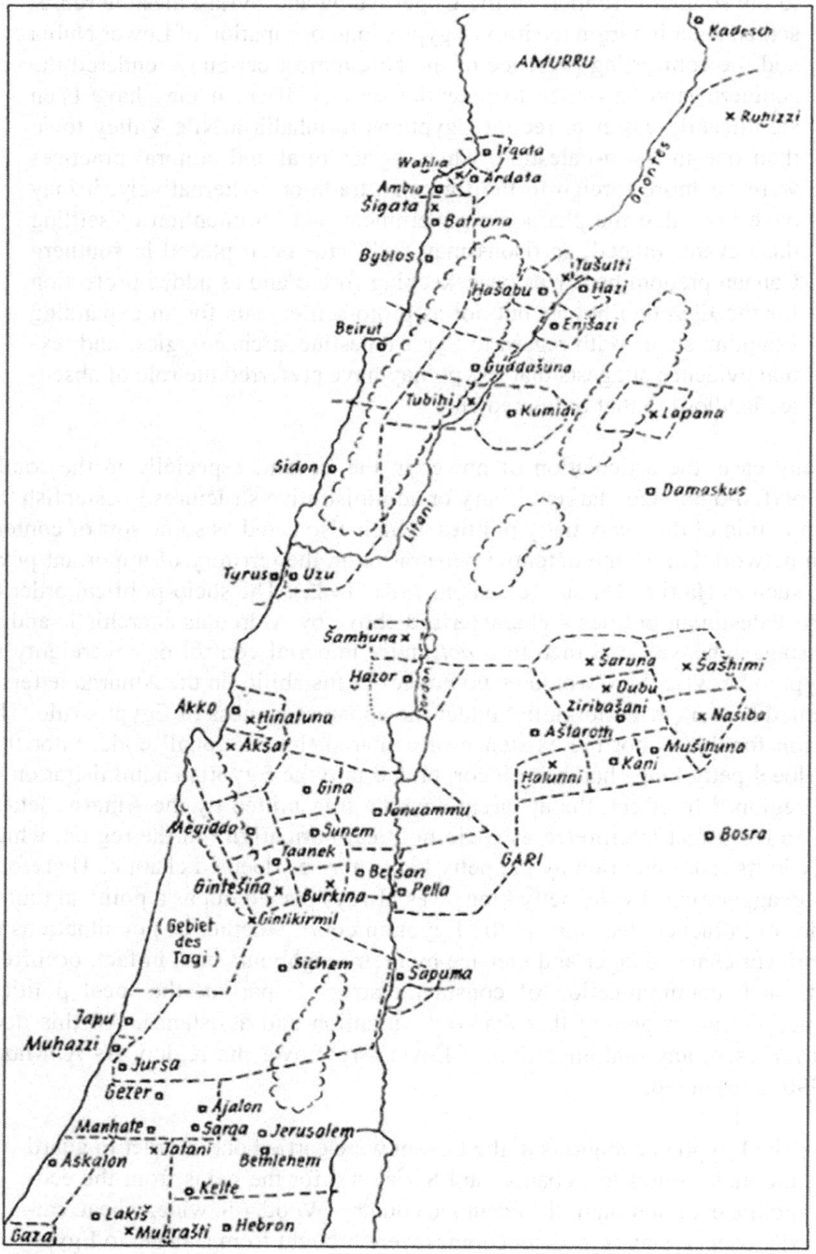


*Map 1.1* Egyptian administrative rule over Syria-Palestine during the Amarna period (taken from W. Helck, *Die Beziehungen Ägyptens zu Vorderasien im 3. Und 2, Jahrtausend v. Chr.* (Wiesbaden: Harrassowitz, 1962, p. 191).

Also, from an economic perspective:

> Our sources offer no evidence of drastic changes in the ownership of land in Canaan as a result of the Egyptian conquest. The whole land became the property of the Pharaoh, but this was only a continuation of the formal ownership upon which the feudal–like Canaanite régime had been based. (Aḥituv 1978: 93)

Actually, the communication maintained between the Pharaoh and the petty local kings ought to be analysed both in formal terms of diplomatic epistolography and according to the views offered by political anthropology. It is through these perspectives that we may fully understand the socio-political logics operating behind the data present in the textual evidence of the period.

## Notes

1 The notion of 'internationalism', as usually referred to in the specialised literature on this period, will be discussed in Chapter 2.

2 For more comprehensive treatments, albeit aiming at presenting synthesis of the history of the region, see *CAH*³ II/1, 417–556; II/2, 1–160; Klengel 1992: 84–180; Lemche 1995a; Liverani 2013: 271–377.

3 On the Hyksos in Egypt, see Redford 1992: 98–122; 1997; Oren 1997. Cf. also *ANET*³, 230–34 for textual documentation. In general, on the Egyptian expansion in south-west Asia during this period, see Redford 1992: 125–213; Bryan 2003; Van Dijk 2003.

4 See Ahlström 1993, 226–32. Cf. the documentation on these campaigns in *Urk.* IV, 647–735; and the translations in *ARE* II §§ 391–574; *ANET*³, 234–45; also in a more succinct manner, Galán 2002: 75–124.

5 The Hittite chronology follows Starke 2005–6: 297.

6 Cf. Starke 2005–6: 238, who refers to the 'federative' nature of Hittite ruling of conquered lands, recognising some sovereignty in some of the polities, as long as there was not rebellion against the empire.

7 Cf. Macqueen 1995: 1097–9; Dothan 1995; Klengel 1999: 309–19; Bryce 2005: 327–55. In general, on the crisis of the twelfth century BCE, see Cline 2014. The crisis has been attributed to the collapse of regional trade in the ancient Near East (Coote and Whitelam 1987: 74–5), to internal social problems (Liverani 1987), and to climate change (Thompson 1992: 215–21; Langgut, Finkelstein and Litt 2013).

8 See Wilhelm 1995; Freu 2003: 25–53; Von Dassow 2014: 11–14.

9 Cf. EA 17:19–30. Cf. also Artzi 2000; and especially Bryan 2000, for the Egyptian perspective.

10 See in general Sommerfeld 1995; also Paulus 2014.

11 The following description is after Liverani 2013: 364–77.

12 About Elam during the Late Bronze Age, see Labat 1975; Liverani 2013: 376–7; and especially Potts 1999: 205–31. On the contacts between Babylonia and Elam, see Paulus 2013.

13 The following description is after Liverani 2013: 347–63.

14 Cf. the overview by Liverani 2013: 325–46; and in greater detail Klengel 1992: 84–180; Bryce 2014: 23–94. One should also consult Klengel 1965; 1969; 1970.

15 The Asiatic campaigns of Thutmose III are studied in detail by Redford 2003. See also Gestoso Singer 2008.

16 The standard ruling procedure of the Hittite kingdom will be properly treated in Chapter 5.

17 On the Egyptian references about Palestine, cf. Abel 1967 I: 329–32, who recognised three terms, partially synonymous: *Ḫ3rw*, meaning above all a coastal zone; *Rṯnw*, the inner country, and *Z3hỉ* or *Ḏ3hỉ*, referring to the Mediterranean coast of Palestine and Phoenicia.

18 See also on the Egyptian presence in Asia, Helck 1962: 109–98. On the nature of the tribute, see Aldred 1970; Bleiberg 1996.

19 Cf. Mazar 1990: 240, who challenges Gonen's conclusions, especially on demographic grounds; see also the discussion in Bunimovitz 1995.

20 On the 'feudal' character Levantine socio-politics, Albright (1975: 104) would indicate that ' . . . there seems to be no doubt that certain princes exercised acknowledged feudal rights over other weaker chieftains.'

21 See Frandsen 1979: 169–79; also Kemp 1978; Hoffmeier 2004; Morris 2005: 27–113; and Drower 1975: 467–83, but the latter only for Syria. Groll (1983) attempted to relativise the administrative differences between the Egyptian rule of Nubia and the Levant, without being convincing though. On the Egyptian rule over Nubia, cf. the important study by Smith 2003.

22 See especially Alt 1959b; also Frandsen 1979: 174–9; Weinstein 1981: 12–17. On the Egyptian impact on Palestine, especially on the iconographic aspect, see Giveon 1978; also Leibowitz 1987.

23 On the term 'Canaan' for the second millennium BCE, see Lemche 1999: 25–52.

24 Cf. the map in this chapter, but only as a heuristic tool, since polity borders in Amarna times, especially in uninhabited areas, were rather variable; cf. Na'aman 1997. On the cartographic representation of ancient polities, see the discussion in Smith 2005, who concludes that ancient empires and states should be seen more 'as networks rather than as homogeneous territorial entities' (845), something that fits well the evidence of political dynamics in the Levant during the Amarna period.

25 See the 'palatial' archaeology of the Late Bronze Age in Nigro 1995: 119–91; also Weippert 1988: 271–6.

26 See Hachmann 1982; Redford 1992: 198–206; Liverani 1998: 38.

27 The translation in Moran 1992: 338; see also Liverani 1998: 66. Frandsen 1979: 175–6: 'As in Nubia the Egyptians ensured the loyalty of their vassals by carrying members of their family off to Egypt as hostages.' On acculturation/deculturation in Syria-Palestine, cf. Liverani 1983b.

28 Cf. also Pintore 1972: 112–15; 1973: 300–302; Na'aman 1988; for the Ramesside phase, Wengrow 1996: 321–3, who holds that the presence of collared-rim *pithoi* in the region was related to the Egyptian demand on local agricultural products, and also the considerations on the Aphek estate in Gadot 2010.

29 Frandsen 1979: 177. As Smith (1991: 84) indicates, 'Nubia was brought completely within the Egyptian social, economic, religious and administrative systems. Settlers were sent from Egypt as well as captive populations from the Levant. Acculturation was encouraged, with indigenous elites allowed virtually full participation in the Egyptian system.' Cf. also Smith 2003, for a treatment of ethnic identities within the Egyptian empire in Nubia.

30 W. Helck, as referred to in Frandsen 1979: 179. Also Aḥituv 1978: 105: 'the geographical position of Canaan was of great importance as a bridge between Egypt and Mesopotamia, and the Lebanon too. The true importance of Canaan for Egypt was the control it allowed over the main trade routes leading to the trading centres in Mesopotamia.' On trade routes in Syria-Palestine, see Sapin 1981: 20–32; Astour 1995: 1414–16; Fales 2002.

31 For a problematisation of Egyptian imperialism, see Vernus 2011: 20, who distinguishes between an 'empirical empire', i.e. the real expansion of the Egyptian state, and 'the pretension of expansion expressed through Egyptian ideology'. Cf. also Morris 2005.

32 See Smith 2003: 24–9, 167–87, on Nubia; and Campagno 2011: 20, 30–31, on Sinuhe and the Egyptian representation of Asiatic people. About the ethnic identification and differentiation in the ancient Near East, see the synthesis in Limet 2005.

33 Frandsen 1979: 175: 'We have here a clear indication of the existence of a shared system of values.' Of course, there were rules of diplomatic communication between the polities of the period (cf. Chapter 2), but such rules left room for cultural distortions and misunderstandings (cf. Liverani 1967; 1983a).

34 I therefore disagree with the kind of interpretation present, for instance, in Gestoso Singer (2007: 46–7), and her reference to EA 51; 161:51–3; 285:5–6; 286:12; 288: 9–15. True, Liverani (1967: 11–12) notes that 'the adoption of the Egyptian conception by the Syro-Palestinian kings is not limited to evident instrumental declarations for achieving their goals, but it seems to penetrate rather profoundly in the sense of assimilation of the position of the vassal king into that of an official. Such assimilation is evident especially in the situation of the defence of the city. The position of the vassal king is to defend the city by himself and to be assisted by his overlord in doing so; the position of the official is instead to defend the city of his overlord, for the lord himself, who has entrusted [him with] such a task'. However, this does not mean, as it will be argued in the following chapters, that the petty Syro-Palestinian kings adopted a socio-political attitude proper of an Egyptian officer. The Pharaoh commanded different things to these petty kings through direct orders of bureaucratic spirit, and they (for instance, the 'king' of Amiya, cf. EA 99:6–9; Rib-Hadda of Byblos, cf. EA 119:15–16; etc.) claim to obey at once in an apparent same fashion; however, the documented fact of asking for reciprocity from the Pharaoh once the orders have been fulfilled places the nature of the political intervention of the petty kings outside of a bureaucratic sphere and is rather marked by inter-personal relations (as Liverani notes as well).

# 2

# 'INTERNATIONAL' DIPLOMACY DURING THE LATE BRONZE AGE

## 2.1. Primary and secondary sources

A formal revision and exposition of textual material and epigraphic *corpora* from the Late Bronze Age in Southwest Asia shall be presented in this chapter. The presentation will focus on the availability of primary and secondary sources for an analysis of socio-political practices in local Syro-Palestinian polities as well as between polities of equal and different status, rank and organisation in Southwest Asia. Our main textual primary sources are constituted by the Amarna letters, the Hittite treaties and by the data retrieved from the archives from Ugarit and Alalaḫ.

### *2.1.1. The El Amarna archive*

In 1887 at the site of Tell el-Amarna in Egypt, some 300 km south of Cairo, an Egyptian peasant discovered a cache of almost 400 epistolary documents written in Akkadian cuneiform script.[1] These documents belonged to the foreign affairs office in the city of Aḫetaten ('horizon of [the solar disc] Aton'), founded by pharaoh Aḫenaten as a new capital for the Egyptian kingdom, replacing Thebes, in the fifth year of his reign (*c.* 1349), following the religious reform he undertook, through which the cult of the solar disc would replace the traditional cult of the god Amun (see Krauss 1995; Vandersleyen 1995: 425–34; Mynářová 2014: 15–19). At present, the so-called 'Amarna letters' are located mostly in the museums of Berlin and Cairo, and in the British Museum and the Louvre. The main edition of these documents was until recently the one by the Norwegian scholar J.A. Knudtzon, who published a volume in 1907 with 358 letters, with transliteration and translation, followed by a second volume published post-mortem in 1915, by O. Weber and E. Ebeling (Knudtzon 1907/1915). The rest of the known epistolary material was later collected and published by A.F. Rainey in 1970/1978 (Rainey 1978). The order and numbering of the letters established by Knudtzon became standard in ancient Near Eastern studies for about a century, as exemplified in the English translation by W.L. Moran of 1992 (Moran 1992). Only recently, M. Liverani published a new translation of the letters in Italian in which the numbering of the letters has been rearranged, but indicating also a concordance with Knudtzon's numbering (Liverani 1998; 1999). The most recent publication of the letters, which includes transcription and translation as well as commentaries, is the posthumous edition by A.F. Rainey (Rainey 2014).

The main historical value of this archive of texts is the data it provides regarding the political relations between the great powers of the mid-fourteenth century BCE and, notably, between Egypt and its Asiatic subjects, from the reigns of Amenḥotep III, Amenḥotep IV/Aḫenaten and the beginning of Tutanḫamun's.[2] Out of a *corpus* of 382 tablets, 32 may be considered as myths and epics (EA 340?, 356–9), syllabaries (EA 348, 350, 379), lexical texts (EA 351–4, 373), a list of gods (EA 374), a Hurrite tale (EA 341), a list of Egyptian words written in syllabic or logographic cuneiform (EA 368), another letter may be an amulet (EA 355) and another group is undetermined (EA 342–7, 349, 360–61, 372, 376–7, 380–81). The rest of the letters constitutes a set of inventories of gifts (EA 13–14, 22, 25, 120). Finally, as Knudtzon organised the letters, a division can be made in letters sent between the Great Kings of contemporary kingdoms and Egypt: Babylonia (EA 1–14), Assyria (EA 15–16), Mittani (EA 17, 19–30), Arzawa (EA 31–2), Alašiya/Cyprus (EA 33–40) and Ḫatti (EA 41–4); and, the largest group, correspondence between Egypt and its Asiatic subjects from Syria-Palestine.[3]

### *2.1.2. Hittite archives*

The discovery in 1834 of monumental ruins of an ancient site by the Frenchman Charles Texeir in the small Turkish village of Boğazköy (now Boğazkale), located to the west of the mid-course of the river Halys, produced some research on the geopolitical role of the site in the Anatolian Peninsula. Until the late nineteenth century, most researchers would associate the site with a socio-political organisation of small relevance. However, in 1906, excavations at the site led by H. Winkler and T. Makridi unearthed some 2,500 tablets belonging to a royal archive or library that evidenced letters and treaties, among other testimonies, exchanged and established between the kingdom of Ḫatti and other polities of equal or unequal rank. A copy in Akkadian of the peace treaty between Ramesses II and Ḫattušili III (1258 BCE)[4] indicated without doubt that the site was the place of the ancient capital of the Hittite kingdom, Ḫattuša.[5] So far, and after successive archaeological campaigns at the site and associated locations, there is a *corpus* of some 25,000 tablets, most of which are written in the Hittite language. They provide information about the administration of the kingdom, relations between the royal court and dignitaries and between Ḫatti and other kingdoms of the Near Eastern regions between the sixteenth and thirteenth centuries BCE, until the destruction of the city by invading forces.[6]

### *2.1.3. Archives from Ugarit*

The site of Ras Šamra on the Syrian coast was excavated in 1928, revealing an ancient urban settlement. The city of Ugarit, as it was known in contemporary sources, had its zenith as a socio-political organisation between the fifteenth and thirteenth centuries BCE. The excavator of the site, Claude Schaeffer, discovered in 1929 the first tablets of what constituted a set of royal archives. The key location of Ugarit, at the crossroads of the Hittite, Mittanian and Egyptian empires during the Late Bronze Age, made the city an important player in the inter-regional relations between the great powers, especially under Hittite subordination (cf. Astour 1981; van Soldt 1995; Yon 1997; 2006; Vidal 2015b).

The archives of Ugarit offer important information especially for the later period of the Amarna period, namely the fourteenth and thirteenth centuries. The extant epigraphic *corpus* reflects the cosmopolitism of the site – expressed also in the use of a number of languages, such as Akkadian (the *lingua franca* of the period; Labat 1962), Hurrite, Hittite, Ugaritic, Cypro-Minoan and Egyptian, which include different systems of writing: syllabic cuneiform, alphabetic cuneiform, Hittite hieroglyphs, Egyptian hieroglyphs and Cypro-Minoan writing. Among the written texts in Akkadian, several literary genres are recognisable: legal texts (treaties, royal documents dealing with internal and external affairs), epistolary documents (some 350 letters of different provenance), administrative, lexicographic, literary and religious texts.[7]

Relevant for the present study, this archive provides data regarding the internal socio-political organisation of a major local polity in northern Syria, but also in regard to the dynamics of subordination to regional powers (the Hittite kingdom) and on the relations of alliance with nearby analogous polities, such as Amurru.

### *2.1.4. Archives from Alalaḫ*

In 1935, after having excavated the ancient Mesopotamian city of Ur, Leonard Woolley was commissioned by the British Museum to conduct archaeological research at a new site. The chosen site in 1936 was Tell Atchana, in the northern angle of the Orontes river, in the modern province of Hatay in Turkey. There, Woolley expected to find clues about cultural connections between ancient Near Eastern and Minoan and Cretan societies in the Eastern Mediterranean, given the strategic location of the site – in fact, the excavations proved the role of the site as a centre of interregional trade on luxury items, i.e. ivory. Shortly after his first discoveries, Woolley found the ruins of the ancient city of Alalaḫ (see the final reports of the excavation seasons from 1937–39 and 1946–49 in Woolley 1955).

The site had been occupied since the late third millennium BCE and Woolley identified eighteen levels of occupation (including level 0), in which temples, palaces and walls appeared, reflecting the prominence the site had had in the second millennium BCE. Significantly, two levels revealed an important number of tablets in Akkadian cuneiform (some in Hittite as well) from royal archives: Alalaḫ VII, when the city was under the political subjection of the kingdom of Yamḫad in the seventeenth century, and Alalaḫ IV, when the city was politically subordinated to the kingdom of Mittani in the fifteenth century (cf. Woolley 1955: 91–131; see also the comprehensive study in Von Dassow 2008). The tablets from the cuneiform archive of Alalaḫ IV, namely a period previous to the Amarna period, contain treaties, letters, records of legal and administrative procedures, adoption and marriage documents, wills, contracts of sales, debt records, along with an important set of lists of people: census, property records, staff and troops.[8] In general, the quantitative data of the archive, together with the famous autobiography in the statue of King Idrimi, found in level IV,[9] offer important evidence about northern Syrian society – especially given the probable Hurrite infiltration within Semitic population – and the political ideology of the Late Bronze Age.

### *2.1.5. Other epigraphic records*

Besides the already cited collections of textual and epigraphic information, data coming from other archives in the ancient Near East from other periods of the Bronze Age are also relevant sources of secondary character. In particular, when references to political situations or socio-political practices analogous to the ones evidenced in the Late Bronze Age are attested, these date shed important comparative light on the interpretation of the politics of the period.

#### *2.1.5.1. Documents from Emar*

The site of Emar (modern Tell Meskene) is located on the right bank of the Euphrates River in Syria, at a crossroads of interregional trading routes between Babylonia, Mari and Anatolia. Until 1972, the city of Emar was known only after its mention in texts from Mari, Nuzi and Ugarit, as a trading or political partner. In that year, and after six consecutive archaeological campaigns (1972–78), some 800 texts were recovered dating from the late fourteenth and early twelfth century BCE, a time in which Emar was mostly under a Hittite protectorate. Some 150 of these texts are of economic nature (records of deliveries, inventories, lists of sacrifices, lists of staff), some 200 are contracts (adoptions, payments of debt, warrants, loans, sales of fields, slaves, payments of ransom, etc.), and some 20 letters belong to the private sphere (cf. Margueron and Sigrist 1997; Huehnergard 1997; see also Arnaud 1991 for an collection of some 200 documents).

#### *2.1.5.2. Archives from Mari*

In 1933, a French archaeological expedition led by A. Parrot initiated excavations in Tell Hariri (Syria), on the western bank of the Euphrates river, near the modern border with Iraq, where the Amorite city of Mari was unearthed. Royal archives were discovered in the palace, containing important diplomatic and political data for the period 1800–1600 BCE in the Near East.[10] To date, some 20,000 tablets in Akkadian and written in cuneiform have been discovered, providing information about the royal court and diplomatic relations with contemporary Mesopotamian polities, both on terms of equality and of dominance and subordination, as well as several aspects of the kingdom's administration. Especially relevant for the present study are the attested political relations of 'tribal' nature, reflected in the inter-polity epistolary evidence, exposing a kind of interregional political system previous to, although less consolidated than the Amarna interregional political system.[11]

#### *2.1.5.3. Archives from Nuzi*

The site of Nuzi, in Yorghan Tepe (some 12 km from Kirkuk in the north of modern Iraq and east of the Tigris river) was under the political sphere of the kingdom of Arrapḫa in the Bronze Age. It was excavated systematically between 1925 and 1931, although already in 1894 some tablets from the site were brought to the British Museum and published since 1896 in specialised studies. The excavation uncovered some 7,000 tablets in Akkadian language of both public and private character (on legal, economic and administrative matters), dating back from the Late Bronze Age and covering some five generations (*c.* 1475–1350 BCE). They represented an immense *corpus* of information on the social practices of the inhabitants of the site, especially at a local or domestic level, but also reflecting political relations between Assyria, Mittani and Arrapḫa.[12]

The information retrieved from the Nuzi archives had its moment of notoriety between the early and mid-twentieth century, when scholars directly linked them to the family customs described in the biblical book of Genesis about the patriarchs. However, the comparative fallacy between the material from Nuzi and the biblical material rested on an isolation of linguistic elements and social practices so they would 'fit in' and sustain the historicity of the patriarchal traditions.[13] Actually, the main relevance of the documents found at Nuzi lies in the possibility of a reconstruction of the historical context of the site in the Late Bronze Age, and of the about social, economic, administrative and political aspects of everyday life. The Nuzi texts reflect on inter-polity relations but also on relations between individuals from Nuzi and Assyria; on the behaviour of local officials; on real-estate transactions through 'fictive' adoptions; and on the *ilku* (*corvée*) system.[14]

## 2.2. On 'international' diplomacy in the Late Bronze Age

Ancient Near Eastern scholars, and historians in particular, have regarded the Late Bronze Age in the history of the ancient Near East as a foundational period of 'international diplomacy', at least for this part of the ancient world.[15] From a critical perspective, however, terms like 'international' and 'diplomacy' must be properly defined and evaluated in their own interpretative potentiality and value for the historian of ancient socio-cultural realities and the specific aspect within them: namely inter-polity contacts and relations. In pharaonic Egypt, there was indeed an institution that can actually be considered a foreign office, dealing with foreign political affairs;[16] however, it is mandatory that an understanding of the nature and functions of such institution results from a historical and anthropological analysis that covers both the 'native' (Egyptian) meaning attributed to the institution and the scholarly interpretation of it. The native understanding cannot equalize the interpretation offered by modern scholarship. In short, it is all about not confusing what social anthropologists call the *emic* perspective of social reality with the *etic* perspective of it.[17] This understanding suggests that Late Bronze Age or Amarna 'diplomacy' should not be placed in the same category as what we in modern times referred to as diplomacy since not only present is a temporal or historical gap of millennia, but essentially a *cultural* gap must be considered. The ideological universe of Amarna's regional politics is ontologically different from modern (i.e. since the Enlightenment onwards) ideas of politics and diplomacy. Further, G. Berridge (2000: 212, 221–2) has defined 'diplomacy' as 'essentially a means of communication designed to promote negotiations, gather information, and clarify intentions, in relation to enemies as well as friends', and he does not find such definition as fitting for the Amarna regional system of political relations since

> the evidence strongly suggests that it is misleading to describe Amarna diplomacy as a full-fledged diplomatic system. It is true that its personnel were in general adequate to their tasks, that its methods for underpinning agreements were impressive, and that a suitable degree of flexibility of form and procedure (associated in this case perhaps with its very underdevelopment) was apparent. Nonetheless, it was marred by an incomplete and weakly held norm of immunity, an absence of resident missions other than those – stunted and crippled – of special envoys temporarily detained, incomplete bureaucratic support, and little in the way of a reflex for mediation between the Great Powers. Most significantly, diplomatic communication between hostile states – the real test of a developed diplomatic system – appears to have been virtually nonexistent.

This interpretative caveat should lead us to consider the relations between the great powers of the Late Bronze Age on their own terms, as a 'brotherhood' (Akk. *aḫḫūtu*), with the cultural and socio-political implications such a notion possessed within the ideological context of the Amarna epistolography.[18]

In a similar manner, the term 'international' as applied to ancient Near Eastern societies may lead to misunderstandings and misrepresentations: the idea of 'nation', as it is usually perceived nowadays, is essentially an anachronism when applied to pre-modern or ancient social realities (cf. the discussions in Hobsbawm 1992; Thiesse 1999; Eriksen 2002; Anderson 2006). Therefore, a term like 'interregional' instead of 'international' might connote a less modern understanding when we are dealing with issues related to identity, politics and territory. In a more strictly political sense, the notion of 'inter-polity' relations might replace too the idea of 'international' when addressing relations between two or more kingdoms, two or more states, a state and a tribal organisation, etc., each located in different regions. This precision in the use of terminology is necessary to avoid the representation of anachronistic realities of the past and to achieve a correct interpretation of symbolic and socio-political practices in ancient societies.

It should be clear by now that each reference to 'diplomacy' in ancient Near Eastern times depends on a particular set of cultural and ideological presuppositions, which are constructed according to the general parameters of ancient Near Eastern worldviews (cf. Liverani 1976c). Liverani has characterised the nature of diplomatic relations in the Late Bronze Age in the following manner:

> Kings exchanging correspondence call each other 'brother' or less frequently 'colleague', and define their alliance as 'brotherhood', a 'goodness (of relation)' (*ṭābūtu*), even a 'friendship' or 'love' (*ra'amūtu*). They insist on the idea of 'loving' each other, 'enjoying' and 'not afflicting' each other's heart, sharing resources and gratifying each other's desires. If a difference in age should make the brotherhood metaphor inappropriate, the image of a father/son relationship is used instead; this is just a sign of personal respect with no political implications. When the royal Ugaritic couple address a high Hittite official as 'father', they are not implying any political subordination; they just wish to honour an old man. The use of the term 'son' as a form of address is also devoid of political significance, though it savours of an irritating 'paternalism'. When a high Hittite official addresses a young and recently enthroned Ugaritic king as his 'son', his object is to make it understand, from the first line of the message, that a novice such as him has to pay more attention and respect to older people . . . Suzerainty is expressed by the lord/servant terminology.[19]

It is, however, possible to dissent from Liverani's observation when he points out that the father-son image does not have political implications because such are expressed instead through the metaphor lord/servant (cf. Schloen 2001: 256–62). In fact, if we attend to the heading of the letter the petty king Aziru of Amurru sends to the Egyptian official Tutu, Aziru addresses Tutu as 'my lord, my father'.[20] In effect, it could be affirmed that the conception of suzerainty in Syria-Palestine was constructed through notions and representations of kinship and friendship, which support the political phraseology of the period's diplomacy and constitute the vehicle of socio-political practices. These Late Bronze Age socio-political conceptualisations can be sketched, with the Akkadian key terms of inter-polity relations, as shown in the chart on p. 37.

### *2.2.1. Egyptian and Asiatic worldviews*

Building on this structural understanding of the characteristics of Late Bronze Age diplomacy, we must now consider the particularities of ancient Near Eastern

| | *Great King – Great King Relation* | *Great King – Small King Relation* |
|---|---|---|
| Character of the relation | Parity, reciprocity | Asymmetrical exchange, dominance of the Great King and subordination of the Small King |
| Terminology of the relation | *aḫḫūtu* [brotherhood]<br>*ra'amūtu* [love]<br>*ṭabūtu* [friendship] | *kittu* [loyalty] (Small King → Great King)<br>*naṣāru* [protection] (Great King → Small King)<br>*balāṭu* [life] (Great King → Small King) |

worldviews. In broad terms, a clear differentiation can be established between an Egyptian worldview and an Asiatic (Mesopotamian, Hittite, Levantine) worldview.

From the perspective of the Egyptian worldview, what we understand as 'diplomacy' or 'international relations' cannot be addressed apart from the nature of Egyptian kingship itself and the attributes and features of the Pharaoh as a god-king. In effect, the Egyptian conception of monarchy saw the Pharaoh as he who guarantees the cosmic order and peace, both in the land of Egypt (*Kmt*) and in foreign lands (*ḫswt*) (Grimal 1986: 53–4). Furthermore, the Pharaoh would provide the 'breath of life' (*ṯꜣw n ꜥnḫ*) to men, Egyptian, or foreigners, through the establishment of order (*mꜣꜥt*) and the pacification of the land, defeating the forces of chaos and guaranteeing the unity of the country. The Egyptian king of the Eighteenth and Nineteenth Dynasties possesses both warrior and demiurgic qualities: he vanquishes the enemy and grants them life, in a symbolic manner – which is also ontological, from the Egyptian perspective – but also in a more concrete way through political acts.[21]

In the Annals of Thutmose III, the defeated Levantine petty kings at the battle of Megiddo are represented exclaiming:

> [Great] is the power of *Mn-ḫpr-Rꜥ*, [the son of Amun]! Grant that we survive: we shall make deliveries to your majesty, and we shall send trade goods (*bꜣkw*) [for your treasury! . . . There has never been a king who did] what your majesty has done in this land!' Then my majesty commanded that the 'breath of life' (*ṯꜣw n ꜥnḫ*)' be given to them.[22]

In the same text it is further noted: 'Lo, the chiefs of this foreign country came on their bellies to 'kiss the earth' to the power of his majesty and to request 'breath (*ṯꜣw*)' for their noses, because of the greatness of his strength and because of the greatness of the power.'[23]

In the Amarna period and the reign of pharaoh Aḫenaten, several letters from the petty kings in the Levant disclose an appropriation of Egyptian phraseology and, in pragmatic terms, also the ideology. Thus, Rib-Hadda of Byblos claims:

> May the king heed the word of his servant. May he grant provisions for his servant and *keep his servant alive* so I may guard his [lo]yal [city], along with our L[ad]y (and) our gods, f[or you]. May [the king] vis[it] his [land] and [his servant]. [May he] give thought to his land. Pac[ify yo]ur [land]![24]

N. Grimal indicates as well that to receive the Pharaoh's breath of life is, above all, political recognition, from the Egyptian perspective, a recognition realised by the duty of labour (*bꜣkw*), by extension obedience, that the now servants owe to the Egyptian Pharaoh:[25] 'Every land bows down to his power, their goods (*ỉnw*) being on their backs, [in return for giving] them the 'breath of life (*ṯꜣw n ꜥnḫ*).'[26] This, however, should not be taken to mean that the Egyptian administration of conquered lands would proceed through some kind of 'vassal oath' or 'vassal treaty', as was the case with Hittite rule. It is true that the nominal and verbal expression *sḏfꜣ tryt* can be translated as 'oath of allegiance' (Faulkner), 'to undertake fealty' (Wilson), or 'to establish the veracity' (Goedicke); but in each case the expression appears as the commitment of the vanquished (or of Egypt's subjects) not to contravene what the Pharaoh orders or decrees.[27] Also as C. Zaccagnini (1990: 53–4) observes about two occurrences on loyalty oaths (*sḏfꜣ tryt*) sworn by the Asiatics to Thutmose III and Amenḥotep II:

> these oaths are still a matter of controversy, but their sporadicity is a strong hint against a regular practice not otherwise attested in the relations between Egypt and Asia. Comparison with loyalty oaths of the Hittite milieu seem to be out of place, because the *sdfꜣ tryt* only concern the Pharaoh as a person and do not include his successors, and moreover because this kind of oath is by no means functionally inserted in the texture of an inner (i.e. Egyptian) administrative structure or in an international setting where third parties engage themselves as 'tributary' subjects.

Thus, this terminology operates more within a ritual sphere of the Pharaoh's attributes over his subjects than as a loyalty oath.

It is also interesting to note the conception according to which the Egyptian king manifests his sovereignty after a condition of possession (something shared with the south-west Asian monarchies): the Pharaoh is the 'lord' (*nb*), he is the 'king' (*nswt*) and the 'sovereign' (*'ỉty*) of Egypt and the 'chief' (*ḥḳꜣ*) of the 'Nine Bows' (*psḏt-pḏwt*), namely the conquered enemies from the foreign lands (Grimal 1986: 564–85; also Lorton 1974: 12–16, 18–21, 21–9). This differentiated terminology on the modes in which the Pharaohs relate to their subordinates by exerting power is most relevant since, from the Egyptian perspective, there is only one king (*nswt*), while other rulers are recognised as princes (*wrw*, lit. 'great ones'),[28] lords (*nbw*) or chiefs (*ḥḳꜣw*)[29] in foreign lands, who would never be on the same ontological level as the Egyptian king (*nswt*).[30] As D. B. Redford (1995: 168–9) argues:

> The monarchy in Egypt constituted a unity, a single function, with universal application. There was but one *nswt*, 'King (of Upper Egypt)'. The mythology rationalizing kingship did not accommodate a plurality of *nswt*s. The case with Akkadian *šarrum* or West Asiatic *malkum*, both 'king', however, was quite different. These were terms which had basically terrestrial reference, and did not suffer the burden of mythological baggage inherited from the period of formulation. A Hammurabi or a Yarim-lim, or a Shamshi-adad, great kings themselves, were served by lesser kings, and the terms *šar šarri* or *melek m*ᵉ*lakim*, 'king of kings', arose spontaneously. Pharaoh, on the other hand, thrust as overlord into the Asiatic sphere, could not conceive of, or tolerate, degrees of kingship. All foreign heads of state, whether they called themselves kings or nor, were but 'chiefs' (*wrw*) to him. 'King of kings' (*nswt nsyw*) or 'ruler of rulers' (*ḥḳ3 ḥḳ3w*) were simply mechanical translations of alien locutions.

In Southwest Asia, inter-polity relations were conceived instead after a much less centralist ideology or worldview than in Egypt, and the wider landscape, both physical and political, was probably one of the main reasons for it. Kingship in this region had characteristics similar to the Egyptian, in regard to palatine structures and material means of socio-political organisation. However, the kingship ideology diverged from the Egyptian concept of kingship.[31] If in ancient Egypt the Pharaoh was a king-god on earth, the Asiatic king – each one of the Great Kings of Late Bronze Age diplomacy – was instead conceived of as a human king with functions mediating the divine and human realms. The Asiatic king was the representative of the human community before the gods, especially through the performance of rituals, and was also the keeper of the divine order on earth, that is, in the kingdom. Celebrative inscriptions about the protective, warrior and brave nature of the king describing the kings of Southwest Asia in the Bronze and Iron Ages, make room – unlike the ancient Egyptian worldview – for the existence of various kings, ontologically alike, in other words, monarchic peers with which to interact through parity or alliance relations (cf. Munn-Rankin 1956; Zaccagnini 1999; Liverani 2001; Podany 2010; Altman 2012).

An example of a parity treaty is the famous peace treaty celebrated between Ḫattušili III of Ḫatti and Ramesses II of Egypt, notably from the Hittite point of view, in which both rulers are referred to as Great Kings of each of their kingdoms and in terms of brotherhood (*aḫḫūtu*), establishing relations of alliance and mutual defensive assistance, guaranteeing the throne succession of each other and the exchange of fugitives from their respective kingdoms. Copies of the tablets with the treaty inscribed were available for both parties. In the Hittite case, they were found in the archives of the imperial capital and, in the Egyptian case, a hieroglyphic version was carved into the walls of the temple of the god Amun in Karnak.[32] However, in the Egyptian version of the treaty, the pharaonic ideology is preponderant over any parity relation and, thus, king Ramesses II is referred to as *pꜣ ḥḳꜣ ꜥꜣ n Kmt* ('great chief of Egypt'), while Ḫattušili III is titulated only as *pꜣ wr ꜥꜣ n Ḫtꜣ* ('great one of Ḫatti') (Langdon and Gardiner 1920: 185; Spalinger 1981: 308; also K*RI* II, 227.2–3).

We may observe, in this context, also an alternative example, a non-parity or asymmetrical treaty between the Hittite king Ḫattušili III and king Bentešina of Amurru. There certainly were instances of mutual assistance in the treaty, of alliance and observations over safe succession to the throne. However, it was the Hittite king who imposed the conditions of the treaty and the king of Amurru who should follow them, with clauses indicating retribution should he not behave as envisaged in the agreement.[33] This kind of subordination relation, through the imposition of a treaty with duties and nominal guarantees, was the standard procedure of Hittite organisation of conquered polities, as attached territories to the kingdom.

The political relations that the kings from Kassite Babylonia established with Egypt during the Amarna period should be understood, in theory, as parity relations, at least from the Asiatic perspective. Nonetheless, as already indicated, the Egyptian centralist ideology would make it highly improbable for the Pharaoh to recognise a relation among equals – at least as it is attested in the Egyptian repertoire of sources. This is evidenced in the complaint that king Kadašman-Enlil of Babylonia writes to paraoh Amenḥotep III:

> [Morove]r, you, my brother, when I wrote [to you] about marrying your daughter, in accordance with your practice of not gi[ving] (a daughter), [wrote to me], saying 'From time immemorial no daughter of the king of Egy[pt] is given to anyone.' Why n[ot]? You are a king; you d[o] as you please. Were you to give (a daughter), who would s[ay] anything?[34]

Accordingly, on the one hand, the diplomatic relations between Egypt and Asiatic polities may be analytically categorised as between Great Kings; but, on the other hand, the Egyptian centralist worldview, imposing an ontological difference between the monarchies and the kingdoms with which Egypt interacts thus widens the gap of normal asymmetrical relations with Small Kings. The situation is not only marked by conditions of political status or prestige or even military power, as would be expected in the Asiatic political landscape, but it is also affected by the cosmic differences between Egypt and its periphery.

The Amarna correspondence illustrates very well the aforementioned situation, especially from the point of view of the Syro-Palestinian petty kings, when they write to the Pharaoh disappointed by his silence to their complaints. As we read in two letters by Rib-Hadda of Byblos:

> [S]ay [t]o the king, my lord: Message of Rib-Hadda, [your] se[rvant]. I fall at the feet of my lord, [my] Su[n, 7 times and 7 times]. Be informed [that] the war aga[inst me] is severe. [He (Abdi-Aširta of Amurru; EP) has taken] all my cities; [Gubla (Byblos; EP)] alone rem[ains].

> [. . .] What can I do by myself? You yourself have been [neg]ligent of your cities [. . .] I have been plundered of [my grain, and] it is [to you] that I have tur[ned].[35]
>
> [Rib-Hadda says to] h[is] lord: I fall [at the feet of my lord, 7 times and 7 times. I wrote to you, 'W]hy have you sat idly by [and] done nothing, so that the *ḫabiru* dog tak[es you]r cities?' [. . .] O king, [listen to me and s]end ar[chers t]o take the land of Amurru.[36]

From a general outlook, the sovereigns of Babylonia, Assyria and Ḫatti, as described above, were considered Great Kings among and by themselves and as such they would politically relate to each other and to minor polities under subordination.[37] Each of the petty kings from Syria-Palestine – but also rulers of greater importance – were called by the Egyptian court *wr* (Eg. pl. *wrw*; lit., 'great ones'); while the petty kings were self-proclaimed in their letters to the Pharaoh as 'servants' (Sum. sing. ÌR = Akk. [*w*]*ardu*)[38] of their distant 'lord' (Sum. EN = Akk. *bēlu*).[39] Nonetheless, and interestingly, the petty kings of the Levant would refer to themselves among their neighbouring peers as 'king' (Sum. LUGAL = Akk. *šarru*),[40] as the 'man' (Sum. LÚ = Akk. *awīlu* → *amī/ēlu*) of a particular town[41] or as the 'great one' (Eg. *pꜣ wr* = Akk. [*p*]*awera/e*).[42] Summing up the relation and building on the ideology of the actors and the structure of communication between the kings of the Late Bronze Age regional system (Liverani 2000), we can place on one side the aforementioned structure of Great Kings and Small Kings interacting, but we must also acknowledge the distinctive character of the Egyptian worldview, especially when interacting with the powers of Southwest Asia and the petty kings from the Levant.

Now, if we consider the profoundly ethnocentric nature of the Egyptian worldview, regarding the essence of kingship but also the nature of those living beyond the borders of the land of Egypt (cf. Galán 1995), how does such worldview coalesce with any notion of 'diplomacy' or 'international relations'? As D. Lorton (1974: 1) asks: 'What did the Egyptians regard as the method of creating this order? What was its specific content? How was their system, i.e. their international law, intelligible both to them and to the foreigners with whom they dealt?' It is in effect evident that the interregional contacts of Egypt denote a certain tension between the mentioned ideology and concrete situations of 'diplomatic' contact with other powers as any state or complex polity would be expected to have. In this sense, we could argue that Egyptian propaganda – in the etymological sense of propagating a worldview through visual and graphics means – establishes a double vision. Towards the internal public, a centralist and triumphalist vision of kingship predominates, while towards the exterior public, namely the diplomatic arena, such centralist and triumphalist vision is tamed and a recognition of a certain parity predominates.[43] However, attending to a proper historical example, we find in the parity relations between Ramesses II and Ḫattušili III, that the tension goes critical between the political construction propagated by the Egyptian ideology, after the Egyptian *topos* of the ever victorious Pharaoh over those peoples dwelling beyond Egypt's borders (the Nine Bows), and the particular historical situation, which denies Egypt its regional political superiority, by placing it as an ally and peer to Ḫatti, through an arranged marriage between the royal houses that sealed the alliance.[44]

The different manner of procedure in Egypt and in Southwest Asia regarding inter-polity contacts produced, on the one hand, a relatively stable mode of socio-political relations – notably, Ḫatti's rule over the northern Levant – and, on the other, political articulations marked by semantic interferences in the political communication between the ruler and the ruled – notably, Egypt's dominance over the southern Levant. Such socio-political dynamics, between the Great Kings themselves, and between Great and Small Kings, may be interpreted within a general framework covering the variety of means for interaction: economic exchanges, marriage alliances, and the exchange of messages and specialists, besides the conceptualisation and articulation of political power and prestige. More than concrete historical facts, the interregional polity interaction during the Late Bronze Age offers a kind of ancient mental scheme, evidenced in the epigraphic and textual record, and after which we may recover an ancient cultural mode of creating and expressing a whole spectrum of social realities as ancient Near Eastern political elites conceived of them.

## 2.3. On the Late Bronze Age epistolographic structure

The analysis of the correspondence between the kingdoms of the Late Bronze Age offers, as indicated above, not only historical data, but above all, the formal aspects of political communication, and their respective ideological configuration, between polities of different rank and status of the period. If we consider the main textual *corpus* for this period regarding political representations, namely the Amarna letters, a formal pattern can be established to understand the nature of such epistolography (cf. Liverani 1998: 40–62).

Traditionally, the Amarna correspondence has been divided between 'international' and 'vassal' or 'imperial' letters (Knudtzon 1907; Moran 1992; Liverani 1998; 1999; Cohen and Westbrook 2000a; also the discussion in Mynářová 2006). The 'international' letters can be divided into letters of the Great Kings (Egypt, Ḫatti, Babylonia, Mittani and Assyria) and letters of the 'independent kingdoms' (Arzawa and Alašiya). Also, the correspondence of the petty Levantine kings can be sub-divided into 'letters of peace and obedience' – coming mostly from Palestine and Phoenicia, a zone of total control by Egypt – and 'letters of war and menace' – coming mostly from Syria, a contested zone with the Hittite kingdom. The external menace in the Syro-Palestinian corridor, mostly on its northern border on account of its topography and human geography (Abel 1967 I: 235–9, 250–58, 261–70; II: 1–42; Rowton 1967; Sapin 1981; 1982), included the semi-nomadic or pastoralist elements, for instance, the Suteans (Eg. *šwtw*) and the politically marginal elements, the *ḫabiru* (Liverani 1965; also Klengel 1972; on the Suteans, Kupper 1957: 83–145; Heltzer 1981), who would attack caravans or sites under Egyptian control but who would also hire themselves out as mercenaries of a petty king under the Pharaoh's orders.[45]

As to the formal structure of the letters and the epistolary mechanism that seemed to be active during the Late Bronze Age, it is possible to distinguish clearly three scribal traditions to address the addressee from the opening of the letter:

1 A Babylonian tradition: 'To [ADDRESSEE]: thus (says) [SENDER]'.
2 A Syro-Palestinian tradition: 'Message from [SENDER] to [ADDRESSEE]'.[46]
3 An Egyptian tradition: '[SENDER] says to [ADDRESSEE]'.

The majority of the Amarna correspondence exposes a 'Babylonian' opening.[47] Due to aspects of rank and formal courtesy, the openings vary according to the region from which the letters come. From Babylonia, where the epistolary courtesy prevails, the name of the addressee is placed first, followed by the name of the sender. From the Syro-Anatolian region, the name of the most important interlocutor is placed first, be it the sender or the addressee. From Egypt, where an ethnocentric worldview prevailed, such epistolary courtesy was hardly followed. Interestingly, there is only one Levantine petty king (Rib-Hadda) who adopted in several letters an 'Egyptian' opening: 'Rib-Hadda says to his lord'.[48]

It is also possible to identify as well a whole set of epithets of exaltation between the Great Kings of the period, together with epithets of auto-humiliation from the Small Kings when addressing, especially, the Pharaoh (Liverani 1998: 55–9). There existed an opposition between rank and function, represented by the binomial 'lord/servant', and also a metaphoric kinship reference exemplified by the binomials 'father/son' and 'brother/brother' (Fensham 1971). These terms are used in the correspondence as indirect approximation. For instance, in the letters from the Small Kings, 'my lord' to say 'you', 'your servant' to say 'I', etc. Also in this correspondence, the formula is always laudatory of the Pharaoh and auto-humiliating of the sender: the Pharaoh is referred to as 'the king, my lord, my god, the Sun'; the local petty kings refer to themselves as 'your servant' or 'the dust/soil under your feet' (Akk. *epru ša šēpē-ka*). When saluting and paying respect, the petty king declared in the letters a bowing or prostration 'seven times and seven times' (Akk. *7-šu 7-ta-a-an*) before the Pharaoh[49]

> *a-na šàr-ri* EN-*ia* $^{d}$UTU *iš-tu* AN *ša-me-e um-ma Sá-ta-at-na* LÚ URU *ak-ka*$^{KI}$ ÌR-*ka* ÌR *šàr-ri ù* SAḪAR.MEŠ *ša* 2 GIR.MEŠ-*šu* KI.MEŠ *ša-ka-ba-ši-šu a-na* 2 GIR.MEŠ *šàr-ri* EN-*ia* $^{d}$UTU *iš-tu* AN *ša-me 7-šu 7-ta-a-an.*
>
> To the king, m[y] lord, the Sun from the sky: Message from Satatna, the ruler of Akka, your servant, the servant of the king, and the dirt at his feet, the ground on which he treads. [I] prostrate myself at the feet of the king, my lord, the Sun from the sky, 7 times and 7 times, both on the stomach and on the back.[50]

The described principles of diplomatic epistolography may certainly be found all over in the ancient Near East, though with minor regional variations. As already indicated, during the eighteenth century BCE a similar inter-polity interaction, as the one found in the Amarna letters, is testified in the Mesopotamian kingdom of Mari, as the diplomatic correspondence excavated from the archives of Tell Hariri shows.[51] In the correspondence of king Zimri-Lim with peer polities and with his 'vassals', we get a clear image of a rudimentary diplomatic system that would later appear enhanced during the Amarna period. The political interaction between kings of equal rank is denominated in terms of 'brotherhood' and the corresponding interaction between Mari's king and his 'vassals' is articulated through the already mentioned binomial 'father/son', as indicated by Munn-Rankin (1956: 76):

> The political relationship between allied rulers was conceived of as one of kinship, either of 'fraternity', *aḫûtum*, *atḫûtum*, or of father and son. It has been suggested that 'brotherhood' was invoked between rulers of equal status, whereas 'paternity', *abûtum*, and 'sonship', *marûtum*, expressed subordination, in particular that of the vassal to his overlord or 'father', a relationship that may alternatively be described as one of 'service', *wardûtum*.
>
> The epistolography from Mari followed the Babylonian diplomatic tradition and, therefore, we find the formula 'Say to [ADDRESSEE]: thus (says) [SENDER]', usually followed by 'your son/your father/your brother', according to the rank of the parties. In the case of communication with a subject or an official of the king of Mari, the recurring formula is 'Say to my lord: thus says [SENDER], your servant'. (Durand 1997: 383–639)

In the kingdom of Ḫatti, besides the interaction with the contemporary great powers, formalised in the already mentioned terms of equality and 'brotherhood',[52] we also find epistolary communication with the subdued polities during Hittite military expansion, between the Hittite king and his 'vassals', or between a Hittite official and a 'vassal' of the king (Beckman 1996). In the instance of a letter sent by the Hittite king to a subject king, the formula is 'Thus says My Majesty: say to [ADDRESSEE]'. In the case of a 'vassal' king or an official writing to the king, the formula used is 'To my Sun, my lord, say: thus (says) [SENDER]'. On some occasions, both 'vassals' and officials of the kingdom are referred to in terms of kinship, i.e. 'son', connoting a hierarchical relationship between sender and addressee.[53]

The archives of Ugarit, on the Syrian coast, have preserved a set of notable examples of inter-polity epistolography. From a structural point of view, it is possible to distinguish between two kinds of epistolary openings of the correspondence. The formula 'To [ADDRESSEE] say: message from [SENDER]', which occurs when the lower-ranking party addresses a superior party; and the formula

'Message from [SENDER]: to [ADDRESSEE] say', having place in a situation of socio-political peers communicating or when a higher-ranking party addresses a lower-ranking party (Cunchillos-Ilarri 1989a: 244–5). We also find prostration and respect formulas: 'at the feet of [ADDRESSEE] I prostrate myself' (*KTU* 2.13, 5–6; 2.30, 4–5; 2.64 recto, 6–7); or 'at the feet of [ADDRESSEE] from afar I prostrate myself/we prostrate ourselves' (*KTU* 2.11, 5–7; 2.33, 3–4; 2.45, 11–12); or 'at the feet of [ADDRESSEE] two times seven (times) I prostrate myself' (*KTU* 2.64 verso, 13–16; 2.70, 8–10; cf. RS 17.383, 4–5; 17.391, 4–5; 17.422, 5–7; 17.425, 6–7, in *PRU* IV, pp. 221, 226, 223 and 218, respectively; RS 20.16, 4–5; 20.151, 2'–4'; 20.219, 5–6, in *Ug* V, pp. 118, 138 and 129, respectively); or 'at the feet of [ADDRESSEE] seven and seven times from afar I prostrate myself' (*KTU* 2.12, 6–11; 2.24, 5–7; 2.40, 5–8; 2.42, 4–5; 2.51, 2–3; 2.68, 4–7; such phraseology is also found in the Amarna correspondence, but without the adverb *mrḥqtm/mrḥqm*, 'from afar', for instance, in EA 213:6–9; 233:9–15; 281: 4–7; 301:5–11; etc.; cf. Cunchillos Ilarri 1989a: 249–50).

The terminology employed consist of terms of kinship or interpersonal, such as *adny* 'my lord' (*KTU* 2.64, 2.); *b'ly* 'my lord' (*KTU* 2.40, 1; 2.42, 1; 2.61, 2; 2.63, 1; 2.64, 10); *b'lh* 'his lord' (*KTU* 2.47, 2); *b'lny* 'our lord' (*KTU* 2.70, 1); *b'lkm* 'your lord' (*KTU* 5.10, 3); *umy* 'my mother' (*KTU* 2.11, 1; 2.13, 2; 2.16, 2; 2.30; 1; 2.34, 2; 5.10, 3); *bny* 'my son' (*KTU* 2.14, 3); *aḫy* 'my brother' (*KTU* 2.14, 3; 2.38, 2); *iḫy* 'my sister' (*KTU* 2.44, 2); *aḫty* 'your daughter' (*KTU* 5.10, 1); *'bdk* 'your servant/s' (*KTU* 2.11, 4; 2.12, 5; 2.24, 4; 2.33, 2; 2.40, 4; 2.42, 3; 2.64, 12; 2.68, 3; RS 34.148, 4); *bnk* 'your son' (*KTU* 2.13, 4; 2.30, 3; 2.64, 5); *aḫk* 'your brother' (*KTU* 2.38, 3). Without denying in principle a possible concrete biological relationship between two persons designating themselves after some of these terms in Ugaritic (as also in Amarna, Mari, etc.) epistolography, the relevance lies at the level of socio-political relations connoted by such terminology, implying a determined set of political practices and expectations from the communication partner.

As in the Mari and Hittite cases, the Ugaritic epistolary *corpus* may be arranged in three groups: internal correspondence, that is, messages exchanged between the court and palace officials; correspondence between peers, that is, messages between Ugarit and kingdoms of similar political rank and status, and 'vassal' correspondence, especially with the kingdom of Ḫatti, but also with Egypt. The correspondence between peers follows the rules of the 'brotherhood ideology', as it can be illustrated in a letter from the king of Tyre to the king of Ugarit:

> *a-na* LUGAL KUR *U-ga-ri-it um-ma* LUGAL URU *Ṣur-ri qí-bi-ma lu-ú šul-mu a-na muh-hi-ka* DINGIR.MEŠ *a-na šul-ma-ni pap-ru-ka ša-ni-tam* ŠEŠ-*ia*.
>
> To the king of the land of Ugarit, thus says the king of the city of Tyre. Say: May the peace be with you! May the gods grant you health/well-being! Further, my brother . . . .[54]

There is also a standard greeting formula, *yšlm l-*, 'may the peace be with [PN]', as can be seen in this letter to the Pharaoh:

> *'m/l . špš . ] mlk . rb . mlk . mṣrm . mlk . n'*]*m . mlk . ṣdq . mlk . mlkm . b'l . kl . ḥwt . mṣr*]*m . rgm . tḥm .* ]*k/r . 'bdk . l . p'n . b'ly . ql*]*t . ln . b'ly . yšlm . xl . inšk . l . ḥwtk . l . `s`sw . l . mrkbtk .* ]*l . kl . d . iṯ . l . špš . m*]*lk . rb . mlk . mṣr[m . mlk . n'm .* ]*mlk . ṣ[dq . mlk . mlkm.*
>
> [To the Sun], Great King, king of Egypt, gracious king, just king, king of kings, lord of all the land of Egypt, say the message from [ ], your servant: at the feet of [my lord I am prostrat[ed. May the peace be with my lord! [ ] with your people, with your land, [with your horses], with your chariots, [. . .] with everything that belongs to the Sun, Great King, king of Egypt, gracious king, just king, king of kings![55]

The description of the formal structure for the exchange of letters between Late Bronze Age polities has presented a general overview of this kind of textual data. A proper socio-political interpretation of this evidence will be provided later, especially in Part III. Now, I would like to offer a synthetic view of the socio-linguistics of the Amarna correspondence as a key feature for understanding the cultural sense of politics during the second half of the second millennium BCE in the Levant.

### *2.3.1. Amarna socio-linguistics*

Apart from two letters in the Hittite language (EA 31 and 32) and a letter in Hurrite (EA 24), the language of the Amarna epistolography is in fact Babylonian Akkadian, notably in the 'international' letters and some of the 'vassal' letters. However, most of the letters sent to the Pharaoh by the Syro-Palestinian petty kings were written in a language often referred to as 'hybrid' or even 'artificial'. Its lexicon was almost completely Babylonian Akkadian, but the grammar was mainly Canaanite, meaning that probably this latter language have 'influenced its syntax and its morphology, and affecting the phonology and semantics' (Izre'el 1995b: 102; on the 'hybridisation' of Amarna Akkadian, cf. Rainey 1996). Also R. Labat had noted that in the Amarna correspondence, 'it is the conjugation that manifests the strongest contamination of the Akkadian by the local language. Moreover, the majority of letters from Canaan corrupt [lit., "fait violence"] the Akkadian phrase and adopt the scheme present in West Semitic' (Labat 1962: 21); namely, verb + subject + object, instead of the Akkadian order, subject + object + verb. The linguistic phenomenon of the glosses in the Amarna correspondence is related to this situation as well, which means that native lexemes in West Semitic or Hurrite (also Egyptian) were associated with other words in order to obtain a correct interpretation by the scribe. Regarding this question, S. Izre'el (1995b: 118) has concluded that

> when considering the Amarna glosses, one should not adhere solely to the accepted view of messengers sent with letters to be read by resident scribes in Egypt, as is evidenced by the letters of Jerusalem or Arzawa . . . The situation may have been more complex than that, allowing for other scenarios, such as messenger-scribes moving between Egypt and the Levant.

Further, E. Von Dassow (against Izre'el, who conceives of a 'Canaano-Akkadian' language; cf. Izre'el 1995b; 2012) understands Amarna Akkadian rather as an artificial or scribal construct, affirming that

> the hybrid of Canaanite and Akkadian in which Canaanite scribes wrote was not a language of any kind, but an artifact of these scribes' use of cuneiform, and furthermore, . . . the language underlying their communication in cuneiform was not Akkadian but Canaanite. The Canaanite use of cuneiform would then be an instance of alloglottography, to borrow a term from Ilya Gershevitch, who defined it as 'the use of one writable language for the purpose of writing another language': the Canaanite scribes used Akkadian words, spelled in cuneiform, to write Canaanite.

This leads Von Dassow (2004: 656, 673–4) to conclude that

> Canaanite, not Akkadian, was the *lingua franca* shared by the scribes of Canaan and their counterparts in Egypt . . . The idea of a dominant language would be replaced by the idea of a dominant writing system, which was implemented in various ways to encode different languages, in diverse regions: not Sumerian and Akkadian, but cuneiform *litterae francae* . . . were the medium of written communication among the multitude of Near Eastern states, with their multiplicity of tongues.

It is also notable that the meaning of the Akkadian term *umma*, used in the opening formula of the correspondence, varies according to the sender. In Babylonian Akkadian, the term is followed by the nominative, expressing the adverbial meaning of 'thus', while in Canaanite Akkadian, the term is followed by the genitive, for which its meaning changes into 'message from'.[56]

However, apart from the morpho-syntactic study of Amarna Akkadian and the influence of the local Canaanite language, the semantic field of Amarna epistolography is open to a wide spectrum of insights and interpretations due to the particular configuration of such epistolography (Vita 2010: 863–6). Scribes in Syria-Palestine were thinking and conceiving of their reality in Canaanite language, conveying this to addressees having an Egyptian worldview and using a means of communication – the letters – produced in what is in principle a foreign language. Hence, a foreign representation of the world for both parties of the communication, who, using Babylonian Akkadian, were at risks of 'communicative contamination' due to the cultural background of the scribes, notwithstanding the epistolary formalism and the rules of diplomatic communication, widespread in this period. K. van der Toorn (2000: 100, 102) has commented on this particular situation:

> The paucity that surrounds the activities of the scribes does not mean that their role was purely instrumental. At the receiving of the letters, scribes were responsible for the booking of the messages, their first screening, their translation, and – finally – the words in which the message would reach its destinatary. We should not forget that the culture of the Amarna Age was an oral one; the decipherment of written texts, especially those written in a foreign tongue, was an arcane science. Letters from allies and vassals of the Pharaoh would eventually reach their destinatary in an Egyptian version spoken by one of the scribes of the Foreign Office at the palace in Amarna . . . It must be remembered that the written letter is never the *verbatim* transcript of the words spoken by the nominal sender, usually a local ruler. Straightforward dictation is excluded by the mere fact that the scribes wrote in Akkadian, i.e. the *koine* Akkadian in use in Syria and Palestine, whereas the rulers who sent the letters spoke Canaanite as their native tongue. Even if it should be assumed that dictation was involved at some level, the scribes wrote down the translated version of their masters' word. And as every translator knows, there is no translation without interpretation. In addition to stylistic choices, the very substance of a letter could be influenced by the scribe on duty.

After presenting a communicative situation like this, we may consider – although without delving further into the nature of linguistic systems – that each language, natural or artificial, creates distinctive realities supported by particular cultural backgrounds, and which reciprocally such language influences. Therefore, a semantic analysis of the diplomatic epistolography of the Amarna period requires not only close attention to the linguistic and cultural divergences between sender and addressee – for instance, a Syro-Palestinian petty king and the Egyptian king or officials – but it also needs a kind of *ethnographic sensitivity* of the modern exegete in regard to language translation and perhaps, most relevantly, a *cultural translation* is mandatory in such interpretation.[57]

Let us consider the formal organisation of the communication between the Pharaoh and his Syro-Palestinian subjects. According to a suggestive hypothesis by M. Liverani – whom I follow closely in this section since he has produced what could be deemed a fine anthropological understanding of Amarna politics in his many contributions to the subject – the Egyptian administration, following a seasonal pattern of messages, would make a forewarning about the arrival of an official for the collection of tribute plus other items each spring. The tribute and the required goods were taken late in the summer or in autumn. Also, the Egyptian messenger announcing the imminent arrival of Egyptian troops, would return to

Egypt with the responses of the local petty kings.[58] This would have been the general pattern of the Amarna epistolography. In a 'structural' sense, according to Liverani, the forewarning letters of the Pharaoh transmitted a sequence that was always anchored in the same key verbs, 'to protect' (*naṣāru*), 'to listen [→ to obey]' (*šemû*) and 'to prepare' (*šūšuru*) (Liverani 1998: 36). Thus, the structure of the letters from the Pharaoh to his Syro-Palestinian subjects would proceed with the imperative formula 'Protect/be on your guard! Listen! Prepare!':

> Say to Endaruta, ruler of Akšapa: Thus [says] the king. He herewith dispatches to you this tablet, saying to you, Be on your guard. You are to guard the place of the king where you are. The king herewith sends to you Ḫanni, the son of Maireya, the stable overseer of the king in Canaan. And what he tells you heed very carefully lest the king find fault in you. Every word that he tells you heed very carefully and carry out very carefully. And be on your guard! Be on your guard! Do not be negligent! And may you prepare before the arrival of the archers of the king food in abundance, wine (and) everything else in abundance. Indeed he is going to reach you very quickly, and he will cut off the heads of the enemies of the king.[59]

As for the petty kings, the structure of the letters usually expresses an affirmative answer to the pharaonic command: 'I protect/am on my guard! I listen/obey! I prepare/am ready!' For instance: 'I am indeed guard[ing/protecting] the place of the king where I am. Whatever the k[ing], my lord, has written me, I have listened to very carefully. Who is the dog that would not obey the orders of the king, his lord, the son of the Sun?'[60]

To this order, three exceptions must be observed: there are in the epistolary record correct but incomplete answers, that is, messages that only assure the protection but that omit any reference to the other two commands, which nonetheless are considered affirmative answers by the Egyptian administration.[61] There are also letters with equivocatory answers: some letters from inner southern Syria express what seems to be a misunderstanding in the command to be prepared with a petition to lead the arriving Egyptian troops (see further below). Finally, there are a few cases of negative responses, for instance, by Rib-Hadda, ruler of Byblos, noting the impossibility of protecting his place and preparing the required goods because of a grave situation of upheaval in his territory and also due to the lack of resources and Egyptian troops:

> I am unable to send my ships there since Aziru [of Amurru, EP] is at war with me, and all the mayors [*ḫazannu*, EP] are at peace with him [. . .] Moreover, why does the king give the mayors, my friends, every sort of provision, but to me not give anything? Previously, money [silver, EP] and everything for the<ir> provisions were sent from the palace to my ancestors, and my lord would send troops to them. But now I write for troops, but a garrison is not sent, and nothing at all is given [to m]e.

> A[s for] the king, my lord's, [having said] 'Gua[rd yourself] and [the city of the king where you are],' how am I to guar[d myself]? I wrote t[o the king, my lord], 'They have taken a[ll] m[y cities]; the son of Abdi-Aširta is their [master]. Gub[la is the only c]ity I have'. I have ind[eed sen]t my mes<sen>ger t[o the king], my lord, but troops are not sen[t], and [my] messenger you do not allow to come out.[62]

There are also letters sent by local initiative – the 'autumn' letter, named so by Liverani due to its timing in the seasonal rhythm of the epistolary exchange – containing notices on the enemies of the petty king, which are also the Pharaoh's, and complaints about the local situation: 'May the king, my lord, know that the war against me and against Šuwardata is severe. So may the king, my lord, save his land from the power of the *ḫabiru*. O[th]erwise, may the king, my lord, send chariots to fetch u[s] lest our servants kill us.'[63]

Liverani proposes to distinguish between two levels of interpretation in the Amarna correspondence. One is the 'factual', with details of events, complaints and manifestations of moods, especially by the local petty kings, and another is the 'structural' level, characterised by the aforementioned sequences (Liverani 1998: 36–7). The 'structural' level allows us to also consider a situation of conflict or clash of ideological and political perspectives between the Syro-Palestinian 'vassals' and the Egyptian court, as indicated in the Introduction and proposed by Liverani (Liverani 1967; 1983a) many years ago:

> The Egyptian court tried to insert and use the Syro-Palestinian kinglets within the framework of its own administrative system and to obtain from the Asiatic subjects answers and actions useful to its own aims. Yet sometimes the Egyptian court was also resigned to entering [into] the complicated meanderings of the Asiatic behavioural conventions in order to obtain, in whatever way, results that cannot be repudiated. Furthermore, the Syro-Palestinian kinglets, in order to guarantee their interests and their local power, were generally resigned to accepting a large part of the Pharaonic ideology and trying to adopt a behaviour fitting to the Egyptian expectations. Yet they always remain strongly conditioned by their own mentality, by their own world view.[64]

As already indicated, the nature of the ideological-political clash is manifested, first, in the divergence between the 'Asiatic' and the 'Egyptian' conceptions of how a master and a servant must behave in political terms, and second, through an interference in the epistolary communication, not so much due to grammar errors or mistakes in the diplomatic Akkadian, but rather on the semantic features of the linguistic apparatus whether the letters are interpreted at the Egyptian court or in the petty kings' palaces. The first situation, regarding the organisation and dynamics of the Egyptian dominance over Syria-Palestine, synthesised by Liverani (1979c: 12):

> Pharaoh – or better: the Egyptian palace – did not conceptualize the exchange of letters with correspondents, but only sent official messages redacted according to well-tried and impersonal formulas, messages which were motivated by certain administrative needs (shifting of functionaries and of troops, payments of tribute, furnishing of goods) and for which one expected as a matter of course affirmative responses, always redacted according to a known formula. The Syro-Palestinian kings on the other hand, while they had indeed learned and used the Egyptian praxis, tended to personalize the relationship and to put it on a basis of parity: just as Pharaoh asks questions, so could they ask questions of him, just as he took the initiative to write, so could they on their own take the initiative to write to him, and above all they could expose to him difficulties, problems, and needs. Pharaoh naturally did not reply, and the continuous need, on the part of the Syro-Palestinian kings, to articulate their difficulties, problems and needs transformed a part of the Amarna correspondence into a sort of personal outlet, inclined to a distant and inert divinity, whom one knew to be distant and inert.

For the second situation, I present and follow closely four examples analysed by Liverani (1983b: 49–56) exposing the semantic disparity of some key Akkadian terms in the Amarna correspondence.

A first example regards the Akkadian verb *naṣāru*, meaning basically 'to protect',[65] which acquires a different meaning, whether interpreted from an Egyptian or an Asiatic viewpoint. According to the first conception, the Egyptian Pharaoh was self-sufficient and the only person capable of granting protection. For the Asiatic conception, the notion of protection would cross through the whole socio-political spectrum with different gradations of reciprocity: the king protected his subjects, and the subjects in turn protected (assisted) him. The problem of ancient translation and interpretation of the Akkadian term, following the semantic field of meaning in Egyptian and Canaanite respectively, is placed between such ideological and socio-political backgrounds. The Egyptian verb *sꜣw* means 'to protect, to pay attention, to be alert' but also, according to Liverani, in the Amarna correspondence it carries the connotation of 'to take care in your work, to be alert, to pay attention to what you are doing', etc.[66] The Canaanite verb *yšʻ* can be translated 'to protect, to keep' but also 'to save, to rescue'.[67] Thus, when a scribe used the verb *naṣāru*, a range of meanings was active, depending on the location of the interpreter of the letter either in the Egyptian or the Asiatic semantic field.[68] This situation would in fact interfere in the communication between sender and addressee in the Amarna epistolography. When the Pharaoh ordered 'be on your guard/protect your post', the Syro-Palestinian petty king would respond 'I am on guard/I protect my post', but he would immediately ask for provisions (*balāṭu*)[69] and troops (*maṣṣartu*,[70] from the verb *naṣāru*) in order to protect his post! This response is therefore attached to the friction between an Egyptian bureaucratic articulation of ruling and subordination, after which the dominance relation is unidirectional in matters executive, and the bilaterally personalised and reciprocal conception of ruling and subordination in south-western Asia. The Pharaoh must provide the local petty kings with provisions and troops so they *in exchange* can protect their posts. This is the reason why, when the Pharaoh's scribe used the verb *naṣāru* as equivalent of the verb *sꜣw*, of wider semantic range, to command a petty king that he 'pay attention', namely that he do what is expected from him (cf. EA 190:1–5; 367:6–21), the petty king would understand the message as an order 'to protect, to guard his place', something validated but on condition that material support is provided, as expressed in EA 88:28–34: 'For my part, I will [no]t neglect the word of [my] lord. But i[f the k]ing, my lord, does [not give heed] to the words of [his] ser[vant], then Gubla will be joined to him, and all the lands of the king as far as Egypt, will be joined to the *ḫabiru*'.[71]

A second example used by Liverani involves the term *balāṭu*, which may be translated as 'to live' but also as 'provisions'. This Akkadian term would be the equivalent to the Egyptian concept of *ꜥnḫ*. Egyptian royal ideology indicated that it is the Pharaoh who makes the foreigners under his rule 'to live', incorporating them into the cosmic order he guarantees (cf. *ARE* II § 819; III § 580, § 638). But such an event operates in an ontological and cosmic level, even if the term *ꜥnḫ* may also mean the more earthly 'provisions'. Although the Syro-Palestinian petty kings would recognise the ideological nature of the Pharaoh's words – for instance, submission in exchange for life (cf. EA 169:7–8; 215:16–17) – through which the 'life' gained is literally a divine grace, most of the time the Syro-Palestinian letters of the Amarna *corpus* would refer to the petition of provisions because they were already loyal servants to the Pharaoh, an exchange that from the Egyptian point of view was unrecognised and constituted an impertinent request (cf. EA 74:53–5; 85: 33–8; 91: 27–30; 121:11–17; 150:14–19; 155:17–23). Curiously, such wording is not reserved for the Pharaoh only, as evidenced in EA 238, in which a petty king (Bayadi, in northern Palestine) concludes his letter to a 'great one' (LU.GAL) of the region saying 'it is you who can keep us alive, and it is you who can put us to death' (ll. 31–3). The use of such phrasing in these contexts might indicate the Syro-Palestinian political pragmatism regarding Egyptian phraseology and, also, the situational (rather than institutional) nature of the socio-political articulation. Liverani notes parallelisms with biblical literature: for instance, Deut. 32:39: 'I kill and I make alive; I wound and I heal; and no one can deliver from my hand'; 1 Sam. 2:6: 'The Lord kills and brings to life' (NRSV; noted by Liverani 1998: 145 n. 68; cf. also Tomes 2005: 74–6, 112–13).

The third example is phraseological. The recurrent phrase in Amarna epistolography *šūšura ana pāni* (+ *ṣābē pitati*) refers to the preparation the petty king had to make before the arrival of the Egyptian troops to the place, especially provisions for the soldiers. According to Liverani, this Akkadian phrase is a translation depending essentially on the Egyptian phrase (*dỉt*) *grg r-ḥꜣt pr-ꜥꜣ* (lit. 'to prepare/make ready before [the arrival] of the Pharaoh').[72] The Egyptian verb *grg*, 'to prepare, make ready',[73] was translated by the Egyptian scribes with the Akkadian verb *šūšuru*, which would have then meant 'to be straight' or, in the sense of moving, 'to go straight ahead'.[74] Further, the Egyptian term *r-ḥꜣt*, 'before', possessed a temporal meaning, and it was translated into Akkadian as *ana pāni*, which had instead a mostly spatial sense, namely 'in front of'.[75] Most of the Syro-Palestinian petty kings would respond 'I am ready!' or 'I am on guard!' However, in a group of letters from Syria, the notice of the imminent arrival of Egyptian troops was misunderstood and it was replied that the petty king will march ahead of the Egyptian troops, because the message from the Egyptian court was interpreted in the imperative 'march straight before the troops!'.[76]

A final example offered by Liverani deals with the connotative aspects of the verb *qâlu*, 'to keep silence'.[77] It is explained that, at a denotative level, the Egyptian verb *gr* and the Canaanite verb *dmm* coincide in meaning 'to keep silence, to stand still'[78] within their respective semantic fields. However, on a connotative level, the Egyptian verb possessed a meaning ranging from a neutral to positive connotation, while the semantics of the Canaanite verb ranged from a neutral to negative connotation. Therefore, the unresponsiveness of the Pharaoh to the demands and petitions from the petty kings of the Levant was interpreted differently according to the interpretive context. From an Egyptian point of view, the silence of the Pharaoh expressed, in socio-linguistic terms, calmness and imperturbability, but also a solemn authority that was not obliged to respond to foreign subjects. From the Syro-Palestinian perspective, the silence from their distant overlord connoted a lack of reciprocity in the lord/servant relationship conceived of locally in the Levant; something that is evident, for instance, in many of Rib-Hadda's letters to the Pharaoh (cf. EA 81; 88; 90–92).

* * *

Our obvious impossibility of conducting ethnographic fieldwork in order to ascertain how much of the overall misunderstanding in the Amarna epistolography belongs to the socio-linguistic aspects of the correspondence and how much simply to political manipulation, must be taken into consideration here (cf. Liverani 2008: 162). Regarding the main features of the Late Bronze Age correspondence in this chapter, we may wonder whether the structural nature of the exchanged messages actually allows for gathering empirical data from the letters with the purpose of writing political history in this period, or whether – and considering here the proliferation of literary *topoi* in the correspondence (Liverani, 1973; 2004a, 2004b, 2004c, 2004d, 2004e; Thompson, 2005) – it will be more cautious to attempt to recover the ideologies and worldviews – in an *emic* sense – and the sociology – in an *etic* sense – of the ancient societies of the Levant, since a considerable amount of the political data in the letters is hard to verify (cf. Liverani 1983a: 46–7). This is far from proposing a general anti-historicism when using written sources. Instead, a different use of the textual data is favoured, in order to overcome the limits of event-centred reconstructions of historical periods. Thus, the socio-linguistic approach within a general socio-anthropological interpretation allows for the identification in the written sources of a variety of ideologies and worldviews and, in general, offers a more complex picture of ancient historical realities. The procedure of reading ancient texts critically is built on a proper philological-linguistic analysis, but it must also proceed with the semantics of the textual data (Cunchillos Ilarri 2005: 25–6; further Cunchillos [Ilarri] and Vita 1998). That is, open the cultural dimension of the text and understand ancient texts as cultural artefacts that must be culturally translated. Finally, any reference to 'ancient Near Eastern diplomacy' ought to be understood as a modern interpretative concept to analyse particular aspects of ancient Near Eastern societies. A similar disposition should be maintained when dealing with other notions, such as 'economy', 'politics', 'religion', 'art', or 'literature', all of which are modern analytical delimitations and arrangements of the ancient data from Southwest Asia (cf. Moscati 1976a).

## Notes

1 In general, on the formal characteristics of the Amarna epistolary *corpus*, see Moran 1992: xiii–xxxix; Izre'el 1995a; Liverani 1998: 9–62; 1999: 311–39; Mynářová 2007: 11–39. It is estimated that the known cache of letters represents only around 10 per cent of the total correspondence exchanged during the Amarna period (Liverani 1998: 52). On the provenance of the tablets, see Goren, Finkelstein and Na'aman 2004, showing how petrographic analysis can aid to locate with more precision the territorial extent of polities.

2 For the chronology of the letters, see the dated but still relevant studies by Campbell 1964; Kühne 1973; and for the Hittite kings, Kitchen 1962; updated now by Rainey 2014.

3 According to Belmonte Marín (2005: 170–71; cf. also Liverani 1998; 1999; Mynářová 2007: 125–46), there are 284 letters, out of which 209 have been identified by their provenience site: Akka (EA 232–5), Akšaf (EA 223 and 367), Amurru (EA 60–62, 156–61, 164–71 and 371), Aškelon (EA 308 and 320–26), Aštartu (EA 364), Beyrut (EA 141–3), Byblos (EA 68–95, 101–40 and 362), Buṣrūna (EA 199–200), Damascus (EA 194–7), 'Enu-Šāsī (EA 187 and 363), Gaza (EA 296), Gintu-Ašna (EA 319), Guddašuna (EA 177), Gezer (EA 267–271, 292–4, 297–300 and 378), Hazor (EA 227–8), Ḫašabu (EA 174), Ḫazi (EA 175 and 185–6), Irqata (EA 100), Jerusalem (EA 285–91), Kumidi (EA 198), Labana (EA 193), Laqiš (EA 328–32), Megiddo (EA 242–7 and 365), Mušiḫunu (EA 180 and 182), Naziba (EA 206), Nuḫašše (EA 51), Piḫilu (EA 255–6), Qadeš (EA 189–90), Qanû (EA 204), Qaṭna (EA 52–6[+ 361]), Ruḫizu (EA 191–2), Sidon (EA 144–5), Shechem (EA 252–4), Ṣiri-bašāni (EA 201), Šamḫuna (EA 225), Šaruna (EA 241), Šas'īmu (EA 203), Taanak (EA 248), Tyre (EA 146–55 and 295), Tunip (EA 59), Ṭūbu (EA 205), Ugarit (EA 45–9), Yurza (EA 314–16), Zuḫru (EA 334) and Zunu (EA 220). Another 65 messages are private: Abdi-Aštarti [from Gintu (successor of Šuwardata)] (EA 63–5 and 335), Abdina (EA 229), Amayaše [from the region of Ḥauran] (EA 202), Baal-mehir (EA 257–9), Baal-mir [from Bit-Tenni] (EA 260), Baal-qarradu (EA 249–50), Baduzanu (EA 239), Bayadi (EA 237–8), Bayawa (EA 215–16), Belet-Nešeti [from Ṣapuna] (EA 273–4), from an Egyptian subject (EA 173), Dagan-takala [probably the successor of Baal-mir] (EA 317–18), Dašru (EA 261–2), a general (EA 96), Ḫibiya [from Biqā'] (EA 178), Ḫiziru (EA 337), Ipte— (EA 207), Maya [Egyptian commisioner] (EA 230), Paapu (EA 333), Šipṭu-riša (EA 226), Šubandu

(EA 301–6), Šum— [from Maḫḫazu?] (EA 272), Šum-Adda (EA 224), Šuwardata [from Gintu] (EA 251, 275–7), Yapaḫ-Adda [from Ardata?] (EA 211–14). Anonther ten letters have no identified address (EA 67, 176, 179, 208, 217–18, 231, 307, 309 and 313). Cf. Helck's map on the political division of Syria-Palestine in Chapter 1.

4 *CTH* 91. See the transliteration and translation in Langdon and Gardiner 1920; and more recently in Spalinger 1981; cf. also the translations in *ANET*[3], 199–203; Beckman 1996: 90–95. On the political interaction between Egypt and Ḫatti during the Late Bronze Age, cf. Warburton 2003.

5 On the history of the discovery of the city, its archives, etc., cf. Bittel 1970: 3–90; on the archaeology of the site, cf. Bryce 2002: 230–56.

6 The standard collections of texts found in Boğazköy are *KBo* and *KUB*, apart from *CTH*. A recent anthology of texts covering the correspondence between the royal court and dignitaries during the Middle and Imperial Kingdoms is found in Marizza 2009. An edition of Hittite alliance and subordination treaties, together with some royal edicts, is found in Beckman 1996. Other relevant anthologies of texts are Bernabé and Álvarez-Pedrosa 2004; Hoffner 2009.

7 Cf. Pardee 1997; Belmonte Marín 2003: 176–7. A recent transliteration of the Ugaritic texts from the archives is found in *KTU*. The diplomatic and internal correspondence of the kingdom in Ugaritic and Akkadian can be found in *PRU* III-V. A recent translation of texts is also Cunchillos [Ilarri]: 1989a: 239–421. See also Cunchillos Ilarri 1989b; 1992; Hawley 2003. The Akkadian documents from Ugarit have been recently published in translation in Lackenbacher 2002. For a technical evaluation of the archival material, cf. Liverani 1988.

8 A first publication of 465 items is found in Wiseman 1953, supplemented by Wiseman 1954. However, the complete cataloguing and publication of the epigraphic material from Alalaḫ is still to be done, with the exception of some current works (Greenstein 1997; Von Dassow 2008: 3 n. 5).

9 The *editio princeps* is in Smith 1949; see also Von Dassow 2008: 23–45. For an ideological and literary exegesis of Idrimi's carrier, see Liverani 2004c.

10 Cf. Dossin 1938. On the Amorite infiltration, cf. the dated but still relevant study by Kupper 1957, and more recently Whiting 1995. On Mari and the royal palace, see Margueron 1995.

11 See Munn-Rankin 1956; Korošec 1967; Fleming 2004. The Old Babylonian documents from Mari are copied in cuneiform, transliterated and translated in the series *ARM* and *ARMT*. Recent translations of the epistolary data are the comprehensive anthologies in Durand 1997–2000; and the selection of documents in Oliva 2008: 15–30, 85–97, 117–459.

12 In general on Nuzi, see Maidman 1995. For a recent transliteration with translation of selected texts from the site, see Maidman 2010.

13 On the inappropriate and methodologically incorrect of such comparison, cf. Maidman 2010: 11–12; and in greater detail, Thompson 1974: 196–297.

14 Besides the evidence noticed so far, we can also refer – although secondarily – to some Egyptian documents can be understood as pseudo-ethnographic as they offer descriptions about socio-political situations in Southwest Asia but always marked by a strong Egyptian worldview in detriment of a rather clear representation of historical realities. These documents, however, are still of high value for the historian of the ancient Near East. The so-called 'Execration Texts' (*c.* 1900–1800 BCE) consist of hieratic writing on

vases describing both domestic and foreign enemies of the Pharaoh, or war prisoners, which through rituals of sympathetic magic would contribute to destroy such enemies or prisoners and the menace they represented. In 1926, K. Sethe published a first edition of texts inscribed on vases, and in 1940 G. Posener published texts inscribed on clay figures (Sethe 1926; Posener 1940; also *ANET*³, 328–9; Dussaud 1940; Briend and Seux 1977: 30–36). In both cases, the relevance of these texts lies in the identification of the enemies of the Pharaoh as 'big ones' (sing. *pꜣ wr*, *wr*), men of prestige and some authority in south-west Asian communities (also in Nubia), leading their local subordinates and creating a foreign political and cosmic threat to the general order in Egypt. Another example is constituted by the story of Sinuhe, according to which an Egyptian official of king Amenemḥet I (*c.* 1960 BCE) is forced to run away, after the Pharaoh's death, to the Levant, where he has to face the local instances of 'tribal' sociability in order to survive (cf. *ANET*³, 18–22; Lichtheim 1973: 222–5). An analogous case to Sinuhe's story is the report by the official/priest Wenamun of his trip to Byblos, on the Phoenician coast (dated *c.* 1100 BCE, as the Egyptian empire on Asia had begun to disappear; cf. *ANET*³, 25–9; Lichtheim 1976: 224–30).

The so-called 'New Kingdom' in Egypt (*c.* 1550–1150 BCE) is, as already noted, a period of incursion into foreign lands, political expansion and domination of most of Syria-Palestine. Accordingly, there exists an abundant quantity of textual and epigraphic material of diverse genres (autobiographies, commemorative inscriptions, etc.) referencing socio-political situations in the Levantine societies and Egyptian political worldviews of that foreign world. A considerable quantity of the Egyptian epigraphic monumental material, from the Eighteenth Dynasty, is transcribed in the series *Urkunden der 18. Dynastie*, edited successively by K. Sethe (*Urk.* 1–4), A. Burkhardt (*Urk.* 5–16) and W. Helck (*Urk.* 17–22). A translation of texts from the Eighteenth and Nineteenth Dynasties is published by J.H. Breasted (*ARE*, II–III), apart from the selection by J.B. Pritchard (*ANET*³, 233–63) and the anthology by K. Kitchen (K*RI*, I–VIII). A recent selection of texts is Galán 2002. For the Egyptian texts of the Amarna period, see Murnane 1995a.

15 See, for instance, the juridical terminology used in Kestemont 1974; see also Cohen 1996; Cohen and Westbrook 2000a; Westbrook 2000; Lafont 2001; Liverani 2001; Cooper 2003; Eidem 2003; and the studies by Podany 2010 and Altman 2012 and the anthology by Westbrook 2003a, in which evidence is presented in order to support the existence of an 'international diplomacy', even an 'international law', in the ancient Near East already in the third millennium BCE, although without the formal components of the Late Bronze Age diplomatic relations.

16 At the site of Tell El Amarna, the so-called 'Building 19', which housed the cache of tablets of the Amarna letters was called 'The Place of the Letters of the Pharaoh – Life, Prosperity, Health', and was effectively the archive of the foreign office of the Egyptian state (see Bryce 2003: 223–27; Mynářová 2007: 11–39). Moran (1992: xvi) observes about this building: '[it] may refer to a larger complex, the more extensive part of which was devoted to affairs of state conducted in the Egyptian language, the smaller (the actual find-spot), to those conducted in foreign languages.' About the site of Tell El Amarna, cf. Kemp 2006: Chapter 7.

17 On methodological grounds, it is thus most relevant the criticism Lévi-Strauss (1950) posed on Mauss's interpretation of the nature of native exchanges; cf. also Sahlins 1972: 149–83. See also Harris 1964; 1976; Feleppa 1986; Laburthe-Tolra and Warnier 2007: 161.

18 Cohen and Westbrook 2000c: 233. The semantic field of the Near Eastern concept of ‘brotherhood’ covers biological and family relations but also socio-political bonds: *CAD* A, 186–8: *aḫḫūtu* 1. ‘brotherly relationship, brotherliness, 2. position of a brother (as legal [a] term, *adoptio in fratrem*), group of persons “of equal status”, 3. brotherhood (referring to a political relationship)’; cf. also *CAD* A, 195: *aḫu* 2. ‘brother, colleague, associate’. For the implications of ‘brotherhood’ in the Ugaritic myths, see Tugendhaft 2012.

19 Liverani 2001: 136. Liverani refers here to the heading of the text RS 19.70. The transcription of the Akkadian as originally appeared in *PRU* IV, 294, follows: *um-ma šàr* $^{mat}$ $^{al}$*u-ga-ri-it ù šarrat*$^{mat}$ $^{al}$*u-ga-ri-it a-na* $^{I}$*ki-la-’e-e a-bi-ni* (transl. ‘thus (says) the King of Ugarit and the Queen of Ugarit: to Kila’e, our father’). On the basic aspects of Bronze Age diplomacy, cf. also Munn-Rankin 1956; Korošec 1967; Liverani 1976a: 378–90; 2001: 128–34 (on the ‘ideology of protection’), 135–8 (on the ‘ideology of brotherhood’); Zaccagnini 1990; 1999; Beckman 2003; Eidem 2003; on epistolary formalities, see the last section in this chapter.

20 EA 158:1; see the translation in Moran 1992: 244; Liverani 1998: 273; Rainey 2014: 787. A corrected transliteration of the phrase after Knudtzon 1907: 642 reads: *a-n[a] Tù-ú-tù* EN-*ia a-bi-[ia]* [‘for Tutu, my lord, my father]; see also Rainey 2014: 786. Knudtzon’s transliteration of the letters did not include the Sumerian pronunciation of the sumerograms, but their equivalent in Akkadian (cf. Huehnergard 2005: 107–11, also 532–6).

21 Cf. Grimal 1986: 229–338; also Lorton 1974: 136–44; Liverani 2010: 162–70; together with the general characterisation of ‘holy war’ and ‘just war’ in Liverani 2002. On the features of Egyptian kingship in the Eighteenth and Nineteenth Dynasties, cf. Redford 1995; and Murnane 1995b respectively; see also Spalinger 2005: 101–9.

22 *Urk.* IV, 759, 8–15; quoted in Lorton 1974: 138. This expression is also found in the Amarna correspondence: *a-na ša* LUGAL EN-*ia* $^{d}$DUTU-*i[a]* DINGIR.MEŚ-*ia ša-ri* TIL.LA-*ia* (EA 141:1–2; cf. Knudtzon 1907: 592; Rainey 2014: 718; transl.: ‘[Say] to the king, my lord, my Sun, my gods, my breath of life’); see also EA 142:1; 143:1–2; 144:1–2.

23 *Urk.* IV, 662, 8–12; quoted in Lorton 1974: 138–9. Cf. also a similar example in, among others, Edgerton and Wilson 1936: 99 = *KRI* V, 81.16–82.1.

24 EA 74:55–9, after Moran 1992: 143 (cf. also Knudtzon 1907: 376–7; and Liverani 1998: 173; Rainey 2014: 455; the emphasis is mine).

25 Grimal 1986: 246. Faulkner (1962: 48) translates *bꜣkw* as ‘work, task; work of craftmanship, labour of captives, revenues, taxes’, semantic variants that can be made one single term, from the Egyptian worldview, meaning all of which is owed to the pharaoh for keeping the cosmic order and guaranteeing life: ‘the natural submission of Egypt to her king makes him to grant automatically to the country “the breath”, the symbol of the protection rewarded for obedience’ (Grimal 1986: 248). In the same sense, the term *bꜣk*, ‘servant’ (Faulkner 1962: 49), may be conceptualised under the same analytical considerations.

26 *Urk.* IV, 896, 15–17; quoted in Lorton 1974: 140. The term *inw* can be translated as ‘produce of region; tribute of subject lands; gifts from palace; diplomatic gifts from foreign powers, dues to be paid’ (Faulkner 1962: 22); see in general, Bleiberg 1996: 90–114, and Chapter 3.

27 Cf. the discussion in Lorton 1974: 132. See also Wilson 1948; Faulkner 1962: 259; Helck 1962: 256–7; Goedicke 1963: 79; and Morschauer 1988: 103, who dismisses the reference of the expression to a loyalty oath and places it in the realm of a royal pardon.

28 Faulkner (1962: 64) translates 'great one, magnate' (cf. *Urk* IV, 62, 2) and 'ruler of a foreign land' (cf. *Urk*. IV, 185, 3; 773, 2); Hannig (2006: 699), translates 'Fürst, Konig (*e. Fremlandes*)'.

29 According to Lorton (1974: 176), 'The crucial change in the terminology occurs in the Hyksos period, with the introduction of *ḥḳꜣ* "ruler" to indicate an independent king who can be an overlord and *wr* "prince" to indicate a king, especially a dependent king. Given the Asiatic provenance of the Hyksos, it seems clear that these terms translate Akkadian *šarru rabû*, "great king, independent king, overlord" and *šarru* "king, dependent king".'

30 Cf. *Urk*. IV, 15, 1292, 1325, 1568, 1756. On the bureaucratic centralism of Egypt, see the dated but still illustrative contribution in Edgerton 1947.

31 Cf. especially the notable study by H. Frankfort (1948), noting the salient features of Egyptian and Mesopotamian kingship. A more recent but less comprehensive synthesis is found in Jones 2005.

32 See the translation in Beckman 1996: 90–95. For the geopolitical background of the treaty, cf. Rowton 1959; Van de Mieroop 2007.

33 Cf. *CTH* 92. See the translation of the treaty in Beckman 1996: 95–8. Cf. also the list of non-parity treaties between Ḫatti and Ugarit in *PRU* IV, and the epistolography of Ugarit in *Ug* V, 20–80. For a discussion on the symbolic rather than socio-politically normative aspects of these treaties, cf. Chapters 5 and 7.

34 EA 4:4–9, after Moran 1992: 8–9 (cf. also Knudtzon, 1907: 72–3; Liverani 1999: 349; Rainey 2014: 73).

35 EA 90:1–9, 22–3, 63–4, after Moran 1992: 163–4 (cf. also Knudtzon 1907: 424–9; Liverani 1998: 195–6; Rainey 2014: 519).

36 EA 91:1–5, 36–8, after Moran 1992: 165 (cf. also Knudtzon, 1907 428–31; Liverani 1998: 196–7; Rainey 2014: 523, 525). It is usual in the Amarna letters to find the term *ḫabiru* as a derogatory epithet for referring to the enemies of the Pharaoh; see Liverani 1979b.

37 Following an established rule of reciprocity in the salutation formula opening the diplomatic letters, for instance, in these letters sent to the Pharaoh: EA 7:1–7; 16:1–5; 19:1–8; 21:1–12; 27:1–6; 29:1–5; 41:1–6.

38 Cf. *CAD* $A_2$, 243: *ardu (wardu, bardu, urdu, aradu)* '1. slave, 2. official, servant, subordinate, retainer, follower, soldier, subject (of a king), worshipper of a deity)'. The semantic difference between 'slave' and 'servant' is, of course, contextual in each case. See, for instance, EA 230:1–8: *a-na* $^{I}$LUGAL BAD-*ia qí-bi um-ma* $^{I}$*ia-ma ÌR-ka a-na* GÌR.MEŠ-*ka am-qut a-mur-mi a-na-ku ÌR-ka i-na aš-ri ša i-ba-ša-ti a-mur aš-ra-nu ša i-ba-ša-ti* URU.DIDLI.ḪIÁ-*ka gáb-bu a-na-ku ÌR* <*ki*>*ti-ka* (trans. after Moran 1992: 290: 'Say to the king, my lord: message from Yama, your servant. I fall at your feet. As I am your servant in the place where I am, the places where I am are all cities belonging to you'; transcription follows Rainey 2014: 970; cf. also Knudtzon 1907: 770–71; and Liverani 1998: 110). It could be said, from the Egyptian ideological perspective, that all the Levantine petty kings are 'slaves', in the sense that they all belong politically to the Pharaoh; however, from the Syro-Palestinian perspective, all the petty kings see themselves as 'servants', as they proclaim their loyalty and request assistance in exchange; cf. Liverani 1967.

39 Cf. *AHw* I, 118: 'Herr; Besitzer (von)'; also *CAD* B, 191: '1. master, ruler, 2. owner (of property), officeholder'. See, for instance, the Akkadian terminology in EA 139:1: *a-na* LUGAL E[N-*ia* $^{d}$UTU-*ia]* (trans. 'to the King, my lord, my Sun'; 149:1: *a-na* LUGAL

EN-*li-ia* $^{d}$UTU-*ia* DINGIR.MEŠ-*ia* (trans. 'to the king, my Sun, my gods'); 233:1–2: *a-na šàr-r[i* EN-*i]a* $^{d}$UTU *iš-tu* A*[*N-*ša-m]e* (trans. 'to the king, my lord, the Sun in the sky'); the three examples in Knudtzon 1907: 586–7, 614–15, 774–5; and Rainey 2014: 712, 752, 976; see also Helck 1962: 515; Moran 1992: xxvii n. 73; Liverani 1998: 39.

40 See, for instance, EA 92:30–34; 147:66; 148:25, 40. Cf. Knudtzon 1907: 434, 610, 614; Rainey 2014: 526, 744, 748.

41 Cf. *AHw* I, 90; *CDA* A, 31. See EA 146:14: [*i-na-n*]*a an-nu-ú* LÚ URU [*ṣí-du-na*] (trans. 'now, indeed, the man/ruler of the city of Sidon'); 154:11–14: *ša-ni-tam iš-tu pa-ta-ri* ERIN.MEŠ LUGAL EN-*li-ia muḫ-ḫi-ia la-a i-na-an-din-ni* LÚ URU *ṣí-du-na* (trans. 'Moreover, since the departure of the people [troops] of the king, my lord, from me, the man/ruler of the city of Sidon does not allow me or my people to go to land to fetch wood'); 155:67–8: *[i-]na* URU *ṣu-mu-ri a-mur* LÚ.MEŠ URU P*[Ú-r]u-ti i-na [1]* GIŠ.MÁ *a-li-ik ù* URU *ṣí-du-[n]a i-na 2* GIŠ.M[Á] (trans. 'as the man/ruler of of Beirut has done service with one ship, and the man/ruler of Sidon is doing service with two ships'). Cf. Knudtzon 1907: 606–7, 632–3, 636–7; Moran 1992: 232, 241, 242; Liverani 1998: 153, 160; Rainey 2014: 738–9, 774–5, 778–9.

42 The term has been frequently overinterpreted as 'prince': see, for instance, EA 149:30: [$^{l}$*e-ta-ga-ma*' *p*]*a-wa-ra*; also EA 151:59. Cf. Knudtzon 1907: 616–17, translating 'Herr von'; Albright 1937: 196, 'foreign prince, chieftain'; Rainey 2014: 755, 'prince'.

43 Cf. Liverani 1990a: 208: 'In effect, the main part of royal 'propaganda' is destined to the internal public, whereas when in contact with the exterior a different attitude is held, having in mind not so much the achievement and consolidation of prestige but the interest of keeping in function a mechanism of relations necessarily based on mutual recognition.' Nonetheless, the term 'propaganda' should not be used having in mind essentially modern totalitarian regimes. In fact, Grimal (1986: 5) affirms, the term 'propaganda' 'applied to pharaonic Egypt is, to the limit, improper. It does not refer, in fact, to a need of demonstration or conversion, because the pharaonic "discourse" addresses exclusively those who participate of the system it describes. It is simply a presentation of facts according to a formula that does not aim at produce violence at them, but quite the contrary, to return them to their essential reality.'

44 Cf. the analysis of this particular situation in Liverani 1990a: esp. 212–13: 'Hattushili must have therefore considered that the enormous celebrative apparatus placed by Ramesses intended to contradict the new spirit of brotherhood – while on the Egyptian side it was considered that the concrete political events had a very limited weight regarding the traditional arrangement of 'sides' in the stereotypical and eternal act of the victory of the Pharaoh over 'vile' and 'rebel' enemies. The fact is that Hattushili decides to protest, and seems to have concentrated his protest mainly (if not exclusively) on the motif of the victorious sole king against the entire Hittite army: '(Really) was there no one else there (with you)?' A recent overview of inter-polity relations during the reign of Ramesses II is Van de Mieroop 2007; and especially with Ḫatti, cf. Pernigotti 2010: 11–49.

45 Cf. EA 195:24–32: *a-un-ma a-na-ku qa-du* ÉRIN.MEŠ-*ia ù* GIŠ GIGIR.MEŠ-*ia ù qa-du* ŠEŠ.MEŠ-*ia ù qa-du* LU.MEŠ SA.GAZ.MEŠ-*ia ù qa-du* LU.MEŠ *su-te-ia a-na pa-ni* ÉRIN.MEŠ *pi-ṭā-ti a-di a-šar yi-qa-bu* $^{I}$LUGAL *be-li-ia* (cf. the translation in Knudtzon 1907: 722: 'Siehe, ich nebst meinen Kriegern und meinen Wagen u[n]d nebst meinen Brüdern und nebst meinen Sa.Gaz-Leuten [*ḫabiru*] und nebst meinen Sutu (ziehe) entgegen den Feldtruppen bis dorthin, wo es befiehlt der König, mein Herr'; cf. also the translations in Moran 1992: 273; Liverani 1998: 251; Rainey 2014: 896.

46 Also attested in Ugaritic epistolography (cf. Cunchillos-Ilarri 1989a; 1989b). Under Babylonian influence, a formula is adopted including the order 'say/speak' (Akk. *qi-bī-ma*): 'To [ADDRESEE] say: message from [SENDER]'.

47 Following Mynářová (2005: 403 n. 10), 19 different kinds of opening passages can be identified: '(1) address, (2) address + prostration, (3) address + prostration + gods' blessing, (4) address + prostration + sender's dehonestation, (5) address + prostration + wish of well-being to the addressee, (6) address + prostration + wish of well-being to the addressee + a wish of well-being to the addressee extended to other members of his household, (7) address + prostration + wish of well-being to the addressee + statement of sender's well-being, (8) address + gods' blessing + prostration, (9) address + sender's dehonestation, (10) address + wish of well-being to the addressee + prostration, (11) statement of the origin + address + prostration, (12) address + gods' concern, (13) address + confirmation of sending the tablet, (14) address + wish of well-being to the addressee, (15) address + wish of well-being to the addressee + a wish of well-being to the addressee extended to other members of his household, (16) address + statement of sender's well-being + wish of well-being to the addressee, (17) address + statement of sender's well-being + wish of well-being to the addressee + a wish of well-being to the addressee extended to other members of his household, (18) address + statement of sender's well-being + a comment on well being to other members of the sender's household + a wish of well-being to the addressee + a wish of well-being to the addressee extended to other members of his household, and (19) address + statement of sender's well-being + wish of well-being to the addressee + a wish of well-being to the addressee extended to other members of his household + statement of sender's well-being + a comment on well being of other members of sender's household'. Cf. further Mynářová 2007.

48 According to Liverani (1983b: 509–10), the reason for this is 'to flaunt Egyptophilic acculturation, but also to put his own name first, before the pharaonic addressee, and to proclaim the life-giving power of the local goddess Belit of Byblos'. Cf. EA 68:1–3; 70:1–3; 74:1–2; 75:1–2; 76:1–3; 78:1–3; 79:1–3; 81:1–2; 83:1–3; 88:1–2; 89:1–2; 91:1–2; 92:1–2; 94:1–2. It is equally true that Rib-Hadda also used a combination of the Babylonian and Syro-Palestinian traditions to open his letters: cf. EA 69:1–3; 71: 1–2; 73:1–2; 77:1–2; 82:1–3; 84:1–3; 85:1–2; 86:1–2; 87:1–3; 90:1–3; 93:1–2; 95:1–2 (perhaps due to scribes with different training backgrounds?).

49 In the case of Ugarit, the local king would prostrate himself before the king of Ḫatti with a variant: 'two times seven'; cf. further below. According to Liverani (1998: 58f.), the duplication of times belongs to the prostration of 'belly and back' (Akk. *kabatumma u ṣirumma*) before the great king. Morris (2006) offers and interesting analysis of what might be called a topography of prostration, indicating different modes of prostration according to the location of Egypt's Levantine subjects.

50 EA 234:1–9; cf. Knudtzon 1907: 776–7; updated in Rainey 2014: 978; the translation in Moran 1992: 292; see also Liverani 1998: 136.

51 See Durand 1997–2000. Cf. Munn-Rankin 1956: 68: 'Until the discovery of the royal archive of Mari belonging to the first half of the eighteenth century B.C., the principal sources for the study of the history of international law and diplomacy in the second millennium B.C. were the diplomatic records of the Egyptian and Hittite empires found at Tell el Amarna and Boğazköy, covering the fourteenth and thirteenth centuries B.C.; few earlier documents of international character were known. The new evidence, combined with that of contemporary texts from Babylonia and Alalaḫ, proves that many of the rules and principles recognised in the fourteenth century B.C.

as governing the relations of civilised [*sic*] states were already established some four centuries earlier.' Together with Mari, Ebla is another important polity during the Bronze Age, cf. Matthiae 2010: 48–63; Podany 2010: 19–36.

52 Cf., for instance, the opening of the letter by Ḫattušili III to Kadašman-Enlil of Babylonia: 'Thus says Ḫattušili, Great King, King of Ḫatti: Say [to] Kadašman-Enlil, Great King, King of Babylonia, my brother' (slightly adapted from Beckman 1996: 133).

53 Cf., for instance, Beckman 1996: 121, 142. On the internal correspondence of the Hittite kingdom (royal family and officials), see Marizza 2009. Regarding the treatment in terms of kinship between the epistolary parties, Marizza (2009: 24) affirms that 'this is almost always a fictive kinship, a rhetorical device to emphasize the good relations between the two subjects of the letter. In the case of seniority in one of the parties, terms like 'father' and 'son' are used, while if age and rank are more or less the same, the term 'brother' is applied instead.'

54 Adapted from Arnaud 1982: 102.

55 Original transliteration and translation into French in Bordreuil and Caquot 1980: 356, 358. This formula, wishing well-being to the king's household, appears as well in the Amarna letters; cf. EA 2:3–5; 19:5–8; etc.

56 Cf. Albright 1942: 33 n 7; Marcus 1948; Liverani 1998: 54. On Canaanite rhetoric in the Amarna letters, see Gevirtz 1973. A general semiotic perspective on such communicational issue is found in Eco 1968.

57 See the ethnographic insights in Asad 1986; on the ethnography of communication see Saville-Troike 2003: 28: 'There is no doubt . . . that there is a correlation between the form and content of a language and the beliefs, values, and needs present in the culture of its speakers. The vocabulary of a language provides us with a catalogue of things considered important to the society, an index to the way speakers categorize experience, and often a record of past contacts and cultural borrowings; the grammar may reveal the way time is segmented and organized, beliefs about animacy and the relative power of beings, and salient social categories in the culture'; cf. also pp. 30–35, 48–59, 251–3.

58 Liverani 1990b; 1998: 34–7. For an alternative point of view regarding this procedure, cf. Na'aman 1990; and esp. 2000. See also on the Egyptian troops (Akk. *ṣābē piṭāti*), Pintore 1972; 1973; Spalinger 2005: 160–68.

59 EA 367:1–21, after Moran 1992: 365 (see also the translation in Liverani 1998: 133–4). Cf. as well EA 99; 141; 142; 226; 252; 302; 303; 330; 369; 370.

60 EA 320:16–25, after Moran 1992: 350 (cf. also Knudtzon 1907: 929; Liverani 1998: 71; Rainey 2014: 1195).

61 Cf. EA 65; 216; 267; 303; 319; 321; 322; etc. See Liverani 1990a: 342–5.

62 EA 126:7–42, after Moran 1992: 205–6 (cf. also Knudtzon 1907: 539, 541; Liverani 1998: 228; Rainey 2014: 657); see the analysis in Liverani 1979c as well.

63 EA 271:9–21, after Moran 1992: 317 (cf. also Knudtzon 1907: 837; Liverani 1998: 102; Rainey 2014: 1071).

64 Liverani 1983a: 47. For a contrary interpretation to Liverani's on the nature of Amarna politics, cf. Moran 1995. Moran understands this ideological-political clash essentially from a bureaucratic perspective (p. 330: 'we must assume that protestations of loyalty and requests for help were made with an understanding consistent with the legal position of an Egyptian vassal and with the considerable evidence that the implications of such status were neither unfamiliar nor rejected'), which ignores the evidence in favour of the existence of a particular 'Asiatic' worldview on the question,

differenced from the 'Egyptian' worldview, as Liverani noted. Cf. Part III for a full discussion.

65 Cf. *AHw* II, 755: 'bewachen, schützen, bewahren'; *CAD* $N_2$, 33: 'to keep somebody under guard, to watch a person, to keep a watch on someone, to wait, 2. to stand guard, to guard a house, a fortress, etc. 3. to take care of, to safeguard . . . 7. to protect, to keep safe'.

66 Faulkner 1962: 207–8: 'guard', 'restrain', 'heed', etc.; Hannig 2006: 2076: 'bewachen, hütten'.

67 Cf. the equivalence of the verb and the noun in Hebrew: ישע nif. '1. receive help; 2. be victorious'; hif. '1. help; 2. help, save, rescue; 3. come to (the) aid'; 'help, liberation, salvation' (Holladay 1971: 147); cf. also Clines 2009: 167.

68 This general semiotic question is treated brilliantly in Eco 1968. As Eco notes in this work, any attempt to determine the referent of a sign forces us to define such referent as nothing but a cultural convention.

69 Cf. *AHw*, I, 98–9: 'Leben'; *CAD* B, 46: '1. life, vigor, good health (held and dispensed by the gods), immortality, 2. life, lifetime, duration of life, 3. coming year, 4. Provisions'.

70 Cf. *AHw*, II, 620–21; *CAD* M, 333: '1. watch, guard (as individual man and as detachment), garrison, 2. watchhouse, post . . . strongroom, defense (of a city)'.

71 Slightly adapted from Moran 1992: 160 (cf. also Knudtzon 1907: 420–21; Liverani 1998: 180; Rainey 2014: 511). Cf. also EA 216; 218; 220; 221; 267; 303; 319–22; etc.

72 Also found in the Ramesside correspondence in Egypt; see Liverani 1983a: 54. On the Ramesside epistolography, cf. Wente 1967, especially on the use of *r-ḥꜣt*, 'before the arrival of' (i.e. p. 68). See also Mynářová 2009, who proposes, nonetheless, to differentiate between an Amarna tradition and a Ramesside tradition of epistolography.

73 Faulkner 1962: 291, 'establish', 'settle', 'provide for', 'set in order', 'be ready', 'make preparation'.

74 Cf. *CAD* $Š_3$, 387: '1. straight, 2. in good condition, prospering, 3. righteous, upright'.

75 Cf. *CAD* P, 84, *panu*: '1. front, front part'.

76 Cf. Chapter 8 for a socio-political interpretation of such misunderstanding.

77 Cf. the notable semantic variation of this verb: *CAD* Q, 72: '1. to become silent, to stay quiet, to be unmindful of, 2. to heed, to pay attention, to listen'. In general, on the denotative and connotative aspects of language, cf. Eco 1968: Section A, 2, VII–VIII; Barthes 1977: 89–94.

78 For the Egyptian term, cf. Faulkner 1962: 290: 'be silent', 'be quiet', 'be still'; for the Canaanite term, cf. the Hebrew variant 'be or grow dumb, silent, still' (Gesenius 1957 [1907]: 198); 'be motionless, stand still' (Holladay 1971: 72); also Clines 2009: 80.

# 3

# ALLIANCES AND EXCHANGES

## 3.1. Anthropology and history: epistemological preliminaries

In his work *Islands of History*, the American anthropologist Marshall Sahlins wrote:

> History is culturally ordered, differently so in different societies, according to meaningful schemes of things. The converse is also true: cultural schemes are historically ordered, since to a greater or lesser extent the meanings are revalued as they are practically enacted. The synthesis of these contraries unfolds in the creative action of the historic subjects, the people concerned. (Sahlins 1985: vii; see further Hartog 2003)

It may be said that within such a dialectical arrangement between structure and process the epistemological point of departure of a *historical anthropology* is to be found. Historical anthropology's primary aim is to study the total social articulation of human groups in the past, according to the testimony provided by written sources and, also, to the methodological tools of the ethnographic practice. Moreover, we may postulate two necessary moments in the analytical procedure implying precisely a basic *rupture épistémologique* – as G. Bachelard called it – consisting essentially in (a) the deconstruction of the object within its social setting (the synchronic aspect) and (b) the historicisation of the object (the diachronic aspect) (cf. Bourdieu, Passeron and Chamboredon 1991: 3–56).

The first moment may indeed remind us of the plea for a structural interpretation of society produced by C. Lévi-Strauss (1962; 1963). Nonetheless, a critical perspective needs to object to the Lévi-Straussian 'ontological structuralism' and propose instead an 'operative structuralism', namely an analytical procedure of the social free of transhistorical essentialisms. In effect, as U. Eco has defined this perspective, the notion of structure does not refer to a real objective structure 'out there' but functions instead as an open semiotic device to understand society and different kinds of communication within it (cf. Eco 1968: Section D).

The second moment leads us to historicise the operative concepts belonging to the society under study but also the data comprising a particular social situation, to make a serial genealogy of the ontological and epistemic matrix involved within it as *emic* and *etic* instances. In sum, to establish the contingency of the historical processes, whose genealogy is always retrospective rather than transcendental and teleological.

Departing from this succinct interpretative scheme, it is possible to address any specific historical situation when the written sources are interpreted ethnographically.[1] This approach may be apprehended after the following semiotic chart exposing the preliminary divergence of both the synchronic and diachronic perspectives, which nonetheless may be integrated in a final analysis:[2]

| | | | |
|---|---|---|---|
| *Connotative level* | Anthropology | Structure of meanings | *Langue* |
| *Denotative level* | History | Process/agency of events | *Parole* |

It is a truism that any theoretical conceptualisation, and its putative universality, must be put to the test and confronted with any historical and anthropological data about a certain society. But the aim here is to offer operative strategies of interpretation of ancient sources and ancient social behaviours, employing a merging of epistemological and methodological procedures from anthropology and history as interpretative disciplines to analyse the total social world of the Late Bronze Age in Syria-Palestine.

## 3.2. Economic anthropology of the Late Bronze Age

The high degree of interconnections, of so-called 'internationalism' or better stated *inter-regionalism*, during the Late Bronze Age in south-western Asia, which can also be understood as the working of diplomacy among various polities, presents us with a series of social aspects that may well be differentiated in concrete compartments of analysis – interrelated though as they are. The epistolographic exchange, especially during the Amarna period, is but one aspect of a historical situation comprising a complex procedure of political contacts and economic exchanges that can be understood, as M. Liverani (1999: 314) already noted, within the tripartite model of Lévi-Strauss: (a) the exchange of gifts, (b) the exchange of women (marriage alliances), and (c) the exchange of formal messages. Each of these practices is attached to one another: the exchanged messages deal with the flow of gifts and women; the gifts accompany the salutatory letter that initiates the epistolary contact and it is an essential part of the marriage arrangements; the inter-dynastic marriage is the goal of this system of interaction and communication. As already indicated in the previous chapter, this system of interaction between the Great Powers of the period is permeated by family metaphors and personal relations: 'brotherhood', 'goodness', 'love', 'alliance', etc., which connote a set of expectations and patterns of behaviour that cannot be neglected as a mere epistolary formality (see further in Part III). Thus, the disaggregation in three parts of this scheme of practices belongs only with the analytical procedure. The exchange dynamics must eventually be understood as a whole.

To begin with, it is necessary to consider the three main interpretative schools of economic anthropology that have addressed the question of exchanges as social practice: Formalism, Substantivism and Marxism. The debate between formalists and substantivists in anthropology during the 1960s, preceded by the debate between primitivists and modernists in the field of economic history, was foundational for a critical understanding of economic phenomena in history (see Aubet 2007: 21–9).

Formalism in anthropology is based in the modern econometric models, and postulates that any economy is, ultimately, an economy of scant resources or of limited means to unlimited ends, which fosters a law of maximisation of benefits through minimal efforts and free choice of individuals, as witnessed in modern market economies (cf., for instance, Burling 1962; Leclair 1962). Regarding ancient or pre-capitalist economies, formalists postulate that the difference with modern capitalist economies was one of grade and not of substance, meaning that in any historical period the law of maximisation of individual or group benefits, depending on the free rational choice of economic behaviour, could be detected to some degree. Without doubt, the ethnocentrism of this perspective did not consider the particular historical processes that produced each of the economic systems that may be identified in different historical periods, social situations and cultural contexts. From an ethnographic point of view, several examples would seriously challenge the universality of the formalist principles, as it can be effectively documented that the subsistence goods of a given society are not the object of competition among its members but rather belong to the social collective, and that competition is limited to the acquisition of exotic or luxury goods for gaining or maintaining prestige or power (Balazote 1998: 147–51; Dupuy 2008: 19–21, and especially Sahlins 1972).

The criticism of formalism by the substantivist approach, led by notable figures such as K. Polanyi and G. Dalton, produced through critical attention to historical processes a restriction of the categories of classical economy to modern Western societies (cf. Polanyi, Arensberg and Pearson 1957; Dalton, 1961; 1969; Polanyi 1977; also Dupuy 2008: 22–5; Rössler 2007). The substantivists observed that the economy of a society is intimately and directly arranged according to social structures and practices of production and circulation of goods at a certain point in its historical existence. In these economies, the market does not dictate the general procedure, but rather instances of *reciprocity*, *redistribution* and *exchange*, following principles of symmetry and centrality as argued by Polanyi.[3] In effect, it is kinship, politics, or religion as the base structure of economy, which is *embedded* in these kinds of social relations.[4] Therefore, economic phenomena should be analysed according to their cultural and historical configuration and not based on a transference of models of later economic realities into previous periods (cf. Aubet 2007: 21–55; also Morris and Manning 2005).

The third school is based on the fieldwork of Marxist ethnographers such as C. Meillassoux and M. Godelier, who renewed criticism towards the formalist postulates, among which the scarcity of resources in 'primitive' societies was a key element (Godelier 1973; Meillassoux 1975, among others; cf. the comments in Dupuy 2008: 25–31). The Marxist approach would also disagree with Substantivism. As Polanyi and his colleagues analysed the modes of circulation and distribution of goods in ancient and 'primitive' societies, Marxist criticism in anthropology would emphasise modes of production in a given society and be determined to find the real structures of the economy, beyond their spontaneous representation. Precisely, the *mode of production* and its concrete manifestation, the *economic and social formation*, constitute the key concepts for understanding the total functioning of societies in different historical periods. The *relations of production* may appear in the shape of kinship relations or political or religious subordination, and the reproduction of these relations of production will be carried out through the reproduction of kinship, political subordination, or ideological relations (Godelier 1973: 27). According to Godelier (1969 II: 205), there are no exclusive economic relations, but social relations functioning as economic relations, or better relations of production interrelated with every aspect of society.

Having in mind these three approaches, briefly characterised here, and instead of siding univocally with any of them, we may proceed now with a pragmatic attitude, choosing the concepts and analytical tools that better fits the conditions of interpretation for the economic realities of the Late Bronze Age. In this sense, the substantivist approach, especially its emphasis on the embeddedness of the economic phenomena in socio-cultural situations and its tripartite conceptualisation of the flow of goods (reciprocity, redistribution and exchange), seems to be pertinent. Given that it shows to be useful in mapping the scheme of social relations of production in ancient societies (cf. the discussion in Peyronel 2008: 13–39), we cannot disregard the key Marxist notion of mode of production, even if it seems contradictory at first sight to the substantivist approach. In fact, the concept of an Asiatic Mode of Production, which K. Marx would sketch to explain the socio-economic structure of pre-capitalist India and China, has been used since the 1970s in ancient Near Eastern economic studies in the notions of 'domestic mode of production' (drawn from M. Sahlins's studies) and 'palatine mode of production' by M. Liverani and C. Zaccagnini to analyse the socio-economic morphology of pre-Classical Near Eastern societies, in which both spheres – domestic and palatine – are interrelated and interdependent.[5] Likewise, and after the mentioned substantivist approach, each reference to 'exchanges' or 'commerce' (Aubet 2007: 101), by the way, analytical concepts that indicate a circulation of goods (for consumption or luxury), must be understood after the proper cultural features of each society in order to explain the circulation of such goods.

In sum, as Sahlins (1972: xii) observed, '"Economy" becomes a category of culture rather than behavior', and the social and political meaning of the circulation of goods in the Late Bronze Age period in general, and in the Amarna period in particular, does not escape this understanding.

## 3.3. Commodities and exchange of luxury goods[6]

According to the archaeological and textual-epigraphic records, the greater flow of exchanges on an inter-regional scale consisted of minerals, especially metals. For the production of bronze, copper was essential, and since it was abundant in Cyprus, it was the island's main export. Tin came from what is now the region of Afghanistan. Silver was used as a price referent and it was found in the mines of Anatolia, exploited by the Hittites.[7] The exportation of gold to all over the Near East was monopolised by Egypt, which extracted it from Nubia. In fact, Egypt was situated in a strategic position, on the route between the products coming from Asia and those coming from Africa. Ebony, ivory and other African commodities were also exported from Egypt, lapis lazuli from Afghanistan, carnelian and agate from India and Iran – although in the Late Bronze Age these latter were replaced to a great extent by artificial stones made of coloured vitreous material (Liverani 2008: 163). Mittani would export combat chariots and horses, bows and woollen textiles, also sent from Assyria and Babylon.[8] As to domestic consumption products, olive oil came from Anatolia and the Levant, sesame seeds from Mesopotamia and flax seeds from Egypt.

From a typological perspective, it is possible to differentiate two main categories of exchanged goods, already mentioned: prestige goods – or the raw matter to produce them – offered as a gift or as tribute, and goods of subsistence in general, offered as tribute or sent as commercial exchange (Zaccagnini 1973: 170; 1976b: 467–93). Certainly, the circulation of prestige goods is closely related to the establishment or the flux of previously established inter-polity relations. Thus, the circumstances in which gifts were exchanged are diverse: the conclusion of marriage arrangements, the ascension to the throne of a king, the conclusion of an alliance treaty, the victory over an enemy, feasting, the arrival of messengers (Zaccagnini 1973: 9–58). On several occasions, the documentation from the period witnesses the practice of reciprocity permeating all kinds of exchanges between the parties, not only of goods but also of salutations and news,[9] and its corollary, the explicit proclamation of 'brotherhood' between them.[10]

Also, the exchange relations were conditioned by various factors, as Zaccagnini indicated in a seminal and important study (1973: 149–93). One of them, and a key element, is the rank of the parts: it is possible to clearly identify (a) peer relations between kings;[11] (b) unequal or asymmetrical relations between a great king and a small king;[12] (c) peer relations between a great king's officer and another great king's officer;[13] (d) unequal or asymmetrical relations between a great king's officer and a small king;[14] (e) peer relations between a small king and another small king;[15] (f) unequal or asymmetrical relations between a small king and a small king's officer;[16] and finally (g) peer relations between a small king's officer and another small king's officer.[17] Another factor is age, or at least the reference to an age difference (Zaccagnini 1973: 157), a situation that inaugurates a rank difference, as manifested in the treatment of others: the treatment of 'father

(/mother)' and 'son' is produced in the following circumstances, respectively: (a) between a great king and a former great king;[18] (b) a great king and the son of a great king;[19] (c) the son of a great king and a small king;[20] (d) a great king's officer and a small king;[21] (e) a small king and another small king[22]; (f) a small king and a small king's officer;[23] (g) a small king's officer and another small king's officer,[24] and finally (h) a particular (not officer) and a small king's officer.[25]

Now, according to the previously noted scheme of 'Great Kings' and 'Small Kings' and also after the 'prestige and interest' model proposed by Liverani, each situation must be assessed attending to the specific location in which the exchange is conceptualised (Liverani 2001: 9–11; Peyronel 2008: 135–58). In a relation between peers, of 'brotherhood' of kings, the person who sends a gift acquires prestige with this act. If the situation is instead one between asymmetric ranks, prestige is acquired by receiving a gift or tribute from an inferior party. Therefore, Egypt would acquire prestige by receiving women (princesses) from Asia in exchange for gold, a precious commodity abundant in pharaonic lands; Babylonia, in need of gold, which it did not possess locally, would get it by sending princesses to the Pharaoh's harem.[26] And the insistence of the Babylonian king, as reflected in one episode of the Amarna epistolography, about obtaining gold makes the Pharaoh respond in a sarcastic tone, connoting the lack of prestige in the requirement from the Babylonian king: 'it is a fine thing that you give your daughters in order to obtain gifts from your neighbours!' (EA 1:61–2; cf. Liverani 1999: 346).

Here we reach an interesting point in our examination of the executed exchange and the cultural dispositions to conceptualise such exchange. In principle, according to Liverani (2001: 183–8), the manner in which the obtained goods were represented in Egypt would vary, depending on the message being addressed to an internal public or an external public. In the correspondence with other great Near Eastern powers, the Pharaoh conceptualised the received goods as gifts in a reciprocal relation, namely between peer polities. However, in the celebrative inscriptions, the Egyptian worldview would take over, exposing a verticality that places the Pharaoh as the only lord of the world and all the goods received as tributes from the periphery. This situation can be illustrated with three examples studied by Liverani – and commented upon briefly here.

*a* *The royal expedition during the reign of Queen Ḥatšepsut to the land of Punt* (Liverani 2001: 166–9; Diego Espinel 2011: 326–90). The incursion without intermediaries to the distant land of Punt (probably, in the Horn of Africa) in search for exotic goods, which convey prestige since, also, they are at a long distance from Egypt,[27] may be understood as a commercial exchange, since the Egyptians had travelled with goods to offer as counter-gifts, as attested in the texts evoking the event (*ARE* II §§ 252–95). However, and in spite of the goods the Egyptians offered in exchange, the products from Punt are considered in the Egyptian sources as *ỉnw*,[28] namely as tribute for the Egyptian queen, and the chiefs of Punt are represented as coming in obedience and bowing their heads to the queen.[29] In sum, what from a historical (i.e. external or *etic*) point of view is considered a commercial exchange between two parties, from the Egyptian worldview (*emic*) it is regarded as a tribute from a barbaric periphery to the civilised centre that is Egypt, source of all life that now also emanates towards Punt, and that is what the texts transmit, especially to its internal public.[30]

*b* *The exchange between Wenamun and Zakar-Baal* (Liverani 2001: 170–75; also *ARE* IV §§ 563–91; *ANET*³, 25–9; Lichtheim 1976: 224–30). The tale of the expedition of the Egyptian officer Wenamun to the city of Byblos, on the Phoenician coast at the beginnings of the eleventh century BCE, in search of cedar wood, allows for detecting another variant of the conception of the exchange relation. Wenamun asks Zakar-Baal for the wood, without naming the goods that he will offer as counter-gifts. In such conditions, Zakar-Baal refuses to supply the wood. Wenamun then declares that the counter-gifts may arrive from Egypt and Zakar-Baal sends a petition of these counter-gifts together with a sample of the cedar wood – showing thus that negotiation is open. Finally, the counter-gifts arrive from Egypt and Zakar-Baal sends the wood. In synthesis, under the appearance of a gift and counter-gift procedure, a commercial negotiation is in fact produced, which has to be equally analysed in its ideological components. If Zakar-Baal (from the Egyptian point of view and according to Wenamun) had not reclaimed his material counter-gift, 'life and health' would have arrived from Egypt, in a cosmic but also a political sense that would have added to Zakar-Baal's local prestige. Besides – now from a more pragmatic perspective – by closing the deal with the demand of an immediate payment, Zakar-Baal, according to the stipulations of reciprocity, lost the opportunity of leaving the other party in debt to him and assuring an extension of his (both cosmic and political) life. From Zakar-Baal's point of view, his complaint was just and his commercial demand satisfied.

*c* *Tribute in the Annals of Thutmose III* (Galán 2002: 75–100; Liverani 2001: 176–82; also *ARE* II §§ 391–540). The annals of the reign of Thutmose III, narrating the victories of the Pharaoh, are carved in the inner walls of the temple of Amun in Karnak. In the annual reports on the goods arriving at Egypt as a consequence of Egypt's military victories over foreign lands, these are classified distinctively as *bꜣkw* (usually interpreted as 'work', but, according to Liverani, the term had the connotation of 'product', that is, what is produced by such work, in this context), *ỉnw* (usually translated as 'tribute', lit. meaning 'that which is brought'), and lastly *biꜣt* (namely, 'wonders', exotic products).[31] The problem does not reside in the translation of the first or the third term, but in the interpretation of the second. Since the Egyptian documentation on the 'tributes' coming from foreign lands is depending on Egypt's centralist ideology, the strong political connotation of this term can be identified. It is possible to translate it both as 'gift' and as 'tribute', depending on the context of representation and the public to which the message is addressed to, although both meanings appeal to something obtained in exchange of something else. Liverani suggests that an internal public would have favoured an interpretation of the term with a connotation of 'tribute', as it is represented by the Egyptian court: all the countries, especially those ruled or influenced by Egypt supply goods for the Pharaoh, who in exchange supplies them with the 'breath of life' (material goods in exchange of symbolic goods, but of equal or superior effectivity, according to the Egyptian perspective). The understanding of this term, obviously in translation, towards an external public, in other words, in the context of a communication between the courts of great kings, would have tended to connote the term as 'gift', which would have confirmed the validity of the 'brotherhood' that binds the Egyptian king with some other foreign king (material or luxury goods exchanged for other material or luxury goods).[32]

This last analysis may be illustrated in the following chart:

| *Genre of communication* | *Sphere of the message* | *Reception of the message* | *Term* | *Socio-political assumption* | *Meaning of the term* |
|---|---|---|---|---|---|
| Letters | Private | External | *inw* | Parity, Reciprocity | Gift |
| Celebrative inscriptions | Public | Internal | *inw* | Verticality, Asymmetry | Tribute |

From a more general perspective on exchanges in the ancient Near East, and according to the diplomatic conventions of the period, a message could not be sent without a greeting-gift (Akk. *šulmānu*),[33] that would prompt the start of communication between the royal courts. It also functioned as an element of induction, a situation that consisted in sending a small amount of the product that is expected to be exchanged in a greater quantity. There was as well a 'rejection gift' mechanism, which consisted in sending a small amount of the required good back to its sender, indicating in this way a rejection of proceeding with the exchange (Liverani 1999: 324–31). Now, from a formal economic perspective, all these aspects of commercial communication constitute 'irrationalities' since, for instance, the exchange of identical products is opposed to the principle of exchanging something needed or desired and therefore lacking (Liverani 1979e: 22–6). However, perceiving the exchanging procedure holistically, from an anthropological perspective that recognises that economic phenomena are expressions of cultural communication, a coherent logic can indeed be found, depending on the native models of exchange.[34] In letter EA 40, for instance, the *rabiṣu* of Alašiya requires from the *rabiṣu* of Egypt a load of ivory to be sent as a counter-gift, and with the petition, elephant's tusks are sent as an inaugural gift. Actually, the apparent irrationality in these practices resides in a ceremonial custom carried out to ask for goods – if ivory, gold or silver are needed, a small amount of each good is sent. Also this practice was valid as a means of stabilisation of personal relations, which prompted future exchanges. Other examples can be read in EA 13 (a small amount of gold and ebony is sent to Egypt), EA 14 (silver and copper objects, and one of lapis lazuli, are sent from Egypt to Babylonia), and in EA 17 (gold and ebony is sent to Egypt). In all these cases, such gifts did not symbolise an exchange, but were only meant to consolidate relationships between the parties.

According to the evidence from the Amarna letters, there existed an 'ideal model' and a 'real anti-model' of exchange, as Liverani explains. The exchange model was based on generosity and hospitality; however, in practice, each king would search for augmenting his personal gain in the exchange, contravening the premises that confer prestige, represented, for instance, in the practice of *potlatch* of the natives from north-west America, or the 'gift and counter-gift' model presented by Mauss. The gift cannot be required, but in the Amarna correspondence is always required; the gift has to be granted, but in the letters resistance and complaints regarding the lack of it are evidenced. The gift has to be accepted and appreciated, but in the letters disappointments are usually manifested due to the small amount of the gift sent (Liverani 1999: 328; 2000: 24–5; Avruch 2000: 160–64; cf. further Bourdieu 1977: 171–83; and see also the survey in Graeber 2001: 23–47). Relevant in this context is the message of the king of Assyria to the Pharaoh:

> I send as your greeting-gift a beautiful royal chariot out[fit]ed for me, and 2 white horses also out[fitted] for me, 1 chariot not outfitted, and 1 seal of genuine lapis lazuli. Is such a present that of a Great King? Gold in your country is dirt; one simply gathers up. Why are you so sparing of it? I am engaged on building a new palace. Send me as much gold as is needed for its adornment . . . If your purpose is graciously one of friendship, send me much gold. And this is your house. Write me so what you need may be fetched.[35]

As Druckman and Güner observe:

> the international negotiations consisted of exchanges of material items (gold, horses, brides) in which attempts were made to enhance one's own benefits *relative* to gains made by the other parties. . . . as negotiators, the kings frequently insisted on *reciprocal* exchanges but seemed mostly concerned with the symbolic implications of these exchanges for their status or prestige. (2000: 176; original emphasis)

Such particular circumstances, attested in the written evidence, certainly contradict the essence itself of the reciprocal practice of gift and counter-gift, since 'gifts, and the spirit of reciprocity, sociability, and spontaneity in which they are typically exchanged, usually are starkly opposed to the profit-oriented, self-centered, and calculated spirit that fires the circulation of commodities' (Appadurai 1986: 11). But, do they imply an impossibility of applying such an interpretative model? The key is found, in effect, in analysing the economic phenomena of the period from a non-ethnocentric perspective, that is, without imposing an interpretive framework based on our own Western, capitalist, market-driven economic system to ancient data, but also without considering concrete ethnographic cases as telling of some 'primitive' or pre-modern universality. The ethnographic case offers a contingent example of the construction of a particular social reality and, as such, provides the researcher a way to comprehend the order of alternative social realities. The ethnographic case is not the ultimate, primordial example to confirm at different locations and periods, but just a model to interpret the diversity of the manifestation of the social. We must also allow for a native mode of conceiving of the system of exchanges during the Late Bronze Age according to the features expressed in the evidence of such exchanges. This system constituted a true commercial exchange, with a certain search for gaining some economic vantage, but it was also structured by ceremonial protocols of exchange of gifts and sending of tributes, which constitute the practice itself and are not mere ideological aspects covering up a more raw profit-searching thirst.[36] As Burnaburiaš of Babylon writes to the Egyptian Pharaoh: 'Among kings there are brotherhood, alliance, peace and [beautiful] words, if there is abundance of [precious] stones, abundance of silver, abundance [of gold]' (EA 11 rev:22–3; cf. Liverani 1999: 359).

These protocols, belonging to a social world that transcends the mere economic sphere evidenced from concrete elements, must be perceived in interaction with political and religious spheres so that we may compose a fuller and more accurate representation of ancient social realities within which the exchanges took place. The ultimate goal of the exchange of prestige goods between great kings seems not to have been economic profit maximisation, but rather a maximisation of status and prestige. In effect, the recurrence of the slight appropriateness of the counter-gifts that we find in the Amarna correspondence and the petition for sending a larger amount did not come from a desire of accumulating goods with exchange value, but instead with luxury goods, granting prestige to the owner: the more prestige gifts are received, the greater the status of the receiver. As Druckman and Güner (2000: 187) suggest:

> the kings were engaged in a competitive game for status. By jockeying for competitive advantage, they avoided confronting the larger substantive issues that had ramifications for the broader regional system. By insisting on reciprocity, they were often unable to agree on a formula for exchange on which agreements could have been based.

## 3.4. Exchange of women

### *3.4.1. Marriage as social and political communication*

The general rules structuring the practices of exchanges of goods – gifts, tributes or instances that may be simply understood as commerce – and which generate bonds of sociability – symmetric alliance, asymmetric alliance, direct subordination – apply as well to marriage practices during the Late Bronze Age. In effect, as already indicated, the inter-dynastic matrimonial bond is only a limited aspect of a greater interactive system with social norms affecting each feature of such a general system.[37]

Social anthropology has studied, since its beginning as a professional discipline in the late nineteenth century, the rules governing matrimony relation in different societies, as a key element in their kinship configuration. Of special interest for the present study is the particular marriage form known by scholars as *exogamy*, namely the obligation of establishing a marriage relation outside of the kinship group (Deliège 2005: 12–15; Testart 2006: 105–12). In brief, it may be said that the main reason of this kind of practice is to produce alliances with non-kinship groups and, by doing so, include them in the reciprocity networks that guarantee the survival of the group in various aspects of the social life. Likewise, the exchange of women would offer a system of relations between groups, which establishes a permanent structure when political ties are rather weak to do it, as J. Pitt-Rivers has argued (1977: Chapter 6). Thus, the establishment of exogamic marriages creates social relations that were previously non-existent, and it generates ways of social communication with different goals, especially political and economic. From the preliminary arrangements of the union until its realisation, the goal of the exogamic marriage basically concerns political alliance and economic exchange.

Since its publication in 1949, C. Lévi-Strauss's *Les structures élémentaires de la parenté* has been foundational in comprehending kinship networks and matrimonial provisions – even after some criticism of his understanding of kinship had appeared. Lévi-Strauss's key argument is that the universality of the prohibition of incest in 'simple' societies does not depend only on biological factors, but also on cultural elements and features leading directly to the practice of exogamy (the so-called 'generalized exchange' of women between different communities), which, at the same time, is mediated by social rules (Lévi-Strauss 1969 [1949]: 12–51; cf. also Marie 1972). The exogamic practice, then, leads on the one hand to forge alliances and establish different modes of hierarchy within a society that is extended by these bonds, and on the other hand, as already noted, establishes bonds and obligations of reciprocity between individuals and communities, manifested by the apparently paradoxical continuation of instances of violent clashes, exchanges of goods and marriages (Lévi-Strauss 1969 [1949]: 29–68).

Attending to the marriage sphere within the general structure of circulation of women, goods and messages in different societies, it is clear that the realisation of marriage generates alliances and reciprocal obligations between the parties, but it also produces a hierarchy between them, and between the husband and his wife, depending on the particular circumstances in which the marriage is celebrated. Eventually, marriage provision, mediated by payments of the bride price and the dowry,[38] represents in this sense a certain and immediate subordination of one party to the other and, likewise, a set of expectations and associated practices to such subordination.[39] The ethnographic record allows for two general forms of status organisation between alliance groups through asymmetrical marriages: *hipergamy*, according to which those who marry are superior to those providing the women, and *hipogamy*, according to which those providing the women are superior to those they marry (Hage and Harary 1996: 110).

This general and synthetic presentation of the ways social anthropology understands and studies marriage provisions as evidenced in the ethnographic record allows for a battery of conceptual tools with which to interpret the textual data on inter-dynastic marriage alliances in the Near East during the Late Bronze Age beyond the literal meaning of the translation and in order to attempt to perceive and understand the social world of the period.

### 3.4.2. Hierarchies and alliances during the Late Bronze Age

In the ancient Near East, inter-dynastic marriages, with the mentioned goals of achieving political alliance and economic exchange, are attested already during the regional hegemony of the city of Ebla in Syria, in the late third millennium BCE, and later also during the regional hegemony of the city of Mari in Mesopotamia, in the first half of the second millennium BCE.[40] Also, in the Code of Ḫammurabi, from the eighteenth century BCE, do we find references to the 'nuptial gift' (from the groom's father to the bride), to the distribution of goods for the wedding banquet, to the dowry in favour of the bride from her father, and to the transference of some goods from the husband to the wife. In sum, a set of practices and dispositions also represented in the ethnographic record from other parts of the world, makes it possible to proceed with the ethnographic analogy as an interpretive tool, when caution is exerted in order to avoid anachronisms and misrepresentations.[41] It is during the Late Bronze Age, and in particular in the Amarna period, that we find at our disposal a considerable amount of textual material about inter-dynastic marriages in the Near East, rich enough to produce a synthesis of a basic structure of procedure.

In the first place, and attending to the arguments of Lévi-Strauss on generalised and restricted exchanges, it is possible to think that the documentation exposes a kind of restricted exchange between the kings of the great kingdoms of the time.[42] Likewise, as Liverani (2001: 189–95) has argued, there were two points of view or, even more, two worldviews at play in marriage exchanges, dictating the procedure between the parties, which were not without friction and negotiations. From the Asiatic perspective, the marriage between the daughter of a great king and a great king is, in fact, a symmetric marriage, between equals or peers (which is evidenced in the irritation of the king of Babylonia while declaring in EA 1:10–17 that his daughter, now wife of the Pharaoh, is lost among the rest of the consorts). But, from the Egyptian perspective, the only person gaining prestige is the Pharaoh, when he receives princesses from distant places – in the same fashion as the products understood to be *inw*. In relation to a small king, marriage with an Asiatic princess did not seem to differ much from the practice of sending tribute, in which the woman seemed to be like any other good or material resource.[43] In relation to a great king, negotiations were complex since both parties pretended to get the greater benefit without big concessions (Meier 2000: 172–3; also Pintore 1978; Schulman 1979; Bryce 2003: 107–20; Podany 2010: 217–42). Actually, it is on this level of interaction that the cultural conceptions of each region are confronted.

The pharaonic court was, as it was observed in a previous chapter, the symbolic centre to which the Asiatic princesses arrived, that is, from a periphery that is both earthly and cosmic. From the Kassite perspective in Babylon is also present the symbolic dichotomy of centre-periphery; but, in this case, the prestige resided effectively in obtaining gold stemming from far-away Egypt in exchange for sending princesses, while emphasising the gaining of a luxury item.[44] Instead, from the Hittite perspective, political pragmatism seemed to be pre-eminent – although without losing its symbolic manifestation or cosmic meaning – as the king's daughters were married to the kings of subordinated lesser kingdoms, probably to increase the Hittite court's influence on the petty rulers within the empire's periphery:[45] 'The Egyptian king, who cannot "export" daughters, prefers to "import" Asiatic princes. But the basic difference is that in the Hittite perspective a vassal is expected to be loyal if he has been educated in Egypt' (Liverani 2001: 192).[46]

At a structural level, marriage relations can be distinguished in three concrete types: (a) *paritary* or *symmetrical*, (b) *asymmetrical*, and (c) *unidirectional* (Pintore 1978; Liverani 1999: 331–5).

a *Paritary* or *symmetrical marriages*: according to the documentary evidence, marriage procedures between the royal houses of Ḫatti and Assyria, and Assyria and Babylon were clearly symmetrical marriages: the marriage between a princess of Babylon with the son of Ḫattušili III finds its reciprocity reflex in the marriage of the king of Babylonia with a daughter of king Ḫattušili himself (*KUB* XXI, 38 Vs 47′–49′, 54′–5′). It is true that reciprocity is relative, since the king of Ḫatti seemed to be better positioned regarding the role the married princess could have had in the royal court; nonetheless, this kind of reciprocal exchange is not documented, or is virtually inconceivable, for Egypt. Another example of symmetry may come from the alliance between the dynasties of small kingdoms, such as Ugarit and Amurru: a document, by which the Hittite king Tudḫaliya IV acts as mediator between the parties, notifies the divorce of the king of Ugarit, Ammistamru II, from the daughter of Bentešina, king of Amurru (RS 17.159 in *PRU* IV, 126–7). Since other alliance treaties between the royal houses of Ugarit and Amurru are available (RS 19.68 in *PRU* IV, 284–6), it is possible to think that marriage exchanges was part, in effect, of the procedure of political alliance; however, it seems that only the kings of Ugarit received princesses from Amurru. Without existing verification of the opposite practice, we might suggest a certain socio-political differentiation of status between these small kingdoms (and would rather place marriage relations between the dynasties of these kingdoms on category [c]; Pintore 1978: 79–87).

b *Asymmetrical marriages*: I already mentioned the marriages between Hittite princesses and Syrian 'vassals' of Ḫatti, which constitute clear examples of unequal bonding. The marriage arrangement undoubtedly serves a calculated geopolitical control strategy, when the Hittite princess is placed at the very centre of the decision-making place in the subordinated kingdom.[47] The textual data allows for evidencing the marriage of a sister of king Šuppiluliuma I with Ḫukkana of Ḫayaša and two daughters of the king with Šattiwaza of Mittani and Maššḫuiluwa of Mira (*CTH* 42 and 51–2; Beckman 1996: treaties no. 3 and 6A–B); a sister of king Muwatalli with an Anatolian 'vassal' of Mašturi (*KUB* XXI 33), and two consecutive marriages with the house of Amurru, the first of them between the daughter of Ḫattušili III and Bentešina (*CTH* 92; Beckman 1996: treaty no. 16).

c *Unidirectional marriages*: considering the number of Asian princesses married to New Kingdom Pharaohs and, as it is said in the Amarna correspondence, 'From time immemorial no daughter of the king of Egypt is given [in matrimony] to anyone' (EA 4), the Egyptian disposition towards other great kings may be characterised as negative in terms of reciprocity. As far as the exchange of women went, it was driven by ethnocentric principles by which foreign princesses became Pharaoh's wives and the counter-gift for that was not Egyptian princesses, but luxury items, such as gold (EA 4:6–7, 7–14; cf. Pintore 1978: 11–13). The Babylonian kings Kurizalzu I and Kadašman-Enlil I each sent a daughter to Pharaoh Amenḥotep III (EA 1:12; 3:7–8; 4:21–2). Also Burnaburiaš III of Babylon sent a daughter to the Egyptian court, in his case for Amenḥotep IV (EA 11:Vs 7–8). From the kingdom of Mittani, a daughter of Artatama was sent to Thutmose IV (EA 29:16–18; 24:III 37–8) and a daughter of Šuttarna II and another of Tušratta were sent to Amenḥotep III,[48] who also married a daughter of the king of Arzawa (EA 31–2). Ramesses II married a daughter of the Hittite king Ḫattušili III (Beckman 1996: letters 22C–22G; Hoffner 2009: text 98). Finally, and this is a rare exception (notably, only appearing in Hittite sources), the widow of Pharaoh Tuthanḫamun requested that the Hittite king Šuppiluliuma sent a son for her to marry and procreate. However, and according to the sources, the prince died on the way to Egypt in strange circumstances. Unfortunately, this has cancelled the possibility to see what kind of influence the Hittite prince would have had in the Egyptian court, when the political projection of the Hittite marriage eventually crashed with Egypt's ethnocentric worldview (cf. Güterbock 1956: 94–7; *ANET*[3], 395).

It is evident that the Egyptian situation differs considerably from the rest of marriage practices found in Southwest Asia. The Egyptian military expansion during the Eighteenth Dynasty to Asia and the consolidation of Egyptian control beyond its natural and historical frontiers had, according to F. Pintore, as a direct consequence the apparition of the 'Egyptian harem' of Asiatic princesses, coming from the subjugated polities (Pintore 1978: 13). Egypt's vantage position in respect to the access to precious metals would have produced a more, let us say, 'authoritarian'[49] behaviour – and certainly fitting with Egypt's centralist worldview, regarding regional geopolitics – in what is referred to as diplomatic norms among the rest of the group of great powers of the period.[50] According to S. Meier (2000), we should attend more to the practices carried out by the Pharaoh than to the worldview supporting them. In effect, Meier (2000: 168) observes that the Egyptian diplomatic disposition during Amarna times was actually forced to give up certain pretensions of its own worldview in order to maintain contacts with the rest of the great powers:

> Pharaoh and his chancery had surrendered on the international level their self-image in order to communicate with second-class humans. What Egypt gained was coexistence with powerful neighbors on the northern fringes of their empire. The public compromise of Egypt's image – demotion from uniqueness to membership in an elite club – suggests that Egypt was not dealing from a position of strength. This posture of compromise marks a real surrender on Egypt's part that is confirmed on other levels. Not only in the areas of kingship and kinship is Egypt publicly (i.e., internationally) compromising its image. One must also not overlook the fact that Egyptians are corresponding in a non-Egyptian language. Instead of foreigners learning Egyptian standards, it is Egypt who learns the mechanics of international communication form others. It is not suggested that there was any competition in this regard. It is simply that when Egypt began to join in the dialogue, the tools for diplomacy had already been forged, and Egypt had to learn the rules set up by others.

A key to Meier's suggestion lies in the fact that Egypt had not imposed completely its rules of relations between powers, but had joined a group of 'international' players who were already operating with agreed rules. Egypt may have attempted to impose its pretensions concerning marriage negotiations, but it did not change the established rules of the inter-regional system. In effect, it is noteworthy that in the Amarna correspondence (for instance, EA 53:40–44), the Egyptian king is called by the Akkadian term for 'king', *šarru,* and placed ontologically in the same category as the Asiatic kings, even when the Egyptian was the most powerful (Meier 2000: 167).

Another clue, according to Meier, is constituted by the practice of anointing the head of a Babylonian princess (EA 11:16–18, rev 15), and of a princess of Arzawa (EA 31:11–14), and of a Hittite princess (Edel 1994: 51.14–16; 53.5–8; 107.4′–7′) with oil on non-Egyptian ground. This would indicate a concession from Egyptian centralism in order to be able to participate in inter-regional politics and avoid complete isolation, something that can also be evidenced by the Egyptian disposition and acceptance of celebrating a peace treaty with Ḫatti in 1258 BCE, although, as shown by Liverani, the treaty contains clear clues of Egypt's pretensions to appear as an ontologically unequal power, distancing itself from Ḫatti (Liverani 1990a). In effect, the Marriage Stele of Ramesses II declares that a marriage with the Hittite princess, agreed upon in the peace treaty, is part of the *ỉnw* of Ḫatti to Egypt; nevertheless, in the previous correspondence, the parties had agreed upon that the princess should become 'Lady [Akk. *bēltu*] of Egypt' (Edel 1994: 62.5). Likewise, the Hittite queen had indicated her desire that the daughter sent to the Pharaoh should be of a higher status with respect to the other daughters of the great kings (Edel 1994: 106.5′–9′).

In conclusion, the preceding characterisation of inter-dynastic marriage provisions during the Late Bronze Age permits us to infer, as a methodological principle and attending to the last Egyptian-Hittite example, that both the native models for understanding the world and the theoretical models we use to explain them must be put to the test constantly, through a critical historical outlook and the sound use of ethnographic analogies. Beyond some doubts and criticism, Lévi-Strauss's general tripartite model of the exchange of women, goods and messages is of heuristic value for interpreting the textual data in cuneiform sources from this period. Nevertheless, Pintore (1978: 138–9) relativised the instance of 'generalised exchange' for the ancient Near Eastern societies, since in these societies the exchange of women was restricted by a series of factors and situations, for which we should best speak of a 'restricted exchange' as the general rule, at least during the Late Bronze Age.

## 3.5. Exchange of specialists

### *3.5.1. Techniques and specialisation*

The appearance of full-time specialists in the societies of the ancient Near East can be traced to the emergence of urbanisation and the socio-economic division of labour in the primary states of the region (Lower Mesopotamia, Egypt) towards the end of the fourth millennium BCE. Full-time specialists were engaged in one of the two 'great organisations', the temple and the palace, key institutions in the whole process.[51] In this context, and following the consolidation of the state organisation, two kinds of specialists may be identified: on one hand, there were the technical specialists already existent before the process of urbanisation, that is, specialists in metalworking, pottery, healers/shamans, etc.; on the other hand, there were new specialists that urbanisation required: administrators and officers of the state apparatus, messengers-ambassadors, etc. Of course, the specialists in pre-urban technologies did not disappear with the rise of the state organisation, but they were integrated within the productive sphere of the cities and, together with the new urban specialists, they would contribute their trades to the productive functioning of the temple or the palace. Their juridical status was that of a 'free' person. However, their function within the state apparatus would have tied them inevitably to a socio-economic dependence on the palace for their subsistence and vice versa.

In effect, both technological and administrative specialists during the Late Bronze Age belonged almost entirely to the palatine sphere of production. In the context of the fluid contacts between polities during this period, such specialists would travel from one court to the other but only within the framework of diplomacy.[52] The stable image of the itinerant specialist in the Near East, as a stable feature, is not confirmed by contemporary documentation before Hellenistic times, although it is possible to think that after the general crisis that affected all the Eastern Mediterranean around 1200 BCE some specialists, who were now not institutionally attached to the palatine sphere, may have contributed to the diffusion of some technologies, in particular metallurgy, during the transition from the second to the first millennium BCE.[53] As noted by C. Zaccagnini (1983: 258), 'their wanderings represented a *temporary* stage of unemployment and not a permanent and institutional condition of life' (original emphasis). W. Burkert (1992: 9–87), on the other hand, favoured the idea of the itinerant specialist (possessing, according to Homer, a *techne* nobody else mastered), particularly artisans, healers-physicians, bards, after the collapse of the palace organisation in the Near East and the Mediterranean world, around 1200 BCE. However, as P.R.S. Moorey (2001: 4) observes, '[There] is no clear evidence for completely independent specialist craftsmen trading on their own account in the Late Bronze Age; but, if they existed, they might be expected to have fallen outside the range of the surviving documentation.' As for the Late Bronze Age, however, it is the palace specialists – artisans and metalworkers – those producing the technology and fostering its advance – notably, the glass industry and the industry of combat chariots driven by horses. They worked with raw materials and virtually with unlimited resources and time:

> It was not an accident that courts were central to technological developments. Only in such places were the necessary resources in terms of labour and materials, tools and workshops readily available on an appropriate scale. It was, moreover, within this environment that vital subsidiary factor fostering technology transfer came to play: craftsmen of all types would have been working closely together in associated workshops, many of them foreigners. (Moorey 2001: 4; cf. also Sherrat and Sherrat 2001)

### *3.5.2. Mobility and hospitality*

Once again, the Late Bronze Age specialist belongs essentially to a palatine realm of production. However, we have also seen that during this period there was an important level of inter-regional contact among the great powers, contacts aiming at exchanging goods, women – as future wives of kings or princes – and, precisely, specialists. According to C. Zaccagnini, the spatial mobility of craftsmen may be understood through patterns following at least two of the modes of economic activity proposed by Polanyi for pre-modern societies, namely redistribution and reciprocity – with the commercial mode discarded for pre-Hellenistic Near Eastern societies.[54]

The redistributive pattern in the mobility of craftsmen can already be evidenced in the correspondence of the kingdom of Mari, although it might be extended as well to the rest of analogous situations in other palatine economies of the Middle and Late Bronze Ages.[55] The textual evidence witnesses then a mobility of specialists – healers and seers, physicians, masons, scribes, builders, architects, musicians, metalworkers, furriers – from the palace to the periphery of the kingdom, where they were required.[56]

The reciprocal pattern is particularly represented in the Amarna epistolary evidence. Comparing the mobility of specialists to the rhythm of the exchange of gifts and women: the specialists would represent a kind of 'symbolic capital' offered as a gift exchanged among the royal courts,[57] as possessors of key techniques but also embodying a prestige that arrived to the court from a distant location, they were imbued with a certain sacredness. Indeed, as Kristiansen and Larsson (2005: 39) note, space and distance possess political and especially also ideological and symbolical connotations, as constructed by each society. Therefore, 'knowledge acquired from travels to such distant places may form part of a corpus of esoteric knowledge controlled by "specialists" (chiefs, artisans, priests) as an attribute and legitimisation of their status, power and authority.' The possession of foreign specialists in the court also helped to obtain prestige.

Some examples can be presented to illustrate this. In EA 35:26, the king of Alašiya asks for a specialist in vulture omens to the king of Egypt; and in EA 49:22–6, the king of Ugarit requests of the Pharaoh the sending of a physician and two black servants (slaves).[58] In the same fashion, in the epistolography between the kings of Ḫatti and the kings of Egypt, we find a petition by Ḫattušili III to Ramesses II of a physician (an obstetrician) so her sister may conceive a child (the Pharaoh shows reluctance concerning the petition and answers back, not without mockery, that only a miracle from the gods would allow for a woman so advanced in age as the Hittite princess to conceive; Beckman 1996: 131–2). Likewise, in a letter from Ḫattušili III to Kadašman-Enlil II of Babylon, the Hittite king declares to have taken care of the physician sent to Ḫatti by the Kassite king, and denies having prevented his return to Babylon (Beckman 1996: 136–7; on the physicians at the Hittite court, cf. Edel 1976). Such assertion has to be contextualised within the common practice in this period of withholding foreign specialists in the courts, as a particular means of ostentation of individuals bearing a singular symbolic capital, which bestows prestige upon their host (see further below).

Another episode in EA 23:13–25, which is not exactly an exchange of specialists, informs about the sending of objects carrying an important symbolic capital: Tušratta, king of Mittani, sends the king of Egypt, his son-in-law, the statue of a goddess: 'Thus [speaks] Šauška of Niniveh, mistress of all lands: "I wish to go to Egypt, a country that I love, and then return". Now I herewith send her, and she is on her way' (Moran 1992: 61; also Liverani 1999: 374; Rainey 2014: 185).

But, perhaps the main figure of the specialist travelling through the kingdoms' capitals in this period is the messenger (Akk. *mār šipri*, Eg. *wpwty*). In fact, the semantic field of the term *mār šipri* is broad and in the Amarna texts it is used to refer both to messengers and couriers properly, but also to ambassadors and ministers.[59] The messenger delivering a letter is the formal and normal manner of communication between the kings of the Late Bronze Age because of the orality of the message, as shown in the very form of the written message (cf. Chapter 2, section 2.2, this volume). The function of the messenger transcended the sole delivery of the message, as he also had to answer questions and explain the intentions of the sender (cf. EA 299:12–14; 302:11–18; 329:13–20). Of course, the messenger had as well a key role in marriage negotiations, which were at the same time commercial negotiations,[60] and acting thus as ambassador and exchange agent:

> The distinction between messenger and diplomat is sometimes blurred. Since along with their messages they often carried goods as 'gifts', which in international diplomatic practice was a major means by which foreign trade of the king was carried on, they can also be seen as merchants. (Oller 1995: 1466)

Two aspects of the mobility of the messengers are worth noting. The first one is the danger that was implied in travelling to foreign courts. Messengers, with the exception of a courier, would travel in convoys of some twenty people or more, which made the trip a long and slow journey – the longer it took, the more the possible danger of an attack by bandits or semi-nomads, or even desert animals: as the Egyptian text 'The Satire on the Trades' (*ANET*³, 433) notes, 'The courier goes out to a foreign country, after he has made over his property to his children, being afraid of lions and Asiatics.' Often, messengers would carry passports with them in order to avoid detention or attacks in the territory they were passing through, as it appears in a letter to the king of Mittani

> To the kings of Canaan, servants of my brothers: Thus [says] the king. I herewith send Akiya, my Messenger, to speed posthaste to the king of Egypt, my brother. No one is to hold him up. Provide him with safe entry into Egypt and hand (him) over to the fortress commander of Egypt. Let (him) go on immediately, and as far as his pre<sents> are concerned, he is to owe nothing. (EA 30; after Moran 1992: 100; cf. also Knudtzon 1907: 268–71; Liverani 1999: 405; Rainey 2014: 325)

The second aspect was related to instances of hospitality when a messenger arrived, as they were not only socio-politically, but also – and equally relevant – symbolically foreign to the host court or community. For instance, in the context of a marriage negotiation, the king of Babylon Kadašman-Enlil, complaints to the Pharaoh for not observing the customs of hospitality and reciprocity between two kings who are bonded by 'brotherhood' (*aḫḫutu*).

> Previously, my father would send a Messenger to you, and you would not detain him for long. You qui[ck]ly sent him off, and you would also

> send here to my father a beautiful greeting-gift [*šulmānu*]. But now when I sent a messenger to you, you have detained him for six years, and you have sent me as a greeting-gift, the only thing in six years, 30 minas of gold that looked like silver . . . When you celebrated a great festival, you did not send your Messenger to me, saying 'Come t[o eat an[d drink'. No[r did you send me] my greeting-gift in connection with the festival. It was just 30 minas of gold that you [sent me]. My g[if]t [does not amount] to what [I have given you] every yea[r].[61]

Messengers, according to the inter-regional diplomacy of the period, were expected to be received according to the rules of hospitality, which implied care and protection of the foreigner during a period of time.[62] In the Amarna letters, there is evidence that this principle of hospitality was overturned in practice in order to execute political pressure, as messengers and ambassadors, as well as other specialists, were withheld in the court in order to gain some advantage from their presence (cf. EA 3:13–14; 7:49–50; 28:16–22; 29; 59:13–14).

In sum, the function of specialists in Late Bronze Age societies was twofold. In the first place, there was the specific task they would perform within the production sphere of the temple or the palace. Without scribes, especially, the relations between the powers would have been much different than what we can reconstruct from the letters and treaties. Second, they would play a key role towards the exterior of their polity, creating contacts between the kingdoms as messengers-ambassadors-exchange agents.

Now, beyond their political role, we must attend to the symbolic status possessed by messengers and ambassadors, and also by traders or specialists in transforming matter (i.e. metalworkers), as they would travel through distant territories and arrive as foreigners to the receptive communities. As such, they were socio-politically strangers; however, in a closer interaction, they were essentially regarded as non-kin to the community. The characterisation made by the Classical historian M.I. Finley in his *The World of Odysseus* (1954), about the ways foreign specialists were perceived in the Homeric world, would also apply to the communities of Late Bronze Age Southwest Asia. They were met with fear and suspicion as they were not kin and they did not belong to the household organisation; but on the other hand, there was the obligation of granting hospitality to foreigners (cf. Finley 1954: 74–154).[63] Precisely, in attending comparatively to the Homeric tales, a similar image about the para-social character of the specialists can be obtained. Homeric literature refers to the *demioergoi* in the Greek world, that is, 'the ones working for the people', a group including metalworkers, bards, physicians, carpenters, etc. They were strangers to the communities they would interact with, but ultimately depended on them for their subsistence. These conditions are illustrated in some passages of the *Iliad* (XXIII, 835–8) and the *Odyssey* (III, 425–38), in reference to metalworkers and to the role they had as strangers within a community.

As indicated, the foreigner's condition was often addressed by means of the practice of hospitality, which was probably a manner of dealing with foreign elements without resorting to violence. According to J. Pitt-Rivers (2012: 513):

> The law of hospitality is founded upon ambivalence. It imposes order through an appeal to the sacred, makes the unknown knowable, and replaces conflict by reciprocal honour. It does not eliminate the conflict altogether but places it in abeyance and prohibits its expression. . . . the custom of hospitality invokes the sacred and involves the exchange of honour. Host and guest must pay each other honour. The host requests the honour of the guest's company – (and this is not merely a self-effacing formula: he gains honour through the number and quality of his guests). The guest is honoured by the invitation. Their mutual obligations are in essence unspecific, like those between spiritual kinsmen or blood-brothers; each must accede to the desires of the other. To this extent the relationship is reciprocal. But this reciprocity does not obscure the distinction between the roles.

Even more, explains Pitt-Rivers (2012: 507–8) that

> by dispensing hospitality honour was acquired within the community and allies outside it and considerations of personal advantage are thereby added to the general utility of the association between the stranger and the sacred. . . . The stranger belongs to the 'extra-ordinary' world, and the mystery surrounding him allies him to the sacred and makes him a suitable vehicle for the apparition of the God, the revelation of a mystery.[64]

By all means, these rules of hospitality and the sociability implied by it must be taken as general instances present in most agrarian or pre-capitalist societies. By evoking situations in which envoys, messengers, or officers arrived to a foreign court, we should understand that the overall instances of reciprocity between the host (a king) and the guest (the messenger, the ambassador) might have been in effect less 'equilibrated' or symmetrical than those attested in the ethnographic record referring to more 'primitive' societies. Nonetheless, the key issue is to be aware of such ethnographic possibilities in order to shed more light when interpreting the textual-epigraphic record, especially of the Amarna period.

* * *

The social world of the Late Bronze Age in the Near East, it was noted, proceeded to the exterior of the political community by means of practices proper of kinship relations, even when real kinship was not attested. Within this conceptual framework, commercial exchanges, but also matrimonial and diplomatic, were performed. In the three aspects of this general circulation, the intangible value attached to the acquisition of luxury items and women from distant lands, and also receiving and withholding messengers or other specialists, is *prestige*. In the correspondence between great kings of the period, it is evident that there was an implicit competition among them for acquiring prestige through these exchanges, which at the same time motioned an inter-regional political sociability with its own cultural features. Building on this description of great kings and small kings and the ways they interacted during this period, we proceed in Part II to describe and characterise the socio-political structures and dynamics of Syro-Palestinian polities.

## Notes

1 See further Viazzo 2009. As Llobera (1999: 21–43) has written, fieldwork is not the ultimate goal of anthropological research (let us think in M. Mauss's *Manuel d'ethnographie* [1926], written by someone who never did fieldwork!), but to interpret the social world, analysing its articulation. Cf. further, on ethnographic theory, the reflexive essays in Clifford and Marcus 1986.

2 This scheme is built upon the interpretations in Barthes 1977 and Eco 1968.

3 Cf. Polanyi 1957. Of course, the instances of reciprocity, redistribution and exchanges (market) cannot be taken as evolutive phases in a lineal historical development. Cf. also Humphreys 1969: 202, stating that Polanyi's model 'certainly applicable to the organization of labor . . . : reciprocal labor patterns are common in primitive societies, corvée labor can be classed as redistributive, and slavery belongs to the householding pattern. (It is more difficult to associate different patterns of land tenure with Polanyi's categories, and he did not deal with this problem). Polanyi seems to have regarded exchange of goods as the primary pattern, and allocation of resources as secondary.' See further in Humphreys 1969; Valensi 1974; Testart 2005; Aubet 2007: 31–55.

4 Cf. Polanyi 1977: 47–56. Without doubt, such embeddedness of the economy in social relations refers directly to the foundational studies on the nature of exchanges in 'primitive' societies by B. Malinowski, *Argonauts of the Western Pacific* (1922), and by M. Mauss, *Essai sur le don* (1990 [1950]), which should be contrasted now with later developments and studies, such as Gregory 1982; 1997; Parry and Bloch 1989; Weiner 1992, and Graeber 2001. Cf. also the criticism in Testart 2006: 85–140; and the notes in Rössler 2007. For the ancient Near East, cf. Aubet 2007: 110–14.

5 Cf. Liverani, 1976b: 3–12 (on the coexistence of a domestic and palatial mode of production in the ancient Near East); 1984; 2005; Zaccagnini 1981. On the Asiatic Mode of Production in general, see the historiographical discussion in Sofri 1969; O'Leary 1989; for the Levant, cf. the discussion in Zamora 1997.

6 I will not deal in this chapter with the internal economic situation in Late Bronze Age Levant since I focus the analysis on the political anthropological aspects of the regional exchange. For an understanding of this period in Syria-Palestine as one suffering from economic decline, see Knapp 1989a; 1989b; 1992; for an opposite conclusion, see Bienkowski 1989. For the question of trade and economic structures, cf. Sugerman 2000; Gestoso Singer 2007, and especially McGeough 2007.

7 Cf. Zaccagnini 1973: 120; Liverani 1979e: 27–30; Aubet 2007: 322–4, on silver as 'money'. The use of silver in this period may be differentiated into commercial (EA 35; 37; *Ug* V, 80–83) and of prestige value (EA 13; 14; 22; 25; 41); see further Peyronel 2014.

8 Cf. on the circulation of these products, Edzard 1960; Helck 1962: 391–460; Zaccagnini 1973: 170–89; Cochavi-Rainey 1999; Aruz 2008.

9 Cf. EA 4:41–3, 44–50; 6:13–16; 7:33–6, 37–9, 59–61; 9:16–18; 10:12–27; 16:32–4; 19:66–70; 20:71–6; 24 III 5–7; 27:16–18; 29:159–60; 168–70, 172; 35: 19–22, 40–42, 43–8; 37:13–17; 40:18–23; 41:36–8; 44:20–28; RS 15.24 + 50:12–21 (*PRU* III, p. 18); RS 17.116:25′–7′, 29′–30′ (*PRU* IV, pp. 133–4); RS 18.54 A:17′–20′

(*PRU* IV, p. 229); *PRU* VI 4:7–9; *PRU* VI 16; RS 20.03:10–13 (= *Ug* V p. 92); similar examples from the Old Babylonian period in *ARM* V 5:18–19 (Durand 1997: 400–1); V 6:19–21 (Durand 1997: 314). Cf. Zaccagnini 1973: 100–108.

10 Cf. EA 4:15–18; 7:37–9; 10:11, 23; 11: Rv 22–3; 16:32–3; 17:51–4; 19:74–9; 20:72–4; 24 I 74–7, 79–82; 26:45; 27:10–11, 64–5; 29:65, 125, 132; 35:19–20; RS 17.116:21′–3′, 28′ (*PRU* IV, p. 133); RS 20.03:7–9 (= *Ug* V p. 92). Cf. Zaccagnini 1973: 108–17.

11 Cf. EA 1–39, 41–2; cf. also EA 48, probably denoting a gift exchange between the queen of Ugarit and the queen of Egypt (Moran 1992: 120 n. 1).

12 Cf. EA 48; 49; 99; 369; *Ug* V, 98, 101–2.

13 Cf. EA 40: the *rabiṣu* of Alašiya writes to the *rabiṣu* of Egypt.

14 Cf. *Ug* V, 97–8, 100.

15 Cf. *PRU* IV, 132–4, 228–9; *Ug* V, 120–21.

16 Cf. *PRU* IV, 222–3; *Ug* V, 117–19, 135, 138, 152.

17 Cf. *PRU* III, 18; IV, 4, 6, 7B, 18; *Ug* V, 122–3.

18 Cf. Klengel 1963; Šattuara II, king of Ḫanigalbat writes to the king of Ḫatti, Ḫattušili III or Tudḫaliya IV.

19 Cf. *KUB* III, 70; Šutaḫapšat, son of Ramesses II writes to Ḫattušili III; EA 44: Zita, son of the king of Ḫatti, writes to the Pharaoh.

20 Cf. RS 17.247 (*PRU* IV, 191): Piḫawalwi, son of the king of Ḫatti, writes to Ibiranu, king of Ugarit.

21 Cf. EA 73; 82; 86: Rib-Hadda of Byblos writes to Amanappa, Egyptian official (note that in EA 87, Rib-Hadda calls him 'lord', instead of 'father'); EA 96: and Egyptian official to Rib-Hadda; EA 158; 164: Aziru of Amurru to Tutu, Egyptian official; RS 20.255 A (= *Ug* V, 101–2) someone at the Hittite court to the king of Ugarit.

22 Cf. RS 17.152 (*PRU* IV, 214): the king of Amurru to the king of Ugarit, his 'son' (note that in RS 17.286 [*PRU* IV, 180] the king of Amurru declares to be the 'brother' of the king of Ugarit); p. 216 (RS 17.83); pp. 217–18 (RS 17.143): the king of Ušnatu to the king of Ugarit, his 'father'; RS 16.111 (*PRU* III, 13–14): the queen of Amurru to the queen of Ugarit, her 'daughter'; RS 20.168 (*Ug* V, 80–82); pp. 87–88 (RS 20.238): the king of Ugarit, the 'son', to the king of Alašiya, his 'father'.

23 Cf. RS 11.730 (*PRU* III, 12–13): the king of Beirut to the prefect of Ugarit, his 'son'; in RS 10.046:7–9 (*PRU* III, 10) a functionary call the king 'father'.

24 Cf. RS 17.78 (*PRU* IV, 196–7): an official of the king of Karkemiš (?) to the prefect of Ugarit, his 'son'.

25 *PRU* VI 7A: a woman to the prefect of Ugarit, his 'son'.

26 The notion of 'harem' (from the Ar. *ḥaram*, 'forbidden, sacred') possesses indeed some Orientalist connotations; cf. Solvang 2006.

27 Regarding the relation between the value or prestige of a material good and the distance of its provenience, cf. Kristiansen and Larsson 2005: 32–41; Aubet 2007: 118–20.

28 The concept of *inw* is analysed in point c).

29 Cf. Bleiberg 1996: 96, 114: 'The Egyptian king clearly did not believe this exchange was occurring between equals. The texts and reliefs depicting these transactions always showed the giver as subservient to the king. Exchanges of *inw* were always made "with bowed head" or "with bowing" on the part of the giver . . . An exchange of *inw* between the king and another prince was an expression of each ruler's place in the social hierarchy of Near Eastern potentates.'

30 Cf. Bleiberg 1996: 90, 96: '*inw* was considered as an aspect of kingship, aside from the general idea that the king owned everything in the world. [Also,] *inw* represented

the results or cementing of a personal relationship between the king and a chief of a particular area.'

31 Janssen 1993; Spalinger 1996: 365–8. Cf. Bleiberg 1996: 96: 'The exchange of *inw* stood in direct contrast to the exchange of *b3k.t* which was always paid by a country or a region.' See also on other aspects of Egyptian economy, Janssen 1975: 173–7 (on taxes); 1982 (on gifts); 1993 (on *bꜣkw*); also more in general, see Bleiberg 1995; Eyre 2010; Moreno García 2014.

32 Spalinger 1996: 363–76, agrees with Liverani's interpretation of these technical terms but only in regard to the Annals of Thutmose III.

33 Cf. Zaccagnini 1973: 202–3; the root of the term is *šlm* and is related to the peace and well-being salutation. Cf. *in extenso* Eisenbeis 1969: 10–34; also *CAD* $Š_3$, 206–30.

34 Cf. Liverani 1979a: 26–7; 1979e: 22. See also, from a juridical perspective on exchange during the Late Bronze Age, Kestemont 1977; and on ceremonial aspects, Zaccagnini 1987.

35 EA 16:9–18, 32–4; after Moran 1992: 39 (cf. also Knudtzon 1907: 128–31; Liverani 1999: 363–4; Rainey 2014: 141).

36 Cf. Zaccagnini, 1989–90; a different perspective is presented in Pfälzner 2007.

37 'According to Lévi-Strauss, social life is above all exchange, namely reciprocity. There is no social life without reciprocity and exchange; men exchange words, goods, but also women' (Deliège 2005: 137). According to Bourdieu (1992a: 143–209), it would be better to speak of 'matrimonial strategies' rather than 'matrimonial rules', as Lévi-Strauss did, in order to confer agency to the actors in marriage relations and to avoid conceiving of the exchanged women as mere objects; in the Amarna correspondence, women appear essentially as a prestige good, yet we cannot discard in principle their potential agency.

38 As attested in the ethnographic record, following the generalisation made by Testart, Govoroff and Lécrivain (2002), the bride price refers to the set of goods offered by the future husband according to tradition and which are destined to the parents of the future wife, in exchange for giving the daughter in marriage (p. 66). On the other hand, the dowry refers to a transfer of goods from the bride's father in occasion of her marriage and destined to the future husband and wife, as a bond between two generations and as the inverse transaction of the bride price (p. 170).

39 According to Testart, Lécrivain, Karadimas and Govoroff (2001), in societies in which debt slavery is allowed, it is logically possible that marriage observes a submission of one party (woman) to the other (man), extending also to the rights of the woman and her children and all her symbolic and material patrimony. Cf. also Testart, Govoroff and Lécrivain 2002: 192.

40 Cf. in general Podany 2010: 34–6, 83–9. On marriage ceremonies and rites during the Old Babylonian period in Mesopotamia, cf. Greengus 1966; also Munn-Rankin 1956: 94–5. Cf. for Mari, *ARM* I 24, 46, 77; II 40; VI 26: Rv 5′–7′; and for marriage ties with Alalaḫ, *AT* 409, 411 and 35.

41 Cf. respectively in the Code of Ḫammurabi §§ 159–61, 138–9, 159–61, 163–4, 166, 137–8, 142, 149, 162–4, 167, 171–4, 176, 178–84, 171–2; see the translation in Roth 1997: 71–142. See too the analysis in Zaccagnini 1973: 12–32; and Westbrook 2005a, including the Greek world (Homeric tales).

42 Cf. Zaccagnini 1973: 15, 16 n 26. The marriage bonds during the Old Babylonian period probably represent the generalised exchange better.

43 Cf. EA 99:10–20: 'Prepare your daughter for the king, your lord, and prepa<re> the contributions: [2]0 first-class slaves, silver, chariots, first-class horses. And so let the king, your lord, say to you "This is excellent", what you have given as contributions to the king to accompany your daughter' (after Moran 1992: 171, who, as noted, translates *tamarāti* as 'contributions', also Rainey 2014: 547; Liverani 1998: 243, translates the term as 'doni', like Knudtzon 1907: 449, who interpreted it as 'Geschenke'); *ARE* II § 447: 'The tribute [*ỉnw*] of the chiefs of Retenu: the daughter of a chief (with) ornaments of – gold, lapis lazuli of [t]his country; 30 [slaves] belonging [to her]; 65 male and female slaves of his tribute; 103 horses; 5 chariots, wrought with gold . . . .'

44 On the symbolism of centre and periphery, cf. in general Eliade 2010: Chapter 1; and for the ancient Near East, Liverani 1976c: 439–62.

45 On the potential political agency of the princesses in the court that received them, cf. Melville 2005: 225.

46 Cf. *ARE* II § 467: 'Behold the children of the chiefs (and) their brothers were brought to be in strongholds in Egypt. Now, whosoever died among these chiefs, his majesty would cause his son to stand in his place.'

47 Cf. Pintore 1978: 71–5; see also Pitt-Rivers (2000: 27) about the contemporary Mediterranean.

48 Cf. EA 17:26–7; 29:18–20; 24:III 35–6; *Urk.* IV, 1738; EA 20–22, 24; after the death of Amenḥotep III, the Mittanian princess became Amenḥotep IV's wife (EA 25–9).

49 Pintore (1978: 56–62) contrasts the model of the giver of women (Asiatic), insecure and inconstant, always concerned for the place the princess will occupy in the Pharaonic court, with the model of the receiver (Egyptian), expressing a 'controllata arroganza' (p. 60) and superiority.

50 'The monopolistic control of the flow of precious goods of African origin and above all the gold from the mines of Nubia into the area of the palatine civilisation, put Egypt in condition of having its own rules in the exchange relations with other countries' (Pintore 1978: 11).

51 See in general Gregoire 1981; and more recently Liverani 2013: 61–80. Cf. also Zaccagnini 1976a: 324–5; and Gunter 1995.

52 Charpin 2004: 52. Of course, certain specialists (metalworkers, carpenters) also travelled with armies for basic maintenance in the war affairs (Moorey 2001: 7). On the circulation of medical specialists, see Couto-Ferreira 2013.

53 On the twelfth-century BCE crisis and its technological impact, cf. Sherrat 2003; Liverani 2013: 381–400; and on metallurgy in the ancient Near East, see Muhly 1995; on its diffusion, Buchholz 1988; on the diffusion of material culture styles, cf. Hitchcock 2005.

54 Zaccagnini 1983: 247; also 257: 'The singling out of a "commercial" pattern of mobility raises extremely complex problems, mainly because the operation of such a scheme must be evaluated in relation to a specific socio-economic background, for which ancient Near Eastern sources offer only partial and still problematic evidence. In short, the crucial point to be examined is the following: to what extent are we entitled to recognize the presence of a free-labor market in the pre-Hellenistic Orient (and the Levant) or at least some embryonic stage of such a socio-economic situation?'

55 Cf. Sasson 1968; Zaccagnini 1983: 247–49; Durand 1992; and for Mari epistolary references to artisans and specialists (ac. *mârû ummênî*), cf. Durand 1997: 221–317.

56 Cf. ARM XIII 147:27–33; II 15:1–29; I 115; XIV 3; II 127:1–13; II 101:8–31; I 7: 32–45; XIV 15 and 16; XIV 5 and 6; IV 65 and 79; XIII 21: rev.1′–12′; XIII 16:11–15; XIII 44 and 139: rev. 4′–20′; XIII 142:37–42; I 44, 68 and 99; V 54; IV 79; etc.

57 Cf. Zaccagnini 1983: 250: 'The sending of specialized workers is well attested in the framework of the diplomatic relations between the "great" kings and, to a certain extent, between the "great" and "small" kings of the Late Bronze Age. The skilled workers who were sent from one court to another were viewed as prestige goods, and their transfers are inserted into the dynamics and formal apparatus of the practice of gift-exchange.' The concept of 'symbolic capital' is applied here according to the theoretical arguments in Bourdieu (1992a: 112–21).

58 According to Zaccagnini (1983: 251–2), the two black servants (slaves) represent in fact a prestige good, 'exotic curiosities to be shown at court among the king's entourage'; furthermore, 'both physicians and diviners were considered luxury goods, whose appreciation was not exclusively based on their "value of use" but primary on their "exchange value": in a way, they were on a level which is not very different from that of the foreign princesses who were part of marriage exchanges.'

59 Cf. Bryce 2003: 63; and Holmes 1975: 376: 'Although the letters mention that a foot soldier filled the [messenger] position in one instance [EA 149:83], generally someone closely associated with the palace was used. One passage states that a Mitanni princess acted as a courier [EA 24:III, 22–3], while another passage indicates that a Mitanni family was used in the messenger service [EA 29:156–62].' In general, see the studies by Meier 1988, for the messengers in the Semitic-speaking world, and Vallogia 1976, for the Egyptian messengers. On the procedures and logistics of long-distance communication in the ancient Near East, see Crown 1974.

60 Cf. EA 5:16–17; 11:7–9; 19:17–23. Holmes 1975: 379–81: 'The messenger functioned as a trade representative for the king. . . . The foreign powers were interested in a messenger exchange with Egypt, not so much for diplomatic reasons, but because of the exchange of gifts . . . The messenger exchange was the main source of trade between Egypt and the other important powers, whereas it did not serve this function between Egypt and her vassals.'

61 EA 3:9–22, after Moran 1992: 7; cf. also Knudtzon 1907: 70–71; Liverani 1999: 348. Food and beverage are elements that were essential for the maintenance of friendship through hospitality and the relation created between host and guest by consuming together a certain substance, as exposed in Pitt-Rivers 2012.

62 On the different attitudes towards (different) foreigners in the ancient Near East, and especially their absorption into the host communities, see now Beckman 2013.

63 Cf. Finley 1954: 74–154. In effect, according to Boudou (2012: 268) this matter involves two questions (or enigmas) to be addressed when dealing with foreigners and hospitality: 'The first [enigma] concerns the place of the stranger: why tales and hospitality practices refer to the sacredness of the stranger, who must be given everything, while in normal times he is considered a morally inferior being among the members of the group? The second enigma refers to the question of the reciprocity involved and of the value of the stranger: what bond has to be installed first with the stranger, and what sense of community does it imply?' See the response in the following lines.

64 Cf. also Grottanelli 1977. Auffarth (1992) relates the moral obligation of providing asylum and protecting strangers in ancient Israel and Greece, rather than with personal honour, with instances akin at honouring the gods. On ethno-historical data on Bedouin hospitality in the Near East during the nineteenth century CE, cf. van der Steen 2013: 120–24. But see further the critical ethnographic remarks on honour and hospitality in Herzfeld 1987.

# Part II

# POLITICAL SYSTEMS IN SYRIA-PALESTINE

# 4

# SOCIO-POLITICS OF SYRIA-PALESTINE (I)

## Analytical concepts

### 4.1. Towards an historical anthropology of Syria-Palestine

Numerous recent examples illustrate the analytical richness of the confluence of the historical discipline and anthropological and ethnographic studies, both in regard to epistemology and methodology. In particular must be mentioned the now-classic interventions by K. Thomas (1963), B.S. Cohn (1980) and N.Z. Davis (1981). Three further examples are the celebrated studies by E.E. Evans-Pritchard, *The Sanusi of Cyrenaica* (1949), N. Wachtel, *La vision des vaincus* (1971), and E. Wolf, *Europe and the People without History* (1982). As N. Farriss (1986: ix) notes:

> Social historians in recent years have been turning to anthropology for theoretical perspectives, as they expanded their interests to include peasants, ethnic minorities – the people without history – the family, and other topics thought to be the traditional domain of anthropologists. For those who wished to do history from the inside out as well as from the bottom up, anthropology offered the necessary dimension of culture, the systems of meaning that people invest in their social forms. Anthropologists' interest in history, although not entirely new, has become more intense and of a different kind. The past, once viewed as a more or less undifferentiated prelude to the ethnographic present, has increasingly come to represent a rich storehouse of information on socio-cultural organization.[1]

Such a confluence is usually presented under the title of *historical anthropology*. However, it is also possible to conceive of this interpretive approach to social situations of the past – which find similar manifestations in a certain ethnographic present – associated as well to the kind of *histoire sociale* to which the co-founder of the French historical school of *les Annales,* Marc Bloch, would refer to in his seminal and posthumous essay *Apologie pour l'histoire*.[2] Nevertheless, the key issue is beyond descriptive tags and the variability of synonyms. To propose an historical anthropology implies an attempt to address different approaches to history and anthropology and to create an interpretive field that problematises social realities both on a synchronic and diachronic axis. Social structure and social change are intertwined in this perspective, as it is the manner in which social actors and agents perceive structure and change and their involvement in the making of their reality. These principles prompt us, in the first place, to acknowledge the contingency of all historical realities and social systems, and in the second place, to proceed with a deconstructive analysis of them in order to construct an analytical description of that historical reality. Over half a century ago, P. Bohannan (1956: 557) would argue for an anthropological epistemology coincident with the historical epistemology here presented:

> (1) Social anthropologists seek to understand the societies they study and the culture of those societies. (2) Such an understanding necessarily implies an understanding of the ways in which the people being studied conceive their own culture and social system. (3) The conceptions of no people can be understood apart from their language because a concept (as differentiated from a thing) can be embodied only in language and language substitutes. (4) Therefore: either (a) we must assume that all systems of thought are identical – the monoglot's assumption – or (b) we are committed to study the semantic aspects of the language of the people we are studying.

Of course, some practical obstacles arise from such a convergence, like the obvious impossibility of conducting ethnographic fieldwork in the past, as it has already been pointed out. Yet, even when the ethnographic view must become forensic to examine extant documents – both textual and archaeological – from the past, the chance of gaining new perspectives and understanding of long-disappeared societies, like in the ancient Near East, is worth the investigative effort (see Farriss 1986: x).

Traditional ancient Near Eastern, and especially ancient Levantine historiography – it must be noted – has been recently marginally updated with the critical perspectives that European historiography had begun to produce from the 1930s onwards, with the work of the historians from the two first generations of the aforementioned *Annales* school (M. Bloch, L. Febvre, F. Braudel). Only in recent years, the now-almost ubiquitous – at least in name – Braudelian perspective of *la longue durée* (long-term history), to refer to one of the most representative examples, has been introduced in the field of archaeology in the Levant as a belated novelty, as well as an effort to overcome and update the scope, methods and results of so-called 'biblical archaeology', hegemonic in the field until the 1970s (cf. Stager 1985; Bunimovitz 1994b; Finkelstein 1994; on the social archaeology of Palestine, cf. Levy 1995; cf. also Lehmann 1999). In the field of Assyriology the situation was not much different. In particular reference to studies dealing with Syria-Palestine, the emphasis was – and to some degree still is – on textual-philological issues together with archaeological questions, governed by a much more empirical than theoretical approach to historical (and socio-anthropological) problems. Of course, this diagnosis is not absolute but defines a general tendency,[3] as the relative absence of anthropological views in methodological procedures has its reasons. First, traditional Assyriology, anchored in Europe's academic standards, privileges the formation of students and specialists in ancient languages with an archaeological variant as complementary knowledge over a wider range of social sciences and the humanities (cf. already Liverani 1966; and more recently Vidal 2015a: 25–8). Second, Near Eastern archaeology, in general, does use the textual record of ancient civilisations but usually not beyond a formal reading, which is 'faithful' to the literal meaning, almost without problematising it.

In this state of research, on its accepted epistemological and methodological standards, the proposal here aims at considering a different, yet complementary approach to the social realities of ancient Near Eastern, and in particular Syro-Palestinian societies, an approach based on what social anthropology can provide to the enhancement of knowledge of these ancient societies, especially analytical frameworks that process textual and to a lesser degree archaeological data. I paraphrase A. Burguière (2006 [1988]: 142–3) here, stating that, just as the ethnographer using the distance between their own culture and that of the fieldwork in order to find out the logical system of a society under study, the historian can operate in the same fashion to explain the logical working of a certain conjuncture or historical period.

The analytical comparison of societies and cultures distanced by millennia and, at times, continents does not seek to produce any kind of ontological continuity ('a primitive or ancient society functions always in the same manner in any place'), but rather an epistemological key to proceed methodologically in order to explain historical phenomena. The study of ethnographic situations of contemporary or modern periods can provide us with clues to interpret fragmentary data from ancient times. Interpretative comparison must proceed with utmost care, however, in order to avoid the risk of proposing the existence of a certain historical rigidity in a particular region (e.g. 'modern Bedouins illustrate pastoralism in biblical times', making thus the ethnographic present a transhistorical reality detached from the observation present; cf. notably Fabian 1983: 37–69). Interpretative comparison, be it historical, sociological, or ethnographic, seeks not to discover immutable behaviour models, but, instead, key factors supporting the analysis of particular historical situations, which are culturally contingent. In particular, as N.P. Lemche (1985: xv) has already noted:

> Of course, it would be both naive and erroneous simply to identify modern or relatively modern social conditions in the Near East with the circumstances which prevailed in the past. I certainly do not propose to do this . . . . On the other hand, at the end of the day I am forced to admit

> that there is surprising continuity between many aspects of these societies then and now, as far as such things as forms of social organization, the forces of social control, the location of ethnic groups within larger contexts, the structure of complex societies, and so forth are concerned. This implies that it *is* permissible to offer a number of conclusions by analogy, conclusions which, however, must in each case observe the distinctive conditions prevailing then and now. (emphasis original)

When the archaeological or textual evidence is scant or ambiguous, or even if we wish to pierce the cultural barrier of meaning of a translated document, the historian must make use of a set of comparative possibilities in order to achieve a sound reconstruction of the past. And we must also in this instance problematise this concept, the idea of the *reconstruction of history*.

In effect, the historical discipline does not *reconstruct* an objectively given historical situation from the past, in spite of the connotation of this often-used term. The historical discipline *interprets* processes and facts and *constructs* meaning about them, that is, it creates such processes and facts while interpreting them from the available extant textual, archaeological, or quantitative data. And, just as historical narratives are created in the present, also ethnographic data possesses a constructive character in the ethnographic fieldwork (Clifford and Marcus 1986). These are the basic epistemological principles of a critical historical anthropology.

Now, even if this approach is far from being hegemonic or widespread in ancient Near Eastern studies, it is certainly not entirely novel. In fact, some four decades ago, in his introduction to that marvellous work *L'alba della civiltà* from 1976, S. Moscati observed that a recognition of the peculiarity of ancient Near Eastern societies, with respect to the 'primitive' societies of anthropology, resides more in the nature of documentation than in the possibility of research, as the method and not the object of research is what characterises social anthropology.[4]

In the present study, a similar research outlook is shared. Furthermore, the interpretative potential of an historical anthropological approach to the total social world of ancient Syria-Palestine manifests a comprehensive understanding of every aspect of social and human lives, both in a synchronic and a diachronic sense, as already indicated. Within this whole perspective, our intention in the chapters comprising Part II of this study, is to focus on the political anthropology of Late Bronze Age Syria-Palestine by attending to the analytical concepts and the interpretative models through which data is analysed and historical explanations and representations are produced. In general, the rule followed by Assyriologists, archaeologists and scholars of the ancient Levantine societies has been to refer to the societal organisations of the territory in ancient times through political concepts such as 'kingdoms', 'city-states', 'states' and 'empires' (cf., among others, Buccellati 1967; Glassner 2000; Hansen 2000; Goldstone and Haldon 2009). However, a critical definition of what is meant and implied by such concepts has been lacking. Every concept carries a semantic range of meaning that, unless clarified, may direct us to represent historical realities in a distorted way, supplemented by our own understandings of what a term refers to instead of attending to how a concept is used to analyse data and thus produce sound historical knowledge. These problems will be addressed in this part of the study, before offering our interpretation of the political anthropology of Syria-Palestine in Part III.

## 4.2. On statehood and state practice in Syria-Palestine

In the study of the societies of the ancient Near East, the emergence of social and political complexity in pristine contexts, like Lower Mesopotamia and Egypt towards the end of the fourth millennium BCE, can be observed by the presence of a series of present elements indicating such complexity. In light of the now-classic classification of V. Gordon Childe, we may note the following distinctive features: (1) a demography of considerable density; (2) a full-time specialisation of labour; (3) the existence of an economic surplus, and its organised centralisation; (4) a social structure based on classes; (5) a hierarchical and institutionalised political organisation, namely a state, in which political association is not based on kinship but on territory. Later, we may also note: (6) monumental public works; (7) long-distance trade; (8) a normalisation of artistic and monumental expressions; (9) writing, as an administrative feature, and (10) a series of specialised trades, applied to engineering, astronomy, etc. (cf. the theoretical line-up in Childe 1950; and for the ancient Near East, Redman 1978: Chapter 7; Maisels 1990).

All these features, appearing or present at the same time, at a certain location and period, and without necessarily subscribing to (neo-)evolutionist perspectives of society (Service 1978; Carneiro 1981), could indicate the existence of a particular social dynamics implying a fundamental break between a non-state society and a state society (cf. Campagno 2002: 21–94). Now, attending to the specialised historiography, the concepts usually applied to the study of ancient Syro-Palestinian societies are mostly dependent on theoretical formulations crafted for or belonging to the analysis of pristine contexts of social complexity, instead of an observation of the particularity of the local or native socio-political practices. In effect, both the socio-political structure and the dynamics of the Syro-Palestinian polities of the Bronze Age, in general, are essentially described in quantitative comparison of characteristics to other polities, such as the Mesopotamian. This means that the general organisation of the big Mesopotamian city-states is reproduced as an interpretative framework for a characterisation of the small urban centres of Syria-Palestine, albeit on a lesser scale. However, the notion of urbanisation in Palestine must be considered in the proper scale of the country. Local settlements or towns in the southern Levant had a regular size of around 10 ha., much smaller than exceptional sites like Hazor (70 ha. In the Middle Bronze Age), Samaria (60 ha. in the Iron Age II), or Jerusalem (50 ha. during the seventh century BCE). During the Late Bronze Age, the average extent of a 'city-state' in Palestine would have occupied a radius of 15–20 km and been at an average of 30 km from each other (Bunimovitz 1993: 447; 1994a: 3; 1995: 326), while Jasmin (2006: 164) reduces the radius to 10 km for the Shephelah. Clearly, these sites are far from comparative with important cities of Mesopotamia like Niniveh (700 ha.) or Babylon (1,000 ha.) (cf. de Geus 2003: 185 *et passim*).

But, let us be clear: the comparison in itself is not totally inappropriate. The problem lies in its quantitative nature, which, when referring to a general model, ignores the local (Syro-Palestinian) particularities. In such a situation, the possibility of identifying or detecting qualitatively different socio-political structures and practices is eliminated, in order to confirm to some degree a variation of a general model. Thus, the presence of small urban centres in Syria-Palestine during the Bronze Age does not necessarily support, in principle, the verification of an equally small state power, quantitatively 'underdeveloped' due to its location in the periphery of the regional political centres such as Mesopotamia. The situation requires, instead, an investigation of the kind of socio-political practices active in these small urban centres.

Beyond the political scenario of Late Bronze Age Syria-Palestine – and the Amarna period as the most representative of the examples – a *longue durée* perspective of the political anthropology of the region could certainly shed some light on the evaluation attempted in this study. In general, the socio-political phenomena in the pre-Hellenistic Levant are interpreted by current history-writing through concepts such as 'city-state' (especially for the political centres of the Bronze Age and in reference to notable socio-political organisations, like Ebla, but also regarding much smaller centres, e.g. Byblos) and 'tribal state' (especially for the Iron Age, *c.* 1200–600 BCE, and the Aramean socio-political organisations, for instance; cf. Dion 1997). Likewise, the transition from the Bronze to the Iron Age around the twelfth century BCE, is usually understood in socio-political terms as a transition from 'territorial states' to 'national or ethnic states'.[5] The differentiation proposed by such descriptive typologies refers mainly to diverse modes of political structuring through different historical periods, but also to a difference in power dynamics in society, which depends on each social organisation.

We may define then what is to be understood as a 'state' or 'statehood'. I will avoid making reference here to the various conceptions and characterisations of the early state (cf. Claessen and Skalník 1978a; 1978b; Claessen and van de Velde 1987; Campagno 1998; 2000; 2002). Instead, I will argue that statehood refers mainly to a confirmation of the concrete reality of a specific socio-political practice at a particular historical period: the legitimate monopoly of coercion in society. This definition, in effect, makes reference to Max Weber's understanding of what constitutes the modern state, which can be detected in a political organisation when 'its administrative staff successfully upholds the claim to the *monopoly* of the *legitimate* use of physical force in the enforcement of its order' (Weber 1978: 54). More recently, Bourdieu (1994: 4) has offered a more comprehensive definition:

> The state is the culmination of a process of concentration of different species of capital: capital of physical force or instruments of coercion (army, police), economic capital, cultural or (better) informational capital, and

> symbolic capital. It is this concentration as such which constitutes the state as the holder of a sort of meta-capital granting power over other species of capital and over their holders.

Even acknowledging this definition as proper to the modern state, its usefulness over many others, even if referring to ancient forms of political hierarchical organisation, is that it allows for immediate detecting, although at a certain abstract level, of what constitutes a state society and what does not. In other words, in a state society, it is possible to identify an institutionalised concentration of political power in a particular sector of such a society. In a non-state society, political power is distributed at different levels and realms and is less institutionally attached to a particular sector of such society. Non-state societies are usually structured and governed by kinship networks and bonds, with key instances of reciprocity as the social articulator of politics and economics, which represents a serious obstacle to the concentration of power. A profound internal change is required to overturn this situation and promote the formation of an institutionalised concentration of political power and, with that, the establishment of the state (cf. on this Clastres 1989; Campagno 1998). How and why such a change from a non-state society to a state society is produced is beyond the scope of this study. What is relevant is the important divergence between both kinds of societies, non-state and state.

It was previously noted that research in both eastern and western Syria generally characterised the archaeological structures of its main sites as states, or more specifically, city-states (cf. Akkermans and Schwartz 2003: Chapters 6–8). But, what is it meant by 'city-state'? The overall disposition in current Near Eastern scholarship may be synthesised in the following definition by Hansen (2000: 19):

> A city-state is a highly institutionalised and highly centralised micro-state consisting of one town (often walled) with its immediate hinterland and settled with a stratified population, of whom some are citizens, some are foreigners and, sometimes, slaves. Its territory is mostly so small that the urban centre can be reached in a day's walk or less, and the politically privileged part of its population is so small that it does in fact constitute a face-to-face society. The population is ethnically affiliated with the population of neighbouring city-states, but political identity is focused on the city-state itself and based on the differentiation from other city-states. A significantly large fraction of the population is settled in the town, the others are settled in the hinterland, either dispersed in farmsteads or nucleated in villages or both. The urban economy implies specialisation of function and division of labour to such an extent that the population has to satisfy a significant part of their daily needs by purchase in the city's market. The city-state is a self-governing but not necessarily an independent political unit.

This definition covers a wide range of socio-political manifestations having urban centralisation. But, it is worth asking, to what extent such definition of city-states is valid for interpreting the textual and mainly the archaeological data from Syria-Palestine? In other words, the concept must be put to the test in order to verify its analytical and descriptive potential for offering a sound historical representation of Syro-Palestinian polities and politics.

## 4.3. City-states in Syria-Palestine?

The most representative example of a city-state in ancient Syria is usually attributed to Ebla (*c.* 2400 BCE). This conclusion is reached essentially through an examination of the archaeological and textual materials discovered *in situ* (Matthiae 2010). Ebla housed one of the biggest archives of the Near Eastern Bronze Age, with data on internal and foreign economics of the kingdom. Thus, in Ebla clear features of state organisation are visible: urbanism, palace officers, administrative documents, political control of the periphery, etc. (cf. Milano 1995; Pinnock 2001; Mazzoni 2003). In its heyday, Ebla occupied 56 ha. (Milano 1995: 1226). Nonetheless, and in spite of having many of the features found in state organisations like those present in Lower Mesopotamia and Egypt, Ebla's socio-political organisation also had features of *tribal* structures. But what is a *tribe*? As Lapidus (1990: 26–7) observes:

> the concept of tribe is unclear and controversial. The word is used to refer to a kinship group, an extended family, or a coalition of related families. It may refer to the elite family from whom some larger confederation gets its name, to a cultural, ethnic, or other non-familial social group, or to conquest movements of pastoral peoples without regard for the internal basis of cohesion. I will not take a position about the meaning of tribe except to make clear that I am not talking about small-scale family groups, cooperative herding, or village communities but about political entities that organize fragmented rural populations – be they small kinship or clientele groups or ad hoc alliances of individuals conceived as an extended family – into large scale alliances. Such large-scale political entities may be conceived by their members in terms of a common mythic ancestry, but usually the leadership is defined in terms of patriarchal, warrior, or religious chieftaincies.

This definition should be kept in mind when addressing the 'tribal' features some early polities seem to possess in the ancient Near East, not as secondary addenda to a state formation but as the key foundation upon which the polity functions.

Regarding Ebla, Milano (1995: 1222) has noted two significant differences in comparison to Mesopotamian city-states:

> While urban consolidation speeded centralization, thus preparing cities to compete politically, a different tempo for social development in Syria helped institutionalize a power system typical of a kinship-based society. Not surprisingly, two important manifestations of royal prerogatives known early in Mesopotamian history are missing so far from Ebla. There are no 'royal inscriptions' (as a literary genre) to legitimate the sovereign and to glorify his power as derived from the gods. We also do not find 'year names' by which kings titled a whole year after the main achievement of the previous year.

It is also interesting to note, as S. Mazzoni (2003: 181–2) indicates regarding the conditions of production in Ebla, that some products were manufactured in the villages or in urban locations that were not under the direct control of the Ebla palace and had, perhaps, a domestic base (cf. also Maisels 1993: 140–55), which makes one wonder about the effective extent of the state power in Ebla, especially if we consider, as P. Michalowski affirms (cf. Schloen 2001: 283), that 'the use of kinship terminology at Ebla . . . suggests that the Ebla kingdom was ruled by a "corporate" dynasty in which the power of the king depended on a network of kin mediated alliances.' For sure, there existed relevant kinship relations in state organisations, especially at the elite level and at the domestic level of the villages, but they did not comprise the backbone of the political organisation. An impersonal and institutional power did, under which kinship relations were subsumed. There is therefore an important difference between an organisation managing its internal affairs exclusively through kin-members of the élite – which does not necessarily stand for a state organisation – and another organisation that, beyond these élite kin-members, functions through officers related to the élite not by kin but by office—which would clearly constitute a state organisation. Therefore, when we think of a site like the kingdom of Ebla, we may propose that, in spite of a series of state-like features, kinship relations were of paramount importance for the organisation of the kingdom and therefore they should be seriously attended in defining the political nature of this polity.

The rest of the urban centres in Syria-Palestine during the Bronze Age are notably much more 'modest' in scale and scope than Ebla and, consequently, the importance of kinship relations and tribal structures may have had a greater gravitation in the definition of their internal and external politics. The kingdom of Mari, with its tribal relations as politics, was under the Mesopotamian, rather than Syrian sphere of political influence (cf. Fleming 2004). In the Late Bronze Age, the kingdom of Ugarit, on the Mediterranean coast, can be seen as a sophisticated example of Syro-Palestinian urbanism, with a solid internal political hierarchy, the presence of administrative archives, commercial and diplomatic, religious specialists, division of labour, etc.[6] Yet, as I will attempt to show in the following chapters, the presence of statehood as a native phenomenon, especially in the southern Levant, is more than elusive, having present the personalised political articulation characteristic of Levantine kingdoms – in fact, to all Levantine polities – in its internal structure and its external relations (see the following chapters).

In Palestine in this period, the question of statehood is not supported by much primary or direct evidence, even less than in Syria. There is certainly evidence of a process of urbanisation since the Early Bronze Age (*c.* 3300 BCE) and through the successive periods (Weippert 1988: 146–81; Mazar 1990: 92–143). However, the sole presence of urban centres is far from being obvious evidence of state formations. From a political anthropological perspective, socio-political practices must be attested as well. No doubt, especially during the Middle Bronze Age (Mazar 1990: 174–231; Kempinski 1992; Ilan 1995; Burke 2010: 44–7), urbanised political centres, with a political hierarchy, are attested, yet state practice is not self-evident in the archaeological record. Again, tribal structures and kin relations may have been present instead. The general political dynamics active during the Late Bronze Age appears to be analogous to the model of *peer polity interaction*, including warfare and 'competitive emulation' among polities (Renfrew 1986: 8), yet within a general framework of foreign rule of the territory, which resulted in a constrain of the potentiality of such interaction from outside and 'from above' (cf. Müller 2011).

The concept of city-state has also been used to characterise the fragmented topography in the Levant, especially in Palestine. Thuesen (2000: 64) notes:

> By contrast with the Mesopotamian alluvial plain . . . the geographic conditions in Syria never favoured centralisation. Most of the towns were situated in regions often limited by natural barriers such as mountains or deserts. To some degree that explains why Syria during antiquity had a tendency to return to a political fragmentation into a number of smaller kingdoms, a structure which can be compared to a city-state system.

While Strange (2000: 67) says of Palestine: 'This country, on the other hand, fragmented into numerous small valleys and with difficult passage between its various parts, is ideally suited to the development of city-states, and was very seldom united into a larger unit except when under foreign rule.'

The political scenario of the period seems to have had an important influence on regional political structuring. In effect, this factor may clarify even more the socio-political landscape we intend to comprehend, with respect to the display of politics, especially in Palestine. The aforementioned topographical condition seems to have created obstacles to the emergence of state-like local organisations sustained through time. Instead, the urban centres would operate politically circumscribed to their hinterland or not far beyond it – with some exceptions, such as Hazor in the Middle Bronze (Weippert 1988: 217–32; Mazar 1990: 192–203, 206, 209–10; Nigro 1995: 29–118) and Shechem in the Late Bronze (Finkelstein and Na'aman 2005: 173–80) – in constant competition for human and political resources. According to A. James, during the Late Bronze Age:

> conditions in Canaan were not conductive to political unity. The coastal plain is discontinuous and often narrow; mountain ranges run parallel with the coast, making lateral communications difficult; and especially in the north, the wooded valleys – more appropriately, gorges – are often steep. Thus, there was a little chance that a significant power, either indigenous or external, would emerge at Egypt's very gate. Authority was likely to be dispersed, and the resultant rulers would be much weaker than Egypt. By the same geographical token, the efforts of a large externally based power like Egypt to exert authority would encounter logistical and tactical complications. Because the terrain was ideal for those who would later be called guerrillas, the checking of their activities would be a formidable task. Furthermore, other external powers might try to win the loyalty of some of the several hundred local principalities and their rulers who exercised authority in Canaan.[7]

Also, M. Jasmin (2006: 177) while describing the main features of 'city-states' in thirteenth-century BCE Palestine, has written:

> The city-state potentially had significant local power, but it could not use it beyond certain limits. It seems as though the Egyptian administration encouraged an equal power distribution among the city-states, so that they might exhaust each other in internal fighting without eclipsing Egyptian control.

Furthermore, Jasmin (2006: 175–7) distinguishes the territorial structure of the city-states if the Coastal Plain, the Shephelah, the Hill Country and northern Negev. The Shephelah had the most hierarchical structure of Palestine, with urban centres and satellite sites and villages, while the sites in the Coastal Plain possessed a smaller hinterland, due mainly to their different economic basis, and the sites in the highlands and the northern Negev were scarcely urbanised, apart from Tel Masos in Late Bronze Age II, with an important pastoralist socio-political element.

In effect, spatial fragmentation must be considered a basic element in understanding how politics and political relations developed, especially in the highlands of the southern Levant. In this sense, the use of the concept 'city-state' to characterise the many centres of Syria-Palestine seems inappropriate, since what is prescribed in the ideal model interferes with what is found in the archaeological and textual data.

During the Late Bronze Age, western Syria was under Hittite, Mittanian (briefly) and Egyptian rule, which meant that the 'kings' of the local political centres held a certain amount of autonomy within their polities but depended ultimately on external political will. The mode of administering the imperial territories would vary, from the Hittite case – in which the king of Ḫatti would establish a political reciprocity pact with his Syrian subjects, through which the political survival of the petty king was guaranteed – to the Egyptian case – in which the Pharaoh would not consider the petitions from his Asiatic subjects at all, for reasons both ideological and administrative, as well as practically, because they were in most instances not important (cf. Klengel 1992: 84–180). We may note in this connection the question of *sovereignty* of the Syro-Palestinian kings, especially within their own political community. And it is fair to wonder whether, under circumstances of effective Egyptian or Hittite control of the region, the term 'sovereign' for the local rulers really applies. If so, it was a very much constricted sovereignty. It is therefore certain that the political manoeuvrability of these petty kings was externally conditioned by the presence, effective or symbolical, of the great powers of the period. The petty king depended on the agreed or imposed conditions with the Hittite king or on the concessions granted by Pharaoh or his officials (i.e. *rabiṣutu*) stationed in the land.[8] To the external conditioning of local sovereignty from above, in the Syrian case an internal limitation is equally observed under the shape of a reciprocity relation of the Ugaritic king with his men, the *bnš mlk* in the Ugaritic texts.[9] Since the Ugaritic king, the king of one of the most important kingdoms of Syria, had to grant lands in exchange for support to the throne, as has been maintained,[10] it might be possible to argue that the Syrian kings of the Late Bronze did not actually hold the monopoly of coercion in their political communities, but they had to articulate a network of exchanges and obligations to secure the internal order of the kingdom.

For Late Bronze Palestine, the situation of a precarious sovereignty is much more evident, if we consider the recurrent socio-political structure, as defined by T.L. Thompson (1992: 58):

> For Bronze Age Palestine, the term 'city' is seriously misleading, and 'city-state' is an immense exaggeration if we think of the normal use of such terms. The size of settlements in ancient Palestine was in direct proportion to their agricultural exploitation of the regions in which they were situated: a pre-eminent characteristic of village culture. The city of ancient Palestine is equivalent to the modern small town; its 'prince,' 'king,' and 'lords' might best be translated as 'village head' (in the sense of *mukhtar)* and 'elders.' The term city-state used to describe the society of ancient Palestine refers to little more than the autonomy of a local village or village cluster from other Palestinian powers. The very largest towns rarely exceed one or two thousand people, and the average only a few hundred.

One can find some ethno-historical analogy in this description with the duties of the *ra'īs al-fallāḥīn*, the leader of the peasants, in Ottoman Jerusalem during the sixteenth century (Singer 1994: 32–45). And it is interesting as well to attend to what B. Scarcia Amoretti (1990: 165) notes for Palestine in much more recent times regarding the figure of the *mukhtar*: 'the *mukhtar* plays an administrative and political role above all in the countryside, where . . . the official expressions of power are lacking.' Here, vis-à-vis the outside world, '[the *mukhtar*] is the representative of the rural community in its entirety; inside he is the mediator of possible disputes.' Thus, the duties of a *mukhtar* actually coincide in many aspects with those of a village's *sheikh*, as demonstrated ethnographically also by M. Shunnaq (1997), for a Jordanian village (cf. also Lutfiyya 1966: 77–100; Antoun 1979). K. Nakhleh (1975: 502), however, further states that

> empirical evidence from Palestine shows the subordination of this position to that of the heads of dominant kinship units. The position of the *mukhtar* in traditional Arab villages was not a leadership position; it was a position created by the central authority to facilitate its contacts with the village without necessarily upsetting the structure of dominance in the village. Therefore, the position was established for the fulfillment of specific functions. Some of these functions were: the preservation of peace and order, the recording of births and deaths, the circulation of government announcements. All in all, the *mukhtar* was the official link between the village and the authorities. . . . Since the occupant of the position was appointed by the authorities, and not elected, and since it was created in the first place so that the authorities would have harmonious relations with the village, the authorities had to take into consideration the specific social structure of each village. Thus, to fulfill those functions, the *mukhtar* either had to be from a dominant group himself, or he had to be supported by one. Once in a while the occupant of the position would be the head of an influential kinship group, but many times the *mukhtar* was the 'lackey' of a specific kinship group; he was merely the holder of the 'rubber stamp.'

It is therefore interesting to confront these ethnographic notices with the documentary evidence provided by the Amarna correspondence and highlight some paradigmatic examples of the fragile constitution of power, or better said, of leaderships at the local level. For instance, Rib-Hadda, ruler of the city of Byblos who faces a crisis in his domains, writes to the Pharaoh 'I am afraid the peasantry will strike me down' (*pal-ḫa-ti* LU.MEŠ *ḫup-ši-ia ul ti-ma-ḫa-ṣa-na-ni*), or also 'What <am I to say> to my peasants?' (*u mi-na a-<qa-bu-na a->na* LU.MEŠ *ḫup-ši-ia*).[11] Faced with evidence like this, one is forced to ask: where is the punitive force of this petty kingdom repressing the rebellion? Why does the petty king have to say anything to his peasants? These questions make us think about the degree of internal socio-political differentiation between the petty kingdoms of the Levant – or at least Rib-Hadda's kingdom – and the presence of a centralised political power as an institutionalised function within them. As a matter of fact, from an ethnographic point of view, Rib-Hadda's testimony, can clearly be seen as that one of a tribal chief, instead of a head of a (city-)state: a tribal chief can be deposed by a peasant rebellion when his prestige does not measure up to his behaviour as a chief; a tribal chief must also respond to his peasantry as he does not have the monopoly of power within the society. One understands this better with Khoury and Kostiner's (1990b: 8) description about chiefdoms in the contemporary Middle East:

> In chiefdoms the bonds between the chief and society are not necessarily institutionalized; they tend more often to be based on personal or ad hoc arrangements. In such circumstances the various societal segments of the chiefdom, notably the tribes, remain intact and still enjoy a considerable degree of political manoeuvrability and cultural and economic autonomy.[12]

We may also reconsider our use of the native terminology about the monarchy in Syro-Palestinian society, to support the present interpretation. As L.K. Handy affirms, one must attend to the connotation of the term commonly translated as 'king' (*mlk*) in West Semitic languages:

> The problem lies not with the word *mlk*, but with the connotations of the term 'king'. The verbal root *mlk* means 'to rule'. It does not mean to be the *sole* ruler. In the ancient Near Eastern political world, it was common for a series of rulers (any of whom might be called *mlk* 'king') to form a hierarchy within an empire. The city-states of Syria-Palestine had long been subject to the rulers of Egypt or to Hittite kings, even before the arrival of the Assyrians, Babylonians, Persians, Greeks, or Romans. The king of a local city-state remained a 'king', even though he served under the authority and at the discretion of the king of the empire. The title used for the king of the empire could quite literally have been 'king of kings'. Therefore, *mlk* was a title used not only on more than one level of the hierarchy of an empire, but even on several people on the same level simultaneously. (Handy 1994: 112; original emphasis)

Therefore, the Amarna evidence might actually be telling us that, even when it can be asserted that the polities of Late Bronze Age Syria-Palestine were something more 'complex' than a kinship society – and social complexity is not the sole patrimony of the state formation (cf. Possehl 1998) – these polities did not seem to be articulated by concrete state structures or even constitute a proper city-state, especially in Palestine. In this sense, the socio-political landscape seem to have been rather similar to previous periods in Syria-Palestine – even if we grant some quantitative variations – according to what can be attested, for instance, in the Execration Texts (*c.* 1800 BCE). Here reference to petty 'tribal' leaderships, and 'tribal' instances of sociability can be found in the story of Sinuhe (*c.* 1960 BCE). This story describes the political landscape of the Levant with reference to hospitality ('The sheikh among them, who had been in Egypt, recognized me. Then he gave me water while he boiled milk for me. I went with him to his tribe. What they did (for me) was good'; vv. 26–9), about marriage alliances ('He set me at the head of his children. He married me to his eldest daughter. He let me choose for myself of his country, of the choicest of that which was with him on his frontier with another country'; vv. 79–81), about tribal integration of the foreigner, once accepted in the community ('This ruler of (Re)tenu had me spend many years as commander of his army'; vv. 99–101), and about public tests of prestige ('A mighty man of Retenu came, that he might challenge me in my (own) camp. He was a hero without his peer, and he had repelled all of it. He said that he would fight me, he intended to despoil me, and he planned to plunder my cattle, on the advice of his tribe'; vv. 109–14).[13]

It therefore seems to be the case that the usual treatment of these petty polities in traditional scholarship on Syria-Palestine as 'city-states' responds perhaps more to certain preconceptions and analogies – for instance, if some monarchic dynastic inscriptions are attested, a state formation should be evident – than to effective analysis of the socio-political practices in action, as partially reflected in the textual record and the archaeological remains. The sole reference to 'kings' (*mlkm*) in the multiple small centres of the southern Levant does not mean that each of them was the head of state and therefore possessed the monopoly of power within a political community. In relatively major centres such as Ugarit or Alalaḫ in Syria (Sapin 1981: 32–46, 59–61; Pfälzner 2012: 774–87), with greater socio-economic organisation than the rest of petty polities of the region, the absence of a firm political autonomy towards the exterior of the kingdom, but also the inner administration of the kingdom, which was nonetheless rather complex, are to be regarded carefully since what is proposed here is not to conceive of the state as a mere addition of features – as noted above – but rather as the concrete manifestation of a particular socio-political practice affecting the whole of society and thus properly defining it.

* * *

If we focus our analytical attention on the concrete socio-political practices that bond individuals (or agents, in sociological parlance) as they are manifested in the epigraphic record of the Late Bronze Age Levant, it is safe to affirm that, with some exception, the evidence for a native state organisation is ambiguous and disputable. In the same fashion, the concept of city-state for understanding the socio-political nature of local polities is far from the most appropriate explanatory tool of socio-politics. Perhaps terms like 'monarchy' or 'kingdoms',[14] even though they lack the descriptive strength of other analytical concepts, may be of greater neutrality and less connotative in characterising Late Bronze Age polities of Syria-Palestine and avoid an over-interpretation that results in false historical (re-)constructions. The Syro-Palestinian 'kings' of these polities are not necessarily leaders of a state formation, holding and displaying the monopoly of power in society. In fact, the concept of 'kingdom', with a king as the articulator of the social whole in its executive but also ideological aspects, may actually provide a better framework to interpret the archaeological and epigraphic evidence of

Syro-Palestinian polities, since it implies the existence of a certain internal social hierarchy and recognises the particularity of the monarchic office, without requiring an institutionalised centralisation of power in order to exist as a polity. The monarchic office in the Semitic world also implies mediation between the divine and earthly realms because the Semitic king is the ritual specialist of first order in the society.[15] Yet, this king is not the holder of absolute political power. The king was at the apex of the societal pyramid but also, as it will be argued in the following chapters, he was a politically limited actor. In a socio-political sense, then, the Levantine king, especially the southern Levantine king, is rather a *primus inter pares*, having a certain amount of authority in society but equally constricted by other social factors. Beyond terminological preferences, what must be emphasised is a correct use of analytical concepts with what they imply and explain, taking also into account the *socio-political practices* over the institutional spheres in which they may be inscribed.

## Notes

1 For a vehement argument for the interpretative potential of historical-anthropological comparativism, cf. Detienne 2009; and considering only anthropology, Herzfeld 2001. Further on ethnohistory and historical anthropology, Axtell 1979; Feely-Harnik 1982; Comaroff and Comaroff 1992: 3–48; Dube 2007; Viazzo 2009.

2 Bloch 1992 [1949]. Numerous are the members of *les Annales* having followed the Blochian criteria of historical reconstruction, producing in fact an *anthropologie historique*, notably for the Middle Ages and later periods. On the 'anthropological turn' in French historiography, cf. Burke 1990: 79–85.

3 Notable exceptions can be found in Oppenheim 1960: 419; Kramer 1962; Gelb 1967; Zaccagnini 1973; Moscati 1976a; Schloen 2001; Bahrani 2008. The influence of the work of K. Polanyi (1957; 1960; 1977) in Assyriological treatments of trade in Mesopotamia and Anatolia is also of special relevance here; cf. Lafont 2005; Michel 2005; also Jursa 2005; Rede 2005.

4 Moscati 1976a I: 7. Moscati would continue in the same page: 'It is true that the research disposition on 'primitive' society is essentially synchronic, whereas in the history realm diachrony is hegemonic. But, the old antithesis of comparative method and historical method now tends to fade [and] a complementary perspective [arises]'. Also M. Rowton (1973a: 250) commented in favour of a merging of anthropology and history for ancient Near Eastern studies, although with the following warning: 'This anthropological approach to history involves, by its very nature, a potentially dangerous procedure. Comparison entails, to some extent at least, projection from a later to an earlier period. This can be useful but on one condition only. Nothing from the later period can be allowed in evidence as proof of a solution in the earlier period. Material from the later period should function only as a trail marker in unfamiliar territory, indicating the possible location of evidence, either entirely new or evidence the significance of which has not been appreciated.'

5 Cf. Buccellati 1967; Herr 1997; Joffe 2002; Liverani 2002. The notion of 'secondary state' (Price 1978) has been used in this context for the Iron Age Levant, although it results somewhat problematic; cf. the discussion in Pfoh 2011.

6 Cf. the description in Yon 2006. The excavated area of the *tell* where Ugarit was situated (some 7 ha. of a total of 21 ha.), comprises the palace area in one-third and the palace factories in the remaining two-thirds (Liverani 2005b: 123).

7 James 2000: 112. See also Finkelstein 1996, and see the criticism in Na'aman 1997 too. On the problem of human resources in Late Bronze Age Palestine, see Bunimovitz 1994a.

8 See further on this in Chapters 5 and 7.

9 Cf. RS 15.111 (*PRU* II 9); RS 15.022 (*PRU* II 24); RS 15.032 (*PRU* II 25); RS 15.115 (*PRU* II 106), RS 18.076 (*PRU* V 66); RS 18.079 (*PRU* V 67); RS 19.016 (*PRU* V 11); *KTU*: 200, 267, 268, 282, 350, 351 and 421f.

10 Cf. Liverani 1974; Lackenbacher 2002: 219–46. Márquez Rowe (2002: 18) states: 'we do not have any contracts that describe the basic stipulations of a *bunušu malki* regarding his duties towards the king, his master', and this was like so given the personal bonding that most probably characterised the relation between the king and his men; it was not a 'legal' agreement, but a personal one, actually a patron–client relation, as Prosser (2010: 178–217) indicates.

11 EA 81:33 and 77:37 (cf. Knudtzon 1907: 394–5, 386–7; Moran 1992: 151, 148; Liverani 1998: 178, 175; Rainey 2014: 469, 483); cf. also EA 271:9–21. Groll (1983; 238) observes that 'Aware of the *ḫazanu*'s vulnerability in the face of local opposition, the Pharaohs supplied their clients with a military and financial aid package, including a garrison.'

12 Against Carneiro 1981, we should not perceive the 'chiefdom' organisation as anticipating inevitably the rise of statehood, but instead use this concept as an analytical tool in itself; cf. Clastres 1989; Yoffee 1993; Campagno 2000.

13 *ANET*³, 18–22, 328–9; also Briend and Seux 1977: 30–36; Lichtheim 1973: 222–35. See also the analysis in Campagno 2011. On the 'tribal' world of Syria-Palestine during the second millennium BCE, cf. Sapin 1982: 1–49; and cf. also about Mari, Anbar 1991: 77–90, 119–57.

14 Klengel (1992) refers to 'principalities' to characterise the Syro-Palestinian polities of this period.

15 Cf. more on this in Chapter 7.

# 5

# SOCIO-POLITICS IN SYRIA-PALESTINE (II)

## Interpretative models

### 5.1. Feudalism and the Asiatic mode of production

The precise way in which Syro-Palestinian polities interacted with the great powers controlling their territories – or having hegemony over them – may indeed provide us with a key to understand how these polities were internally organised. The differentiation of the internal organisation of a Levantine kingdom and its 'foreign policy' is, in fact, only analytical, since in the concrete realm of its realisation we may verify a particular unity of conception, as reflected in the relevant textual data. This statement may be equally descriptive of the socio-economic organisation of these polities.

Two interpretative models have been mainly used to explain the internal socio-economic functioning of the polities of Syria-Palestine, having the kingdom of Ugarit as a paradigmatic example of such models, namely a feudal model and a model referred to as the 'two-sector model'. As J.D. Schloen has observed,[1] until the 1960s a model crafted from medieval feudalism was used to describe Old Babylonian society, Kassite Babylonia, Middle Assyrian society, Nuzi and the kingdom of Arrapḫa, the Hittite kingdom and its empire and Middle and Late Bronze Age Syria-Palestine. Following the theoretical path of Marxism, many scholars – not necessarily Marxists – such as J. Gray, G. Boyer, A. Alt and A. Rainey,[2] would propose this interpretative model for the Levant, implying that in these societies there was no private land, property being exclusively the king's, while the land labourers did not own the means of production – which, in fact, places this model within the realm of a slave society, as Marxian theory indicates, rather than as a feudal society, where the labourers did own some of the means of production.

> For Rainey, as for Alt and Boyer, the 'feudalism' of Ugarit essentially consisted of a land-tenure system characterised by hereditary rights of usufruct in return for service or payment. Unlike Gray, Rainey attributes no special political role to the *maryannu*-charioteers or any other

> military corps. On the contrary, he places heavy emphasis on royal authority, in a way that tends to contradict the usual picture of feudal government as a somewhat decentralised arrangement in which powerful nobles wield substantial influence . . . Rainey . . . goes so far as to call the king of Ugarit 'a typical oriental despot', a comparison sharply at odds with the normal use of the term 'feudal'. But this comparison may be more apt than the feudal model itself. In my opinion, 'Oriental despotism', properly defined, is not a bad description of Ugarit . . . The royal service system of Ugarit, as Rainey describes it, resembles not so much feudalism as a miniature version of Ottoman sultanism and other Middle Eastern political systems like it – examples of what Max Weber called patrimonial regimes. (Schloen 2001: 218)

This model would assert that the king would grant lands ('fiefs') with hereditary status to his men ('vassals'), who would in return be at his service through a sworn bond ('fealty'). Those receiving the land may divide it in order for it to be exploited by their own servants. The resulting scheme is a kind of hierarchy of feudal appearance, but lacking in fact the juridical and political framework of European feudalism, which depended on the contract between free men with institutionalised rights and duties for both parties, something non-existent in the Near East in ancient times.[3]

Departing from a different strand of Marxism, the Russian orientalist I.M. Diakonoff had, since the 1950s, proposed in a series of studies a socio-economic model for the ancient Near Eastern societies: the 'two-sector model', which stood aside from the more orthodox interpretations of Marxist theory and which, according to Diakonoff, would explain the working of society in Mesopotamia, Anatolia and Syria-Palestine since the beginnings of urbanisation until the second millennium BCE. From a traditional Marxist point of view, as noted above, the feudal mode of production implies the ownership of the means of production by the labourers of the land, and since traditional Marxist interpretations regarded ancient Near Eastern society as slave-centred, namely no ownership of the means of production by the labourers (Struve 1969 [1933]), the feudal model was rejected as inappropriate for analysing the available documents. Diakonoff, against such Marxist orthodoxy, then proposed a model that differentiated society into two sectors: besides the productive unit of the temple or the palace, there existed a productive unit of the communal-kinship base that possessed private land and that was legally free from the temple or the palace. According to Diakonoff, the king, rather than 'owner', was 'sovereign' of the territory and its inhabitants and thus he required 'taxes' instead of 'rent' from the free population of the kingdom. This model, on one hand analogous in its working to the Marxian 'Asiatic Mode of Production' (Marx 1965 [1857–58]), implied on the other hand a rejection of the connotation of 'oriental despotism' available in the records and images of nineteenth-century European writers Karl Marx had consulted for elaborating his model (which dealt mainly with colonial India and China; cf. O'Leary 1989; Curtis 2009: 217–57). Without going further, what is relevant is the manner in which this model has been enhanced by M. Heltzer and M. Liverani in the course of various studies of the kingdom of Ugarit, as a paradigm of Levantine society during the Late Bronze Age.[4]

If we attend in detail to the characterisation made by Liverani,[5] at a structural level, society was organised through the superimposition of two different levels, with different technological development and forms of production: at the lower level, villages or local communities, and at the upper level the palace organisation. The 'city', or better the urban village (Akk. *ālu*) was a relatively closed world and was composed of a group of houses and families.[6] The executive organisation was in the hands of a council of elders or notables (Akk. *šibūtu*), the chiefs of the main houses, with internal rules of solidarity and collective responsibility (cf. *AT* 2:27; *AT* 3:38 [Wiseman 1953: 27, 29, 32]; RS 20.239:21–7 [*Ug* V, 142–3]); and the palace, besides, would designate a *ḫazannu* residing in the village and managing in accordance with the orders from the capital (Liverani 1983c: 175–8; Van Soldt 2010: 255–6).[7] There was no productive differentiation in the village, which was self-sufficient. The palace (Akk. *ekallu*), instead, would control the territory (Akk. *mātu*) where the villages were found economically as well as politically.[8] The palace (and the city surrounding it), unlike the village, would preserve the effects of the 'urban revolution': division of specialisations, accumulation of productive surplus, cult and administration specialists, etc. (cf. Liverani 2013: 61–80). The palace would then concentrate the economic production of the self-sufficient villages and the exploitation of the royal farms (Liverani 1979f; 2005b). Thus, in a Weberian fashion, Liverani (1974: 331) would indicate: 'The palace, through the monopoly of collecting the surplus and through the monopoly of the organised and legal use of force, presents itself as like "the state".'

The palace organisation revolved around the king (Ug. *mlk,* Akk. *šarru*), of whom all the population depended. There was then the 'prefect' (Ug. *sakinu*, Akk. *šakin māti*; cf. del Olmo Lete and Sanmartín 2003: 757–9), an official in charge of managing the duties of the rest of the kingdom's officials. The members of the palace organisation are the 'king's men' (Ug. *bnš mlk*, Akk. *arde šarri*). They would not possess the means of production but, instead, would depend economically on the palace, and therefore were not actually 'free'. The texts of Ugarit distinguish categories among the 'men of the king': the *rabutu*, men closest to the king, probably direct kin; the *maryannu*s, the warrior class; and then the lower-rank specialists, such as artisans, administrators, etc. (cf., for instance, RS 17.133:15 = *PRU* IV, 119; Liverani 1974: 334). Further, the documents from Alalaḫ, distinguish clearly between *maryannu* and the rest of the palace dependants, the *eḫelena,* besides the rest of the population (two-thirds in all) constituted by *ḫupše*, that is, 'clients', if we include the *ḫaniaḫḫe* ('poor') as a sub-class in the latter group (cf. Von Dassow 2008: 233–348).[9] Men from the villages were economically free but not politically, by which is meant that they had to offer tribute of a certain amount of economic surplus or perform *corvée* in labour or military service to the king (Liverani 1974: 329–32).

This basic description of the Ugaritic society has recently been challenged by Schloen's important contribution *The House of the Father as Fact and Symbol* (2001). In particular, Schloen appeals to the Weberian formulation of the patrimonial society for interpreting economic and political documents from the Bronze Age Near East, thus confronting formulations anchored in the feudal model and the two-sector model/Asiatic Model of Production, especially as to what concerns the executive and hierarchical aspect of Near Eastern society:

> a patrimonial ruler, according to Weber's definition, organizes his domain as an extension of his own household. Government officials are his personal servants and members of his household. In theory, all property belongs to the ruler because the entire kingdom is viewed as a single 'household' of which the king is master and owner.[10]

The Patrimonial Household Model, as Schloen (2001: 255) himself calls it, 'agrees with the very durable native terminology used for all manner of political and social relationships throughout the Near East in the pre-Hellenistic period'. This patrimonial model was anchored in a political terminology drawn from family and kinship relations but also 'familiar household relationships provided the pattern not only for governmental authority and obedience but also for the organization of production and consumption and for the integration of the gods with human society' (2001: 255). As to the extent of such political terminology:

> Household language – the use of terms such as 'house,' 'father,' 'son,' 'brother,' 'master,' and 'servant' in an extended political sense – carries more significance than is usually thought, for it reveals the self-understanding of the social order that was at work in these societies. These terms were used metaphorically, to be sure, but this does not mean that they were merely casual figures of speech or euphemisms for 'real' economic and political relationships. They were widely used because alternative conceptions of social hierarchy were not readily available. In the absence of the rather abstract idea that an impersonal political constitution or universal egalitarian social contract might underpin the social order, personal relationships patterned on the household model served to integrate society and to legitimate the exercise of power.[11]

Thus, it is most important to take into account the native (*emic*) model for conceiving of political relations. It is not correct to consider it an expression of mere personalised metaphors covering up a more impersonal order, but in the manifestation of such a native model through kinship and household terminology there lies precisely the key of the total social configuration of the polities of Syria-Palestine.

The patrimonial characterisation so far is enough to consider a better alternative to the feudal and two-sector models. In Part III of this study, the patrimonial model is further explained as uncovering the socio-political matrix of Syro-Palestinian society as reflected in the textual documentation of the period.

## 5.2. On Hittite 'vassalage'

The image of a feudal order in several of the main societies of the ancient Near East, as we have seen, had a general acceptance to some degree among scholars towards the mid-twentieth century. In the particular case of the kingdom of Ḫatti, in effect, the existence of a feudal-like relation in the internal organisation seemed to be confirmed, especially by the presence of a powerful king, to whom officials had to swear loyalty and who would grant lands in return and who also would replicate this practice towards the exterior of the polity, when a conquered king had to swear an oath of loyalty to the Hittite king as a proper means of political subordination.

A classical formulation of Hittite (and Near Eastern) feudalism is provided by K. Ebeling in his entry 'Feudalismus' in the *Reallexikon der Assyriologie* from 1971:

> Also in Hatti the social formation can be characterised as feudal. On the top, there is the king and the aristocracy (landowners and court dignitaries, Hit. *panku*). The latter stand before the king as in a relation between a feudatory and a feudal lord, although with rights. In the following steps of the state pyramid one finds the free[men] (merchants and priests), half-free [men] (warriors, craftsmen and peasants) and finally the slaves (the state administration [sic!]).[12]

Nonetheless, the idea of a Hittite feudalism must be revised and probably discarded as an interpretative possibility. I have advanced some of the reasons for setting aside the feudal model for the Levant some paragraphs above; but one should also consider serious objections from the arrangement of medieval feudal relations in Europe. Already half a century ago, the French medievalist R. Boutruche (1968) had observed that Hittite treaties had in principle a certain similitude with Euro-Franc feudal-vassal bonds. But such bonds did not imply the particularities of the western European feudal concession, first of all because the lord-vassal bond was a private affair in feudalism, while in Ḫatti the treaty with foreign subjects was a public political matter. Further, on legal grounds, there was legislation on the nature of the feudal order, between lords and vassals, and each party could have appealed to it in a dispute. This did not exist in the Hittite empire, as the legal terms of the socio-political transaction represented by the treaty were actually personal: those of the Hittite king. Further, as another notable medievalist, M. Bloch, asserted in his monumental work *Feudal Society* (Bloch 1989: 172):

> Vassal homage was a genuine contract and a bilateral one. If the lord failed to fulfil his engagements he lost his rights. Transferred, as was inevitable, to the political sphere – since the principal subjects of the king

> were at the same time his vassals – this idea was to have a far-reaching influence, all the more so because on this ground it was reinforced by the very ancient notions which held the king responsible in a mystical way for the welfare of his subjects and deserving of punishment in the event of public calamity.

Hittite treaties hardly fall into this presentation of 'lord-vassal' treaties and therefore their historical presentation as expressions of Hittite feudalism and vassalage is in fact misleading and anachronistic. In the field of Hittitology, the notion of Hittite feudalism was partially rejected in the 1970s, especially by A. Archi (1977) and F. Imparati (1982) – although most of the terminology still remains in current treatments. Both authors proposed to consider the general layout of the organisation of the Hittite kingdom by appealing to the two-sector model, or the Asiatic Mode of Production. However, in this instance we can also consider the criticism made by Schloen for the case of Ugarit and apply it to Ḫatti, proposing thus a patrimonial understanding of the organisation of the kingdom, by which not only royal officials but also external subordinated kings are incorporated in the royal Hittite household, although with a different standing:

> [Enough] evidence exists to support the view that Hittite rule was legitimated and implemented according to a model of political authority based on personal 'household' relationships rather than an impersonal bureaucratic model. As elsewhere in this period, the entire state and its administrative apparatus was regarded as the king's 'house' and royal officials were the king's dependent servants or, at the highest level, his 'sons'. (Schloen 2001: 311)

Now, it is from this perspective, of a patrimonial kingdom with a political power conceived of as personal and hierarchical, that we may attend to the specific nature of the so-called 'vassal treaties' and to the role they had regarding the political subordination of the conquered or subjugated polities.

The political scene of the fourteenth and thirteenth centuries BCE was the general context of the 'vassal treaties' and, precisely, the structural fragility or volatility of the political relations established in the northern Levant due to military interventions from different powers may provide us with a clue as to the need for expressing ritual and symbolic formulas of subordination, loyalty and obedience and their respective punishments for acts of treason on behalf of the subordinated party.

In ancient Near Eastern historiography, the study of the ways of bonding two polities (or individuals, or an individual and a deity in the case of Old Testament literature or the Meša stele in the epigraphy of the Levant; cf. Fensham 1963; McCarthy 1963; Kalluveettil 1982; Thompson 2007) by means of a pact or a treaty finds it first antecedent of importance in the seminal study of V. Korošec, *Hethitische Staatsverträge* from 1931, dealing with Hittite treaties essentially from a juridical perspective.[13] Accordingly, the formula of Hittite treaties would comprise:

1 A preamble with the name of the sovereign, thus legitimating his dynastic position and noting that the treaty is actually at his initiative.
2 A historical prologue, in which the former conditions leading a (Syrian or Anatolian) prince to the treaty, i.e. to have relations with the Hittite king, are narrated.
3 The stipulations; namely, a list of mutual obligations, always heavier on the subordinated or 'protected' party: a) the obedience of the petty king or prince to the Hittite king; b) the prohibition to the 'vassal' of having an independent policy in his relations with other polities; c) mandatory military assistance of the Hittite king; d) the return to Ḫatti of eventual Hittite fugitives, without reciprocity from the Hittite king; e) the payment of tribute (which can be light or heavy) to the Hittite sovereign; f) material assistance to the Hittite troops settling in or passing by the petty king's or prince's territory. Observing such instances would secure stability in the throne and dynastic succession for the petty king or prince.
4 The dispositions relating to the placement of the document in a temple and its regular public reading, especially in the presence of the protected king or prince, to remind him of his duties as well as of his alliance with Ḫatti;
5 A list of gods as witnesses (cf. Freu and Mazoyer 2007: 375–8), whose wrath would come down over the party that did not observe the agreement. It should be noted that the list of Hittite gods was far larger that the list of gods of the protected king or prince.
6 A series of curses on the petty king or prince who does not respect the treaty, and blessings to whomsoever does.[14]

Most of the known Hittite treaties belong to the so-called 'protected' kingdoms. When a polity entered spontaneously or after a conquest into the Hittite political realm, the Hittite king would impose on his new ally a protectorate treaty (Hit. *isḫiul*; lit. 'bond'). Nonetheless, it was not a treaty between two polities or states, but an arrangement of political personal relations that had to be observed '*cum bona fide*'.[15] Also, in spite of a rhetoric of symmetry and reciprocity of obligations bound by an oath (Hit. *lingai*), always sworn by the subordinate king – although on some occasions the Hittite king might have also sworn it (Altman 2003; Beckman 2006: 283; Miller 2013: 2), it was evident that the Hittite king was the party imposing the political conditions of the relation and the subordinated king the party that had to observe them.[16]

Similar conditions were detailed in the treaties with other minor polities of the Levantine coast, like the kingdoms of Amurru and Ugarit.[17] The loyalty of Amurru to the Hittite king was essential for the rule of Syria by Muršili II, especially as revolts erupted in the region of Nuḫašše and in Qadeš. Likewise, in the Ugarit archive, a copy of the treaty between Muršili II and Niqmepa (1313–1267 BCE) was found, stipulating analogous conditions of loyalty, obedience and (apparent) reciprocity (*CTH* 66; Beckman 1996: 59–64; Lackenbacher 2002: 78–85).

Now, from a strictly social anthropological perspective, it is possible to assert that the main impetus of the imposition of these treaties over subordinated polities was ritual, symbolic and ideological – which nonetheless had a potent incidence in reality and was far from being a mere superstructural covering of concrete socio-political practices. The treaties were not legal documents by which actions were determined – as in our modern Western juridical world – but they represented instead a royal will, a manifestation of the king's authority in a symbolic and ritual manner. It would have been, in the words of P. Bourdieu (1992b: 82), a 'rite of institution':

> The act of institution is therefore an act of communication, but of a particular kind: it signifies to someone his identity, but at the same time as it expresses that identity and imposes it on him, it expresses it before everyone . . . and authoritatively informs him of what he is and what he must be.

The treaty then possesses an intrinsic 'symbolic efficacy' and performs a kind of 'social magic', it represents 'the "magical" consecration of a difference' (Bourdieu 1992b: 83, 87, 82) between the Hittite king and his subordinate, creating and manifesting the subordination of the petty king to the Hittite king, the sole owner of political power in the established bond.

Thus, in the face of a lack of observation of the treaty by one of the parties, there was no external judgment or intervention in the relation by a third party. The king of Ḫatti would have used the monopoly of coercion he exerted, punishing any treason, and the subject king could do little in response, apart from perhaps finding a new master.

In a recent and important study on the 'historical prologue' of the Hittite subordination treaties, A. Altman (2004: 13) describes the character of such a prologue 'to present legal arguments justifying the imposition of obligations by the overlord on the inferior party to the treaty, and depriving that party of the ability to contest the treaty's validity or legality'; later (2004: 184), it is asserted:

> In order to justify the subjugation, the 'true' circumstances that led to it were recorded in the treaty; the subjugated king had to take an oath on the treaty, thereby confirming its version of the political events that had led to the subjugation; and copies of the treaty were placed in the temple of the main god of each of the parties. Should the subordinated king decide in the future to renounce his vassal treaty and appeal to the gods, claiming the illegality of his subjugation, this confirmed version of the events would stand against him. Admittedly, the supposed rule, according to which a subordinate king could be released from his obligations on the grounds of a claim that his political subjugation was illegitimate, is nowhere explicitly stated.

From the socio-anthropological perspective advance here, we may disagree with these statements.[18] First, the explicit discourse, i.e. the ideology of the Hittite treaty, is applied as an analytical model of the historical socio-political situation. Second, the treaty is assumed to have had a juridical potency that results in being, in fact, anachronistic, since the treaty is regarded as a document with which one of the parties could have appealed to a third party to solve a dispute or a conflict. Actually, what is really under scrutiny is the legally prescriptive character of the Hittite subordination treaties, since the ultimate disposition to accept what is agreed upon in a treaty, especially from the point of view of the subordinated party, derives from the implicit arrangement of political forces in the very treaty, which is guaranteed by a group of Hittite (and other) deities. What forces the 'vassals' to accept the treaty is not a juridical or legal prescription, nor the existence of a divine court – before which a case could have been appealed. The coercion comes rather from the latent violence represented by the treaty, namely a potential Hittite military incursion in the land of the protected king, should the latter transgress the treaty, which would have been considered a *personal treason* to the Hittite king, rather than a juridical infraction (*post tractatus*) to the state as an impersonal institution. True, the gods would have acted as guarantors of the treaty; but it would be reasonable to think that the Hittite king's *Realpolitik* – to fulfil or transgress what is explicit in the treaty – would have coincided precisely with the will of the divine court. It was the Hittite monopoly of coercion in the bond of alliance that drove the political order of the situation, not the assumed legality of the treaty.

Hittite treaties would have therefore constituted a medium for and a symbolic expression of the monopoly of coercion that Ḫatti exerted over the petty kingdoms of the northern Levant. In sum, and as D. Lorton (1974: 178) has indicated from a more general viewpoint:

> in ancient Near Eastern law, both domestic and international, documents were regarded only as evidentiary, and not as dispositive. . . . The modern notion of the 'treaty' as a dispositive document which becomes valid with the signatures of the parties is inapplicable to the usages of law in the ancient Near East.

* * *

The application of the model of the Asiatic Mode of Production, or two-sector model, may actually provide us with a certain analytical scheme for the internal socio-economic working of Levantine societies of the Late Bronze Age, even if the patrimonial model seems to express in a much better way the socio-political meaning of the written evidence (as we shall see). The main objections one could raise to the Asiatic Mode of Production model reside in its implicit mechanicism – as formulated by Marx – but also in its theoretical subordination of the native socio-political conception to the functional predominance of the socio-economic structure. In effect, if that were the case, all the political terminology of the period as expressed in letters, treaties and other documents would be reduced to a simple metaphor of a basically economic exploitation in society. Also in this chapter, I have noted that referring to the kind of political relations that the kingdom of Ḫatti established with the small polities of the northern Levant as 'vassalage', together with other feudal analogies, is inappropriate for several reasons, not least because it imposes in a different spatial and temporal context such as the ancient Near East a particular mode of economic and political subordination belonging to medieval Europe.

After considering these two interpretative models, it is necessary to address the socio-political relations established between various and different actors and polities of the regional scene of the Late Bronze Age through a sound evaluation of the data in the textual sources and through ethnographically attested practices, which represent for the historian a repertoire of analytical tools for understanding ancient politics. Thus, two interpretative concepts are proposed here to explain and understand the evidence of socio-political practices during this period in the Levant: in the first place, the already mentioned patrimonial model of society, and second, patron–client relations, as the ethnographic fieldwork has documented them, especially in the Mediterranean region but also in the modern Middle East.

Part III of this study will make explicit the use of both of these concepts in order to show their interpretative usefulness when addressing diplomatic texts expressing socio-politics in the Syria-Palestine of the Late Bronze Age.

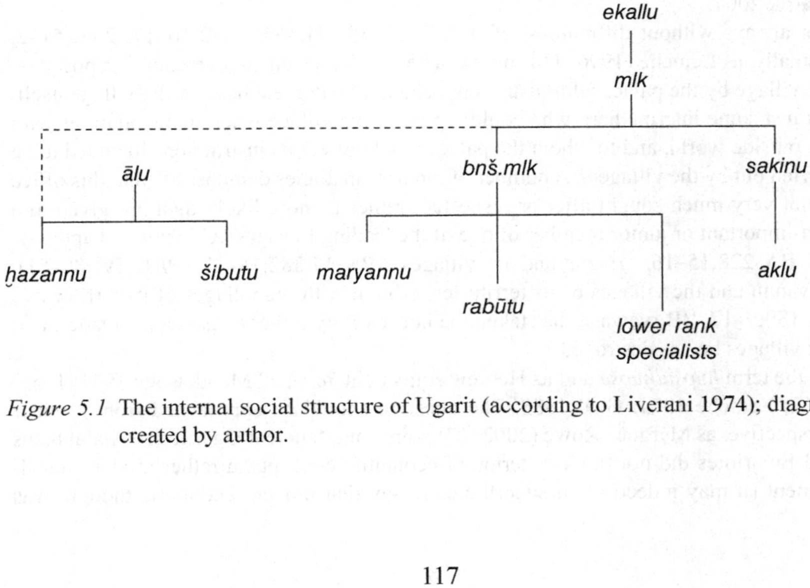


*Figure 5.1* The internal social structure of Ugarit (according to Liverani 1974); diagram created by author.

## Notes

1 The following description is after Schloen 2001: 187–94, 201–19 (feudalism in Ugarit), 221–54 (Asiatic mode of production in Ugarit); cf. also the historiographic analysis in Zamora 1997: 7–47, 53–65; and Vidal 2006a, who opposes Schloen's Patrimonial Household Model (cf. further Chapter 7).

2 Gray 1952a; 1952b; Boyer 1955; Alt 1959d; 1959e; Rainey 1962. See further on the historiographic construction of a feudal Ugaritic economy, McGeough 2007: 42–8. Cf. also the general analysis already in Abrahamian 1975.

3 The relatively recent anthology of feudalism cases, edited by Bournazel and Poly (1998), still nominates as valid examples of feudal situations instances of economic and political dependence in the ancient Near East from the third to the first millennium BCE; cf. especially Lafont 1998. See also, on Ugarit's economy, McGeough 2007: 49–59.

4 See, for instance, Diakonoff 1982; Heltzer 1976; 1982; Liverani 1974; 1975; 1976b; 1979f; 1984; 2005a; 2005b; and Zaccagnini 1981, who accepts the model especially as an heuristic tool. On the notion of 'oriental despotism' in modern Europe, cf. Curtis 2009; on the related idea of 'hydraulic societies' the key work is Wittfogel 1957, now refuted, for instance, by Vidal-Naquet 1964. For a critical re-evaluation of these ideas for the history of the ancient Near East, cf. Liverani 1993; Briant, 2002; Charpin, 2002; Durand, 2002. On the Asiatic mode of production in general, cf. the historiographic discussion in Sofri 1969; and for Ugarit, Zamora 1997; and Vidal 2006a.

5 The following characterisation is based essentially on Liverani 1974, also Bordreuil 1981; Van Soldt 2010; cf. Figure 5.1 on p. 117. See also, from a rather juridical perspective, the descriptions, for Ugarit, in Márquez Rowe 2003b; for Alalaḫ, in Márquez Rowe 2003a; for Emar, in Westbrook 2003b; and compare too with the description of the Nuzi palace in Cassin 1974.

6 Cf. now Von Dassow 2008: 131–232. As discussed in the previous chapter, we should not conceive of Syrian cities through Mesopotamian analogies; without doubt, urban sites in Syria-Palestine are much more modest, apart from some exceptions. Cf. also the ethnographic discussion on cities/villages/population in Africa in Holder and Peatrik 2004.

7 Not always without difficulties; cf. EA 73:23–33; 74:35–6; 272:10–17; 286: 51–2. Actually, as Lemche (1996: 114) notes, 'The official headman, eventually imposed on the village by the palace administration, need not be the real head of the village itself, but just some intermediary who could represent the village when in negotiations with the outside world, and to whom the palace would direct its instructions intended to be carried out by the villagers. A number of modern analogies demonstrate that this office is not very much sought after or respected; rather is more likely than not given to a non-important or junior member of one of the leading lineages.' Cf. *supra* Chapter 4.

8 Cf. EA 228:15–16, 'Hazor and its villages'; RS 17.382:14–17 (*PRU* IV, 80–81), 'Siyannu and the villages of its territories, Ušnatu with the villages of its territories'; EA 189:9–12, '(Biryawaza) has taken the house of my father (= palace) at Qadeš, and my villages he has destroyed.'

9 On the term *ḫupšu*/*ḫupše* and its Hebrew equivalent *ḥofšî*, cf. Mendelsohn 1941; 1955; 1962; Lemche 1974; Gaál 1988. The question should be approached from a wider perspective, as Márquez Rowe (2002: 17) points out, 'ancient Ugariteans, Alalakhians and Emariotes did not think in terms of economic concepts, a rather modern development (it may indeed seem superfluous to say that modern economic thought was

absent in antiquity). They probably understood and had a notion of hierarchy (even if they did not have the word for it); but not an economic hierarchy which probably did not go farther beyond the distinction between rich(er) and poor(er). The evidence clearly shows that they rather thought and surely acted in the concrete terms of rights and obligations, their real scale of hierarchy. Their own social categories and terminology should therefore reflect a juridical, rather than an economic, divide (in accordance with the nature of the textual material). Indeed, we have suggested that the *bunušu malki* in Ugarit and the *e[ḫ]ellena* in Alalakh shared, like the *amīlūtu* in Emar, similar duties that originated from similar circumstances, namely unpaid debts (rather than service to the crown).'

10 Schloen 2001: 218. Cf. also Weber 1978: 370–84, 1006–69. See also Curtis 2009: 258–98. Naderi (1990: 77–9) accuses Weber of 'orientalism' in his characterisation of Islam as 'sultanism' (a particular style of patrimonialism), linking it, according to Naderi, to 'oriental despotism'. Still, the concept of patrimonialism, instead of reflecting a particular historical reality, is rather more useful as a template for understanding social practices, and this is how is used in this study.

11 Schloen 2001: 255. See already Thompson 1974: 203–97. On the concept of household, as domestic unit and family residence, see Bender 1967; Sacchi and Viazzo 2014; on the household as behaviour, cf. Jongsma and Greensfield 2002. An historical example of a major household polity is Ottoman Egypt (cf. Hathaway 1997; see also Eychenne 2005; 2008).

12 Ebeling 1971: 54. Possibly, 'palace dependants' is a much better term to refer to what Ebeling calls 'slaves' (*Sklaven*), as to allow the category of those individuals deprived of all freedom, for instance, war prisoners, even though *every* subject to the king were his servants: cf. Liverani 1976b: 80–81; Diakonoff 1987: 1–2.

13 Cf. Korošec 1931; also 1960; further McCarthy 1963: 2–50; von Schuler 1969: 112ff.; Imparati 1999: 359–63, 365ff. ('protectorate' or subordination relations), 363–4 ('brotherhood' or paritary relations); Starke 2005–6: 219ff. Further on Hittite treaties Beckman 2006; Balza 2008; further on edicts, Devecchi 2012; and on royal instructions, see now Miller 2013.

14 Cf. Korošec 1931; Briend, Lebrun and Puech 1994: 5–6, 16–17; Beckman 1996: 1–6. Also, as Korošec (1960: 66) noted, these treaties obliged the 'vassals' to go each year to Ḫattušaš, the Hittite royal residence, to pay their homage to the sovereign and rendering the annual tribute.

15 Lebrun, in Briend, Lebrun and Puech 1994: 16. Cf. Korošec 1931: 21–35; Starke 2005–6: 218. Cf. also Imparati 1999: 358–87.

16 This is evident, for instance, in the treaty between Ḫatti and Kizzuwatna (fourteenth century BCE). Cf. the thorough analysis in Liverani 2004b: 57–61 (symmetrical clauses), 61–3 (asymmetrical clauses). Cf. also McCarthy 1963: 33ff.; and Singer 1999: 628, for an asymmetrical alliance between Amurru and Ugarit (cf. *CTH* 54; Lackenbacher 2002: 64–6; Freu 2006: 76, 177). We may propose here that, between such small polities, a treaty might have been, not only a political, but also a ritual channel to accord mutual assistance. But, why did Ḫatti, being able to exert directly control over small polities, make subordination treaties with them? The answer might be found in the military logistics of ruling conquered territory.

17 Cf. Liverani 1962; Singer 1991; 1999; Starke 2005–6: 255; in general, on the history of Syria-Palestine, cf. Ahlström 1993: 217–81; and the synthesis in Lemche 1995a.

18 From a Hittitological point of view, cf. Devecchi 2008.

# Part III

# PATRONS AND CLIENTS IN THE LEVANT

# 6

# PATRONAGE RELATIONSHIPS

## A theoretical overview

In the previous chapters, a general characterisation of socio-political relations and bonds during the Late Bronze Age was offered, together with criticism towards traditional concepts and models used by current Near Eastern historiography, for describing and defining Syro-Palestinian polities. In this chapter, basic features of patron–client or patronage relationships are presented, having in mind its intimate configuration within and outside kinship networks. The so-called 'anthropology of the Mediterranean' was pivotal in this understanding of patronage as a socio-political phenomenon, also related to social instances of honour and prestige. These insights will be put to the service of interpreting anthropologically ancient Levantine socio-politics.

### 6.1. On Mediterranean societies

It has been rightly noted that social anthropology has placed the Mediterranean basin under ethnographic scrutiny only since the 1950s, in spite of an already existing European intellectual tradition concerned with the study of the region's societies, especially the Classical past. Further, as noted by S. Silverman (2001: 43):

> Modern anthropological fieldwork in the Mediterranean began only in the 1950s, by which time most of the world had already been encompassed within the scope of the "ethnographic record". Yet, as others have pointed out – and as John Davis [1977] explicated especially well – the Mediterranean material had attracted anthropologists earlier and in greater numbers than that of perhaps any other region in the world. Maine, Fustel de Coulanges, Robertson-Smith, Frazer, Durkheim, Mauss, and other luminaries drew on the Mediterranean for seminal ideas that had a profound influence on the analysis of remote societies. Their work was based primarily on literary, historical and archaeological sources, and was only occasion[al]ly connected to living peoples.

Also, D. Gilmore (1982: 175) argued that 'Anthropology *in* the Mediterranean area [was] nothing new; some of the earliest ethnographies took place there.

But an anthropology *of* the Mediterranean area which includes both Christian and Muslim sides [was] both new and controversial' (emphasis original; cf. further Horden and Purcell 2000: 485–523).

The now-classic ethnography by Julian Pitt-Rivers, *The People of the Sierra*, inaugurated the study of Mediterranean societies by British social anthropologists (Pitt-Rivers 1954). Yet, maybe 1959 is the true foundational date of the anthropology of the Mediterranean, with the celebration of a conference in Burg Wartenstein, Austria, on peasant societies in the Mediterranean basin. This academic event gave impetus to several successive academic meetings, which generated the publication of several foundational texts on Mediterranean anthropology: *Mediterranean Countrymen: Essays in the Social Anthropology of the Mediterranean* (Pitt-Rivers, ed. 1963a); *Honour and Shame: The Values of Mediterranean Societies* (Peristiany, ed. 1965); *Contributions to Mediterranean Sociology: Mediterranean Rural Communities and Social Change* (Peristiany, ed. 1968) and *Mediterranean Family Structures* (Peristiany, ed. 1976).

Eventually, fieldwork on both sides of the Mediterranean produced a considerable amount of ethnographic material possible of being compared in each of its details, themes and topics. In parallel, these studies unfolded a concrete ethnographic genre, the 'anthropology of the Mediterranean', which seemed to represent a particular Mediterranean ethos in its different manifestations, anchored in factors like honour and shame, 'amoral familism', hospitality, feuding, revenge (*vendetta*) and patron–client relations, in a somehow essentialist manner and tending to an overall homogeneity, in spite of regional differences in Turkey, Lebanon, Egypt, Spain, Italy, Greece, Morocco, or Algeria.[1] This understanding was aided by the geomorphological and ecological characteristics of the Mediterranean basin, giving place to common elements or circumstances in different communities, several kilometres apart, as to the environment, local economy and cultural features. Such common landscape characteristics, which seemed to be (erroneously) rather constant through time, allowed for speculations on the little change social conditions would have experienced in the last millennia. As D. Albera and A. Blok affirm, regarding L.E. Sweet's contributions to eastern Mediterranean ethnography:

> Sweet argues that in the past the Mediterranean basin was characterized by a 'distinctive Mediterranean culture pattern or civilization', which displays a structural, an ecological and a cultural distinctiveness [cf. Sweet and O'Leary 1969: v–xxii], including pre-industrial city-states, and urban character of peasant life (agro-towns), the predominance of large estates for the production of grains, and transhumant pastoralism of sheep and goats. Sweet emphasizes 'the recurrence of a similar climate, mountain topography, flora and fauna – natural or culturogenic (especially the vine-fig-olive, wheat-barley-beans, small-scale fishing, sheep and goat specializations) – from the Neolithic base to the present' [cf. Sweet and O'Leary: 1969: i]. In passing, she mentions Mediterranean

> 'stereotypes', including gender segregation and the subordination of women. Whether stereotypical or not, the cultural emphasis on virginity and chastity of women together with the exclusion of women from public space (men:women/public:private/dominance:subordination) is often singled out as a most telling and diagnostic feature of the forms of life on both shores of the Mediterranean. (Albera and Blok 2001: 18)

As would have been expected, such a homogeneous description of Mediterranean social fabric, both in spatial and temporal factors, configuring a kind of 'cultural area'[2] (even though this particular concept, as Pitt-Rivers (2000: 25) himself notes, was never used by British social anthropologists working in the Mediterranean), produced a stereotypical image soon to be criticised by Mediterranean anthropologists themselves, especially during the 1980s, accusing their predecessors of the promotion of exoticism, tendentious cultural homogenisation and limited comparativism, besides the expected ethnocentrism from the countries of northern Europe, where most Mediterranean anthropologists came from (cf. Herzfeld 1980; 1984; Wikan 1984; Pina-Cabral 1989; Llobera 1999: 63–101). Nonetheless, the Mediterranean genre was not totally discarded in social anthropology – only its analytical 'deviations' – as Albera and Blok (2001; see also Davis 1977) have recently recognised, exposing a healthy social-anthropological reflexivity:

> It seems that a spectre is haunting those who write on the Mediterranean area: the trait-list. Two well-known dangers underlie these characterizations. First, by emphasizing common features you play down differences. Differences between religious beliefs and practices in the Mediterranean region are obvious, but so are the basic differences in kinship, marriage and inheritance practices, as for instance, [J.] Goody argued in his essay 'Two Sides of the Mediterranean' [1983: 10–12]. A second and perhaps even greater danger of attempts to define the Mediterranean area is presenting an ahistoric, essentialized picture of something that is obviously in a state of flux – forms of life that have experienced a uniquely documented continuity and change over more several millennia. (Albera and Blok 2001: 18–19)

In this sense, criticism towards some aspects of the anthropology of the Mediterranean did not delegitimise its validity as a research field,[3] but – and once discarding the essentialist perspective, proper of a social approach based on the notion of a *Mediterranean culture area*[4] – it was rather reformulated under a more reflexive constitution

> without necessarily essentializing or reifying the concept, it is possible to conceptualize the Mediterranean area as a field of ethnological study – as a historical formation, as a historically-constituted unit – showing enough differences and similarities for fruitful comparative research. (Albera and Blok 2001: 20)

Attending too to the historical geography of the Mediterranean region and its dynamics may actually allow for a heuristic comparison of social practices and environmental adaptability through time, without resorting to any ecological determinism. A clear feature of Mediterranean geography, for instance, is what Horden and Purcell call 'the connectivity of microregions',[5] which seem to be a constant background as societies remain and change through time. Thus, a critical approach to the Mediterranean landscape would first attest to particular social practices according not only to their environment but also to their historical context, in order to establish changes and continuities in a proper historical manner. In this way, it is legitimate to propose a comparison of practices active in modern or present times and practices detected in more ancient times, given a proper control of the comparison; i.e. without extracting universal laws from observing two analogous practices in similar ecological or economic settings. The question is if we are able to understand ancient socio-political practices placed in a certain environment by analysing current socio-political practices set in similar environments. My answer is definitely positive as long as we keep in mind the heuristic purpose of the analytical effort.

So, for example, the livelihood of many communities in the ancient southern Levant depended on growing olives, goat and sheep herding and horticulture; a certain interdependence of farmers and semi-nomads was established. Many urban settlements of relative size had a rural periphery which depended politically on them, according to the topographical fragmentation, especially in Palestine, where a cantonal landscape was evident. As M. Liverani explains:

> The first evident consequence of this topographic and ecologic fragmentation is political fragmentation, at least during all the period in which the dimension of political formations will be strongly conditioned by the modes of exploitation of the territory, dependent on agriculture and husbandry. . . . Thus, the dimension that we may qualify as 'cantonal' (a city with its hinterland destined to agriculture and husbandry) cannot be exceeded unless other factors of [territorial] unification (ethno-linguistic, religious) appear from within or proceed from external interventions. Each 'canton' remains isolated from the others due to a weakly inhabited landscape (hills, steppes, woods) quantitatively predominant.[6]

This scenario is still found – or was until not so long ago – in some parts of the Mediterranean, and the relationship between an urban centre and the rural space makes us think of the *agro-towns* of the Italian ethnographic record.[7] Now, if we extend the scope of our historical perspective, it is possible to see a continuum from the pastoralist semi-nomad to the peasant to the urban dweller, not only in the eastern Mediterranean but also in the Middle East, at least until the mid-twentieth century. Said continuum is traversed by relationships of economic or political dependence, which are essentially vertical – through schemes of tribal ascendancy, family networks, neighbourhood and patron–client bonds – rather than horizontal, as in a class order.[8] This ethnographic panorama creates, as was already observed, a spectrum of analytical possibilities through which to interpret ancient textual data.

In one of the aforementioned foundational works of Mediterranean anthropology, Pitt-Rivers (1963b: 9) wrote:

> The geographical form [of the Mediterranean basin] therefore favours unification by military force, settlement and, as soon as the commanding power relaxes, rebellion, but not integration into a homogeneous culture. As a result, political and religious hierarchies were able to replace one another while leaving the local community, if not unaltered, nevertheless faithful in large parts to its traditions.

These words, read decades after being written, may now be objected to for their blatant generalisation. However, they capture two constant realities in the history of Syria-Palestine in antiquity: in the first place, the occupation or domination of the territory by successive imperial powers since the middle of the second millennium BCE until recent times – almost four thousand years! – especially due to the geopolitical location of the region, as a commercial and military bridge between continents (Aharoni 1979: 3–6, 43–63; Astour 1995: 1415–16); and in the second place, what we may call the ubiquity of vertical ties of political dependence, i.e. patron–client relations, through different periods, verified by ethno-historical work until the mid-twentieth century. Traditional historiography of the ancient world is confident in detecting ancient patronage only with Roman expansion, in our case, towards the East.[9] However, patron–client relations are much older in the region and have been permanent through different periods (cf. Pfoh 2013).

One could ask, however, whether Pitt-Rivers's words do not betray some geographical determinism. But we should not confuse geographical determinism with the permanence of some socio-political practices through time in the same region due, essentially, to some geographic factors. If patronage relations are encountered in the Levant, articulating the local community, but also the community and the regional power, by ethnography throughout the twentieth century and even some centuries before (cf. Cohen 1973; Khoury 1983; Doumani 1995; Rabinowitz 1997; Philipp 2001), and there is data from ancient textual sources that reflects clues that can be understood through a conceptualisation of patron–client relations, such an analytical operation is legitimate and is far from exposing an ethnocentric essentialism proper to the societies of the region. As indicated by R.B. Coote and K.W. Whitelam (1987: 114):

> Peasant factionalism shaped according to patterns of elite patronage, at both village and urban levels, appears to be endemic in Palestine. Once this feature has been examined in materials dating from the seventeenth to the early twentieth centuries, it becomes quite noticeable whenever historical sources for rural life in Palestine exist in any detail.

Contemporary examples of patronage may indeed help us explain and understand the ideological and political worldview active in the ancient Levant through a careful employment of analytical analogies and being aware of the temporal and cultural distance between ancient Levantine peoples and modern ones. As Horden and Purcell (2000: 464) have indicated, 'We can then go on to enquire what ways remain in which the ethnographic present might instruct us about the historic past.'

## 6.2. Kinship and patron–client relationships

Building on the Mediterranean ethnographic record, our first attestation we can make is the close relation between patron–client bonds and the ideological and political realm of kinship (cf. especially Campbell 1964). From a more general perspective, it is possible to assert that a key factor articulating kinship relations is reciprocity. Reciprocity is found in the ethnographic record as traversing political and economic realities, notably in non-state societies, and 'a norm of reciprocity, in its universal form, makes two interrelated demands: (1) people should help those who have helped them, and (2) people should not injure those who have helped them', as A. Gouldner suggests.[10] Likewise, M. Sahlins has observed that the degree of reciprocity is conditioned by the range or the absence of a kinship relation between two individuals or two groups: the closer the degree of kinship or friendship, the greater the reciprocity exerted (*generalised* and *balanced reciprocity*); when the kinship relation is weak or non-existent, *negative reciprocity* is expected (Sahlins 1972: 185–230). This characterisation, although usually used for the study of kinship societies (hunter-gatherers to chiefdom societies), may well be applied to the study of societies showing a considerable social stratification and in which a certain centralisation of resources is expected, thus distancing themselves from societies in which kinship is the backbone of social life (cf. Rodríguez López and Pastor 2000).

Kinship networks are also vehicles of political practices. After considering a number of particular situations, G. Balandier exposed the intrinsic relation between kinship bonds and power display in segmentary societies.[11] In segmentary lineage systems, political phenomena such as alliances between lineages are based on a genealogical 'fusion' that makes both lineages act like one polity. Descent and territory are also key factors in determining political behaviour (Balandier 1972: 50–77). But, what seems to be most relevant is the place some individual have in a kinship network or in a lineage, which grants them prestige if they know how to exploit it. Such prestige is a key factor in political dynamics in the community and a key relation establishing social ties since, as Balandier (1972: 72–7) argues, in segmentary societies political life is expressed more through situations than political institutions.

In the ethno-historical record of the Middle East, the most representative example is perhaps constituted by Ibn Khaldun (1332–1406), a Maghrebi writer who produced what might be considered one of the first examples of a sociological explanation of state formation and civilisational decay. A key concept in Ibn

Khaldun's theory, exposed in his *Muqaddimah* (1377) or 'prolegomena', is the *'aṣabīya*, that is, the tribal group solidarity on which a whole social system and a state is based. Ibn Khaldun stated that such *'aṣabīya* was based on kinship, in a biological but also ideological sense, and therefore was extended to the relationship between a ruler and his subjects. In ideal conditions, there is a mutual protection and assistance between the ruler and the subjects; and if the ruler starts accumulating power or oppressing his subjects, such *'aṣabīya* is interrupted and the end of the polity is then at hand (Ibn Khaldun 1958; cf. further Lemche 1985: 91–3; Gellner 2007). This patrimonial understanding of society is to be found, with variations though, in many Middle Eastern scenarios until the mid-twentieth century (cf. Leca and Schemeil 1983; Khoury and Kostiner 1990a; Bonte, Conte and Dresch 2001).

This brief ethnographic presentation suffices to consider kinship relations of greater importance than a mere biological link. They actually are a specific idiom for social relations – political, economic, religious – in many pre-modern societies with a basic hierarchical structure based on gender and age, but also in such complex societies as chiefdoms or tribal kingdoms.[12] In fact, the Islamic Middle Eastern ethnographic record attests instances of 'agnatic illusions' that allow for situations of non-kinship (like patron–client bonds) to be conducted after the same reciprocity and prestige norms present in a kinship society and articulated as well by premises of honour and shame:

> elective kinship is often enacted between parties, be they individuals or groups, divided by an asymmetry of status. A classical saying indirectly stresses this by recalling that 'the relation of clientship is a [form of] kinship (*luhma*), just as kinship by agnatic descent (*nasab*).' The compass of tolerable differentiation is, however, bounded by the imperative of 'honour preserved'. Disparity must not attain a degree of intensity such that it would be debasing for the initially 'higher' party to engage the 'entering' party into a relation other than of durable subordination. Inversely, the acceptance of sanctuary is not compatible with condescending patronage, for this would disgrace the 'host' as well as the 'protected neighbour'. (Conte 2003: 39–40)[13]

Examples like this show that the extended network of kinship that articulates politics in society allows also patron–client relations to be manifest. At a domestic or communal level, there is a structural, but also symbolic, linkage between kinship and patronage: patronage ties use kinship ties and networks, but they also transcend the kinship realm producing a political logic of their own. Reciprocity is still a key factor in both kinship and patronage. However, in kinship societies, the reciprocity principle forces the return of goods or services offered, and the demand not to injure or offend those who helped (Gouldner 1960; also Pitt-Rivers 1954: 137). In other words, there is a generalised or balanced reciprocity (Sahlins 1972: 193–5). In patronage societies, or in societies in which patronage is the hegemonic socio-political practice, such reciprocity is arranged in an unbalanced or asymmetrical manner. It is the patron who is the one disposing the conditions of reciprocal exchange, not the client. Nevertheless, the patron, in the same fashion as the *big man* ethnographically attested to in non-state societies (Sahlins 1963), must maintain his position in the kinship community. He must keep his prestige and his honour through acts that expose him as a 'good patron' (Pitt-Rivers 1954: 63; Goodell 1985).

The existence of a socio-political party having a certain control over another party, by means of asymmetrical reciprocity (cf. Orenstein 1980), leads us to consider that patronage is not simply a distorted variant of kinship relationship. The patron, in a non-state society, can actually exert violence towards his clients, who may well be his relatives, and impose some dependency ties.[14] Patronage, in effect, is something else, something different. For certain, the patron–client articulation is based on a scheme analogous to a kinship network, but its function in society makes it different from kinship ties. Patronage is also far from being a kind of state practice in the making,[15] since reciprocity, which characterises the practice although asymmetrically, prevents a direct evolution towards the institutionalisation of the monopoly of coercion – a violent rearrangement of society would be necessary for the rise of state practice. Thus, the idiom of patronage unfolds from a kinship realm and uses kin-related terminology to express itself, but constitutes a particular kind of socio-political practice in between kinship and statehood (although not in an evolutionary scheme, only in an analytical exposition).

Approaching patronage from a common-sense perspective – especially in modern urban environments, when addressing the sociological phenomenon of contemporary political clientelism – might place it within a sphere of political corruption or as a deviation from the legally expected socio-political practices in civil society. Such evaluation, dependent more on the ethics of modern liberal political philosophy, is actually ill-suited to comprehend patronage as a political relation in non-Western and especially pre-modern societies. Clientelism and corruption are not synonyms, even though corrupt behaviour has clientelism as a vehicle to reach its goals. Corruption must essentially be understood within an ethical and juridical framework in modern states, while clientelism should be seen and understood in a historical perspective, as a socio-political strategy of survival (see further Médard 1998). In fact, such preconceptions ought to be avoided and, as S. Silverman (1977: 9–11) suggested, the practice of clientelism/patronage should be studied both from the *etic* pint of view and the *emic* point of view, taking into account the cultural values of the societies in which patrons and clients operate.

As already stated, if in 'primitive' societies a generalised reciprocity is in theory ubiquitous between the community members (Sahlins 1972: 191–210), in the relationship between a patron and a client, said reciprocity adopts an unbalanced or asymmetrical structure (cf. the ethnographic insights in Lévi-Strauss 1944; Rosenfeld 1974). Possibly, from an *emic* perspective, the protection granted by the patron to each of his clients – and we must keep in mind that patronage is initially a *personal* and *individual* relation, configuring a basic dyadic unit (Foster 1961; 1963) – may be perceived as the equivalent element of loyalty and assistance the latter owe to him. However, from an *etic* perspective, it is clear that the patron sets the conditions for the exchange, not the client(s). This dyadic exchange structure, however, is not fixed but rather circumstantial since, given the chance of obtaining the necessary resources (both material and immaterial, wealth and prestige), any client can become a patron, and a patron can fall in socio-political disgrace, thus becoming someone else's client.

It is also relevant to note that a patron–client relationship can transcend the dyadic bond that has created it and become a template for the whole social world of the members of a community and their operative scheme of behaviour. Exchange through patron–client links contributes to the creation of particular means to conceive and recreate the world of social actors. In fact, it is possible to think of patronage as a particular socio-political *habitus*,[16] which enables a configuration of social reality through imaginary collective figures – 'the patron' and 'the client' – and their combination in a series of possible situations.

## 6.3. Honour, prestige and patronage

The presence of public social behaviours attached to a certain concept of individual and group honour, as evidenced in the practice of patronage, has been attested in almost every ethnographic study on Mediterranean societies (cf. Peristiany 1965; Davis 1969; Pitt-Rivers 1997; Blok 1981; 2001; Gilmore 1987; Horden and Purcell 2000: 489–501). As Pitt-Rivers (1977; 1997) has noted in his contributions, honour ties the ideals of a society with their reproduction in the individual and his or her desires personify them. But further, and more relevant for our present enquiry, are the words of Cassar (2005: 14), who noted that 'The language of honour is a political language used for describing the distribution of power and wealth.' Building on this base, it is possible to create patronage relations in society, exchanging protection for loyalty, in order to meet a certain particular ends. The exchange is always configured as a friendship or even family relationship – in *emic* terms – but it is of course based on a concrete difference of status, wealth and resources (Pitt-Rivers 1954: 137–59; Campbell 1964: 263–320), which creates a certain unbalance among personal relations.

In his foundational ethnography, *The People of the Sierra*, Pitt-Rivers (1954: 140) indicated:

> the more friends a man can claim the greater his sphere of influence; the more influential his friends are the more influence he has. Friendship is thereby connected with prestige, and boastful characters like to assert how many friends they have, how extensive is the range of their friendships. So while friendship is in the first place a free association between equals, it becomes in a relationship of economic inequality the foundation of the system of patronage. The rich man employs, assists and

> protects the poor man, and in return the latter works for him, gives him esteem and prestige, and also protects his interests by seeing that he is not robbed, by warning him of the machinations of others and by taking his part in disputes.[17]

Then, after this ethnographic synthesis, the honour and prestige gained by a particular individual enables him to create patronage bonds with others, so gaining even more prestige and influence and, lastly, political power in the community. Likewise, the client also acquires some prestige from the relationship, since he is associated with a prestigious patron, and in certain circumstances this allows him to act as a broker between his patron and other individuals, thus extending the original dyadic unit of interaction into a triadic unit of patron–broker–client. According to Sharon Kettering (1988: 425–6):

> [a] patron–broker–client relationship in contrast is a three-party transaction in which a broker acts as a middleman to arrange an exchange of resources between two parties separated by geographic or personal distance such as differences in rank or office. Brokers bridge distances separating patrons and clients. A broker is a mediator in an indirect exchange, an agent who does not control what is transferred but who influences the quality of the exchange in negotiating the transfer. He is more than an intermediary or go-between because he has resources of his own that he can add to the exchange, and he does more than transmit the negotiations: he can also influence them, doing his own manipulating and lobbying. Brokers are usually important individuals in their own right with independent resources and numerous dependents, which is why they become brokers. Their new role adds to their status. A broker's essential resources are people he knows who can provide access to power and place in exchange for loyalty and service: a broker introduces those with power to those seeking its use who are willing to give favors in return for it, and arranges an exchange. He brings people and opportunities together, allowing them to trade resources, and, in conducting these negotiations, he facilitates the use of power and the distribution of resources. A broker frequently uses resources he does not directly control himself.[18]

Ethnographic examples of brokerage are numerous in Ottoman Syria and Palestine, showing how local 'men of prestige' would act as mediators between the state and the community (cf. Khoury 1983; Krämer 2002: Chapter 4, Section 3; Hourani 2004). But we can also attend to what O. Roy (1989: 1) observes regarding modern Afghanistan:

> A traditional leader is someone who has been able to establish a personal patron–client relationship, at the expense of a real political party structure.

> He is not a feudal lord, but uses his influence to protect and promote the interest of his own segmentary group, thus enhancing his own status in terms of wealth and prestige. These *khan* and *malek* (as they are called) act as middlemen between state and local groups, taking some financial and symbolic advantages from both, in exchange for maintaining peace and preserving the group from encroachment by the state.

Similarly, P.C. Salzman (1974: 206) indicates, while analysing the relation between a colonial rule and tribal structures in the Middle East:

> What is the consequence of indirect rule through the traditional centralized authority structures of tribes? What impact does the function of middlemen have upon the traditional role of tribal chief? The major points to keep in mind here are that the chief as middleman represents his tribe as a corporate body and that he is in consequence the primary if not the exclusive channel of information and resources as they flow between the tribe and the agencies of the encapsulating power. This means that the chief has control over valuables that he did not have in the tribal system.

Patronage in its dyadic form, but also working as brokerage, is then to be seen not as an immutable relationship in society but rather as a situational practice, building on kinship ties but going beyond them to exert some sort of authority and even power over certain individuals, or clients (see a clear ethnographic example of this in Jabbra and Jabbra 1978). A client may profit from his role as a broker to eventually break free from the moral and material attachments to his patron to become himself an autonomous patron, something favoured by the non-institutional condition of patronage. In the same fashion, a patron may deviate from the behaviour he is expected to have in society and become tyrannical or oppressive, although this would go against the prescriptions of social honour and the conditions for maintaining a loyal clientele, who may then, given the chance, start looking for better patrons. In order to understand the phenomenon correctly, each situation requires that we contemplate the ideal conception of patron–client relations and its adjustment to concrete and particular historical and social conditions.

## 6.4. The concept of patronage and Late Bronze Age Syria-Palestine

The general and theoretical sketch of patronage presented so far in this chapter considered the structuring of politics through kinship relations, which act as the basis for creating patron–client relations by means of kin-related terms and reciprocity instances, although in a singular manner, thus achieving an ultimate differentiation of kinship and patronage relations. The logical step to take here is to see the potentiality of these conceptual tools for analysing inter-polity interaction during the Late Bronze Age in Syria-Palestine. Kinship structures and relationships are documented during the whole history of the ancient Near East by archaeology and, especially, by texts.[19] I will not address each aspect and detail of ancient Near Eastern kinship but will make rather a general description of its main features as related to socio-political intervention.

The individual in ancient Near Eastern societies cannot be characterised apart or independently from his family group. To understand such an individual we must also understand the kinship network that defines it as such. Ancient Near Eastern family structure was strictly hierarchical, with the father figure at the top (patriarchy), who gave the primary identity to individuals (patrilineality or agnatic descent) and who received in his household the women his sons married (patrilocality). In this hierarchical order of kinship, verticality is also marked by gender and age factors. From an ideal and formal point of view, the eldest members of a family had authority over the youngest, and male members over female ones, resulting in a finite spectrum of intra-family permutations, designating the male elders as the sector in charge of the decision-making process, as well as the authority in the extended family and the youngest women as the members of least authority of all and subject to the will of the elders.[20]

Beyond the family, as F.M. Fales (1976: 251–61) pointed out, two categories appear: the supra-family, considered an emanation of the inner family group sociability and based on common descent, and the extra-family, namely non-kin members who interact with the kinship group and with whom the principle of negative reciprocity applied. Regarding, in particular, supra-family sociability, lack of biological connection did not prevent the presence of the norms that regulate kinship. Reciprocity actions are more or less as mandatory for distant kin as for clients or dependents related through personal ties – but less with slaves. The supra-family organisation implies, in effect, a patrimonial sociability proper of the household.[21] It is precisely within this social realm that we may find such patron–client relationships.

What I have been describing so far is the fact that patron–client ties are articulated within small communities. Yet, patronage as an interpretive and explanatory model may indeed be applied within a much larger context, such as the socio-political organisation and relationships the Syro-Palestinian kingdoms and polities had during the second half of the second millennium BCE. The dynamics found in the ruling structure of these polities, from a local or native perspective, may also be perceived in further detail by examining the relationships established between petty kingdoms with contemporary great regional powers. Patronage could then be effective as an analytical concept for explaining the asymmetrical interaction between small Levantine kings and Ḫatti, on the one hand, and – now in conflict with the means of foreign rule – with Egypt, on the other. In the following chapters, it will be argued that the socio-political conception governing the political behaviour of the petty kings of the Levant was anchored in a patron–client interaction, within a framework of patrimonialism as the organisation of the kingdoms, rather than in proper statehood features.

## Notes

1 See especially Banfield 1958, where the concept of 'amoral familism' is coined (Chapter 5) to describe these societies; but cf. Silverman 1968. See further Roque, 2000; 2005.

2 On the 'culture-area', a key term in American anthropology of the early twentieth century, cf. Wissler 1927; 1928; also Hill 1941. Wissler, through the study of American native societies, would conceive of defined 'culture-areas', in which ecology and material culture corresponded. To this, Hill added the concept of 'culture type', to deepen the characterisation of culture-areas. Later, A. Kroeber would use the concept of culture-area in opposition to the studies of F. Boas on the natives of California (cf. Buckley 1998). Of course, the risk of cultural essentialism and ecological determinism is very much expressed in these formulations – as it is in the foundational study of F. Braudel (1972) on the Mediterranean area.

3 The perspective has been revalidated in more recent times, with a reflexive spirit, both anthropological and historical: cf. Boissevain 1979; Gilmore 1987; Albera 1999; Horden and Purcell 2000; Roque 2000; Albera, Blok and Bromberger 2001; Harris 2005; Albera and Tozy 2006a.

4 The same criticism can be applied to characterisations of the Middle East: cf. the essentialist description by R. Patai (1952) on the Middle East as a 'culture area'.

5 Defined as 'the various ways in which microregions cohere, both internally and also one with another – in aggregates that may range in size from small clusters to something approaching the entire Mediterranean' (Horden and Purcell 2000: 123); cf. also Bresson 2005; Abulafia 2011; and for the Late Bronze Age, Knapp 1990; Hitchcock 2005.

6 Liverani 1990c: 15. Cf. further Sapin 1981; 1982; Thompson 1992: 316–34; 1999: 130–54.

7 On Mediterranean *agro-towns*, cf. Blok 1969. There is certainly an urban–rural continuum in the Mediterranean basin at the level of socio-economic units. As Caro Baroja (1963: 31) indicates: 'In spite of the classical authors' [Plato, Strabo] insistence on the particular quality of rural as opposed to urban life, they had very distinct ideas on the close relations of the city with the country and on their necessary connections. And it is worth noting that when they do the works of sociologists (rather than historians, geographers or moralists), they begin to see clearly something that can be defined as a linking of functions between the city and the country.' Cf., for a Middle Eastern comparison, Eickelman 2002: Chapters 3–5.

8 Cf. Lindholm 2002; Eickelman 2002: Chapters 6 and 7. After analysing ethnographies carried out in Tell Toqaan (Syria), Al-Munsif (Lebanon) and Kufr el-Ma (Transjordan), Lemche (1985: 178) notes: 'The preceding analysis has shown that in dealing with the Middle East the relationship between city and village is not a dichotomy, but rather a continuum.' See further about this question in Lemche 1985: 164–201.

9 The Roman period is generally considered the first historical example illustrating patronage as a well-extended phenomenon (and from that period comes the basic terminology of the phenomenon): see, for instance, in general Eisenstadt and Roniger, 1984; Mączak 2005; Lécrivain, 2007a; 2007b. For patronage in ancient Rome, Wallace-Hadrill 1989; Deniaux, 2007; in ancient Greece, Finley 1983: 24–49; Pébarthe 2007; in absolutist France, Kettering 1986, and modern Europe, Giry-Deloison and Mettam, 1990; also Mączak 2005: 105–58; Boltanski 2007; Duma 2007. For patronage in rural

settings, cf. Garnsey and Woolf 1989, for the Roman world; and Thompson 1971, for a much modern period; on the moral economy of the peasantry and solidarity networks, cf. Fafchamps 1992. Patronage in the Middle East is well documented, cf. especially Leca and Schemeil 1983; and the studies in Gellner and Waterbury 1977. For patronage in the Mediterranean basin, cf. besides the already indicated literature, Campbell 1964; Boissevain 1966; Silverman, 1968; Weingrod 1968; Blok, 1969; 1974; Schneider, 1969; Di Bella, 1984. On the related phenomenon of political clientelism, cf. Briquet and Sawicki 1998.

10 Gouldner 1960: 171; also Befu 1977: 259: 'The norm as stated by Gouldner is an etic concept and an abstraction in approximation of culture-specific norms exhorting participants to reciprocate.'

11 Segmentary societies are those societies articulated by extended kinship networks based on lineages and descent schemes. They lack an institutionalised political centralisation and only during certain circumstances (i.e. conflict) a hierarchical leadership is arranged, to be dissolved when normality is restored. See Evans-Pritchard 1940; Dresch 1988; Southall 1988.

12 Besides the definition of 'tribe' by Lapidus (1990), already noted in Chapter 4, we may also consider the definition by M. Godelier, who understands the tribe as 'a form of society constituted by groups of men and women who understand themselves as kin-related, in a real or fictive manner, by birth or alliance, who are united and cooperate among themselves in order to control a territory and exploit the resources, commonly or separately, and who are ready to defend it by means of violence' (Godelier 2010: 13).

13 Cf. further for the Middle East, Jabar and Dawod 2003. For a Scottish ethno-historical example of the articulation of kinship and patronage/clientage, within the clan and also towards the exterior, cf. Cathcart 2006: 59–128.

14 The practice of physical and symbolic violence between kin relatives, and in a context of patronage, has been documented, for instance, in Persian Luristan in the twentieth century; cf. Black 1972. See also on kinship and violence, Black-Michaud 1975: 228–34; Wilson 1988: 129–57. Further, on kin and patronage, see Wolf 1966; and on patronage as rural exploitation, see Scott 1977.

15 Even though states, at some stage, can indeed make use of patronage ties to rule over peripheral territories.

16 Bourdieu (1992a: 53) defines the *habitus* as 'systems of durable, transposable dispositions, structured structures predisposed to function as structuring structures, that is, as principles which generate and organize practices and representations that can be objectively adapted to their outcomes without presupposing a conscious aiming at ends or an express mastery of the operations necessary in order to attain them'.

17 Whether patron–client relations appear in society after a scarcity of resources (as suggested, for instance, by Foster 1965; and González Alcantud 1997: 199–200; cf. the discussion in Gregory 1975; Black-Michaud 1975: 190–207) is beyond our point here. However, an explanation based only on material conditions must be complemented with a proper understanding of the symbolic and political elements involved in personal relations.

18 Cf. further Kettering 1986: 40–67; and Befu 1977: 268: 'Brokerage differs from patronage analytically in that a broker is able to obtain from another source (through personal contact, etc.) whatever resources are desired by his client, whereas a patron possesses himself resources desired by his clients'; also Littlewood 1974: 48–50. On patron–client ties as strategy of imperial rule, cf. Newbury 2000.

19 Cf. the still most valid general synthesis in Fales 1976: 180–261; also Pinch 1995; Campagno 2009 (Egypt); Stol 1995 (Mesopotamia); Imparati 1995, and Bryce 2002 (Ḫatti), on aspects of family and marriage.

20 '[The] ancient Near Eastern family presents a relatively clear physiognomy: it is based on a precise consciousness of family hierarchy and on the many social rights and duties tied to the different positions in such a hierarchy [. . .] Socially, the extended family is structured as a group in which the person has a limited individuality and responsibility: all the hierarchy of family relationships (eldest brother–youngest brother, brother–sister, husband–wife, parents–children) and supra-family relationships (family–slaves) are inscribed within the sphere of the superior power of the oldest head of the family' (Fales 1976: 182, 190). On the basics of the anthropology of kinship (lineages, tribes, marriage, residence, etc.) cf. Deliège 2005: 7–23.

21 'To be part of the group (clan or tribe) is an element of social recognition in itself, further precisions are not necessary; and such participation may be extended to clients or servants, assimilated to their patrons through the tradition of hospitality' (Fales 1976: 253).

# 7

# PATRIMONIALISM IN THE LATE BRONZE AGE

In the previous chapter, the characterisation of patronage relationships was made with an emphasis on praxis, in an actualisation of socio-political asymmetrical bonds. Yet, when addressing ancient Levantine societies, patronage should be understood within the context of patrimonialism as well, as the social structure into which patron–client relations are articulated. It is thus proposed to understand the internal organisation of Levantine polities through a patrimonial base upon which patron–client ties are active as the key socio-political dynamic, both inside and outside the kingdoms.

## 7.1. Syria-Palestine as a patrimonial society

If we recall Liverani's characterisation of Syrian monarchy in the Late Bronze Age, it is actually possible to find some aspects that partially coincide with J.D. Schloen's Patrimonial Household Model, in spite of the fact that this latter model is presented in discussion with Liverani's two-sector model (Liverani 1974; Schloen 2001). Liverani states that 'The king is the chief and the beneficiary of an administrative organisation of the territory under his control. He is the owner of a large company corresponding to the state (*oikos*).'[1] If we are led only by such definition, the two-sector model steps into a secondary status for describing the ultimate socio-political nature of the state, or in Liverani's own words, the *oikos*. Likewise, when we scrutinise most of the factors of the state organisation Liverani makes explicit, we may ask again to what extent the Ugaritic king possessed the monopoly of coercion in society. According to the textual data, during the Late Bronze Age the king possesses a function of management and administration in the kingdom but, it seems, that figure has lost the judicial function and was instead taken over by the *sakinu*. The judiciary role of the king in Late Bronze Age Syria is evanescent. Many of the 'juridical' documents from Ugarit do not expose much more than a rather administrative role for the king. In fact, the model of the 'just king' in the Ugaritic poems could be but only literary rhetoric, as in the practice the people resolved their problems through the judgment of the elders (all this according to Liverani 1974: 333).[2]

In the same fashion, the military function was encountered rather in a warrior *corps d'élite*, the *maryannus*, to whom it was conceded; nonetheless, the Ugaritic king could grant the position of *maryannu* to any particular individually, that is, as a non-hereditary position.[3] In Alalaḫ, however, this concession seemed to have been hereditary (*AT* 15; Wiseman 1953: 39).

The only role in which the king of Ugarit seemed to have been irreplaceable is the liturgical one, as a priest, a ritual function that established a brokerage between the community the king embodies and the gods of the land (Liverani 1974: 334). And also, as P. Xella (2002: 416) asserts, the Ugaritic king was the centre and the source of all powers in the society, comprised by the religious power he possessed, as the head of the cultic matters in the kingdom.[4]

Another important aspect highlighted by Liverani is the limits of the power of the Ugaritic king (Liverani 1974: 347–56; see also Solans 2011: 398; and for Emar, Fleming 1992). There was, of course, during this period, a limitation 'from above', related to the military and political interference from Egypt and Ḫatti in the region, conditioning the political autonomy of the local king. The Ugaritic king under Hittite rule was subordinated to the Hittite king by means of a loyalty treaty, owing him personal (the kingdom's) assistance and service, for which the Hittite king would protect the Ugaritic dynasty in the throne and would not intervene in general in matters domestic to the kingdom, unless necessary. Yet, the expansive potential of Ugarit as a polity was seriously limited, together with its political interaction with other peer kingdoms, and conditioned by the geopolitical scenario under Hittite supervision. Furthermore, 'Actually, for the important decisions, at the inside and the outside [of the kingdom], the king of Ugarit did not seem to have a free hand' (Nougayrol 1963, 116; cf. also Vita 1995: 25–30), as seen in Ḫattušili III's edict on the presence of the merchants of Ura in Ugarit (cf. *PRU* IV, 102–5 = *CTH* 93). In the Ugaritic court, we would find another factor of political autonomy and manoeuvrability's limitation to the king. This is most evident in the relation the king had with the 'nobility' and especially with the war specialists, the *maryannus*, to whom I have already referred above. In exchange for their personal service to the king (*ilku*), the nobility would receive lands to exploit. In the particular case of the *maryannus*, the service was differentiated into (a) 'assistance or help' (*reṣūtu*), essentially military,[5] (b) the replacement of the personal service for a certain amount of silver,[6] or (c) the explicit exemption from the service.[7] The main danger with the concession of lands was the empowerment of the receiving party and the chance of treason or abandoning the king in order to associate with another or to achieve political independence.[8] There is evidence of conspiracies in the Ugaritic court in which the king's brothers sought to take the throne;[9] also, south of Ugarit, in the court of Byblos, the king's brother, taking advantage of the absence of the king in the city, took the throne for himself.[10]

Last, there existed limitations 'from below', that is, from the population in the villages, which could certainly exert passive resistance to the king or resist administrative measures at a more individual level by leaving the village and joining disruptive social elements known in the documentation of the period as *ḫabiru*.[11] There is one episode, the case of Abdi-Aširta of Amurru and the villages of Byblos, in which there was an instigation to rebel against the king (specifically, Abdi-Aširta asked them to 'kill your masters!').[12] Finally, at least on four occasions the council of elders (*šibūtu*) of the city replaced the king in his functions.[13] We can highlight, for instance, EA 59, relating that the inhabitants of Tunip in western Syria wrote to the Egyptian king and asked him to appoint a ruler to the city, in fact the son of the previous ruler, since Aziru of Amurru (then a Hittite subject) threatened to take the city over and expand the Hittite sovereignty over the land. Also in EA 100, the council of elders of Irqata, in modern northern Lebanon, asked the Pharaoh for a new ruler, since the previous was killed under treason charges.[14] These examples, far from being evidence of some kind of 'republican' or 'democratic' spirit in certain locations of the Levant, as once was speculated,[15] may be better interpreted in the light of the personal character of local politics and of what we may understand as the collective feature of traditional politics in certain scenarios of the modern Middle East (cf. Gilsenan 2000: 95–115). In other words, the very existence of a council of elders making executive decisions instead of the king, or in spite of the existence of a king,[16] does not indicate this collective government as an end in itself. In both instances, the council of elders asked the Pharaoh for a new ruler, for someone who would bring the monarchic order back to the community, but without appealing to some form of budding despotism. Quite the contrary, the appointment of a king (*mlk*) would restore the traditional order of the community, since it must have a leading figure for political and religious reasons (see further below).

So, considering all these instances, it is possible to think that the social order in Ugarit, at the time of the archives (fourteenth century BCE) was conditioned by several levels of potential conflict and challenge to the monarchic authority. As already indicated, perhaps the most important role of the king was as a priest, wielding religious prestige and social relevance, due to his liturgical actions. These are cosmic, establishing the social order through the symbolic performance proper for the king as brokering agent between the gods and the community's well-being. If we then consider the constrictions to the monarchic autonomy, the king's figure appears more as socially prestigious than absolutely powerful. His function was by no means most relevant, of course, as in any of the ancient Near Eastern hierarchical structures of society, but we should also consider his importance as the ultimate ritual specialist in the community, which granted the king his standing at the top of a pyramidal patrimonial network. Furthermore, Schloen (2001: 252) states:

> If Ugarit was indeed a patrimonial regime, the existence of official titles and delimited duties should not be taken as evidence of the operation of an impersonal bureaucracy . . . Although we call certain men 'officials,' we should not imagine that their 'offices' could be easily separated from their personal status and the constellation of social relationships in which they were embedded.

Ugarit appears as the paradigmatic Levantine kingdom, especially because of the important amount of information gained by the discovery of its archives in 1929 and subsequent translations of its various administrative, diplomatic and ritual texts (Van Soldt 1995; Vidal 2015b), which prompted ancient Near Eastern historiography to consider Ugarit as a representative Levantine 'city-state'. However, we may indeed reconsider such socio-political status in the light of the preceding discussion, together with our common understanding of the rest of the Syro-Palestinian polities. Instead of 'city-states' and 'cities', the notion of *patrimonial kingdom* seems to fit best the evidence for Ugarit, and within the same typological range, the rest of the lesser polities in the region of the Levant may be conceived of as *patrimonial* polities, in order to avoid the connotations that terms like 'state' and 'city-state' have, which might lead us to think of ancient Greek examples. My proposal is, instead of looking at ancient Greece, that we search for analogies in the ethnographic record of the Middle East as a much better record of interpretative possibilities, like the kind of personal and vertical political interactions, present in ancient textual data.

Now, Ugarit presents several features proper to ancient state formation: normalised writing, official administration, social hierarchy and division of labour. It would be difficult to deny that some kind of established political centralisation was present in the kingdom, but it would also be debatable to see this centralisation – considering the external and internal factors of limitation to the Ugaritic king's autonomy – as indisputably absolute. In this may reside the difference between a *kingdom* and a *state*. But, if we now turn to the rest of the smaller polities of the Levant, especially in its southern part, where only a few of the features attested in Ugarit are found, the socio-political status according to the practices and representations expressed in the written and archaeological material remains must be closer to that of the tribe than to the state. It is true that several polities in Syria-Palestine during the Amarna period possessed scribes in their courts, but these specialists were not necessarily the product of a local socio-economic development in all of the polities. In most of the smaller (Palestinian) polities, scribes could have certainly been provided by the Egyptian domination of the territory as agents of interaction with the petty kings, which means that their presence does not attest state formation per se in these polities, but rather only borrowed or adopted features for external contact.[17]

The socio-political configuration of Levantine polities seems to have been, according to the ubiquitous presence of household terminology in diplomatic exchanges, based on inter-personal ties denoting a patrimonial hierarchy. In fact, as Schloen notes, the household terminology is a most important key to figure out the socio-political organisation that gave voice to it: 'father', 'son', 'brother', 'master', 'servant'. In the Amarna epistolographical repertoire we find plenty of evidence of this: in the letters EA 158 and 164, Aziru, ruler of Amurru, addresses the Egyptian officer Tutu as 'my lord, my father' (EN-*ia a-bi-i[a]*), while he presents himself as 'your son, your servant' (DUMU-*ka* ÌR-*ka*[*ma*]).[18] In EA 73 and 82, Rib-Hadda, ruler of Byblos, writes to the Egyptian officer Amanappa in similar terms: Rib-Hadda is the son and Amanappa his father (cf. Fensham 1971). An analogous case is present in an Ugaritic letter found in Aphek, where an Egyptian officer, Ḫaya, is addressed 'my father, my lord', and the Ugaritic officer responds proclaiming himself 'your son, your servant' (Horowitz and Oshima 2006: 35–6). In Ḫatti too, the viceroy of Karkemiš, called Piḫawalwi, and introducing himself as 'son of the [Hittite] king', writes to 'Ibiramu, king of Ugarit, calling him 'my son'.[19] And in a treaty between king Muwattalli II and Talmi-Šarrumma, ruler of Aleppo, Muwattalli says 'for we are all the progeny of Šuppiluliuma, Great King. So let our house be one.'[20]

The presence of internal hierarchical relations in Ugarit may be deducted too from an edict issued by Ḫattušili III for the kingdom of Ugarit.[21] In ll. 3–10 of the text, the Hittite king declares:

| | | |
|---|---|---|
| 3 | *šumma* ÍR LUGAL $^{\text{KUR}}$*ú-ga-ri-it* | If a servant of the king of Ugarit |
| 4 | *ù lu-ú* DUMU $^{\text{KUR}}$*ú-ga-ri-it* | or a dweller of Ugarit |
| 5 | *lu-ú* ÍR ÍR LUGAL $^{\text{KUR}}$*ú-ga-ri-it* | or a servant of a servant of the king of Ugarit |
| 6 | *ma-am-ma i-te-eb-bi-ma* | sets in motion |
| 7 | *ana* ŠÀ$^{\text{BI}}$ A.ŠÀ $^{\text{LÚ}}$SA.GAZ $^{\text{d}}$UTU$^{\text{ŠI}}$ *ir-u-ub* | and enters the territory of *ḫabiru* of the Sun |
| 8 | LUGAL GAL *ú-ul a-la-aq-qí-šu* | (I), the Great King, shall not accept him |
| 9 | *a-na* LUGAL $^{\text{KUR}}$*ú-ga-ri-it* | to the king of Ugarit |
| 10 | *ú-ta-ar-šu* | I shall return him. |

Even if the perspective is Hittite, the testimony may be representative of how Ugarit's political organisation was perceived. In particular, the reference in l. 5 to 'a servant of a servant of the king' might be interpreted as denoting a vertical hierarchy, analogous to patron–client ties or better to the triad patron–broker–client in its constitutive political dynamic. The political configuration expressed in the edict could be read too as patrimonial, where the kingdom of Ugarit is a household made of interpersonal dyads hierarchically articulated, integrated, at the same time, in a 'fractal' (Lehner 2000) fashion in the greater household of the Hittite kingdom. Once more, as Schloen (2001: 252) argues:

> This text refers to 'any servant of a servant of the king of Ugarit,' revealing a social hierarchy consisting of the king, his immediate servants, and their servants. The king of Ugarit himself was likewise the servant of his Hittite master; thus the patrimonial hierarchy of households extended as far as the imperial court. The social and political organization of vassal kingdom and empire alike was structured on the simplest possible basis as a self-replicating household of households, in which the social actors' understanding of household-based relationships of authority and obedience remained the same at every level.

The terminology of the period, especially when it expresses the relations between great and small kingdoms, was built on household concepts. This terminology and its profound connotation of personal relations would have indicated, precisely, that political power in south-western Asia was conveyed *through* personal relations between polities. The native terminology referred to 'fathers', 'sons' and 'brothers' asking protection and assistance, through reciprocity principles, or at least the expectation of such reciprocal instances. Similar orders of vertical hierarchy through personal relations can be imagined for the Levantine polities, externally and internally, from the great king to the petty king and then, within the kingdom, down to the last member of the societal pyramid. In fact, Schloen (2001: 258) argues that 'there is no evidence for an abstract conception of the impersonal state as a political agent during the Late Bronze Age; this is an entirely anachronistic notion.' It was not the 'national community' which was the subject of international treaties – as once defended by G. Kestemont (1974: 48–9) from a, somewhat anachronistic, juridical reading – but the reigning dynasty, as can be observed in the treaty between Muršili II of Ḫatti and Niqmepaʿ of Ugarit: the king of Ugarit must love the Hittite king, his sons and the land of Ḫatti (*māt* $^{\mathrm{URU}}$*Ḫatti*) as he loves himself, his wives, his troops and his land (*mātu*), and must be in peace with the king of the land of Ḫatti, the king's sons, the sons of the king's sons and the land of Ḫatti.[22]

In concluding this section, we may note that Schloen's patrimonial understanding of society and Liverani's (and others') two-sector model may actually not be as incompatible as at first one may think, since what is emphasised in both interpretations are different aspects of ancient Levantine society and the elements that configure it. The two-sector model approaches the organisation of Syro-Palestinian polities, especially their socio-economic structure, from an external (*etic*) perspective, whereas Schloen's patrimonial model addresses mainly the native comprehension (*emic*) of socio-political and socio-economic phenomena in these kingdoms – even though he disputes the two-sector model's understanding of the internal working of labour and production. In effect, Schloen (2001: 255) suggests that

> the native understanding of society is of prime importance in socio-historical reconstruction because the symbolically mediated interpretations attached to social relationships by those who take part in them invariably affect social behavior, with the result that such behavior cannot be appropriately explained without taking this interpretations into account.

Without the intention of formulating a forced hybridisation of perspectives, it might be possible to find an interpretive disposition that takes what is most useful of both models, even though Schloen's model seems to make more sense of a political terminology that reflects political praxis, like patronage, as will be shown in the next chapter. Schloen's model provides also a general unity and coherence to the socio-political articulation of the Levantine kingdoms that is lacking in the implied separation between urban dwellers and village peasants of the two sectors model.[23]

## 7.2. Patrimonialism and patronage

The *political culture*[24] of Late Bronze Age Syria-Palestine seems to be better expressed by models of patrimonialism and patronage, according to what has been already exposed in the previous chapters. Patronage relations imply the existence of a realm of influence between an individual with political and economic prestige and power in society and a plurality of other individuals subject to him by ties of asymmetrical reciprocity. The bond between patron and client is basically dyadic, but its praxis allows for an expansion of the bond into a pyramidal network of dyadic units, ascending and descending, where a small patron is at the same time client of a greater patron – acting then as a broker between the two spheres. The inherent asymmetrical reciprocity of this kind of relationship establishes that the patron will exert protection over his clients, and these will respond with personal loyalty. Otherwise, should the relation fail, the patron can punish the personal treason of a client, or the client can search for, or be forced to choose, a new patron. This scheme seems to explain the basics of Levantine socio-political order and it can be found in some Hittite treaties and in the Amarna corpus.

In EA 53:11–16, for instance, a subject of Egypt makes explicit his personal subordination and loyalty to the Pharaoh: 'And now [Aitukam]a has written me and said, "[Come] with me to the king of Ḫa[tti." I s]aid, "How could [I go to the ki]ng of Ḫatti? I am [a ser]vant of the king, my lord, the king of Egypt".'

Also, in a more explicit manner, in EA 51 rev.:1–6: 'And the king of Ḫatti [wrote to me about an alliance]. My lord, [I rejected] (the offer of) tablets of treaty obli[gations], and [I am still a servant of] the king of Egypt, [my lord].'[25]

The first to suggest that this kind of evidence could in fact be interpreted as patronage relations for the societies of ancient Syria-Palestine was N.P. Lemche:

> In the spatially more affluent Syrian states such as Ugarit, the village structure which embraced 80 to 90 per cent of the population would probably encourage a system to be established, in which the king would be reckoned the head patron – the 'capo di capi'. The village itself, however, formed a subsystem, which would be subject to a patron who could either be the king or some local potentate, eventually a high-ranking client of the king who was entrusted with this village as his personal fief. However, on the local basis the village may at many occasions have functioned almost like an acephalous tribal system without officially appointed leaders, where decisions were made on a communal basis. Some juridical documents point in this direction as in certain cases (the infamous cases of unsolved murders of merchants) they treat the village as a collective rather than looking for an individual offender. In Palestine, the village system hardly existed in the LBA. Instead we encounter a

> system of small scale townships (the normal scholarly term 'city' is a most unfortunate one, as it directs our ideas in the wrong direction) ruled by so-called 'kings', tiny political structures which probably allowed for a personal system of relationships between ruler and subject. No intermediary organization was necessary, and only a most rudimentary administrative system was needed. . . . Nothing comprehensive was needed to control these societies: a scribe and a few soldiers [were] sufficient.[26]

Further, the kind of political behaviour that the Hittite overlords had on their external subjects seemed to follow tacitly the premises of patronage relations, even though these practices could be embedded in the ritual and formulaic presentation of the imposed subordination treaties. The necessity of making explicit the subordination through treaties may have been related to the fragile nature of political bonds in the northern Levant, but it would also carry a symbolic and cosmological expression of the might of Ḫatti over its conquered or protected subjects.

The general social organisation of villages and rural communities of Syria-Palestine was dependent on a kinship and patrimonial structure,[27] according to which the political life of the village or the community was expressed and the relations to the capital city of the kingdom were established. As L. Marfoe has indicated in regard to the socio-political organisation of southern Syria – in particular the Beqa‘ valley – during the Late Bronze Age:

> within the south Syrian cities (except for Hazor) there was simply no room for the sort of state bureaucracy that can be discerned from the large north Syrian and Mesopotamian cities. It may then be conjectured that instead of a multitiered hierarchy of rigidly stratified social roles (as at Ugarit), the social organization among the small populations under consideration required that multiple roles be undertaken by a small urban elite group . . . Royal lineages, government bureaucracy, priesthood, army, and mercenaries were probably less differentiated than in the larger north Syrian cities . . . Socially, culturally, and economically, the urban elite – embodied in the conspicuous display and consumption of wealth in the palace-temple complex – stood more at the center than at the apex of a large but for the most part socially undifferentiated population. In this respect, the royal lineages may only have been the largest and wealthiest of a number of smaller and more fragmented kinship groups, whose principal occupations were in subsistence farming. . . . these 'city-states' did not form a patchwork of segmented social pyramids of power that engaged in 'foreign relations' across well-defined borders, much less consolidated territorial units of hierarchically tiered villages over which rival centers perpetually competed in border disputes. Neither the 'territories' nor the villages of the state were defined by land as much as they were by people. And the social framework that tied these people together may have been in fact relatively uniform kinship groups that solidified into more tightly

> organized units only within the palace-temple complex. . . . The state, in other words, was not 'oriental despotism' writ small; nor was it a genuine territorial unit, much less a unified one. It was in effect a network of personal and political ties centered on the palace-temple, where perhaps the king was not merely the last arbiter but possibly the sole arbiter.[28]

The bureaucracy to which Marfoe refers may indeed be understood in patrimonial terms, as Schloen has argued, instead of a properly impersonal group of officers and administrators. It is within this context that patron–broker–client relations might have had their gravitation in society as the internal articulator of Levantine polities, from the contact of the peasant with the head of the village or a petty officer from the capital city to the relation these latter had with more important agents of the kingdom or even a Syrian king or prince; when the country was under foreign rule, we should think of an Egyptian commissioner in Palestine. In Syrian occupied territory, the Hitittes would have accepted this kind of relationships as a means of governability; in Egypt's occupied Palestine, this sort of personal conception of politics was ignored or discarded by the Egyptian court, as many of the Amarna letters show.

* * *

To be part of the socio-political world of the household in Syria-Palestine implied to perform a set of domestic, communal, kin-related – in other words, patrimonial – practices when addressing the exterior world of the local community or the kingdom. Anthropological literature is very well documented with this sort of relational strategy, illustrated, for instance, with the notion of 'fictive kinship' in the practices of patronage and *compadrazgo*.[29] If, in a kinship community, reciprocity is the rule of social articulation, with the appeal to 'fictive kinship' there is an intention of extending such reciprocity into a non-kinship realm, for various reasons (political alliance, economic interests, gaining prestige, etc.). In an inter-communal or inter-polity political contact through family and friendship terminology we have a key to understanding the socio-political foundation that creates such interpersonal practices. Calling someone 'father', 'son', or 'brother' implies a set of expectations regarding political behaviour which transcends the biological link – regarding it as ultimately irrelevant for the purposes of the contact. Therefore, socio-political relations and contacts in the Late Bronze Age Levant respond to a personalised terminology not because of a mere diplomatic protocol based on family metaphors, but because of the active manifestation of a conception of politics constituted by a patrimonial scheme (Schloen 2001: 63–89, 255–316).

Having in mind the exposition and discussion so far, we proceed in the next chapter to evaluate how the concepts of kinship, state practice and patrimonialism can be used to interpret the epigraphic data from the Late Bronze Age and characterise the Levantine polities and their socio-political praxis. As *state practice* has been defined and used in this study, as the exercise of the monopoly of physical and symbolic coercion by means of an impersonal bureaucratic apparatus, it should be safe to consider New Kingdom Egypt as a prime representative of this. The kingdom of Ḫatti, in spite of the patrimonial characterisation of its internal organisation, did exert a monopoly of coercion towards its foreign subjects, by means of the 'protectorates' and the imposition of alliance treaties. For Syria-Palestine, the archaeological and epigraphic evidence is much more ambiguous and problematic, from a political anthropological perspective. Without doubt, Ugarit constitutes a clear example of a much more complex socio-economic organisation than a tribal or chiefdom structure. Yet, the diplomatic or inter-polity textual data also shows the existence of particular ties of personal dependence and asymmetrical reciprocity in its relation to other polities, peer and larger, which cannot be understood from institutional instances but must be analysed from the conditions of the practice itself.

These last considerations require that we revisit the categories employed to express the nature of socio-political practices in Syria-Palestine. From a patrimonial perspective, it could be said that thinking of a *patrimonial kingdom*, instead of a (city-)state or even a patrimonial state, would best explain the organisation and dynamics of the most important Levantine polities. Smaller polities, with much less signs of state features, might also be understood as *patronage kingdoms*, when patron–client relations are attested as forming the backbone of socio-political life. We proceed now to analyse some of the textual evidence from these theoretical considerations.

## Notes

1 Liverani 1974: 332. This author has revisited such perspective in recent times (Liverani 2005b), without altering much of its characterisation.

2 Márquez Rowe (2003b: 721) thinks otherwise, by following closely the documentary evidence; Liverani, instead, sees this as the projection of a monarchic ideal no longer existent (cf. Liverani 1974: 339), apart from the traditional judicial attributes of ancient Near Eastern monarchy: cf. Pintore 1976: 467–73; Whitelam 1979; Niehr 1997.

3 Cf. RS 16.132 (*PRU* III, 140–41). The term *corps d'élite* is used by Drower (1975: 494–5, 501) in her portrayal of the *maryannu*. See further Liverani 1974: 333–4: 'the military role seems to be proper of the nobiliary caste (*maryannu*), rather than of the king. . . . In fact, the military role was essentially delegated by the king to the 'brothers' and to the *maryannu*, and that was one of the many special duties that the 'king's men' had in exchange for payment. The king is thus the chief of professional military led by him, rather than the chief of the people in arms'; cf. also *PRU* II 12 and *Ug* V, 69–76. The reference to a 'caste nobiliaire' is rather problematic in both terminology and connotation (cf., however, Herrenschmidt 2010). According to Rainey (2003: 173), the *maryannu* were a part of each Syro-Palestinian polity, even though the term, recurrent in the texts from Ugarit and Alalaḫ, does not appear everywhere (but cf. EA 107:45–6; 108:13–17). On the army in Ugarit, see now Vita, 1995: 89–132; Vidal 2006b.

4 A similar opinion can be found in Wyatt 2001; see also del Olmo Lete 1993; Niehr 1998: 40–42; Zamora López 2006: 66–8. Yet, one should not think of the Ugaritic monarchy as sacred kingship (cf. Petersen 1998: 99–100), as it was the case in pharaonic Egypt, even though the Ugaritic king had access to the divine realm (cf. Wyatt 2007).

5 Cf. RS 16.239:14 (*PRU* III, 80); RS 16.132:17 (*PRU* III, 140).

6 Cf. RS 16.239:17–19 (*PRU* III, 80); RS 16.143:20–21 (*PRU* III, 82); RS 16.157:20–21 (*PRU* III, 84); RS 16.250:15–16 (*PRU* III, 85); RS 16.353:30–31 (*PRU* III, 114); RS 15.137:13–14 (*PRU* III, 135); RS 16.348:7–8 (*PRU* III, 162); RS 16.386:14′–15′ (*PRU* III, 166).

7 Cf. RS 16.239:31–3 (*PRU* III, 81); RS 16.157:22–3 (*PRU* III, 84); RS 16.250:17–19 (*PRU* III, 86); RS 15.137:15–16 (*PRU* III, 135); RS 16.132:16–24 (*PRU* III, 140–41).

8 See the case in RS 16.269:7–10 (*PRU* IV, 68).

9 Cf. RS 17.352 (*PRU* IV, 121–2).

10 Cf. EA 137:15–25; 142:15–24; 162:2–6.

11 Cf. EA 35:27–9; 89:39–43; 136:8–13; 137:46–8; 138:35–47, 71–3. See more in Liverani 1965; 1979b; Fleming 2012. On such limitations from below, understood as 'politics from below', cf. Pfoh 2014.

12 Cf. EA 73:26–9; 74:25-9; 81:11-23; cf. the analysis in Barreyra 2006.

13 Cf. EA 59; 100; 136–8; 139; 149:57–60. Cf. Jankowska 1969; Reviv 1969. Artzi (1964) saw in these revolts clues of a 'primitive democracy' (cf. Jacobsen 1943); but cf. Liverani 1993.

14 Cf. EA 75: 25ff.; Momrak 2013: 441–2. See Bunnens 1982, analysing episodes of local dissidence in Ugarit and Alalaḫ. On archaeological evidence for collective governance in Middle and Late Bronze Age Syria, cf. Otto 2012.

15 Cf. Landsberger 1954: 61 n 134. But cf. the study by Solans 2011. Also Momrak (2013: 504), who concludes: 'The picture that emerges of city-state organisation under foreign empire in the Near East is that the inhabitants had their own separate decision-making bodies that could act independently of their governors and officials and have direct contact with foreign rulers. These decision-making bodies do not appear to have been formally constituted. Little is known about how they were organised. It seems that the people took part in or at least were witnesses to decisions, but that the authority in the town or city was with a more limited body of heads of households or representatives of élite families. Thus, there were popular politics in the city-states under foreign empire: there is evidence for semi-autonomous cities in the Levant in the Late Bronze Age and in Mesopotamia in the Iron Age, where the people could reach decisions independent of officials and rulers. However, the relationship between the people and the more limited decision-making body is difficult to unravel and the two often cannot be separated in the sources'.

16 Cf. the textual data from Alalaḫ in *AT* 2:27; *AT* 3:38 (Wiseman 1953: 27, 29; 32); and Ugarit in RS 20.239: 21–7 (Nougayrol 1968: 142–3). See Solans 2011: 283–337.

17 Cf. the study by Moran (1975) on the Syrian scribe of Amarna Jerusalem; cf. also Mynářová 2014: 27–8. Further, as noted by Van Soldt (2013: 25), this phenomenon is related to what J. Goody (1986: 100) named 'external use of writing'.

18 The tribal-pastoral socio-political nature of Amurru does not explain the presence of kinship terminology in the Amarna correspondence, since all the Amarna petty polities would use such terminology. On Amurru, cf. Liverani 1979d; Bryce 2003: 145–68. On the relation between the human geography of mountains and socio-politics, cf. Braudel 1972 I: 25–53; and in particular on Amurru, see the discussion in Morris 2010.

19 Cf. RS 17.247:3 (*PRU* IV, 191) = *CTH* 110.

20 *CTH* 76. Cf. Beckman, 1996: 90 (n. 13). It is interesting that Liverani (2001: 128–38) has addressed himself the meaning of the kinship and household terminology in the contacts between the Late Bronze Age polities without considering the sociological

connotation found by Schloen: 'Liverani not only fails to appreciate the political significance of familial terms other than "brother", as we have seen; he also fails to include within the family model (or, better, the "household" model, which includes the master–servant relationship) another set of terms belonging to what he calls the "ideology of protection"' (Schloen 2001: 261).

21 Cf. RS 17.238 (*PRU* IV, 107–8) = *CTH* 94. Cf. also the discussion in Vargyas 1988; Zamora 1997: 117–48.

22 Cf. Schloen 2001: 259 footnote 5; the text in Beckman 1996: 60 (= *CTH* 26). As Westbrook (2000: 36–7) indicates: 'In the domestic legal systems of the ancient Near East, a contract between heads of household would bind their respective households. . . . A treaty between kings was simply a contract that would bind their "households" in the same way.' On the connotation of the verb 'love' in the ancient Near East, including the Old Testament, see Moran 1963; Thompson 1974; 1977; Ackerman 2002.

23 'The implication is of a clear sociological separation, in terms of both way of life and ethos or ideology, between rural peasants and urban dwellers. No thought is given to the possibility that this dichotomy is an illusion fostered by the modern concept of urbanism' (Schloen 2001: 267). For examples of socio-political articulation between (semi-)nomads and sedentaries, cf. Rowton 1973a; 1973b; 1974; 1977; although the Rowton's *dimorphic* understanding should be better understood as a *polymorphic continuum*: see Lemche 1985: 84–244; Silva Castillo 2005.

24 The concept of 'political culture' derives from political science and sociology studies (cf. Lehman 1972; Meisel 1974; Dittmer 1977; Chilton 1988); the concept is used in the present study meaning 'particular pattern of orientations to political action' (Almond 1956: 396); or better, as a culturally conditioned mode of political action.

25 After Moran 1992: 125 and 122 respectively. Cf. also Knudtzon 1907: 324–5, 320–21; Liverani 1998: 299, 292; Rainey 2014: 391, 385. As Moran (1992: 122 n. 2) notes, it is actually improbable that the Hittite king had sent the tablets of the 'treaty' (*rikiltu*/*rikistu*; *CAD* R, 345–6) before a demonstration of loyalty by the subject since, as patron in the relation, he is the one imposing the conditions of the political exchange.

26 Lemche 1995b; 1995c; 1996; 2013; here 1996: 114–15.

27 Cf. Sapin 1981: 35–8; Buccellati 1967: 64–72. Studies that see the presence of 'statehood' over the village organisation: Heltzer 1969; 1976; Liverani 1975; van Soldt 1995: 1260–61, among others.

28 Marfoe 1979: 15–16; cf. Alt 1959c: 20ff.; Schloen 2001: 329–42. Further, Savage and Falconer (2003: 42) have recently argued that the Levantine region was a 'fractious and volatile countryside balkanized into a relatively large number of modestly sized polities that varied considerably in extent and composition'. At this micro-scale, the topographic landscape of the *polities* coincides with the observations by A. Cohen (1965) on the 'patronymic association' in the organisation of Arab villages in Palestine. Further, Schloen (2001: 112) notes that 'the patronymic association of households that make up residential quarters is often organized around a leading household, whose patriarch acts as the patron of the poorer households nearby'. On household archaeology in the Levant, cf. now Chesson 2003; Yasur-Landau, Ebeling and Mazow, 2011; Hardin, 2011.

29 Cf. Coy 1974. The *compadrazgo*, as Coy (1974 470) points out, is the creation of an extension of kinship relations through ritual practices (e.g. baptism). Cf. further Pitt-Rivers 1968; Ingham 1970.

# 8

# POLITICAL RELATIONS IN LATE BRONZE AGE SYRIA-PALESTINE

Patronage relations seem to be present in the Amarna correspondence and other contemporary textual documents as the socio-political 'idiom', expressing and transmitting the means of Syro-Palestinian political behaviour in front of Egyptian domination, but also in its subordination to Hittite rule. Egypt, however, manifested its ruling of the Levantine territory through an imperative phraseology, proper of bureaucratic or state-like behaviour of domination. When the Syro-Palestinian and the Egyptian polities interacted, they would generate 'semantic interferences' in the communication (cf. Chapter 2, section 2.3.1), which can be understood as a patronage-driven and a state-driven conception of political clashes of power. This did not happen when Syrian polities interacted with Ḫatti since, in its relationship, there was a shared conception of how a relation between a ruler and his subjects should proceed. In this way, they avoided the episodes of miscommunication that were often the case with Egypt. Vertical interaction between great and small kings would differ from the protocols of horizontal diplomatic communication between the great powers of the period. Yet, both kinds of communication were part of a shared patrimonial understanding of how regional political contacts should proceed.

## 8.1. Alliance and subordination – loyalty and reciprocity

In the regional system of the Late Bronze Age, the logical means of formulating and expressing alliance between two great kingdoms were manifested through a protocol of personal relations. Thus, the Egyptian king, making use of diplomatic protocols, which placed him as just another player in the regional game of politics, would write in the following terms to the king of Babylonia:

> Say [t]o Kadašman-Enlil, the king of Karadun[i]še [Babylonia], my brother: Thus Nibmuarea, Great King/the king of Egypt, your brother. For me all goes well. For you may all go well. For your household [E-*ka*], for your wives, for your sons, for your magnates, your horses, your chariots, for your countries, may all go very well. For me all goes well. For my household, for my wives, for my sons, for my magnates,

> my horses, the numerous troops, all goes well, and in my countries all goes very well.[1]

As expected, the Babylonian king would respond in the same terms, illustrating the reciprocity proper of a parity of kingships:

> [Say] to Mimmuwareya, the king of Egypt, [my] brother: Thus [K]a[d]aš[m]a[n-En]lil, the king of Kara[duniyaš]. For me and [m]y country all goes very [well]. For you, for [yo]ur wi[ves], for your sons, fo[r your magnates], your horses, your chariots, and your entire country, may all go very we[ll].[2]

The forging of alliance relations between the two great kingdoms begins, as noted in previous chapters, with the sending of gifts aiming at establishing exchange relations between the countries; as the Assyrian king would express to the Pharaoh:

> Say to the king of E[gypt]: Thus Aššur-ubal[lit, the king of As]syria. For you, your household, for your [coun]try, for your chariots and your troops, may all go well. I send my messenger to you to visit you and to visit your country. Up to now, my predecessors have not written, today I write to you. [I] send you a beautiful chariot, 2 horses, [and] 1 date-stone of genuine lapis lazuli, as your greeting-gift. Do [no]t delay the messenger whom I send to you for a visit. He should visit and then leave for here. He should see what you are like and what your country is like, and then leave for here.[3]

Tušratta, king of Mittani, wrote to Pharaoh Amenḥotep III in similar terms, although with the antecedent of formerly held relations between royal houses, which are meant to be renewed:

> Since you were friendly with my father, I have accordingly written and told you so my brother might hear of these things and rejoice. My father loved you, and you in turn loved my father. In keeping with this love, my father [g]ave you my sister. [And w]ho els[e] stood with my father [a]s you did? . . . I herewith send you 1 chariot, 2 horses, 1 male attendant, 1 female attendant, from the booty from the land of Ḫatti. As the greeting-gift of my brother, I send you 5 chariots, 5 teams of horses. And as the greeting-gift of Kelu-Ḫeba, my sister, I send her 1 set of gold toggle-pins, 1 set of gold (ear)rings, I gold *mašḫu*-ring, and a scent container that is full of 'sweet oil'. I herewith send Keliya, my chief minister, and Tunip-ibri. May my brother let them go promptly so they can report back to me promptly, and I hear the greeting of my brother and rejoice. May my brother seek friendship with me, and may my brother send his messengers to me that they may bring my brother's greetings to me and I hear them.[4]

A similar intention is behind Šuppiluliuma's address to Pharaoh Amenḥotep IV:

> Now, my brother, [yo]u have ascended the throne of your father, and just as your father and I were desirous of peace between us, so now too should you and I be friendly with one another. The request (that) I expressed to your father [I shall express] to my brother, too. Let us be helpful to each other.[5]

Diplomacy in this period is conducted through protocols proper of the social order of a household, as already indicated, in which personal instances of friendship and reciprocity are of utter importance to convey the socio-political bond established or sought after. The kings were 'brothers' and as such, especially in the Asiatic perspective, reciprocity was always expected.

Alliances and relationships between great and small kings in south-western Asia are conducted too by patrimonial protocols. However, when polities of different status or rank are involved, socio-political instances of patron–client relations appear, as evidenced, for instance, in the proposal of alliance that Šuppiluliuma of Ḫatti presented to Niqmadu of Ugarit, in a geopolitical context of struggle with other small polities for the control of northern Syria:

> Since Nuḫaš[še] and Mukiš are at war with me, you, Niqmadu, do not believe them: Trust yourself! Since previously your fathers were friends and not enemies of Ḫatti, you, Niqmadu, are of my enemy, enemy, and of my friend, friend! If you, Niqmadu, know the words of the Great King, your lord, and you are loyal to them, you shall have the favour of the Great King, by which the Great King, your lord, shall gratify you.[6]

The conditional proposition, offering an exchange of political loyalty to the Hittite king for protection and gratification to the Ugaritic king, may actually be linked to instances of patronage, and it is an offer the Ugaritic king hardly could have rejected since Ḫatti's military power would have coerced the little kingdom to accept it in some way or the other.

The documentation shows that Niqmadu accepted the offer of a Hittite alliance, as king Šuppiluliuma tells in the decree issued to such effect:

> As all the kings of Nuḫaš[še] and the king of Mukiš are at war with the Sun, Great King, his lord, Niqmadu, king of Ugarit, was a friend to the Sun, Great King, his lord; not enemy. The kings of Nuḫaš[še] and the king of Mukiš had talked to Niqmadu, king of Ugarit, in the following terms: 'Why don't you move away from the Sun and make war [to him] with us?'. But Niqmadu did not want to be at war with the lord, Great King, his lord; and the Sun, Great King, his lord knew (in this manner) Niqmadu's loyalty. So Šuppiluliuma, Great King, king of Ḫatti, has made an agreement with Niqmadu, king of Ugarit, in the following

> terms: 'your tribute to the Sun, Great King, your lord, shall be: . . . [a description of the tribute follows]'. [. . .] The Sun, Great King, had knew Niqmadu's loyalty when he came a prostrated to the feet of the Sun, Great King, his lord. The Sun, Great King, his lord, has granted this agreement in these terms. May these words, written on the tablet, be recognised in truth by the Thousand Gods! May the Sun in the sky, the Adad of Arinna, the Adad of heaven, the Adad of Ḫatti, truly know of any who modifies the words on this tablet![7]

The alliance treaty, as we have argued in a previous chapter, did not represent a properly legal instance of an agreement between two equal parties, but rather the concession from the Hittite king to his subject or client king of a kind of tribute and guarantees for the subordinated kingdom which otherwise, in the case of a formal Hittite military conquest of the territory, would have been absent. This is a clear Hittite ruling strategy that reduced the general military, logistic and administrative costs for Ḫatti and represented a relative benefit for Ugarit, within a context of political subordination. The functioning of such an asymmetrical relationship between kings may indeed be understood as a kind of inter-polity patronage.

A similar dynamic is evidenced in the arbitrage that the Hittite king Muršili II exerts over territorial disputes in Syrian land under his control and sovereignty:

> Formerly the city of Iyaruwatta belonged to the land of Barga. Then it was taken away by force from the grandfather of Abiradda into the power of the king of the land of Ḫurri, who gave it to the grandfather of Tette, the *ḫabiru.* Then it happened that Tette and EN-urta fought a war with My Majesty, while Abiradda went over to My Majesty's side. He chased EN-urta, the enemy of My Majesty, out of the land, and himself came to the land of Ḫatti, to My Majesty. Kneeling at my feet, he said to me as follows: 'Because the city of Iyaruwatta formerly belonged to my grandfather, give the empty city of Iyaruwatta back to me with its bare walls, gods, and ancestral spirits.' . . . And I, My Majesty, utterly destroyed EN-urta, together with his household and his land. But his kingship, throne, household, and land which I spared, I gave to Abiradda and made him king in the land of Barga. And Abiradda installed for himself his son Ir-Teššup as their crown prince. In the future, when Abiradda dies, he shall leave to his son Ir-Teššup his kingship, throne, land, and household.[8]

Once again, the loyalty of a subject king is compensated, in this case with his installation on the throne of a conquered territory of his dynasty. The edict as a communicative means, like the subordination treaties, represents the Hittite king's will, performing his role of Great King over conquered territory and as a true patron of his loyal client kings.

On this point, a differentiation between patronage as a political system and as a socio-political relation must be made.[9] In the case of Hittite-ruled Syria, the attested patronage constituted a political system, as the Syrian kings were subordinated to the king of Ḫatti. The kind of socio-political bond the petty kings from the southern Levant attempted to establish with the Egyptian king belongs in the regular set of rules proper of ethnographically attested patronage – they actually intended to channel their subordination in patron–client terms, as a personal relation with the Pharaoh. In both cases, a political asymmetry and an expectation of reciprocity are verified in the textual documentation. However, in the Hittite dominion, the king of Ḫatti exerted the monopoly of coercion over a certain subordinate, who may in theory expect to be reciprocated if his loyalty to the king is maintained, as the Hittite treaties stipulated. The situation of the Syro-Palestinian petty kings was different: the Pharaoh also exerted the monopoly of coercion over them, but he channelled it through impersonal instances of domination, rendering the petty kings' actual expectation of reciprocity – attested in the Amarna correspondence – ultimately invalid and ignored or uncontested.[10]

If political alliance relations between the great kings of the Late Bronze Age were carried out through formalities of parity and reciprocity, and the relation between a great king and a small king was manifested by asymmetric exchange and reciprocity, ultimately dictated by the great king, we observe that the relations between small kings reproduced the same patterns of parity and symmetrical reciprocity found in the diplomatic exchange between the great kingdoms. In effect, in a letter to the king of Ugarit, the king of Amurru expressed: 'My brother, look: you and I are brothers. Sons of the same man, we are brothers. Why then would we not be in good terms? Every wish you require from me, I shall satisfy it. And you shall satisfy my wishes. We are but one. Every [wish] you have, I shall satisfy it for you.'[11]

The general idiom of political alliance is therefore the idiom of family and that of the patrimonial household: 'lord/master' and 'servant', to indicate the dynamic of the behaviour; 'father', to make reference to a king of superior status or rank, from whom protection and assistance was expected; 'son', to address a king of inferior status or rank, from whom subordination and political loyalty was expected; 'brother', to treat with kings of the same status or rank, among which balanced reciprocity was the expected behaviour. In the Hittite epistolographic repertoire we find a letter from prince Piḫa-walwi to king Ibiranu of Ugarit, where the patrimonial terminology is manifested together with a complaint for the lack of protocol of subordination on behalf of the Ugaritic king:

> Thus says prince Piḫa-walwi: say to my son, Ibiranu: At the moment all is well with His Majesty. Why have you not come before His Majesty since you have assumed the kingship of the land of Ugarit? And why have you not sent your messengers? How His Majesty is very angry about this matter. Now send your messengers quickly before His Majesty, and send the king's gifts together with my gifts.[12]

Likewise, the Amarna epistolary documentation transmits protocols and formulae of obedience, loyalty and petitions of reciprocity coming from proper expectations of a patrimonial order in which patron–client ties appear as the means to express politics. The petty king Ba'lu-mehir of Mikmate, would write to the Pharaoh in the terms of a loyal client:

> As I am the loy[al] servant [o]f the king, may the king, my lord, know [th]at [h]is [city], along with his servant, is safe and sound. As I have placed my [n]eck in the yoke that I carry, may the king, my lord, know that I serve him [with c]omplete devotion and [. . .] [Gmate [s]erves him with complete devotion.[13]

And in similar terms, Yidya, ruler of Ašqalon, would proclaim his loyalty: 'I am indeed guar[ding] the place of the king where I am. Whatever the k[ing], my lord, has written me, I have listened to very carefully. Who is the dog that would not obey the orders of the king, his lord, the son of the Sun?'[14]

Interesting as well is the manner in which Abdi-Ḫeba, ruler of Jerusalem, acknowledged the Pharaoh's patronage (or what the small king understood as the Pharaoh's patronage), proclaiming 'neither my father nor my mother put me in this place, but the strong arm of the king brought me into my father's house'.[15] And also, in a letter to the Pharaoh: 'Behold, I am not a mayor [*ḫazannu*]; I am a soldier of the king, my lord. Behold, I am a friend of the king and a tribute-bearer of the king. It was neither my father nor my mother, but the strong arm of the king that [p]laced me in the house of [my] fath[er].'[16]

The relevance of these testimonies – be they actually true, in a modern historicist fashion, or coming from the intention to manifest an absolute subordination to the Pharaoh – resides in the recognition of the accession to the throne of this petty king through the 'mighty arm of the Pharaoh'. Such legitimacy is evidently clientelistic. Likewise, Abdi-Ḫeba's self-identification as a 'friend of the king' did not mean he considered himself a peer to the Egyptian king; namely a Great King, but the reference is akin to a patronage phraseology by which a patron and his client are 'friends', from an *emic* point of view, even when both acknowledge the asymmetry of their political status. Examples of native terminology should be interpreted in the light of the implicit realities created by the praxis of socio-politics; namely, patronage.

The presence or existence of a socio-political worldview anchored in patron-client relations may also be witnessed after the non-corporate character the expressed subordination to a great king by petty kings. Precisely, the verticality of social bonds was the dominant political practice in Syria-Palestine in this period, within a context of individual proclamation of loyalty by one ruler together with accusations of treason from the rest of the subordinated petty kings. Such strategy was aimed at gaining political capital (i.e. trust) from the Pharaoh or the Hittite king, enabling a relative autonomy, of local range. As Rib-Hadda, ruler of Byblos, proclaimed to the Pharaoh: 'Look, Gubla is not like the [other] cities; Gubla is a loyal city of the king, [my] lo[rd], from most ancient times.'[17]

In the letter from Aziru of Amurru to Tutu, an Egyptian officer, a patronage association is clearly detected in the words of the Levantine ruler:

> T[o] Tutu, my lord, [my] father: Message of Aziru, your son, your servant. I fall at the feet of my father. For my father may all go well. Tutu, I herewi[th gr]ant the re[ques]t of the ki[ng, m]y l[or]d, [and] whatever may be the request [o]f the king, my lord, he should write and I w[ill g] rant it. Moreover, a[s] you in that place are my father, whatever may be the request of Tutu, my f[at]her, just write and I will grant it. [A]s you are my father and my lord, [and] I am your son, the land of Amurru is your [lan]d, and my house is your house. [Wr]ite me any request at all of yours, and I will grant your [eve]ry request. [And] you are in the personal service [of the king], my [lord. Hea]ven forbid that treacherous men have spoken maliciously [again]st me in the presence of the king, my lord. And you should not permit them. [And a]s you are in the personal service [of the king, m]y lord, representing me, you should not permit malicious talk [ag]ainst me. I am the servant of the king, my lord, and I will [n]ot deviate from the orders of the king, my lord, or from the orders of Tutu, my father, forever. [But i]f the king, my lord, does not love me and rejects me, then what a[m] I to s[a]y?[18]

Notable is the distinction made in the patrimonial treatment towards his superiors: the Pharaoh is obviously Aziru's ultimate lord and he is his servant; but Tutu is also called *father* by Aziru, who presents himself as his *son*. In the context of inter-personal relations, we may propose that such a differentiation responded to an attempt by Aziru of persuading Tutu to act like his broker in the Egyptian court, defending Aziru's loyalty to the Pharaoh before accusations of treason. Aziru maintains in his letter that Tutu represents his words in the Egyptian court and, since Tutu is 'in the personal service' of the Pharaoh, he must intervene by defending his case. Aziru's words, and those of many other petty kings, grant us access to a personalised worldview of politics native to Syria-Palestine.

We have already noted that reciprocity was expected in the political transactions between great kings and also between a great and a small king. However, there are several examples that document in which such expected reciprocity fails to materialise or is seriously limited by misunderstandings in the inter-polity communication or by semantic clashes proper of a friction between different worldviews. In a letter, probably by Šuppiluliuma, to the Pharaoh we read:

> And now, as to the Tablet that [you sent me], why [did you put] your name over my name? And who (now) is the one who upsets the good relations [between us], and is su[ch conduct] the accepted practice? My brother, did you write [to me] with peace in mind? And if [you are my brother], why have you exalted [your name], while I, for my part, am tho[ught of as] a [co]rpse.[19]

It would seem here that the personal honour of the letter's addressee has been touched by altering the correct representation of his name in the tablet where the message is written. In the appropriated terms of an alliance between political 'brothers', this event disrupts the flow of representations of parity between the kings – something actually not surprising since the letter came from Egypt, where the centralist self-perception when it comes to diplomatic communication would vary between an absolute superiority towards Asian polities and a situational acceptance of the formal protocols and rules of the regional system of the Late Bronze Age.

In Chapter 2 we noted the semantic variation in the epistolography regarding concepts like 'to protect', differently interpreted in Egypt and in Syria-Palestine. Such misunderstanding is manifested, for instance, in a letter from Rib-Hadda, answering a letter from the Pharaoh:

> Why does the king, my lord, write to me, 'On your guard! Protect (yourself)!' With what shall I protect? With my enemies, or with my peasantry? Who would protect me? If the king protects his servant, [then I will survi]ve. [But i]f the [ki]ng does not [pro]tect me, who will protect me?[20]

Beyond the semantic variation in the interpretation of the term, it is possible to assert that the puzzlement of the petty king came also from a political incomprehension of the order given by his patron: if a patron is the one who protects the clients, how can a client protect himself? This matter captures in a nutshell what power and politics are all about in ancient Syria-Palestine.

In the same fashion, but now in terms bordering on insolence towards a superior party, Rib-Hadda wrote in a letter to the Pharaoh: 'L[ook], as to the king, my lord's, having written, "Troops have indeed come out," you spo[ke] lies [*ka-ma-mi(?)*]. There are no archers; they do not come out.'[21] And in another letter, the same petty ruler questions the silence of his overlord in Egypt: 'Why do you not send back word to me that I may know what I should d[o]? I sent a man of mine to my lord, and both his horses were taken. . . . Listen t[o m]e! Wh(y) are you negligent so that your land is being taken?'[22]

The ruler of Byblos is complaining here over the absent reciprocity from the Pharaoh in order to attempting to gain politically in his own turf, under Egyptian sovereignty. The instigation to Egypt to send troops and end the threat from the 'enemies of the Pharaoh' seems to have the goal of improving Rib-Hadda's position before the rest of small polities under Egyptian domain.[23]

Another interesting situation is found in Aziru of Amurru's rise to the throne of his land, illustrating a critical episode in which a local petty king must choose one of two possible patrons. After the capture and death of Abdi-Aširta of Amurru, one of his sons, Aziru became the ruler of the polity, exerting a relatively important influence towards expansion, as attested in the constant complaints by Rib-Hadda of Byblos to the Pharaoh, warning of the imminence of Aziru's invasion of the territory (EA 136–8). In principle, Aziru appeals for recognition as a loyal servant to the Pharaoh (EA 157). However, after the Hittite king Šuppiluliuma's intervention in Syria, Aziru would hold an ambiguous relation to the Pharaoh, moving inside his territory and failing to meet the messenger of the Pharaoh, diluting his acceptance of the Pharaoh's orders or demands. As Liverani (2004e) has observed, Aziru behaved like a 'servant of two masters', avoiding the Egyptian messenger while interviewing the Hittite messenger. Aziru's behaviour, and the weighing of opportunities, is actually expected in a dramatic moment of choosing an overlord:

> [Aziru's] politics of movement, of wedging himself between the two opposing political blocks, clearly aims at achieving a rise in status, a condition of *de facto* independence from both great kings. At the same time he also aims for the status of great king by establishing asymmetrical relations to his own advantage with the surrounding kings. He is actively involved from Ugarit to Byblos, from Tunip to Arwad, and even to the Qadesh area. He uses military action, offers a type of protection that was rather a protectorate, and ambiguously assumes the function of the Egyptian *rābiṣu* in Sumura. (Liverani 2004e: 143)

The events, and probably also the geographical proximity brought Aziru finally to choose the Hittite overlord. This 'political game' offers an example of a situation in which a political agent, incapable of rising as a regional patron himself, is forced to choose subordination under one of the greater powers in order to maintain political control over his own polity. In this respect, we may consider the words by G. Simmel (1950: 232):

> Subordination under external, mutually opposed or alien, powers certainly becomes entirely different if the subordinate possesses any spontaneity whatever, if he can invest in the relationship with some power of his own. . . . An essential difference between the medieval bondsman and the medieval vassal consisted in the fact that the former had, and could have, only one master, whereas the latter could take land from several lords and make the feudal vow to each of them. Through this possibility of entering several feudal service relations, the vassal gained solidity and independence in regard to the single feudal lord, and, thus, was compensated very considerably for the basic subordination of his position.

Of course, as we have argued in Chapter 5, medieval analogies of subordination should not be employed directly to explain ancient Near Eastern situations. Nevertheless, Simmel's words are useful for considering Aziru's situation: Aziru enhances his political autonomy when he does not submit to one of the potential overlords. Yet, this situation cannot be extended in time; it is structurally short-spanned and, eventually, he has to decide (as he did!) on a new master/patron. Considering the manner in which Aziru avoids answering directly to the Pharaoh's demands, a conscious political agency should be acknowledged, as Aziru seems to manipulate willingly the semantic interferences between the Asiatic and Egyptian political worldviews in order to gain some advantage in such a political game.[24] But even if Aziru was a conscious agent, manipulating the results of inter-polity communication, that does not invalidate the very existence of such semantic interference between the Egyptian court and the Syro-Palestinian petty kings.[25]

## 8.2. Prestige as authority and power

The political scene of the Syro-Palestinian petty kings was indeed conditioned by their personal subordination to the Egyptian or Hittite power, as representatives of their respective political communities. In this context, the range of their political manoeuvrability was notably circumscribed to situations in which personal ability and political skills – in a local game of treasons, accusations, skirmishes, etc. – were their main political capital outside of their own small kingdoms. Given perhaps the modest socio-economic structure upon which they were organised, these petty kings, especially in Palestine, did not possess the monopoly of coercion in their polities. Quite the contrary, the power of the petty kings appeared rather precarious and in several Amarna letters, internal confrontation to the monarchic authority is evident (EA 59; 74; 100; 136; Artzi 1964). In effect, the Syro-Palestinian petty kings operated politically as men of prestige, protecting the community they represent and attempting to gain as much benefits as possible from that distant patron that was the Pharaoh. The accumulation of political prestige was all the power that could possibly be wielded by the petty kings with the support of their own community. The ostentation of such prestige by the petty king was the necessary ground of legitimacy to that local ruling as 'king'.[26] As such, local monarchic power, especially in small settlements, was fragile and circumstantial, attached to the king's performance as a leader of the community. Precisely, as noted in Chapter 4, the term 'king' (*mlk*) in Syria-Palestine did not mean an absolute ruler but, more generally, someone in charge of government. This 'king' may have certainly been a client of a higher status king, or have other minor kings under his command. He could also be replaced from within the polity if the expectations of his charge were not met.

There are some episodes in the Amarna correspondence that can be understood as reflecting strategies of the petty kings to gain prestige inside their communities. For instance, in a letter to the Pharaoh, Abi-Milku of Tyre wrote: 'May the king send 20 soldiers to guard his city in order that I may go in to the king, my lord, and see his face. What is the life of a soldier when breath does not come forth from the mouth of the king, his lord? But he lives if the king writes [t]o his servant, and he lives [for]ever.'[27]

Usurpation of the throne or a city under attack were real dangers in Amarna Palestine. But it should also be considered that the sole chance of meeting the Pharaoh in person would have placed Abi-Milku in a special situation of prestige in his community. An analogous instance might be identified in the petition made by Abi-Milku for *a single soldier* in another letter:

> The king gave his attention to his servant and gave soldiers t[o] protect the city of the kin[g, m]y [lord]. I am like th[i]s m[a]n. Should a single soldier protect the city of the king, my lord, then I would go in to behold the face of the king, my lord. May the king give his attention [t]o his servant and give him Usu that he may live and [dr]ink w[ate]r.[28]

What other reason could have existed for having just one soldier in Tyre, but for his status as a permanent representative of the Pharaoh's authority, thereby granting prestige to Abi-Milku for having brought him?

Another interesting example, linked to the manifestation of a semantic clash in the epistolary communication of Rib-Hadda, is found in a set of letters from different petty kings of the plateau of Ḥauran, in Transjordan, where the common answer to a letter from the Pharaoh, announcing the arrival of troops is the following: 'As you have written me to make preparations before the arrival of the archers . . . I am herewith, along with my troops and my chariots, I shall march ahead of the Egyptian troops.'[29]

Likewise, Biryawaza, ruler of Damascus, responds to the Pharaoh: 'I am with my troops and chariots, with my brothers, my *ḫabiru* and my Suteans, (I shall march) ahead of the (Egyptian) troops, wherever the king, my lord, orders me to go.'[30]

These answers expose the notification that the petty kings will march ahead of the Egyptian troops, leading the march. But beyond the semantic confusion – already analysed in Chapter 2 – it is possible to interpret such equivocal declarations of obedience to the Pharaoh – since the answers refer to something actually not required by the Pharaoh – as the conscious creation of circumstances through which a polity chieftain might acquire prestige in his community, showing off his circumscribed but functional leadership in such situation (cf. Lemche 2010). In the case of Biryawaza, together with the potential prestige of marching ahead of the Egyptian troops, we detect the network of political allies Biryawaza makes available to the Pharaoh. The king of Damascus not only provides his own troops and men, but also his *ḫabiru* and his Suteans, which can be understood as elements of a local clientelistic network of the king, their patron,[31] who also acts as the Pharaoh's client.

## 8.3. On the socio-religious imagination in Syria-Palestine

As A. Weingrod (1977) has suggested, if we attend to the dimension of power manifested in patron–client relations, we may also extend the range of inquiry to the cultural representation of such relations. In the Levant, patronage seems to have played, as we have seen, a decisive role as a vehicle for politics and social subordination. We could also consider the general worldview of Syria-Palestine as anchored in a structural hierarchy akin to patronage. The paradigmatic example is to be found in the Ugaritic pantheon, organised through a divine hierarchy that reached also human society: on the top of the hierarchy we find El (*'l*), creator of the universe and father of the gods, and husband of Ašerah; then, the higher divinities, Ba'al, Anat and Mot; next, the artisan deities; and last, the messenger deities. It is significant too that this four-level hierarchy coincided with some social hierarchies in Levantine society, including the king, the men of the palace, peasants and specialists, and finally, servants and slaves (Handy 1994; Niehr 1998: 25–32; also Sapin 1983; Zamora López 2006: 61–2). But perhaps even more important is that the political hierarchy – making servants and slaves depend on a higher status figure, which depends ultimately on the king – is extended from the king and his dynasty to deities (cf. Levine and de Tarragon 1984), who depended lastly on the supreme god El (see Figure 8.1 on p. 164).

In sum, the way in which the cosmic order was conceived in Ugarit reproduces the ideal of the patrimonial household and a personal bond between the different stages of the hierarchy (Handy 1994: 169–72; Thompson 1999: 168–78; Zamora López 2006: 61–2). L.K. Handy (1994: 169–70) affirms that 'the Syro-Palestinian perception of the cosmos also included human rule, which was incorporated into the theology along with bureaucratic divine rule. At the top of the organization was the ultimate divine authority of all of the cosmos, while at the bottom were human slaves.' Actually, such reference to a divine 'bureaucracy', extending to the human sphere through the king, is better understood in patrimonial terms as:

> a society structured as a hierarchy of households, one within another, of which the household of the supreme god is the most inclusive. He is king over all because he is the father of all. Each ruler, at any level of the hierarchy, is the master and father of his subordinates, who owe him filial support and service on a highly personal basis. Kingship and kinship are not in opposition to one another; they are two sides of the same coin. This is possible because kinship is not static, rooted in the facts of biology, but dynamic, employing the genealogical metaphor to represent all manner of social and political relations of authority and dependence. Thus the symbolism of the patriarchal household can be both a motif of literary discourse and a template for practical action. (Schloen 2001: 350)

The ubiquitous royal ideology in the ancient Near East, in particular the Old Babylonian monarchic ideal of the *šar mīšarim*, the 'just king', also present in Syro-Palestinian inscriptions and in Old Testament stories, characterising the monarchy with justice and righteousness as constitutive elements and represented by the obligation of protecting the widow, the orphan and the poor, in proper patronage terms, and guaranteeing a just social order, is to be perceived as well in patrimonial fashion.[32] The ultimate nature of such justice and righteousness does not originate in codified laws, but rather such laws come down from the gods to the king as a divine grace: establishing kingly justice and righteousness on earth is but the divine will fulfilled. In this sense, the subordination of the king to a divine figure reproduces the subordination and political loyalty scheme proper of the bond a client maintains with his patron: a good patron is a just and righteous patron, who protects his client, and whose expected behaviour brings honour and prestige upon his social persona. In the sphere of the representation of the divine, the notion of justice and righteousness is derived precisely from an earthly patron–client relation, expressed and represented as the cosmic order established by a godly father and guaranteed on earth by his client, the king, through rituals, but also by a behaviour emulating the gods. I shall not discuss, in this context, whether the mythical compositions from Ugarit (notably the Baʻal cycle and the legends of *Aqht* y de *Krt*) represent a 'script' for a cultic drama performed in the temples (as the consensus in Ugaritic studies maintain; cf. Parker 1997; Pardee 2002; Smith and Pitard 2009: 1–23, 35–67) or whether, on the contrary, they do not actually reflect cultic aspects of the Ugaritic religion, as argued by Liverani (1970; cf. also Wyatt 2005: 246–7). What is relevant here is that Ugaritic texts express a religious imagination anchored in a patrimonial order of the cosmos, which includes humanity and corresponds with the socio-political scheme of the kingdom of Ugarit.[33]

Liverani has suggested that in Late Bronze Age Syria-Palestine this monarchic ideology changed according to the transformation which occurred in the socio-political scenario around 1500 BCE. In effect, the appearance of a king related to the *maryannu* class, owning lands and with peasants working in them, represented a kind of political order which the ancient Near Eastern historiography has traditionally referred to as 'feudal', but which coincided best with the constitutive relations of patronage in society. The key term of the secular documentation of the period is the Akkadian *kittu*, in its connotation of 'loyalty', from its previous Old Babylonian denotation of 'justice, truth'.[34] In spite of this socio-political process, instances of divine and royal patronage are clearly identified in the epigraphic data from the period, as we have already shown.

The practice of establishing subordination treaties and the swearing of loyalty oaths, not only by Ḫatti, but by other political actors, and not only during the Late Bronze Age, but also during later periods, can be understood as a procedure involving the divine sphere through loyalty commitments and expectations of protection (McCarthy 1963; Weinfeld 1976; Magnetti 1978; Kalluveettil 1982; Tadmor 1982; Wiseman 1982; Christiansen and Devecchi 2012). Far from being mere political documents, treaties and loyalty oaths possessed a ritual and symbolical value for establishing a patrimonial order of alliance through personal bonds of patronage between a superior and an inferior party. In sum, the ideological and religious representation found in the corpus of ritual and political texts from the period manifests the order of the cosmos and the earthly realm building on the basics of socio-political structure. And this is clearly reflected in the ethnographic record of the Mediterranean, as J. Boissevain's (1977) study on the causal relation between social change in the island of Malta, order after patron–client networks, and Catholic religiosity, with its appeal to the intercession of saints, has shown, reflecting the same understanding of heavenly and earthly brokers; or further, the analysis of M. Caisson on popular religiosity in the Mediterranean region, according to which 'The religious practices and beliefs, at least on the European coast of the Mediterranean, present a complexity analogue to that described by the ethnology of clientelism in the same area' (Caisson 2001: 400; cf. also Testart 2006: 150–52). And analogies may be found too in the medieval period, as A. Testart (2006: 11) notes:

> Faith, which for today's man does not evoke but the belief in God, was a rather different thing in the Middle Ages: it was a ritual by which a man became the vassal of another, promising 'by his faith' he will be faithful. Everybody was faithful to his God as he was to his lord. The relation of fidelity was both secular and religious. And the same term 'lord', *dominus*, was applied both to the Lord of Heavens and the lord on earth, powerful master of a lordship. Such a correspondence, if not such an identity, between the forms of religious engagement and those of social engagement, go beyond the vocabulary into gesture: joined hands, which have today a religious meaning, were integrated in the medieval period into the ritual of vassalage, the dependent clasping his hands in those of his lord as a sign of submission.[35]

As on earth, so it is in the heavens. That seems to be the implicit structural scheme shaping the religious imagination in ancient Syria-Palestine and the exchanges between gods and humans: 'Honor, shame, and reciprocity are essential in understanding how the relationship between humanity and divinity was understood in the ancient Mediterranean and Near East' (Bolin 2004: 42).

* * *

Patrimonialism seemed to spread through all aspects of society in Late Bronze Age Syria-Palestine. Even more, the bonds of personal subordination, arranged in dyads, which could be integrated into a greater pyramidal network, established a form of socio-political articulation shaped by a particular behaviour and expression of how to be a master and how to be a servant. It is interesting to note in this context – although it would deserve a proper treatment – that the intermittence of foreign powers intervening in the Syro-Palestinian territory since the Early Bronze Age might have enabled a socio-political emulation of several of these powers but without constituting formally an institutionalisation of such characteristics, like the permanent rule over communities through the monopoly of coercion – in other words, state practice itself – as a native phenomenon. Precisely, the notion of 'elite emulation', as proposed by C. Higginbotham (1996; 2000), especially for Ramesside times in Palestine, is also useful to think of Amarna Syria-Palestine as a period of local emulation, especially of Egyptian features (i.e. epistolary phraseology), yet with a strong background on the local traditions of socio-politics, built on patrimonialism and patronage, as the main vehicle for expressing political hierarchical communication.

But whatever the reasons enabling patron–client relations in Syria-Palestine might have been, the preponderance of these relations in the region during this

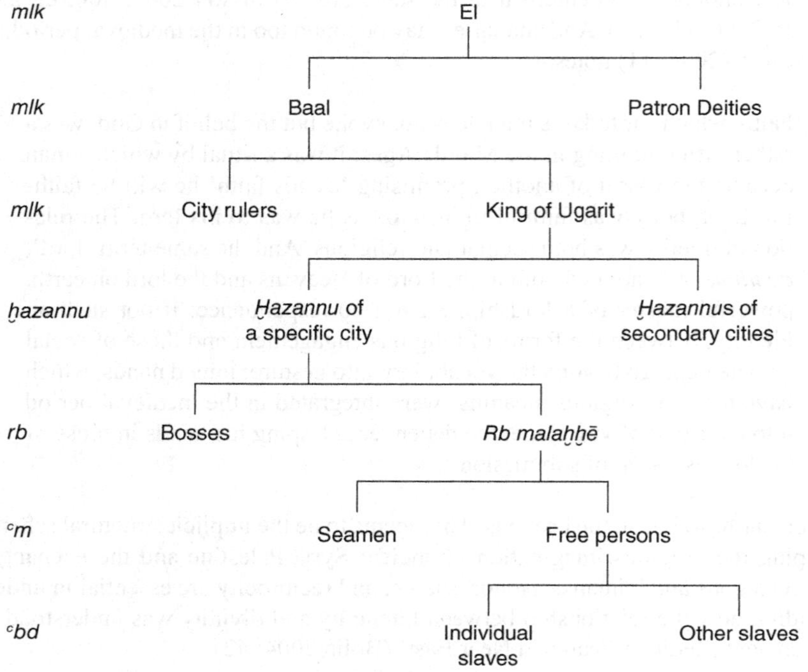


*Figure 8.1* The divine and human hierarchy according to the texts from Ugarit (adapted from L.K. Handy, *Among the Host of Heaven* (Winona Lake, IN: Eisenbrauns, 1994, p. 173).

period seem to be evident, not only as a vehicle for political praxis: we may affirm that the practice of patronage in Syria-Palestine created a native *political ontology* indicating how to behave politically, as a protecting master and as a protected servant, two basic interdependent socio-political poles whose expansion in society maintained the whole socio-political order.[36] In sum, patron–client relations produced a particular mode of political behaviour, or better a distinctive native *political culture* through which to interpret political events and religious dramas.

## Notes

1 EA 1:1–9, after Moran 1992: 1 (cf. also Knudtzon 1907: 60–61; Liverani 1999: 344; Rainey 2014: 59). An analogous patrimonial terminology is also found in the correspondence of the kingdom of Mari in the eighteenth century BCE; cf. Durand 1997: 383–98, 429–58, 458–94.

2 EA 2:1–5, after Moran 1992: 6 (cf. also Knudtzon 1907: 66–9; Liverani 1999: 347; Rainey 2014: 67).

3 EA 15, after Moran 1992: 38 (cf. also Knudtzon 1907: 124–7; Liverani 1999: 362; Rainey 2014: 129).

4 EA 17:21–9, 36–54, after Moran 1992: 41–2 (cf. also Knudtzon 1907: 132–5; Liverani 1999: 367; Rainey 2014: 135, 137).

5 EA 41:16–22, after Moran 1992: 114 (cf. also Knudtzon 1907: 300–301; Liverani 1999: 410; Rainey 2014: 359).

6 RS 17.132:3–18 (*PRU* IV, 35–6). In other political centres of Syria, like Emar, we also find a Hittite 'protectorate', accomplished through a subordination oath (*mamītu*; *CAD* $M_1$, 189–95); cf. Arnaud 1987.

7 RS 17.227 (*PRU* IV, 40–43) = *CTH* 47.

8 *CTH* 41 and 49; slightly adapted from Beckman 1996: 156, nn. 2 and 5.

9 Cf. Testart 2007: 219–20 *et passim*. Likewise, Weingrod (1977: 41) distinguishes between sociological studies of political clientelism and its articulation as a social system, and social anthropology studies of patronage as a social system, for instance, between landlords and tenants.

10 It is noteworthy that Schloen (2001: 313–16) understands Egypt as having been a patrimonial state and also rejects Liverani's (1967) proposal of the clash of political and ideological worldviews between Egyptians and Asiatic peoples. Of course, the patrimonial model is most valid for analysing the internal working of the Egyptian state (cf. Lehner 2000); yet, as for the Egyptian administration of Syria-Palestine, a state-like – impersonal, bureaucratic – dominance seems to have been active, as Liverani noted. Moreover, Assmann (2002: 91, 96–7, 100–101, 103–6) verified the existence of patron-client relations in Egypt during the First Intermediate Period (*c.* 2150–2040 BCE) in a context of weak state control; nonetheless, patronage relation did exist in Egypt in periods of strong central authority: cf. Eyre 2004; and especially Campagno 2014.

11 RS 17.116:21′–30′ (*PRU* IV, 133–4).

12 Slightly adapted from Beckman 1996: 121.

13 EA 257:7–19, after Moran 1992: 310 (cf. also Knudtzon 1907: 818–19; Liverani 1998: 122; Rainey 2014: 1041).

14 EA 320:16–25, after Moran 1992: 350 (cf. also Knudtzon 1907: 926–9; Liverani 1998: 71; Rainey 2014: 1195). A similar formulation is found in EA 316, 319, 321 and 322.

15 EA 286:9–13, after Moran 1992: 326 (cf. also Knudtzon 1907: 860–61; Liverani 1998: 95; Rainey 2014: 1107). The synecdoche 'the strong arm of the king' indicates a strong Egyptian influence on the scribes of the letters from Jerusalem and Tyre (Izre'el 1995a: 2416). Further on the Egyptian influence on the Akkadian texts from the fourteenth and thirteenth centuries BCE, cf. Cochavy-Rainey 1990. For uses of this phrase in biblical stories, cf. Hoffmeier 1986; Hess 1989: 253, 257.

16 EA 288:11–15, after Moran 1992: 331 (cf. also Knudtzon 1907: 868–9; Liverani 1998: 97; Rainey 2014: 1117). See also Hess 1989: 256f.

17 EA 88:42–5, after Moran 1992: 160–61 (cf. also Knudtzon 1907: 420–21; Liverani 1998: 180; Rainey 2014: 511). Probably, Rib-Hadda refers to the Egyptian relations with Byblos, active since the Middle Bronze Age; cf. Ahlström 1993: 160–74; and for the presence of patronage relations in Byblos at that period, see Flammini 2010.

18 EA 158, after Moran 1992: 244 (cf. also Knudtzon 1907: 642–5; Liverani 1998: 272–3; Rainey 2014: 787, 789). Rainey (2014: 787) translates ll. 20–21 of the letter, '[ú-a-m] *ur at-ta a-na pa-ni* [LUGAL EN]-*ia aš-ba-ta*' '[And lo]ok, you abide in the presence of [the king]', instead of 'you are in the personal service of the king', as Moran does. From the perspective of a personalised conception of politics active among the Levantine petty kings, Moran's translation makes more sense.

19 EA 42:15–26, after Moran 1992: 115–16 (cf. also Knudtzon 1907: 302–3; Liverani 1999: 411; Rainey 2014: 363).

20 EA 112:7–18, after Liverani 1998: 214 (cf. also Knudtzon 1907: 490–91; and Moran 1992: 186; Rainey 2014: 599).

21 EA 129:35–8, after Moran 1992: 209 (cf. also Knudtzon 1907: 548–9; Liverani 1998: 232; Rainey 2014: 667). On Rib-Hadda's strategic rhetoric, cf. the analysis in Pryke 2011.

22 EA 83:7–11, 14–16, after Moran 1992: 153 (cf. also Knudtzon 1907: 400–401; Liverani 1998: 189; Rainey 2014: 491).

23 Cf. also EA 71; 73; 76; 93.

24 Herman's (1995) study on the 'language of fidelity' in seventeenth-century France shows how a particular terminology was used as a means through which patrons and clients communicated their political intentions and aspirations, beyond the sincerity behind such intentions. This certainly contributes to analyse Aziru's expressions of loyalty to the Pharaoh. See further on this Jönsson 2000; David 2000.

25 According to Liverani (1983a: 45): 'It is difficult to point out a clear border between consciousness and unconsciousness in this interaction made up of misunderstandings and of limited understanding. The semantic equivocality proceeding from inadequate translation is generally unconscious: each of the two different lexical systems is so deeply imbedded in the "world view" of its bearer that he cannot even perceive that the lexical system and world view of his dialogue-partner are different. But sometimes an additional use of equivocality takes place, wilful in character, aimed at a cunning exploitation of the possibilities offered by linguistic ambiguity (and especially of translation ambiguities) in order better to resist the arguments of our dialogue-partner, or to better support our own arguments.'

26 Cf. the reflections in Geertz 1983, on the leader's need of displaying charisma and prestige in order to maintain internal political power.

27 EA 149:17–27, slightly adapted after Moran 1992: 236 (cf. also Knudtzon 1907: 616–17; Liverani 1998: 155; Rainey 2014: 753).

28 EA 150:4–21, slightly adapted after Moran 1992: 237 (cf. also Knudtzon 1907: 620–21; Liverani 1998: 156–7; Rainey 2014: 759). The reference to the possibility of 'being alive' (*ba-la-ṭi-šu*) and drinks water is probably related to proper instances of hospitality.

29 The translation follows Liverani 1998: 246–8. The same response is found in EA 201:11–23; 202:7–18; 203:9–19; 204:9–20; 205:9–18; 206:9–17 (cf. Knudtzon 1907: 734–41; Moran 1992: 277–80; Rainey 2014: 912–23).

30 EA 195:24–32, after Liverani 1998: 251 (cf. also Knudtzon 1907: 722–33; Moran 1992: 273; Rainey 2014: 897). See further EA 76:17; 132:19–21; 246: rev. 5–10.

31 Rainey (2003: 175) suggests that the distinction between *ḫabiru* and Suteans comes from the different social extraction of both elements: the Suteans are semi-nomads, while *ḫabiru* are 'para-social' (Rowton) elements, at times hired as mercenaries; see further on Sutean warfare, Vidal 2010.

32 Cf. Liverani 1971. In Ugarit, although exceptionally, the couple *ṣdq mšr* is attested in a list of gods (RS 24.271 = *Ug* V, 585) and also the Ugaritic terms *ṣdq yšr* (KTU 1.14:12–13), related semantically to the Hebrew *ṣedāqāh w$^e$mišpāt* ('righteousness and justice'), present in the Old Testament (cf. Psalm 33:5; 72:1–2; 99:4; etc.), and to the Akkadian *kittum u mīšarum* ('truth and justice') in Mesopotamia; cf. Weinfeld 1995:

25–56. In Late Bronze Age Syria-Palestine, according to Liverani (1971: 61–2), the ideology of the 'just king' seems to be eclipsed. See further the studies by Fensham 1962; Niehr 1997; Thompson 2007.

33 Cf. further Wyatt 2001; 2007; for a characterisation of north-west Semitic monarchy. See also Petersen 1998: Chapters 1–4, for a comparative evaluation of Ugaritic compositions and the Psalms.

34 Cf. Liverani 1971: 61–2. On the semantic variation of the Akkadian *kittu*, cf. Knudtzon 1915: 1441: 'a) Treue . . . ; b) Recht . . . ; c) Wahrheit . . . ; d) Bund . . . '; *CAD* K, 468: 'truth, justice, correct procedures, loyalty, fidelity'. For connotations of 'loyalty' in the political documents of the Late Bronze, cf., for instance, EA 47:21; 51: rev. 12; 68:11; 73:42; 74:7, 11; 101:38; 105:83; 106:4; 107:9; 108:22; 109:42; 114:54, 67; 116:29, 55; 118:56; 119:25, 45; 127:25; 132:9; 138:87; 155:48; 180:18; 185:71; 189:15; 192:4; 198:10; 241:19; 242:5; 243:4; 246:4; RS 17.227:15 y 43; 17.340: r. 15′. See also Thompson 2005: 323–5.

35 The idea that particular religious beliefs correspond to particular social orders is of course old, and may be traced back at least to Durkheim (1993 [1912]).

36 In effect, G. Lenclud (2001: 295–300) refers to a *psychologie du protecteur* and a *psychologie du protégé*, to characterise patronage. See also the ethnographic analysis in Johnson 1997.

# CONCLUSIONS

The presentation and arguments in the preceding chapters have attempted to show that perspectives, insights and methodologies proper of ethnography and social anthropology can constitute a legitimate way of writing history, an anthropological history. The historical realities of the ancient Near East – we should remember – are culturally alien to us, in spite of the Near Eastern heritage claimed by the Western world for collective memory and cultural identity reasons.[1] The latter is, from an anthropological perspective, what the Western world finds in the ancient Near East as a place and time of origins does not invalidate the cultural otherness of ancient Near Eastern cultures and civilisations, and this we should keep in mind when approaching the cultural remains (textual compositions and records). These cultures and civilisations have therefore been interpreted and understood through analytical strategies able to recognise cultural difference as historical data on its own. Anthropological perspectives allow for this, at least in their epistemological makeup and interpretative intentions, bridging cultural distances that, in our case, temporal and spatial distance have produced. Interpreting an ancient text, codified in an ancient and dead language belonging to a now non-existent social world, demands a predisposition akin to that of the ethnographer documenting an alien culture. In both instances, the foreign language must be understood, details of the socio-cultural context acting as a framework for social practices must be attended, and the sense of such practices for the actors under study must be deciphered, together with what constitutes the native worldview. Apart from the obvious statement that the ethnographer may (and must) conduct fieldwork and that the ancient Near Eastern historian has only access to the remaining written and archaeological artefacts left by long-gone societies, we may affirm that both disciplines share a common epistemology to analyse society and its actors, although one in the present and the other in the distant past.

If we summarise the analyses and discussions presented in this study, a general outline of the different yet inter-connected aspects of Late Bronze Age Syro-Palestinian polities can be presented.

Syria-Palestine between the sixteenth and twelfth centuries BCE is at the very centre of the territorial expansion of the great powers of the period. Both Egypt and Ḫatti – and, in a modest way, Mittani – conquered and ruled the Levantine lands, interacting in their own way with the small local polities. Precisely, during the Amarna period, a constant flow of interaction between the Great Kings is documented, an 'international' diplomacy that, through its particular configuration, implied a commercial exchange between distant regions, the creation of inter-dynastic marriage alliances and a traffic of specialists and messengers. In this socio-political and cultural context, patron–client relations found a key expression through a variety of manifestations according to the involved actors.

Petty Syro-Palestinian kings would conceive of the expansive territorial powers like Egypt and Ḫatti and also the individual and collective subjects of subordination in exclusive terms of patrons and clients. In fact, all the population of the Levant would have operated after a socio-political conception crafted according to the differential place they occupied in a network of personalised ties of kinship and patronage.

The kingdom of Ḫatti, by means of an analogous socio-political conception of politics and power, channelled the state's rule over northern Levantine polities employing an operative logic and practices proper to patronage and patrimonialism. In effect, it is Ḫatti's political and military might that allows the Hittite king to act like a powerful patron over his Syrian subjects, imposing the rules of political interaction according to his will and the geopolitical interests of the kingdom. The client king in this relation was actually unable to question or challenge such imposition and had no other option than to submit himself to the expectations of the political reciprocity of the relation.

Egyptian domination of Syria-Palestine differed from Hittite rule: the Pharaoh did not share the scheme of reciprocity with his Levantine subjects. Unlike the Hittite king, behaving politically through a patrimonial conception and patronage relations to manifest the monopoly of coercion, the Egyptian king was unwilling even to consider a reciprocity of any kind, exerting instead a one-directional dominion over Syro-Palestinian petty kings, who would conceive of the Pharaoh as a powerful and distant patron who was reluctant to compensate the loyalty of his subjects with words and material protection. Little could the petty kings have done before this situation in which the political culture of the Levant was unacknowledged by the Pharaoh, but to complain, as we read in the Amarna correspondence. Small political figures like Rib-Hadda did question in fact Pharaoh's lack of proper response to petitions of assistance and political attention. However, it is not the foreign rule that is being questioned here, but only the absence of realisation of what is expected in a lord-servant interaction, from a political ontology of patronage.

Thus, the interaction between great kings, and that between great and petty kings, evidences a particular inter-subjectivity, anchored at the same time in shared global conceptions and in divergent worldviews: the Egyptian ethnocentric centralism, the pluralist centralism of great kings in Southwest Asia and the poly-centralism of the small Syro-Palestinian kings. In each of these perspectives, a differentiated representation of the political other was crafted, with each party having a specific place in the regional political hierarchy.[2]

The analysis of these historical and sociological situations refers too to scrutinising the aforementioned social practices and the structures making them possible. Kinship practices, with its instances of reciprocity and hospitality, transcend the nuclear family or the community forged by biological ties, in order to express the backbone of socio-politics. In the world of the Late Bronze Age, and especially in Syria-Palestine, such practices constituted a key factor in the political organisation of polities and also in their interaction. The available documentation evidences situations in which Syro-Palestinian monarchies, notably in the southern Levant, appear more to follow tribal instances of political sociability, with a chief subject of being seriously contested or disputed by his community, but also by the foreign powers ruling over him. That the king was questioned seemed to notably constrain the reach of his concrete political power. In effect, in Late Bronze Palestine, if we attend to the Amarna notices, state formation is highly disputable, given the weak political figure these kings represent, apart from material constraints. However, when we perceive the political world of Syria-Palestine as patrimonial, in which a kingdom (what is often called a 'state' by ancient Near Eastern scholarship) is not only organised as, but also perceives itself as an extended kinship group, ruled by a 'father' with authority over the members of the community, the native monarchy appears more as constituted by a *primus inter pares* and his kin rather than by an elite with the proper monopoly of coercion over the rest of society. Of course, major kingdoms like Ugarit are not mere chiefdoms societies; but when compared to other proper states, like Egypt or Ḫatti and to the urban centres in Mesopotamia, its 'statehood' needs to be relativised and tailored according to the socio-political practices that seem to be hegemonic in society, instead of attending primarily to features like public buildings or administrative records as state formation indicators, since such state-like features might indeed be the product of a socio-political practice like patrimonialism.

Political power in Syria-Palestine is better defined as dependent on a network of inter-personal relations, a hierarchy of personal loyalties, in which authority is conditioned by instances of asymmetrical reciprocity, especially in Palestine. In sum, patron–client relations constituted the conceptual, symbolic and socio-political matrix of the Syro-Palestinian societies' ontology. At the same time, such ontology was manifested, performed and reproduced in a dynamic of patron and client.

Mario Liverani (1967: 16) would conclude in his seminal study on Syro-Palestinian politics: 'the El Amarna period was not a period of particular political crisis in the Syro-Palestinian zone under Egyptian control: the situations to which the letters refer did not represent other than normality.' The petitions and complaints, the loyalty proclamations and the impersonal commands explicit in the Amarna correspondence did not express administrative inefficiency by Egypt due to an internal situation of political crisis or the neglect for the imperial periphery, as ancient Near Eastern scholarship affirmed around the mid-twentieth century. These Amarna notices indicate instead a clash of socio-political worldviews, a difference in political ontologies between Egypt and the Levant. The key to understanding the working of native politics in Syria-Palestine rests in attending to the personal components of relationships, the lack of impersonal offices *qua* bureaucracy, and focusing on what is done, what is said to be done and how it is done; namely the practices themselves and their representations in letters, treaties and edicts, rather than detecting only an alleged institutional framework of socio-political practice.

The Amarna correspondence gives anthropological historians evidence for socio-political conditions in the region of the Levant, rather than particular historical events. The letters expose the procedures carried out by the petty kings in order to survive as political actors, and they represent, although as performed rather than explicitly, the native value system driving interpersonal bonds. The lack of impersonal administrative behaviour by these petty kings – beyond some native emulation of Egyptian formulas and phraseology – is also informative of the political worldview in Late Bronze Age Syria-Palestine.

Patronage as an interpretive concept is also useful to shed light on a socio-political dynamic in the Levant, which seems to be recurrent in several periods of its history, many of which were marked by successive imperial domination under Assyrians, Babylonians, Persians, Greeks, Romans, Arabs and Ottomans – foreign masters who actually used patronage as a means of domination and control of the local society.[3]

The recurrence of patron–client structures in the region should not lead us, of course, to postulate some kind of political or cultural essentialism. Yet we cannot underestimate either the presence of patronage in the history of Syria-Palestine, as it was a key factor structuring society. Its recurrence through many periods might be explained by its flexibility in adapting the patron–client dyad to articulate domestic politics, but also regional control, and at the same time representing the functioning of the divine hierarchies. But apart from patronage as a concrete socio-political phenomenon, patronage as an analytical concept is a most effective tool for understanding how people in the ancient Levant behaved politically and imagined politics through a vertical hierarchy of patrons and clients.

## Notes

1 On this subject, cf. Maier 1995; Liverani 2013: 3–5.

2 On poly-centralism in the Middle East and in the Levant, cf. LaBianca 2009. On the anthropology of intersubjectivity, in relation with the particular ontologies that interaction generates, cf. the formulations in Jackson 1998: 1–36.

3 On the long-term history of Palestine, cf. Knauf 1987; Giardina, Liverani and Scarcia Amoretti 1990.

# BIBLIOGRAPHY


Abdul-Kader, M. 1959. 'The Administration of Syria-Palestine during the New Kingdom'. *Annales du Service des Antiquités de l'Egypte* 56: 105–37.

Abel, F.M. 1967 [1933/1938]. *Géographie de la Palestine. Tome 1: Géographie physique et historique, Tome 2: Géographie politique. Les villes*. Paris: Gabalda Éditeurs.

Abrahamian, E. 1975. 'European Feudalism and Middle Eastern Despotism'. *Science & Society* 39: 129–56.

Abulafia, D. 2011. *The Great Sea: A Human History of the Mediterranean*. Cambridge: Cambridge University Press.

Ackerman, S. 2002. 'The Personal Is the Political: Covenantal and Affectionate Love (*'āhēb, 'hăbâ*) in the Hebrew Bible'. *VT* 52: 437–58.

Aharoni, Y. 1979. *The Land of the Bible: A Historical Geography* (Rev. and enlarged edn). Philadelphia, PA: The Westminster Press.

Aḥituv, S. 1978. 'Economic Factors in the Egyptian Conquest of Canaan'. *IEJ* 28: 93–105.

Ahlström, G.W. 1993. *The History of Ancient Palestine from the Palaeolithic Period to Alexander's Conquest* (ed. by D.V. Edelman; JSOTSup, 146). Sheffield: Sheffield Academic Press.

Akkermans, M.M.G. and G.M. Schwartz. 2003. *The Archaeology of Syria: From Complex Hunter-Gatherers to Early Urban Societies (ca. 16,000–300 BC)*. Cambridge: Cambridge University Press.

Albera, D. 1999. 'The Mediterranean as an Anthropological Laboratory'. *Anales de la Fundación Joaquín Costa* 16: 215–32.

Albera, D. and A. Blok. 2001. 'Introduction: The Mediterranean as an Ethnological Field of Study: A Retrospective'. In *L'anthropologie de la Méditerranée/Anthropology of the Mediterranean*, D. Albera, A. Blok and C. Bromberger (eds). Paris: Maisonneuve and Larose-MMSH: 15–37.

Albera, D., A. Blok and C. Bromberger (eds). 2001. *L'anthropologie de la Méditerranée/ Anthropology of the Mediterranean*. Paris: Maisonneuve and Larose-MMSH.

Albera, D. and M. Tozy (eds). 2006a. *La Méditerranée des anthropologues: Fractures, filiations, contiguïtés*. Paris: Maisonneuve and Larose.

Albera, D. and M. Tozy. 2006b. 'Introduction: Fractures, filiations, contiguïtés'. In *La Méditerranée des anthropologues. Fractures, filiations, contiguïtés*, D. Albera and M. Tozy (eds). Paris: Maisonneuve and Larose: 7–39.

Albright, W.F. 1937. 'The Egyptian Correspondence of Abimilki, Prince of Tyre'. *JEA* 23: 190–203.

Albright, W.F. 1942. 'A Case of Lèse-Majesté in Pre-Israelite Lachish, with Some Remarks on the Israelite Conquest'. *BASOR* 87: 32–8.
Albright, W.F. 1975. 'The Amarna Letters from Palestine'. In *CAH*[3], II/2: 98–116.
Aldred, C. 1970. 'The Foreign Gifts Offered to Pharaoh'. *JEA* 56: 105–16.
Aldred, C. 1975. 'Egypt: The Amarna Period and the End of the Eighteenth Dynasty'. In *CAH*[3], II/2: 49–97.
Aldred, C. 1988. *Akhenaten, King of Egypt*. New York: Thames & Hudson, 1988.
Almond, G. 1956. 'Comparative Political Systems'. *Journal of Politics* 18: 391–409.
Alt, A. 1959a. 'Hettitische und ägyptische Herrschaftsordnung in unterworfenen Gebieten' [1949]. In *KS*, III: 99–106.
Alt, A. 1959b. 'Das Stützpunktsystem der Pharaonen an der phönikischen Küste und im syrischen Binnenland' [1950]. In *KS*, III: 107–40.
Alt, A. 1959c. 'Völker und Staaten Syriens im frühen Altertums' [1936]. In *KS*, III: 20–49.
Alt, A. 1959d. 'Hohe Beamte in Ugarit' [1953]. In *KS*, III: 186–97.
Alt, A. 1959e. 'Menschen ohne Namen' [1950]. In *KS*, III: 198–213.
Altman, A. 2003. 'Who Took the Oath on the Vassal Treaty: Only the Vassal King or also the Suzerain? – The Hittite Evidence'. *ZABR* 9: 178–84.
Altman, A. 2004. *The Historical Prologue of the Hittite Vassal Treaties: An Inquiry into the Concepts of Hittite Interstate Law* (BISNELC). Bar-Ilan: Bar-Ilan University Press.
Altman, A. 2012. *Tracing the Earliest Recorded Concepts of International Law: The Ancient Near East (2500–330 BCE)* (Legal History Library, 8/Studies in the History of International Law, 4). Leiden: Martinus Nijhoff.
Anbar, M. 1991. *Les tribus amurrites de Mari* (OBO, 108). Friburg: Universitätsverlag/Göttingen: Vandenhoeck & Ruprecht.
Anderson, B. 2006. *Imagined Communities: Reflections on the Origin and Spread of Nationalism* (Rev. edn). London: Verso.
Antoun, R. 1979. *Low-Key Politics: Local-Level Leadership and Change in the Middle East*. Albany: State University of New York Press.
Appadurai, A. 1986. 'Introduction: Commodities and the Politics of Value'. In *The Social Life of Things: Commodities in Cultural Perspective*, A. Appadurai (ed.). Cambridge: Cambridge University Press: 3–63.
Archi, A. 1977. 'Il 'feudalesimo' ittita'. *SMEA* 18: 7–18.
Arnaud, D. 1982. 'Une lettre du roi de Tyr au roi d'Ugarit: milieux d'affaires et de culture en Syrie à la fin de l'âge du Bronce Récent'. *Syria* 59: 101–7.
Arnaud, D. 1987. 'La Syrie du moyen-Euphrate sous le protectorat hittite: Contrats de droit privé'. *AuOr* 5: 211–41.
Arnaud, D. 1991. *Textes syriens de l'âge du Bronce Recent* (AULAOS, 1). Sabadell: AUSA.
Artzi, P. 1964. ''Vox Populi' in the El Amarna Tablets'. *RA* 58: 159–66.
Artzi, P. 2000. 'The Diplomatic Service in Action: The Mitanni File'. In *Amarna Diplomacy: The Beginning of International Relations*, R. Cohen and R. Westbrook (eds). Baltimore, MD: The Johns Hopkins University Press: 205–211, 264–5.
Aruz, J. 2008. 'The Art of Exchange'. In *Beyond Babylon: Art, Trade, and Diplomacy in the Second Millennium B.C.*, J. Aruz, K. Benzel and J.M. Evans (eds). New York: The Metropolitan Museum of Art: 387–94.
Asad, T. 1986. 'The Concept of Cultural Translation in British Social Anthropology'. In *Writing Culture: The Poetics and Politics of Ethnography*, J. Clifford and G.E. Marcus (eds). Berkeley: University of California Press: 141–64.

Assmann, J. 2002. *The Mind of Egypt: History and Meaning in the Time of the Pharaohs*. Cambridge, MA: Harvard University Press [orig. German edn 1996].

Astour, M.C. 1981. 'Ugarit and the Great Powers'. In *Ugarit in Retrospect: Fifty Years of Ugarit and Ugaritic*, C.H. Gordon (ed.). Winona Lake, IN: Eisenbrauns: 3–29.

Astour, M.C. 1995. 'Overland Trade Routes in Ancient Western Asia'. In *Civilizations of the Ancient Near East*, J.M. Sasson (ed.). New York: Scribner's Sons, III: 1401–20.

Aubet, M.E. 2007. *Comercio y colonialismo en el Próximo Oriente antiguo. Los antecedentes coloniales del III y II milenios a.C.* Barcelona: Bellaterra.

Auffarth, C. 1992. 'Protecting Strangers: Establishing a Fundamental Value in the Religions of the Ancient Near East and Ancient Greece'. *Numen* 39: 193–216.

Avruch, K. 2000. 'Reciprocity, Equality, and Status-Anxiety in the Amarna Letters'. In *Amarna Diplomacy: The Beginning of International Relations*, R. Cohen and R. Westbrook (eds). Baltimore, MD: The Johns Hopkins University Press: 154–64, 256–8.

Axtell, J. 1979. 'Ethnohistory: An Historian's Viewpoint'. *Ethnohistory* 26: 1–13.

Bahrani, Z. 2008. *Rituals of War: The Body and Violence in Mesopotamia*. New York: Zone Books.

Bailey, F.G. 1972. 'Conceptual Systems in the Study of Politics'. *Rural Politics and Social Change in the Middle East*, R. Antoun and I. Harik (eds). Bloomington: Indiana University Press: 21–44.

Balandier, G. 1972. *Political Anthropology*. Harmondsworth: Penguin Books [orig. French edn 1967].

Balazote, A. 1998. 'El debate entre formalistas y sustantivistas y sus proyecciones en la Antropología Económica'. In *Antropología económica: Ficciones y producciones del hombre económico*, H.H. Trinchero (ed.). Buenos Aires: Eudeba: 145–66.

Balza, M.E. 2008. 'I trattati ittiti: Sigillatura, testimoni, collocazione'. In *I diritti del mondo cuneiforme (Mesopotamia e regioni adiacenti, ca. 2500–500 a.C.)*, M. Liverani and C. Mora (eds). Pavia: Istituto Universitario di Studi Superiori di Pavia: 387–418.

Banfield, E.C. 1958. *The Moral Basis of a Backward Society*.Glencoe, IL: The Free Press.

Barreyra, D. 2006. ''Maten a su señor'. Los oscuros orígenes del reino de Amurru en el período de El-Amarna'. *Estudios de Asia y África* 41: 255–76.

Barthes, R. 1977. *Elements of Semiology*. New York: Hill & Wang [orig. French edn 1964].

Beal, R.H. 1995. 'Hittite Military Organization'. In *Civilizations of the Ancient Near East*, J.M. Sasson (ed.). New York: Scribner's Sons, I: 545–54.

Beckman, G. 1995. 'Royal Ideology and State Administration in Hittite Anatolia'. In *Civilizations of the Ancient Near East*, J.M. Sasson (ed.). New York: Scribner's Sons, I: 529–43.

Beckman, G. 1996. *Hittite Diplomatic Texts* (WAWSBL, 7). Atlanta, GA: Scholars Press.

Beckman, G. 2003. 'International Law in the Second Millennium: The Late Bronze Age'. In *A History of Ancient Near Eastern Law* (HdO, 72), R. Westbrook (ed.). Leiden: E.J. Brill, I: 753–74.

Beckman, G. 2006. 'Hittite Treaties and the Development of the Cuneiform Treaty Tradition'. In *Die deuteronomistichen Geschichtwerke: Redaktions – und religionsgeschichtliche Perspektiven zur 'Deuteronomismus'– Diskussion in Tora und Vorderen Propheten*, M. Witte, K. Schmid, D. Prechel and J.C. Gertz (eds). Berlin: W. de Gruyter: 279–301.

Beckman, G. 2013. 'Foreigners in the Ancient Near East'. *JAOS* 133: 203–15.

Befu, H. 1977. 'Social Exchange'. *Annual Review of Anthropology* 6: 255–81.

Belmonte Marín, J.A. 2005. 'Los dialectos acadios y su presencia en Siria-Palestina'. In *Escrituras y lenguas del Mediterráneo en la antigüedad*, G. Carrasco Serrano y J.C. Oliva Mompeán (coord.). Cuenca: Ediciones de la Universidad de Castilla-La Mancha: 149–89.

Bender, D.R. 1967. 'A Refinement of the Concept of Household: Families, Co-Residence, and Domestic Functions'. *American Anthropologist* NS 69: 493–504.

Bernabé, A. and J.A. Álvarez-Pedrosa (eds). 2004. *Historia y leyes de los hititas. Textos del Reino Medio y del Imperio Nuevo* (Akal/Oriente, 8). Madrid: Akal.

Berridge, G. 2000. 'Amarna Diplomacy: A Full-Fledged Diplomatic System?'. In *Amarna Diplomacy: The Beginning of International Relations*, R. Cohen and R. Westbrook (eds). Baltimore, MD: The Johns Hopkins University Press: 212–24, 265–7.

Bienkowski, P. 1989. 'Prosperity and Decline in LBA Canaan: A Reply to Leibowitz and Knapp'. *BASOR* 275: 59–61.

Bittel, K. 1970. *Hattusha: The Capital of the Hittites*. New York: Oxford University Press.

Black, J. 1972. 'Tyranny as a Strategy for Survival in an 'Egalitarian' Society: Lurid Facts versus an Anthropological Mystique'. *Man* NS 7: 614–34.

Black–Michaud, J. 1975. *Cohesive Force: Feud in the Mediterranean and the Middle East*. Oxford: Basil Blackwell.

Bleiberg, E.L. 1995. 'The Economy of Ancient Egypt'. In *Civilizations of the Ancient Near East*, J.M. Sasson (ed.). New York: Scribner's Sons, III: 1373–85.

Bleiberg, E.L. 1996. *The Official Gift in Ancient Egypt*. Norman: University of Oklahoma Press.

Bloch, M. 1989. *The Feudal Society. Vol. 2: Social Classes and Political Organization*. London: Routledge, 1989 [orig. French edn 1940].

Bloch, M. 1992. *The Historian's Craft*. Manchester: Manchester University Press [orig. French edn 1949].

Blok, A. 1969. 'South Italian Agro-Towns'. *CSSH* 11: 121–35.

Blok, A. 1974. *The Mafia of a Sicilian Village, 1860–1960: A Study of Violent Peasant Entrepreneurs*. Oxford: Basil Blackwell.

Blok, A. 1981. 'Rams and Billy-Goats: A Key to the Mediterranean Code of Honour'. *Man* NS 16: 427–40.

Blok, A. 2001. 'Patronage, 'Networking' and the Social Context'. In *L'anthropologie de la Méditerranée/Anthropology of the Mediterranean*, D. Albera, A. Blok and C. Bromberger (eds). Paris: Maisonneuve/Larose-MMSH: 351–4.

Bohannan, P. 1956. 'On the Use of Native Language Categories in Ethnology'. *American Anthropologist* 58: 557.

Boissevain, J. 1966. 'Patronage in Sicily'. *Man* NS 1: 18–33.

Boissevain, J. 1977. 'When the Sainst Go Marching Out: Reflections on the Deline of Patronage in Malta'. In *Patrons and Clients in Mediterranean Societies*, E. Gellner and J. Waterbury (eds). London: Duckworth: 81–96.

Boissevain, J. 1979. 'Towards a Social Anthropology of the Mediterranean [+ Comments and Reply]'. *CA* 20: 81–93.

Bolin, T.M. 2004. 'The Role of Exchange in Ancient Mediterranean Religion and Its Implications for Reading Genesis 18–19'. *JSOT* 29: 37–56.

Boltanski, A. 2007. 'Un grammaire des comportaments clientélaires. Une exemple des relations patron clients dans la deuxième moitié du XVIe siècle'. In *Clientèle guerrière, clientèle foncière et clientèle électorale: Histoire et anthropologie*, V. Lécrivain (ed.). Dijon: Éditions Universitaires de Dijon: 115–35.

Bonte, P., É. Conte and P. Dresch. (eds). 2001. *Emirs et presidents. Figures de la parente et du politique dans le monde arabe*. Paris: Centre National de la Recherche Scientifique.

Bordreuil, P. 1981. 'Production-pouvoir-parenté dans le royaume d'Ougarit (14ème–13ème siècle av. J.C. environ'. In *Production, pouvoir et parenté dans le monde mediterranéen: De Sumer à nos jours*, C.-H. Breteau, C. Lacoste-Dujardin, C. Lefebure and N. Zanolli (eds). Paris: P. Geuthner, 1981: 117–31.

Bordreuil, P. and A. Caquot. 1980. 'Les textes en cunéiformes alphabétiques découverts en 1978 à Ibn Hani'. *Syria* 57: 343–73.

Bottéro, J. 1954. *Le problème des Ḫabiru à la 4e rencontre assyriologique internationale* (Cahiers de la Societé asiatique, 12). Paris: Imprimerie Nationale.

Boudou, B. 2012. 'Éléments pour une anthropologie politique de l'hospitalité'. *Revue MAUSS* 40: 267–84.

Bourdieu, P. 1977. *Outline of a Theory of Practice* (Cambridge Studies in Social and Cultural Anthropology, 16). Cambridge: Cambridge University Press [orig. French edn, 1972].

Bourdieu, P. 1992a. *The Logic of Practice*. Stanford, CA: Stanford University Press.

Bourdieu, P. 1992b. 'Rites as Acts of Institution'. In *Honor and Grace in Anthropology*, J. Peristiany and J. Pitt-Rivers (eds). Cambridge: Cambridge University Press: 79–90.

Bourdieu, P. 1994. 'Rethinking the State: Genesis and Structure of the Bureaucratic Field'. *Sociological Theory* 12: 1–18.

Bourdieu, P., J.-C. Chamboredon and J.-C. Passeron. 1991. *The Craft of Sociology: Epistemological Preliminaries*. Berlin: W. de Gruyter.

Bournazel, E. and J.-P. Poly (eds). 1998. *Les féodalités* (Histoire générale des systèmes politiques). Paris: Presses Universitaires de France.

Boutruche, R. 1968. *Seigneurie et féodalité. I: Le premier âge: Des liens d'homme à homme*. Paris: Éditions Montaigne.

Boyer, G. 1955. 'La place des textes d'Ugarit dans l'histoire de l'ancien droit oriental'. In *Le palais royal d'Ugarit. Vol. 3* (Mission de Ras Shamra, 6), C. Schaeffer (ed.). Paris: Imprimerie Nationale, 283–308.

Braudel, F. 1958. 'Histoire et sciences sociales: la longue durée'. *Annales: Economies–Sociétés–Civilisations* 13: 725–53.

Braudel, F. 1972. *The Mediterranean and the Mediterranean World in the Age of Philip II. 2 Vols.* London, Collins [translation from the 2nd French edn 1966].

Bresson, A. 2005. 'Ecology and Beyond: The Mediterranean Paradigm'. In *Rethinking the Mediterranean*, W.V. Harris (ed.). Oxford: Oxford University Press, 94–114.

Briant, P. 2002. 'L'État, la terre et l'eau entre Nil et Syr-Darya: Remarques introductives'. *Annales: Histoire, Sciences Sociales* 57: 517–29.

Briend, J. and M.-J. Seux. 1977. *Textes du Proche-Orient ancient et histoire d'Israël*. Paris: Éditions du Cerf.

Briend, J., R. Lebrun and É. Puech. 1994. *Tratados y juramentos en el Antiguo Oriente Próximo* (Documentos en torno a la Biblia, 23). Estella: Verbo Divino [orig. French edn 1992].

Briquet, J.-L. y F. Sawicki (eds). 1998. *Le clientélisme politique dans les sociétés contemporaines*. Paris: Presses Universitaires de France.

Bryan, B. 2000. 'The Egyptian Perspective on Mitanni'. In *Amarna Diplomacy: The Beginning of International Relations*, R. Cohen and R. Westbrook (eds). Baltimore, MD: The Johns Hopkins University Press: 71–84, 244–47.

Bryan, B. 2003. 'The Eighteenth Dynasty before the Amarna Period (c. 1550–1352 BC)'. In *The Oxford History of Ancient Egypt*, I. Shaw (ed.). Oxford: Oxford University Press: 218–71.

Bryce, T. 2002. *Life and Society in the Hittite World*. Oxford: Oxford University Press.

Bryce, T. 2003. *Letters of the Great Kings of the Ancient Near East: The Royal Correspondence of the Late Bronze Age*. London: Routledge.

Bryce, T. 2005. *The Kingdom of the Hittites* (2nd edn). Oxford: Oxford University Press.

Bryce, T. 2014. *Ancient Syria: A Three Thousand Year History*. Oxford: Oxford University Press.

Buccellati, G. 1967. *Cities and Nations of Ancient Syria: An Essay on Political Institutions with Special Reference to the Israelite Kingdoms* (Studi Semitici, 26). Roma: Istituto di Studi del Vicino Oriente – Università di Roma.

Buccellati, G. 2013. *Alle origini della politica: La formazione e la crescita dello stato in Siro-Mesopotamia* (Il paese delle quatro rive). Milano: Jaca Book.

Buchholz, H.-G. 1988. 'Der Metallhandel des Zweiten Jahrtausends im Mittelmeerraum'. In *Society and Economy in the Eastern Mediterranean* (OLA, 23), M. Heltzer and E. Lipinski (eds). Leuven: Peeters: 187–228.

Buckley, T. 1988. 'Kroeber's Theory of Culture Areas and the Ethnology of Northwestern California'. *Anthropological Quarterly* 61: 15–26.

Bunimovitz, S. 1993. 'The Study of Complex Societies: The Material Culture of Late Bronze Age Canaan as a Case Study'. In *Biblical Archaeology Today, 1990: Proceedings of the Second International Congress on Biblical Archaeology, Jerusalem, June 1990*, A. Biran and J. Aviram (eds). Jerusalem: Israel Exploration Society: 443–51.

Bunimovitz, S. 1994a. 'The Problem of Human Resources in Late Bronze Age Palestine and Its Socioeconomic Implications'. *UF* 26: 1–20.

Bunimovitz, S. 1994b. 'Socio-Political Transformations in the Central Hill Country in the Late Bronze-Iron I Transition'. In *From Nomadism to Monarchy: Archaeological and Historical Aspects of Early Israel*, I. Finkelstein y N. Na'aman (eds). Jerusalem: Israel Exploration Society: 179–202.

Bunimovitz, S. 1995. 'On the Edge of Empires – Late Bronze Age (1500–1200 BCE)'. In *The Archaeology of Society in the Holy Land*, T.E. Levy (ed.). New York: Facts on File: 320–31.

Bunnens, G. 1982. 'Pouvoirs locaux et pouvoirs dissidents en Syrie au IIe millénaire avant notre ère'. In *Les pouvoirs locaux en Mésopotamie et dans les régions adjacentes*, A. Finet (ed.). Bruxelles: Institut des Hautes Études de Belgique: 118–37.

Burguière, A. 2006. 'L'anthropologie historique'. In *La nouvelle histoire*, J. Le Goff (dir.). Paris: Éditions Complexe [orig. edn 1988]: 137–64.

Burke, A.A. 2010. 'Canaan under Siege: The History and Archaeology of Egypt's War in Canaan during the Early Eighteenth Dynasty'. In *Studies on War in the Ancient Near East: Collected Essays on Military History* (Alter Orient und Altes Testament, 372), J. Vidal (ed.). Münster: Ugarit–Verlag: 43–66.

Burke, P. 1990. *The French Historical Revolution: The Annales School, 1929–89*. Stanford, CA: Stanford University Press.

Burkert, W. 1992. *The Orientalizing Revolution: Near Eastern Influence on Greek Culture in the Early Archaic Age* (Revealing Antiquity, 5). Cambridge, MA: Harvard University Press.

Burling, R. 1962. 'Maximization theories and the Study of Economic Anthropology'. *American Anthropologist* 64: 802–21.

Caisson, M. 2001. 'Le Terre et le Ciel: Complexité des représentations religieuses dans le monde méditerranéen'. In *L'anthropologie de la Méditerranée/Anthropology of the Mediterranean*, D. Albera, A. Blok and C. Bromberger (eds). Paris: Maisonneuve/ Larose-MMSH: 387–405.

Campagno, M. 1998. 'Pierre Clastres y el surgimiento del Estado. Veinte años después'. *Boletín de Antropología Americana* 33: 101–13.

Campagno, M. 2000. 'Hacia un uso no-evolucionista del concepto de 'sociedades de jefatura'. *Boletín de Antropología Americana* 36: 137–47.

Campagno, M. 2002. *De los jefes-parientes a los reyes-dioses. Surgimiento y consolidación del Estado en el antiguo Egipto* (Aula Ægyptiaca-Studia, 3). Barcelona: Aula Ægyptiaca.

Campagno, M. 2009. 'Kinship and Family Relations'. In *UCLA Encyclopedia of Egyptology*, E. Frood and W. Wendrich (eds). Los Angeles: University of California in Los Angeles, http://escholarship.org/uc/item/7zh1g7ch.

Campagno, M. 2011. 'De Egipto al Asia y de regreso a Egipto: las migraciones de Sinuhé y los contactos interétnicos'. In *Movilidad y migraciones: Actas de las III Jornadas Multidisciplinarias, llevadas a cabo en Buenos Aires, del 22 al 24 de octubre de 2008*, A. Guiance (ed.). Buenos Aires: CONICET: 19–31.

Campagno, M. 2014. 'Patronage and Other Logics of Social Organization in Ancient Egypt during the IIIrd Millennium BCE'. *Journal of Egyptian History* 7: 1–33.

Campbell, E.F. 1960. 'The Amarna Letters and the Amarna Period'. *BA* 23: 1–22.

Campbell, E.F. 1964. *The Chronology of the Amarna Letters: With Special Reference to the Hypothetical Coregency of Amenophis III and Akhenaten*. Baltimore, MD: The Johns Hopkins University Press.

Campbell, J.K. 1964. *Honour, Family, and Patronage: A Study of Institutions and Moral Values in a Greek Mountain Community*. Oxford: Clarendon Press.

Carneiro, R. 1981. 'The Chiefdom: Precursor of the State'. In *The Transition to Statehood in the New World*, G.D. Jones and R.R. Kautz (eds). Cambridge: Cambridge University Press: 37–79.

Caro Baroja, J. 1963. 'The City and the Country: Reflexions on Some Ancient Commonplaces'. In *Mediterranean Countrymen: Essays in the Social Anthropology of the Mediterranean*, J. Pitt-Rivers (ed.). Paris: Mouton: 27–40.

Cassar, C. 2005. *L'honneur et la honte en Méditerranée* (Encyclopédie de la Méditerranée, 32). Aix-en-Provence: Édisud.

Cassin, E. 1974. 'Le palais de Nuzi et la royauté d'Arrapḫa'. In *Le palais et la royauté* (XIXe RAI), P. Garelli (ed.). Paris: P. Geuthner: 373–92.

Cathcart, A. 2006. *Kinship and Clientage: Highland Clanship 1451–1609* (The Northern World, 20). Leiden: E.J. Brill.

Chaney, M.L. 1983. 'Palestinian Peasant Movements and the Formation of Premonarchic Israel'. In *Palestine in Transition: The Emergence of Ancient Israel* (SWBAS, 2), D.N. Freedman and D.F. Graf (eds). Sheffield: Almond Press: 39–90.

Charpin, D. 2002. 'La politique hydraulique des rois paléo-babyloniens'. *Annales: Histoire, Sciences Sociales* 57: 545–59.

Charpin, D. 2004. 'La circulation des commerçants, des nomades et des messagers dans le Proche-Orient amorrite (XVIIIème siècle av. J.-C.)'. In *La mobilité des personnes en Méditerranée de l'antiquité à l'époque moderne: Procédures de contrôle et documents d'identification* (Collection de l'École Française de Rome), C. Moatti (dir.). Roma: L'École Française de Rome: 51–69.

Chesson, M.S. 2003. 'Households, Houses, Neighborhoods and Corporate Villages: Modeling the Early Bronze Age as a House Society'. *Journal of Mediterranean Archaeology* 16: 79–102.

Childe, V.G. 1950. 'The Urban Revolution'. *Town Planning Journal* 21: 3–17.

Chilton, S. 1988. 'Defining Political Culture'. *The Western Political Quarterly* 41: 419–45.

Christiansen, B. and E. Devecchi. 2012. 'Die hethitischen Vasallenverträge und die biblische Bundeskonzeption'. *BN* 156: 65–87.

Claessen, H. and P. Skalník (eds). 1978a. *The Early State*. The Hague: Mouton.

Claessen, H. and P. Skalník. 1978b. 'The Early State: Models and Theories'. In *The Early State*, H. Claessen and P. Skalník (eds). The Hague: Mouton: 637–50.

Claessen, H. and P. van de Velde (eds). 1987. *Early State Dynamics*. Leiden: Brill.

Clastres, P. 1989. *Society against the State: Essays in Political Anthropology*. New York: Zone Books [orig. French edn 1974].

Clifford, J. and G.E. Marcus (eds). 1986. *Writing Culture: The Poetics and Politics of Ethnography*. Berkeley: University of California Press.

Cline, E.H. 2014. *1177 B.C.: The Year Civilization Collapsed*. Princeton, NJ: Princeton University Press.

Clines, D.J.A. (ed.). 2009. *The Concise Dictionary of Classical Hebrew*. Sheffield: Sheffield Phoenix Press.

Cochavi-Rainey, Z. 1990. 'Egyptian Influence in the Akkadian Texts Written by Egyptian Scribes in the Fourteenth–Thirteenth Centuries B.C.E.'. *JNES* 49: 57–65.

Cochavi-Rainey, Z. 1999. *Royal Gifts in the Late Bronze Age, Fourteenth to Thirteenth Centuries B.C.E.: Selected Texts Recording Gifts to Royal Marriages* (Studies by the Department of Bible and Ancient Near East, 13). Beer-Sheva: Ben-Gurion University of the Negev Press.

Cohen, A. 1965. *Arab Border Villages in Israel*. Manchester: Manchester University Press.

Cohen, A. 1969. 'Political Anthropology: The Analysis of the Symbolism of Power Relations'. *Man* NS 4: 215–35.

Cohen, A. 1973. *Palestine in the 18th Century: Patterns of Government and Administration*. Jerusalem: The Magness Press/The Hebrew University of Jerusalem.

Cohen, R. 1996. 'All in the Family: Ancient Near Eastern Diplomacy'. *International Negotiation* 1: 11–28.

Cohen, R. 2000. 'Intelligence in the Amarna Letters'. In *Amarna Diplomacy: The Beginning of International Relations*, R. Cohen and R. Westbrook (eds). Baltimore, MD: The Johns Hopkins University Press: 85–98, 247.

Cohen, R. and R. Westbrook (eds). 2000a. *Amarna Diplomacy: The Beginning of International Relations*. Baltimore, MD: The Johns Hopkins University Press.

Cohen, R. and R. Westbrook. 2000b. 'Introduction: The Amarna System'. In *Amarna Diplomacy: The Beginning of International Relations*, R. Cohen and R. Westbrook (eds). Baltimore, MD: The Johns Hopkins University Press: 1–12, 237.

Cohen, R. and R. Westbrook. 2000c. 'Conclusion: The Beginnings of International Relations'. In *Amarna Diplomacy: The Beginning of International Relations*, R. Cohen and R. Westbrook (eds). Baltimore, MD: The Johns Hopkins University Press: 225–36, 267–8.

Cohn, B.S. 1980. 'History and Anthropology: The State of the Play'. *CSSH* 22: 198–221.

Comaroff, J. and J. Comaroff. 1992. *Ethnography and the Historical Imagination*. Boulder, CO: Westview Press.

Conte, E. 2003. 'Agnatic Illusions: The Element of Choice in Arab Kinship'. In *Tribes and Power. Nationalism and Ethnicity in the Middle East*, F.A. Jabar and H. Dawod (eds). London: Saqi: 15–49.

Cooper, J. 2003. 'International Law in the Third Millennium'. In *A History of Ancient Near Eastern Law* (HdO, 72). R. Westbrook (ed.). Leiden: E.J. Brill, I: 241–51.

Coote, R.B. and K.W. Whitelam. 1987. *The Emergence of Early Israel in Historical Perspective* (SWBAS, 5). Sheffield: Almond Press.

Couto-Ferreira, E. 2013. 'The Circulation of Medical Practitioners in the Ancient Near East: The Mesopotamian Perspective'. In *Mediterráneos: An Interdisciplinary Approach to the Cultures of the Mediterranean Sea*, S. Carro Martín et al. (eds). Newcastle upon Tyne: Cambridge Scholars Publishing: 401–16.

Coy, P. 1974. 'An Elementary Structure of Ritual Kinship: A Case of Prescription in the Compadrazgo'. *Man* NS 9: 470–79.

Crown, A.D. 1974. 'Tidings and Instructions: How News Travelled in the Ancient Near East'. *JESHO* 17: 244–71.

Cunchillos [Ilarri], J.-L. 1989a. 'Correspondance'. In *Textes ougaritiques. II: Textes religieux, rituels, correspondance* (LAPO, 14), A. Caquot, J.-M. de Tarragon and J.-L. Cunchillos. Paris: Éditions du Cerf: 239–421.

Cunchillos Ilarri, J.-L. 1989b. *Estudios de epistolografía ugarítica*. Valencia: Institución San Jerónimo.

Cunchillos Ilarri, J.-L. 1992. *Manual de estudios ugaríticos*. Madrid: Consejo Superior de Investigaciones Científicas.

Cunchillos Ilarri, J.-L. 2005. 'Las nuevas tecnologías y las escrituras (y lenguas) del Próximo Oriente Antiguo'. In *Escrituras y lenguas del Mediterráneo en la antigüedad*, G. Carrasco Serrano and J.C. Oliva Mompeán (coord.). Cuenca: Ediciones de la Universidad de Castilla-La Mancha: 11–32.

Cunchillos [Ilarri], J.-L. and J.-P. Vita. 1998. *Introducción a la lectura crítica de documentos antiguos. Textos semíticos noroccidentales del II y I milenio a.C.* (Banco de Datos Filológicos Semíticos Noroccidentales – Monografías, 4). Madrid: Consejo Superior de Investigaciones Científicas.

Curtis, M. 2009. *Orientalism and Islam: European Thinkers on Oriental Despotism in the Middle East and India*. Cambridge: Cambridge University Press.

Dalton, G. 1961. 'Economic Theory and Primitive Society'. *American Anthropologist* NS 63: 1–25.

Dalton, G. 1969. 'Theoretical Issues in Economic Anthropology'. *CA* 10: 63–102.

David, S.R. 2000. 'Realism, Constructivism, and the Amarna Letters'. In *Amarna Diplomacy: The Beginning of International Relations*, R. Cohen and R. Westbrook (eds). Baltimore, MD: The Johns Hopkins University Press: 54–67, 244.

Davis, J. 1969. 'Honour and Politics in Pisticci'. *Proccedings of the Royal Anthropological Institute of Great Britain and Ireland 1969*: 69–81.

Davis, J. 1977. *People of the Mediterranean: An Essay in Comparative Social Anthropology*. London: Routledge Kegan & Paul.

Davis, N.Z. 1981. 'Anthropology and History in the 1980s: The Possibilities of the Past'. *Journal of Interdisciplinary History* 12: 267–75.

Dawod, H. (dir.). 2004. *Tribus et pouvoirs en terre d'Islam*. Paris: Armand Colin.

De Geus, C.H.J. 2003. *Towns in Ancient Israel and in the Southern Levant* (Palaestina Antiqua, 10). Leuven: Peeters.

del Olmo Lete, G. 1993. 'Royal Aspects of the Ugaritic Cult'. In *Ritual and Sacrifice in the Ancient Near East* (OLA, 55), J. Quaegebeur (ed.). Leuven: Peeters: 51–66.

del Olmo Lete, G. and J. Sanmartín. 2003. *A Dictionary of the Ugaritic Language in the Alphabetic Tradition* (HdO, 67). Leiden: E.J. Brill.

Deliège, R. 2005. *Anthropologie de la famille et de la parenté* (2nd edn). Paris: Armand Colin.

Deniaux, É. 2007. 'Clientèle et éthique à Rome à l'époque républicaine'. In *Clientèle guerrière, clientèle foncière et clientèle électorale: Histoire et anthropologie*, V. Lécrivain (ed.). Dijon: Éditions Universitaires de Dijon: 161–72.

Detienne, M. 2009. *Comparer l'incomparable: Oser expérimenter et construire* (2nd edn). Paris: Éditions du Seuil.

Devecchi, E. 2008. 'La funzione del prologo storico nei trattati ittiti. Ipotesi e discusione'. In *I diritti del mondo cuneiforme (Mesopotamia e regioni adiacenti, ca. 2500–500 a.C.)*, M. Liverani and C. Mora (eds). Pavia: Istituto Universitario di Studi Superiori di Pavia: 361–85.

Devecchi, E. 2012. 'Treaties and Edicts in the Hittite World'. In *Organization, Representation, and Symbols of Power in the Ancient Near East: Proceedings of the 54th Rencontre Assyriologique Internationale at Würzburg, 20–25 July 2008*, G. Wilhelm (ed.). Winona Lake, IN: Eisenbrauns: 637–45.

Diakonoff, I.M. 1982. 'The Structure of Near Eastern Society before the Middle of the Second Millennium B.C.'. *Oikumene* 3: 7–100.

Diakonoff, I.M. 1987. 'Slave-Labour vs. Non-Slave Labour: The Problem of Definition'. In *Labor in the Ancient Near East* (AOS, 68), M.A. Powell (ed.). New Haven, CT: American Oriental Society: 1–3.

Di Bella, M.P. 1984. 'La 'violence' du silence dans la tradition sicilienne'. *Études rurales* 95/96: 195–203.

Diego Espinel, A. 2011. *Abriendo los caminos de Punt: Contactos entre Egipto y el ámbito afroárabe durante la Edad del Bronce (ca. 3000–1065 a.C.)*. Barcelona: Bellaterra.

Dion, P.-E. 1997. *Les araméens à l'âge du fer: Histoire politique et structures sociales* (Études Bibliques, Nouvelle Série. N° 34). Paris: Gabalda.

Dittmer, L. 1977. 'Political Culture and Political Symbolism: Toward a Theoretical Synthesis'. *World Politics* 29: 552–83.

Dossin, G. 1938. 'Les archives épistolaires du palais de Mari'. *Syria* 19: 105–26.

Dothan, T. 1995. 'The "Sea Peoples" and the Philistines of Ancient Palestine'. In *Civilizations of the Ancient Near East*, J.M. Sasson (ed.). New York: Scribner's Sons, II: 1267–79.

Doumani, B. 1995. *Rediscovering Palestine: Merchants and Peasants in Jabal Nablus, 1700–1900*. Berkeley: University of California Press.

Dresch, P. 1988. 'Segmentation: Its Roots in Arabia and Its Flowering Elsewhere'. *Cultural Anthropology* 3: 50–67.

Drower, M. 1975. 'Syria *c.* 1550–1400 B.C.'. In *CAH*³, II/2: 417–525.

Druckman, D. and S. Güner. 2000. 'A Social-Psychological Analysis of Amarna Diplomacy'. In *Amarna Diplomacy: The Beginning of International Relations*, R. Cohen and R. Westbrook (eds). Baltimore, MD: The Johns Hopkins University Press: 174–88, 262–3.

Dube, S. 2007. 'Llegadas y salidas: la antropología histórica'. *Estudios de Asia y África* 42: 595–645.

Duma, J. 2007. 'Saisir clientèles et fidélités à l'époque moderne'. In *Clientèle guerrière, clientèle foncière et clientèle électorale: Histoire et anthropologie*, V. Lécrivain (ed.). Dijon: Éditions Universitaires de Dijon: 99–113.

Dupuy, F. 2008. *Anthropologie economique* (2nd edn). Paris: A. Colin.

Durand, J.-M. 1992. 'Unité et diversité au Proche-Orient à l'époque amorrite'. In *La circulation des biens, de personnes et des idées dans le Proche-Orient ancien. Actes de la XXXVIIIe Rencontré Assyriologique Internationale (Paris, 8–10 juillet 1991)*, D. Charpin and F. Joannès (eds). Paris: Éditions Recherche sur les Civilisations: 97–128.

Durand, J.-M. 1997–2000. *Documents épistolaires du palais de Mari* (3 vols.; LAPO, 16–18). Paris: Éditions du Cerf.

Durand, J.-M. 2002. 'La maîtrise de l'eau dans les régions centrales du Proche-Orient'. *Annales: Histoire, Sciences Sociales* 57: 561–76.

Durkheim, É. 1993. *Les formes élémentaires de la vie religieuse*. Paris: Presses Universitaires de France [orig. French edn 1912].

Durkheim, É. 1893. *De la division du travail social*. Paris: Félix Alcan.

Dussaud, R. 1940. 'Nouveaux textes égyptiens d'exécration contre les peuples syriens'. *Syria* 21: 170–82.

Ebeling, E. 1971. 'Feudalismus'. In *Reallexicon der Assyriologie und Vorderasiatischen Archäeologie*, E. Ebeling, B. Meissner and D.O. Edzard (eds). Berlin: W. de Gruyter, III: 54–5.

Eco, U. 1968. *La struttura assente: La ricerca semiotica e il metodo strutturale*. Roma: Bompiani.

Edel, E. 1976. *Ägyptische Artze und ägyptische Medizin am hethitischen Königshof.* Opladen: Westdeutscher Verlag.

Edel, E. 1994. *Die ägyptisch-hethitische Korrespondenz aus Boghazkoï in babylonischer und hethitischer Sprache. Vol. 1: Umschriften und Übersetzungen* (Abhandlungen der Rheinischer-Westfälischen Akademie der Wissenschaften, 77). Opladen: Westdeutscher Verlag.

Edgerton, W.F. 1947. 'The Government and the Governed in the Egyptian Empire'. *JNES* 6: 152–60.

Edgerton, W.F. and J.A. Wilson. 1936. *Historical Records of Ramses III: The Texts in Medinet Habu. Volumes I and II* (SAOC). Chicago, IL: The University of Chicago Press.

Edzard, D.O. 1960. 'Die Beziehungen Babyloniens und Ägyptens in der mittelbabylonischen Zeit und das Gold'. *JESHO* 3: 38–55.

Eickelman, D.F. 2002. *The Middle East and Central Asia: An Anthropological Approach.* Upper Saddle River, NJ: Prentice Hall.

Eidem, J. 2003. 'International Law in the Second Millennium: Middle Bronze Age'. In *A History of Ancient Near Eastern Law* (HdO, 72), R. Westbrook (ed.). Leiden: E.J. Brill, I: 745–52.

Eisenbeis, W. 1969. *Die Wurzel* שלם *im Alten Testament* (BZAW, 113). Berlin: W. de Gruyter.

Eisenstadt, S.N. and Roniger, L. 1984. *Patrons, Clients and Friends. Interpersonal Relations and the Structure of Trust in Society*. Cambridge: Cambridge University Press.

Eliade, M. 2010. *Le sacré et le profane*. Paris: Gallimard [orig. edn 1957].

Eriksen, T.M. 2002. *Ethnicity and Nationalism: Anthropological Perspectives* (2nd edn). London: Pluto Press.

Evans-Pritchard, E.E. 1940. *The Nuer: A Description of the Modes of Livelihood and Political Institutions of a Nilotic People*. Oxford: Clarendon Press.

Evans-Pritchard, E.E. 1949. *The Sanusi of Cyrenaica*. Oxford: Clarendon Press.
Evans-Pritchard, E.E. 1950. 'Social Anthropology: Past and Present'. *Man* 50: 118–24.
Evans-Pritchard, E.E. 1961. *Anthropology and History*. Manchester: Manchester University Press.
Eychenne, M. 2005. 'Le sultan Al-Ašraf Ḫalīl et son vizir: Liens personnels et pratiques du pouvoir dans le sultanat mamlouk'. *Annales islamologiques* 39: 249–73.
Eychenne, M. 2008. 'Le *bayt* à l'époque mamlouke: Une entité sociale à revisiter'. *Annales islamologiques* 42: 275–95.
Eyre, C.J. 2004. 'How Relevant was Personal Status to the Functioning of the Rural Economy in Pharaonic Egypt?'. In *La dependence rurale dans l'Antiquité égyptienne et proche-orientale* (Bibliothèque d'Étude, 140), B. Menu (ed.). Cairo: Institut Français d'Archéologie Orientale: 157–86.
Eyre, C.J. 2010. 'The Economy: Pharaonic'. In *A Companion to Ancient Egypt*, A.B. Lloyd (ed.). Oxford: Wiley-Blackwell, I: 291–308.
Fafchamps, M. 1992. 'Solidarity Networks in Preindustrial Societies: Rational Peasants with a Moral Economy'. *Economic Development and Cultural Change* 41: 147–74.
Fabian, J. 1983. *Time and the Other: How Anthropology Makes Its Object*. New York: Columbia University Press.
Fales, F.M. 1976. 'La struttura sociale'. In *L'alba della civiltà. Società, economia e pensiero*, S. Moscati (ed.). Torino: UTET, I: 147–273.
Fales, F.M. 2002. 'Vie di transito in Siria centrale tra il II e il I millennio a.C.'. In *Andata e retorno dall'Antico Oriente*. Milano: Centro Studi del Vicino Oriente: 79–122.
Farriss, N. 1986. 'Foreword'. In *The Social Life of Things: Commodities in Cultural Perspective*, A. Appadurai (ed.). Cambridge: Cambridge University Press: ix–xi.
Faulkner, R.O. 1962. *A Concise Dictionary of Middle Egyptian*. Oxford: Griffith Institute - Ashmolean Museum.
Faust, A. 2013. 'Villages, Cities and Towns'. In *Oxford Encyclopedia of Bible and Archaeology*, D. Master, B. Alpert-Nakhai, A. Faust, L.M. White and J.K. Zangenberg (eds). New York: Oxford University Press: 203–11.
Feely-Harnik, G. 1982. 'Is Historical Anthropology Possible? The Case of the Runaway Slave'. In *Humanizing America's Iconic Book*, G.M. Tucker and D.A. Knight (eds). Chico, CA: Scholars Press: 95–126.
Feleppa, R. 1986. 'Emics, Etics, and Social Objetivity'. *CA* 27: 243–55.
Fensham, F.C. 1962. 'Widow, Orphan and the Poor in Ancient Near Eastern Legal and Wisdom Literature'. *JNES* 21: 129–39.
Fensham, F.C. 1963. 'Clauses of Protection in Hittite Vassal Treaties and the Old Testament'. *VT* 13: 133–43.
Fensham, F.C. 1971. 'Father and Son as Terminology for Treaty and Covenant'. *Near Eastern Studies in Honor of William Foxwell Albright*, H. Goedicke (ed.). Baltimore, MD: The Johns Hopkins University Press: 121–35.
Finkelstein, I. 1994. 'The Emergence of Israel: A Phase in the Cyclic History of Canaan in the Third and Second Millennia BCE'. In *From Nomadism to Monarchy: Archaeological and Historical Aspects of Early Israel*, I. Finkelstein and N. Na'aman (eds). Jerusalem: Israel Exploration Society: 150–78.
Finkelstein, I. 1996. 'The Territorial-Political System of Canaan in the Late Bronze Age'. *UF* 28: 221–55.
Finkelstein, I. and N. Na'aman. 2005. 'Shechem of the Amarna Period and the Rise of the Northern Kingdom of Israel'. *IEJ* 55: 172–93.

Finley, M.I. 1954. *The World of Odysseus*. New York: The Viking Press.
Finley, M.I. 1983. *Politics in the Ancient World*. Cambridge: Cambridge University Press.
Flammini, R. 2010. 'Elite Emulation and Patronage Relationships in the Middle Bronze: The Egyptianized Dynasty of Byblos'. *TA* 37: 154–68.
Fleming, D.E. 1992. 'A Limited Kingship: Late Bronze Emar in Ancient Syria'. *UF* 24: 59–71.
Fleming, D.E. 2004. *Democracy's Ancient Ancestors: Mari and Early Collective Governance*. Cambridge: Cambridge University Press.
Fleming, D.E. 2012. 'People without Town: The *'apiru* in the Amarna Evidence'. In *Language and Nature: Papers Presented to John Huehnergard on the Occasion of His 60th Birthday* (SAOC, 67), R. Hasselbach and N. Pat-El (eds). Chicago, IL: The Oriental Institute of the University of Chicago, IL: 39–49.
Foster, G.M. 1961. 'The Dyadic Contract: A Model for the Social Structure of a Mexican Peasant Village'. *American Anthropologist* 63: 1173–92.
Foster, G.M. 1963. 'The Dyadic Contract in Tzintzuntzan, II: Patron-Client Relationship'. *American Anthropologist* 65: 1280–94.
Foster, G.M. 1965. 'Peasant Society and the Image of the Limited Good'. *American Anthropologist* 67: 293–315.
Frandsen, P.J. 1979. 'Egyptian Imperialism'. *Power and Propaganda. A Symposium on Ancient Empires* (Mesopotamia, 7), M.T. Larsen (ed.). Copenhagen: Akademisk Forlag: 167–81.
Frankfort, H. 1948. *Kingship and the Gods. A Study of Ancient Near Eastern Religion as the Integration of Society and Nature*. Chicago, IL: The University of Chicago Press.
Freu, J. 2003. *Histoire du Mitanni* (Collection Kubaba). Paris: L'Harmattan.
Freu, J. 2006. *Histoire politique du royaume d'Ugarit* (Collection Kubaba). Paris: L'Harmattan.
Freu, J. and M. Mazoyer. 2007. *Les débuts du Nouvel Empire Hittite: Les Hittites et leur histoire* (Collection Kubaba). Paris: L'Harmattan.
Gaál, E. 1988. 'The Social Structure of Alalaḫ'. *Society and Economy in the Eastern Mediterranean* (OLA, 23), M. Heltzer and E. Lipinski (eds). Leuven: Peeters: 99–110.
Gadot, Y. 2010. 'The Late Bronze Egyptian Estate at Aphek'. *TA* 37: 48–66.
Galán, J.M. 1995. *Victory and Border: Terminology Related to Egyptian Imperialism in the XVIIIth Dynasty* (Hildesheimer Ägyptologische Beiträge, 40). Hildesheim: Gerstenberg.
Galán, J.M. 2002. *El imperio egipcio: Inscripciones, ca. 1500–1300 a.C.* (Pliegos de Oriente, 7). Madrid: Trotta.
Garnsey, P. and G. Woolf. 1989. 'Patronage of the Rural Poor in the Roman World'. *Patronage in Ancient Society*, A. Wallace-Hadrill (ed.). New York: Routledge: 153–70.
Geertz, C. 1983. 'Centers, Kings, and Charisma: Reflections on the Symbolics of Power'. In C. Geertz, *Local Knowledge: Further Essays on Interpretive Anthropology*. New York: Basic Books: 121–46.
Gelb, I. 1967. 'Approaches to the Study of Ancient Society'. *JAOS* 87: 1–8.
Gellner, E. 1977. 'Patrons and Clients'. In *Patrons and Clients in Mediterranean Societies*, E. Gellner and J. Waterbury (eds). London: Duckworth: 1–6.
Gellner, E. 2007. 'Cohesion and Identity: The Maghreb from Ibn Khaldun to Émile Durkheim'. *Government and Opposition* 10: 203–18.
Gellner, E. and J. Waterbury (eds). 1977. *Patrons and Clients in Mediterranean Societies*. London: Duckworth.
Gesenius, W. 1957. *A Hebrew and English Lexicon of the Old Testament*. Oxford: Clarendon Press [orig. edn 1907].
Gestoso, G.N. 1992. *La política exterior egipcia en la época de El Amarna* (Colección Estudios, 4). Buenos Aires: Consejo Nacional de Investigaciones Científicas y Técnicas.

Gestoso Singer, G.N. 2007. *El intercambio de bienes entre Egipto y Asia anterior. Desde el reinado de Tuthmosis III hasta el de Akhenatón*. Buenos Aires: Universidad Católica Argentina.

Gestoso Singer, G.N. 2008. 'Egipto y sus periferias en el Levante durante la Dinastía XVIII'. *Cahiers Caribéens d'Egyptologie* 11: 129–43.

Gevirtz, S. 1973. 'On Canaanite Rhetoric. The Evidence of the Amarna Letters from Tyre'. *Or* 42: 162–77.

Giardina, A., M. Liverani and B. Scarcia Amoretti. 1990. *La Palestine: Histoire d'une terre* (Comprendre le Moyen-Orient). Paris: L'Harmattan.

Gilmore, D.D. 1982. 'Anthropology of the Mediterranean Area'. *Annual Review of Anthropology* 11: 175–205.

Gilmore, D.D. (ed.). 1987. *Honor and Shame and the Unity of the Mediterranean* (A Special Publication of the American Anthropological Association, 22). Washington, DC: American Anthropological Association.

Gilsenan, M. 2000. *Recognizing Islam: Religion and Society in the Modern Middle East*. London: I.B. Tauris.

Giry-Deloison, C. and R. Mettam (eds). 1990. *Patronages et clientélismes, 1550–1750 (France, Anglaterre, Espagne, Italie)* (Histoire et Littérature Régionales, 10). Lille: Université Charles de Gaulle.

Giveon, R. 1978. *The Impact of Egypt in Canaan: Iconographical and Related Studies* (OBO, 20). Fribourg: Universitätsverlag/Göttingen: Vandenhoeck and Ruprecht.

Glassner, J.-J. 2000. 'Les petits Etats mésopotamiens à la fin du 4e et au cours du 3e millénaire'. In *A Comparative Study of Thirty City-State Cultures* (Historisk-filosofiske Skrifter, 21/Det Kongelige Danske Videnskabernes Selskab), M.H. Hansen (ed.). Copenhagen: C.A. Reitzels Forlag: 35–53.

Gledhill, J. 2000. *Power and Its Disguises: Anthropological Perspectives on Politics* (2nd edn). London: Pluto Press.

Godelier, M. 1969. *Rationalité et irrationalité en économie*, 2 vols. Paris: Maspéro.

Godelier, M. 1973. 'Préface'. In *Sur les sociétés précapitalistes: Textes choisis de Marx, Engels et Lenine*, M. Godelier (ed.). Paris: Centre d'Études et de Recherches Marxistes: 13–142.

Godelier, M. 2010. *Les tribus dans l'Histoire et face aux États*. Paris: CNRS Éditions.

Goedicke, H. 1963. 'Was Magic Used in the Harem Conspiracy against Ramesses III? (P. Rollin and P. Lee)'. *JEA* 49: 71–92.

Goetze, A. 1974. *Kulturgeschichte Kleinasiens* (2nd augmented edn). München: C.H. Beck'sche Verlagsbuchhandung.

Gofman, A. 1998. 'A Vague but Suggestive Concept: The "Total Social Fact"'. In *Marcel Mauss: A Centennary Tribute* (Methodology and History in Anthropology, 1), W. James and N.J. Allen (eds). New York and Oxford: Berghahn Books: 63–70.

Goldstone, J.A. and J. Haldon. 2009. 'Ancient States, Empires, and Exploitation: Problems and Perspectives'. In *The Dynamics of Ancient Empires: State Power from Assyria to Byzantium*, I. Morris and W. Scheidel (eds). Oxford: Oxford University Press: 3–29.

Gonen, R. 1984. 'Urban Canaan in the Late Bronze Period'. *BASOR* 253: 61–73.

González Alcantud, J.A. 1997. *El clientelismo político. Perspectiva socioantropológica*. Barcelona: Anthropos.

Goodell, G.E. 1985. 'Paternalism, Patronage, and Potlatch: The Dynamics of Giving and Being Given To'. *CA* 26: 247–66.

Goody, J. 1983. *The Development of the Family and Marriage in Europe*. Cambridge: Cambridge University Press.

Goody, J. 1986. *The Logic of Writing and the Organization of Society*. Cambridge: Cambridge University Press.

Goren, Y., I. Finkelstein and N. Na'aman. 2004. *Inscribed in Clay: Provenance Study of the Amarna Tablets and Other Ancient Near Eastern Texts* (Emery and Claire Yass Publications in Archaeology). Tel Aviv: Tel Aviv University.

Gouldner, A.V. 1960. 'The Norm of Reciprocity: A Preliminary Statement'. *American Sociological Review* 25: 161–78.

Graeber, D. 2001. *Toward an Anthropological Theory of Value: The False Coin of Our Own Dreams*. New York: Palgrave.

Gray, J. 1952a. 'Canaanite Kingship in Theory in Practice'. *VT* 2: 193–220.

Gray, J. 1952b. 'Feudalism in Ugarit and Israel'. *ZAW* 64: pp. 49–55.

Greenberg, M. 1955. *The Ḫab/piru* (AOS, 39). New Haven, CT: American Oriental Society.

Greengus, S. 1966. 'Old Babylonian Marriage Ceremonies and Rites'. *JCS* 20: 55–72.

Greenstein, E.L. 1997. 'Alalakh Texts'. In *OxEncANE*, I: 59–61.

Gregoire, J.-P. 1981. 'L'origine et le dèveloppement de la civilisation mésopotamienne du troisième millénaire avant notre ère'. In *Production, pouvoir et parenté dans le monde mediterranéen: De Sumer à nos jours*, C.-H. Breteau, C. Lacoste-Dujardin, C. Lefebure and N. Zanolli (eds). Paris: P. Geuthner: 27–101.

Gregory, C.A. 1982. *Gifts and Commodities* London: Academic Press.

Gregory, C.A. 1997. *Savage Money: The Anthropology and Politics of Commodity Exchange*. London: Routledge.

Gregory, J.M. 1975. 'Image of Limited Good, or Expectation of Reciprocity'. *CA* 16: 73–92.

Grimal, N.-C. 1986. *Les termes de la propagande royale égyptienne: De la XIXe dynastie à la conquête d'Alexandre* (Mémoires de l'Académie des Inscriptions et Belles-Lettres, Nouvelle Série, Tome VI). Paris: Imprimerie Nationale/Diffusion de Boccard.

Groll, S.I. 1983. 'The Egyptian Administrative System in Syria and Palestine in the 18th Dynasty'. In *Fontes atque Pontes. Festschrift Hellmut Brunner*, M. Görg (ed.). Wiesbaden: Harrassowitz: 234–42.

Grottanelli, C. 1977. 'Notes on Mediterranean Hospitality'. *Dialoghi di Archeologia* 9–10: 186–94.

Gunter, A.C. 1995. 'Material, Technology, and Techniques in Artistic Production'. In *Civilizations of the Ancient Near East*, J.M. Sasson (ed.). New York: Scribner's Sons, III: 1539–51.

Güterbock, H.G. 1956. 'The Deeds of Suppiluliuma as Told by His Son, Mursili II'. *JCS* 10: 94–7.

Hachmann, R. 1982. 'Die ägyptische Verwaltung in Syrien während der Amarnazeit'. *ZDPV* 98: 17–49.

Hage, P. and F. Harary. 1996. 'The Logical Structure of Asymmetric Marriage Systems'. *L'Homme* 36 num. 139: 109–24.

Halpern, B. 2011. 'Voyage to Yarimuta'. In *The Fire Signals of Lachish: Studies in the Archaeology and History of Israel in the Late Bronze Age, Iron Age, and Persian Period in Honor of David Ussishkin*, I. Finkelstein and N. Na'aman (eds). Winona Lake, IN: Eisenbrauns: 141–57.

Handy, L.K. 1994. *Among the Host of Heaven: The Syro-Palestinian Pantheon as Bureaucracy*. Winona Lake, IN: Eisenbrauns.

Hannig, R. 2006. *Ägyptisches Wörterbuch II. Mitteleres Reich und Zweite Zwischenzeit*. Mainz am Rhein: Verlag Philipp von Zabern.

Hansen, M.H. 2000. 'Introduction: The Concepts of City-State and City-State Culture'. In *A Comparative Study of Thirty City-State Cultures* (Historisk-filosofiske Skrifter, 21/Det Kongelige Danske Videnskabernes Selskab), M.H. Hansen (ed.). Copenhagen: C.A. Reitzels Forlag: 11–34.

Hardin, J.W. 2011. 'Understanding Houses, Households, and the Levantine Archaeological Record'. In *Household Archaeology in Ancient Israel and Beyond* (CHANE, 50), A. Yasur-Landau, J.R. Ebeling and L.B. Mazow (eds). Leiden: E.J. Brill: 9–25.

Harris, M. 1964. *The Nature of Cultural Things*. New York: Random House, 1964.

Harris, M. 1976. 'History and Significance of the Emic/Etic Distinction'. *Annual Review of Anthropology* 5: 329–50.

Harris, W.V. (ed.). 2005. *Rethinking the Mediterranean*. Oxford: Oxford University Press.

Hartog, F. 2003. *Régimes d'historicité. Présentisme et expériences du temps* (Librairie du XXIe siècle). Paris: Éditions du Seuil.

Hasel, M.G. 1998. *Domination and Resistance: Egyptian Military Activity in the Southern Levant, 1300–1185 BC* (Probleme der Ägyptologie, 11). Leiden: E.J. Brill.

Hathaway, J. 1997. *The Politics of Households in Ottoman Egypt: The Rise of the Qazdağlıs* (Cambridge Studies in Islamic Civilization). Cambridge: Cambridge University Press.

Hawley, R. 2003. *Studies in Ugaritic Epistolography*, PhD Dissertation. Chicago, IL: The University of Chicago.

Helck, W. 1962. *Die Beziehungen Ägyptens zu Vorderasien im 3. und 2. Jahrtausend v. Chr.* (Ägyptologische Abhandlungen, 5). Wiesbaden: Harrassowitz.

Heltzer, M. 1969. 'Problems of the Social History of Syria in the Late Bronze Age'. In *La Siria nel Tardo Bronzo* (Orientis Antiqvi Collectio, IX), M. Liverani (ed.). Roma: Centro per la Antichità e la Storia dell'Arte del Vicino Oriente: 31–46.

Heltzer, M. 1976. *The Rural Community in Ancient Ugarit*. Wiesbaden: Reichart Verlag.

Heltzer, M. 1981. *The Suteans* (Istituto Universitario Orientale. Seminario di Studi Asiatici. Series Minor XIII). Napoli: Istituto Universitario Orientale.

Heltzer, M. 1982. *The Internal Organization of the Kingdom of Ugarit*. Wiesbaden: Reichert Verlag.

Herman, A.L., Jr. 1995. 'The Language of Fidelity in Early Modern France'. *The Journal of Modern France* 67: 1–24.

Herr, L.G. 1997. 'The Iron Age II Period: Emerging Nations'. *BA* 60: 114–83.

Herrenschmidt, O. 2010. 'Caste'. In *Dictionnaire de l'ethnologie et de l'anthropologie*, P. Bonte and M. Izard (dir.). Paris: Presses Universitaires de France: 129–31.

Herzfeld, M. 1980. 'Honour and Shame: Problems in the Comparative Analysis of Moral Systems'. *Man* NS 15: 339–51.

Herzfeld, M. 1984. 'The Horns of the Mediterraneanist Dilemma'. *American Ethnologist* 11: 439–54.

Herzfeld, M. 1987. '"As in Your Own House": Hospitality, Ethnography, and the Stereotype of Mediterranean Society'. In *Honor and Shame and the Unity of the Mediterranean* (A Special Publication of the American Anthropological Association, 22), D.D. Gilmore (ed.). Washington DC: American Anthropological Association: 75–89.

Herzfeld, M. 2001. 'Performing Comparisons: Ethnography, Globetrotting, and the Spaces of Social Knowledge'. *Journal of Anthropological Research* 57: 259–76.

Herzog, Z. 1992. 'Settlement and Fortification Planning in the Iron Age'. In *The Architecture of Ancient Israel: From the Prehistoric to the Persian Periods*, A. Kempinski and R. Reich (eds). Jerusaem: Israel Exploration Society: 231–74.

Hess, R.S. 1989. 'Hebrew Psalms and Amarna Correspondence from Jerusalem: Some Comparisons and Implications'. *ZAW* 101: 249–65.

Higginbotham, C. 1996. 'Elite Emulation and Egyptian Governance in Ramesside Canaan'. *TA* 23: 154–69.

Higginbotham, C. 2000. *Egyptianization and Elite Emulation in Ramesside Palestine: Governance and Accommodation on the Imperial Periphery* (CHANE, 2). Leiden: E.J. Brill.

Hill, G.W. 1941. 'The Use of Culture-Area Concept in Social Research'. *The American Journal of Sociology* 47: 39–47.

Hitchcock, L. 2005. '"Who Will Personally Invite a Foreigner, unless He Is a Craftman?": Exploring Interconnections in Aegean and Levantine Architecture'. In *Emporia: Aegeans in the Central and Eastern Mediterranean: Proceedings of the 10th International Aegean Conference/10e Rencontre égéenne internationale, Athens, Italian School of Archaeology, 14–18 April 2004 II* (Aegeaum, 25), R. Laffineur and E. Greco (eds). Liège: Université de Liège/Austin: University of Texas: 691–99.

Hobsbawm, E.J. 1992. *Nations and Nationalism since 1780: Programme, Myth, Reality* (2nd edn). Cambridge: Cambridge University Press.

Hoffmeier, J.K. 1986. 'The Arm of God versus the Arm of Pharaoh in the Exodus Narrative'. *Biblica* 67: 378–87.

Hoffmeier, J.K. 2004. 'Aspects of Egyptian Foreign Policy in the 18th Dynasty in Western Asia and Nubia'. In *Egypt, Israel, and the Ancient Mediterranean World: Studies in Honor of Donald B. Redford* (Probleme der Ägyptologie, 20), G.N. Knoppers and A. Hirsch (eds). Leiden: E.J. Brill: 121–41.

Hoffner, Jr., H.A. 1995. 'Legal and Social Institutions of Hittite Anatolia'. In *Civilizations of the Ancient Near East*, J.M. Sasson (ed.). New York: Scribner's Sons, I: 555–69.

Hoffner, Jr., H.A. 2009. *Letters from the Hittite Kingdom* (WAWSBL, 15). Atlanta, GA: Society of Biblical Literature.

Holder, G. and A.-M. Peatrik. 2004. 'Cité, centre, capitale: Pour une anthropologie du statut politique de la ville'. *Journal des africanistes* 74: 9–34.

Holladay, W.L. 1971. *A Concise Hebrew and Aramaic Lexicon of the Old Testament: Based upon the Lexical Work of Ludwig Koehler and Walter Baumgartner*. Leiden: E.J. Brill.

Holmes, Y.L. 1975. 'The Messengers of the Amarna Letters'. *JAOS* 95: 376–81.

Horden, P. and N. Purcell. 2000. *The Corrupting Sea: A Study of Mediterranean History*. Oxford: Blackwell Publishing.

Horowitz, W. and T. Oshima. 2006. *Cuneiform in Canaan: Cuneiform Sources from the Land of Israel in Ancient Times*. Jerusalem: Israel Exploration Society/The Hebrew University of Jerusalem.

Hourani, A. 2004. 'Ottoman Reform and the Politics of Notables'. In *The Modern Middle East*, A. Hourani, P.S. Khoury and M.C. Wilson (eds) (2nd edn). London and New York: I.B. Tauris: 83–109.

Huehnergard, J. 1997. 'Emar Texts'. In *OxEncANE*, II: 239–40.

Huehnergard, J. 2005. *A Grammar of Akkadian* (2nd edn). Winona Lake, IN: Eisenbrauns.

Humphreys, S.C. 1969. 'History, Economics, and Anthropology: The Work of Karl Polanyi'. *History & Theory* 8: 165–212.

Ibn Khaldun. 1958. *The Muqaddimah: An Introduction to History* (3 vols; translated by F. Rosenthal). Princeton, NJ: Princeton University Press.

Ilan, D. 1995. 'The Dawn of Internationalism – The Middle Bronze Age'. In *The Archaeology of Society in the Holy Land*, T.E. Levy (ed.). New York: Facts on File: 297–319.

Imparati, F. 1982. 'Aspects de l'organisation de l'État Hittite dans les documents juridiques et administratifs'. *JESHO* 25: 225–67.

Imparati, F. 1995. 'Private Life among the Hittites'. In *Civilizations of the Ancient Near East*, J.M. Sasson (ed.). New York: Scribner's Sons, I: 571–86.

Imparati, F. 1999. 'Die Organisation des hethitischen Staates'. In H. Klengel, *Geschichte des Hethitischen Reiches*, unter mitwirkung von F. Imparati, V. Haas y Th.P.J. van den Hout (HdO; Abt. 1; Nahe und Mittlere Osten, Bd. 34). Leiden: E.J. Brill: 320–87.

Ingham, J.M. 1970. 'The Asymmetrical Implications of Godparenthood in Tlayacapan, Morelos'. *Man* NS 5: 281–89.

Izre'el, S. 1995a. 'The Amarna Letters from Canaan'. In *Civilizations of the Ancient Near East*, J.M. Sasson (ed.). New York: Scribner's Sons: 2411–19.

Izre'el, S. 1995b. 'The Amarna Glosses: Who Wrote What for Whom? Some Sociolinguistic Considerations'. *Israel Oriental Studies* 15: 101–22.

Izre'el, S. 2012. 'Canaano-Akkadian: Linguistics and Socio-Linguistics'. In *Language and Nature: Papers Presented to John Huehnergard on the Occasion of His 60th Birthday* (SAOC, 67), R. Hasselbach and N. Pat–El (eds). Chicago, IL: The Oriental Institute of the University of Chicago, IL: 171–218.

Jabar, F.A. and H. Dawod (eds). 2003. *Tribes and Power: Nationalism and Ethnicity in the Middle East*. London: Saqi.

Jabbra, J.G. and N.W. Jabbra. 1978. 'Local Political Dynamics in Lebanon: The Case of 'Ain al-Qasis'. *Anthropological Quarterly* 51: 137–51.

Jacobsen, T. 1943. 'Primitive Democracy in Ancient Mesopotamia'. *JNES* 2: 159–72.

Jackson, M. 1998. *Minima Ethnographica: Intersubjectivity and the Anthropological Project*. Chicago, IL: The University of Chicago Press.

James, A. 2000. 'Egypt and Her Vassals: The Geopolitical Dimension'. In *Amarna Diplomacy: The Beginning of International Relations*, R. Cohen and R. Westbrook (eds). Baltimore, MD: The Johns Hopkins University Press: 112–24, 252.

Jankowska, N.B. 1969. 'Communal Self-Government and the King of the State of Arrapḫa'. *JESHO* 12: 233–82.

Janssen, J.J. 1975. 'Prolegomena to the Study of Egypt's Economic History during the New Kingdom'. *SAK* 3: 127–85.

Janssen, J.J. 1982. 'Gift-Giving in Ancient Egypt as an Economic Feature'. *JEA* 68: 253–58.

Janssen, J.J. 1993. '*B3kw*: From Work to Product'. *SAK* 20: 81–94.

Jasmin, M. 2006. 'The Political Organization of the City-States in Southwestern Palestine in the Late Bronze Age IIB (13th Century BC)'. In *'I Will Speak the Riddles of Ancient Times': Archaeological and Historical Studies in Honor of Amihai Mazar on the Occasion of his Sixtieth Birthday*, A.M. Maeir and P. de Miroschedji (eds). Winona Lake, IN: Eisenbrauns: 161–91.

Joffe, A.H. 2002. 'The Rise of Secondary States in the Iron Age Levant'. *JESHO* 45: 425–67.

Johnson, A. 1997. 'The Psychology of Dependence between Landlord and Sharecropper in Northeastern Brazil'. *Political Psychology* 18: 411–38.

Jones, P. 2005. 'Divine and Non-Divine Kinship'. In *A Companion to the Ancient Near East* (Blackwell Companions to the Ancient World), D.C. Snell (ed.). Oxford: Blackwell: 330–42.

Jongsma, T. and H.J. Greensfield. 2002. 'The Household as Behaviour: An Anthropological Perspective'. In *Material Evidence and Cultural Pattern in Prehistory: Contributions to the Theory and History of the Household and Burial Customs*, L. Nikolova (ed.). Salt Lake City, UT: International Institute of Anthropology: 1–11.

Jönsson, C. 2000. 'Diplomatic Signaling in the Amarna Letters'. In *Amarna Diplomacy: The Beginning of International Relations*, R. Cohen and R. Westbrook (eds). Baltimore, MD: The Johns Hopkins University Press: 191–204, 263–4.

Julliard, J. 1974. 'La politique'. In *Faire de l'histoire, II. Nouvelles approches* (Bibliothèque des histoires), J. Le Goff and P. Nora (eds). Paris: Gallimard: 229–50.

Jursa, M. 2005. 'Money-Based Exchange and Redistribution: The Transformation of the Institutional Economy in First Millennium Babylonia'. In *Autour de Polanyi: Vocabulaires, théories et modalités des échanges*, P. Clancier, F. Joannès, P. Rouillard and A. Tenu (eds). Paris: De Boccard: 171–86.

Kalluveettil, P. 1982. *Declaration and Covenant: A Comprehensive Review of Covenant Formulae from the Old Testament and the Ancient Near East* (AnBib, 88). Roma: Biblical Institute Press.

Kemp, B.J. 1978. 'Imperialism and Empire in New Kingdom Egypt'. In *Imperialism in the Ancient World*, P. Garnsey and C. Whittaker (eds). Cambridge: Cambridge University Press: 7–57.

Kemp, B.J. 2006. *Ancient Egypt: Anatomy of a Civilization* (2nd edn). London: Routledge.

Kempinski, A. 1992. 'Middle and Late Bronze Age Fortifications'. In *The Architecture of Ancient Israel: From the Prehistoric to the Persian Periods*, A. Kempinski and R. Reich (eds). Jerusalem: Israel Exploration Society: 127–42.

Kestemont, G. 1974. *Diplomatique et droit internationale en Asie occidentale (1600–1200 av. J. C.)* (PIOL, 9). Louvain-la-Neuve: Institut Orientaliste – Université Catholique de Louvain.

Kestemont, G. 1977. 'Remarkes sur les aspects juridiques du commerce dans le Proche-Orient du XIVe siècle avant notre ère'. *Iraq* 39: 191–201.

Kettering, S. 1986. *Patrons, Brokers, and Clients in Seventeenth-Century France*. New York and Oxford: Oxford University Press.

Kettering, S. 1988. 'The Historical Development of Political Clientelism'. *Journal of Interdisciplinary History* 18: 419–47.

Khazanov, I.M. 1992. *Nomads and the Outside World* (2nd edn). Madison: The University of Wisconsin University Press.

Khoury, P.S. 1983. *Urban Notables and Arab Nationalism: The Politics of Damascus 1860–1920* (Cambridge Middle East Library). Cambridge: Cambridge University Press.

Khoury, P.S. and J. Kostiner (eds). 1990a. *Tribes and State Formation in the Middle East*. Berkeley: University of California Press.

Khoury, P.S. and J. Kostiner. 1990b. 'Introduction: Tribes and the Complexities of State Formation in the Middle East'. In *Tribes and State Formation in the Middle East*, P.S. Khoury and J. Kostiner (eds). Berkeley: University of California Press: 1–22.

Kitchen, K.A. 1962. *Suppiluliuma and the Amarna Pharaohs* (Liverpool Monographs in Archaeology and Oriental Studies). Liverpool: Liverpool University Press.

Klengel, H. 1963. 'Zum Brief eines Königs von Ḫanigalbat (IboT I 34)'. *Or* NS 32: 280–91.

Klengel, H. 1965. *Geschichte Syriens in 2. Jahrtausend v.u.Z. Teil 1: Nordsyrien* (Deutsche Akademie der Wissenschaften zu Berlin. Institut für Orientforschung. Veröffentlichung, 40). Berlin: Akademie-Verlag.

Klengel, H. 1969. *Geschichte Syriens in 2. Jahrtausend v.u.Z. Teil 2: Mittel- und Südsyrien* (Deutsche Akademie der Wissenschaften zu Berlin. Institut für Orientforschung. Veröffentlichung, 70). Berlin: Akademie-Verlag.

Klengel, H. 1970. *Geschichte Syriens in 2. Jahrtausend v.u.Z. Teil 3: Historische Geographie und allgemeine Darstellung* (Deutsche Akademie der Wissenschaften zu Berlin. Institut für Orientforschung. Veröffentlichung, 40). Berlin: Akademie-Verlag.

Klengel, H. 1972. *Zwischen Zelt und Palast: Die Begegnung von Nomaden und Seßhaften im alten Vorderasien*. Wien: Schroll.

Klengel, H. 1992. *Syria, 3000 to 300 B.C.: A Handbook of Political History*. Berlin: Akademie Verlag.

Klengel, H. 1999. *Geschichte des Hethitischen Reiches* (unter mitwirkung von F. Imparati, V. Haas and T.P.J. van den Hout; HdO; Abt. 1; Nahe und Mittlere Osten, Bd. 34). Leiden: E.J. Brill.

Knapp, A.B. 1989a. 'Complexity and Collapse in the North Jordan Valley: Archaeometry and Society in the Middle-Late Bronze Ages'. *IEJ* 39: 129–48.

Knapp, A.B. 1989b. 'Response: Independence, Imperialism, and the Egyptian Factor'. *BASOR* 275: 64–8.

Knapp, A.B. 1990. 'Ethnicity, Entrepreneurship, and Exchange: Mediterranean Inter–Island Relations in the Late Bronze Age'. *The Annual of the British School at Athens* 85: 115–53.

Knapp, A.B. 1992. 'Independence and Imperialism: Politicoeconomic Structures in the Bronze Age Levant'. In *Archaeology, Annales and Ethnohistory*, A.B. Knapp (ed.). Cambridge: Cambridge University Press: 83–98.

Knauf, E.A. 1987. 'Berg und Tal, Stadt und Stamm – Grundzüge der Geschichte Palästinas in den letzen fünftausend Jahren'. In *Pracht und Geheimnis: Kleidung und Schmuck aus Palästina und Jordanien*, G. Völger, K. v. Welck and K. Hackstein (eds). Köln: Rautenstrauch-Joest Museum: 26–35, 417–18.

Knudtzon, J.A. 1907/1915. *Die el-Amarna-Tafeln mit Einleitung und Erlauterungen* (Anmerkungen und Register bearbeitet von O. Weber und E. Ebeling; Vorderasiatische Bibliothek, 2; 2 vols). Leipzig: J. Hinrichs.

Korošec, V. 1931. *Hethitische Staatsverträge: Ein Beitrag zu ihrer juristischen Wertung* (Leipziger rechts-wissenschaftliche Studien, 60). Leipzig: T. Weicher.

Korošec, V. 1960. 'Les Hittites et leurs vassaux syriennes à la lumière des nouveaux textes d'Ugarit (PRU IV)'. *Revue Hittite et Asianique* 18: 65–79.

Korošec, V. 1967. 'Les relations internationales d'après les lettres de Mari'. In *La civilisation de Mari* (XVe Rencontre Assyriologique Internationale), J.-R. Kupper (ed.). Paris: Société d'Édition 'Les Belles Lettres': 139–50.

Kramer, S.N. 1962. 'Cultural Anthropology and the Cuneiform Documents'. *Ethnology* 1: 299–314.

Krämer, G. 2002. *Geschichte Palästinas. Von der osmanischen Eroberung bis zur Grundung des Staates Israel*. München: C.H. Beck.

Krauss, R. 1995. 'Akhetaten: A Portrait in Art of an Ancient Egyptian Capital'. In *Civilizations of the Ancient Near East*, J.M. Sasson (ed.). New York: Scribner's Sons, II: 749–62.

Kristiansen, K. and T.B. Larsson. 2005. *The Rise of Bronze Age Society: Travels, Transmissions and Transformations*. Cambridge: Cambridge University Press.

Kühne, C. 1973. *Die Chronologie der internationale Korrespondenz von El-Amarna*. Vluyn: Butzon & Bercker Kevelaer.

Kupper, J.-R. 1957. *Les nomades en Mésopotamie au temps des rois de Mari* (Bibliothèque de la Faculté de Philosophie et Lettres de l'Université de Liège, 142). Paris: Société de Édition 'Les Belles Lettres'.

Labat, R. 1962. 'Le rayonnement de la langue et de l'écriture akkadiennes au deuxième millénaire avant notre ère'. *Syria* 39: 1–27.

Labat, R. 1975. 'Elam, *c.* 1600–1200 B.C.'. In *CAH*³, II/2: 379–416.

LaBianca, Ø.S. 2009. 'The Poly-Centric Nature of Social Order in the Middle East: Preliminary Reflections from Anthropological Archaeology'. In *Studies on Iron Age Moab and Neighbouring Areas in Honour of Michèle Daviau* (Ancient Near Eastern Studies – Supplement, 29), P. Bienkowski (ed.). Leuven: Peeters: 1–5.

Laburthe-Tolra, P. and J.-P. Warnier. 2007. *Ethnologie, Anthropologie* (2nd edn). Paris: Presses Universitaires de France.

Lackenbacher, S. 2002. *Textes akkadiens d'Ugarit. Textes provenant des vingt-cinq premières campagnes* (LAPO, 20). Paris: Les Éditions du Cerf.

Lafont, B. 2001. 'International Relations in the Ancient Near East: The Birth of a Complete Diplomatic System'. *Diplomacy & Statecraft* 12: 39–60.

Lafont, B. 2005. 'De l'influence de Karl Polanyi en assyriologie'. In *Autour de Polanyi: Vocabulaires, théories et modalités des échanges*, P. Clancier, F. Joannès, P. Rouillard and A. Tenu (eds). Paris: De Boccard: 113–20.

Lafont, S. 1998. 'Fief et féodalité dans le Proche-Orient ancient'. In *Les féodalités*, E. Bournazel and J.-P. Poly (eds). Paris: Presses Universitaires de France: 517–630.

Landsberger, B. 1954. 'Assyrische Königsliste und 'Dunkles Zeitalter' (Continued)'. *JCS* 8: 47–73.

Langdon, S. and A.H. Gardiner. 1920. 'The Treaty of Alliance between Ḫattušili, King of the Hittites, and the Pharaoh Ramesses II of Egypt'. *JEA* 6: 179–205.

Langgut, D., I. Finkelstein and T. Litt. 2013. 'Climate and the Late Bronze Collapse: New Evidence from the Southern Levant'. *TA* 40: 149–75.

Lapidus, I.M. 1990. 'Tribes and State Formation in Islamic History'. In *Tribes and State Formation in the Middle East*, P.S. Khoury and J. Kostiner (eds). Berkeley: University of California Press: 25–47.

Leca, J. and Y. Schemeil. 1983. 'Clientélisme et patrimonialisme dans le monde arabe'. *International Political Science Review* 4: 455–94.

Leclair, E.E., Jr. 1962. 'Economic Theory and Economic Anthropology'. *American Anthropologist* 64: 1179–203.

Lécrivain, V. (ed.). 2007a. *Clientèle guerrière, clientèle foncière et clientèle électorale: Histoire et anthropologie*. Dijon: Éditions Universitaires de Dijon.

Lécrivain, V. 2007b. 'Le rapport de clientèle dans la perspective comparative'. In *Clientèle guerrière, clientèle foncière et clientèle électorale: Histoire et anthropologie*, V. Lécrivain (ed.). Dijon: Éditions Universitaires de Dijon: 13–31.

Lehman, E.W. 1972. 'On the Concept of Political Culture: A Theoretical Reassessment'. *Social Forces* 50: 361–70.

Lehmann, G. 1999. 'Biblische Landeskunde versus kultur- und sozialgeographische Raumanalyse? Aktuelle Entwicklungstendenzen in der historischen Geographie von Palästina'. In *Fluchtpunkt Uruk: Archäologische Einheit aus methodischer Vielfalt. Schriften für Hans Jörg Nissen*, H. Kühne, R. Bernbeck and K. Bartl (eds). Berlin: Leidorf: 95–124.

Lehner, M. 2000. 'Fractal House of Pharaoh: Ancient Egypt as a Complex Adaptive System, a Trial Formulation'. In *Dynamics in Human and Primate Societies: Agent-Based Modeling of Social and Spatial Processes*, T.A. Kohler and G.J. Gumerman (eds). New York: Oxford University Press: 275–353.

Lemche, N.P. 1974. 'חפשי in 1 Sam. XVII 25'. *VT* 24: 373–4.

Lemche, N.P. 1985. *Early Israel: Anthropological and Historical Studies on the Israelite Society before the Monarchy* (VTSup, 37). Leiden: E.J. Brill.

Lemche, N.P. 1995a. 'The History of Ancient Syria and Palestine: An Overview'. In *Civilizations of the Ancient Near East*, J.M. Sasson (ed.). New York: Scribner's Sons, I: 1195–218.

Lemche, N.P. 1995b. 'Justice in Western Asia in Antiquity, or: Why No Laws Were Needed!'. *Chicago Kent Law Review* 70: 1695–716.

Lemche, N.P. 1995c. 'Kings and Clients: On Loyalty between the Ruler and the Ruled in Ancient "Israel"'. *Semeia* 66: 119–32.

Lemche, N.P. 1996. 'From Patronage Society to Patronage Society'. In *The Origins of the Ancient Israelite States* (JSOTSup, 228), V. Fritz and P.R. Davies (eds). Sheffield: Sheffield Academic Press: 106–20.

Lemche, N.P. 1999. *The Canaanites and Their Land: The Tradition of the Canaanites* (JSOTSup, 110; 2nd edn). Sheffield: Sheffield Academic Press.

Lemche, N.P. 2010. 'Notes on the Amarna Letters', paper read at the *European Association of Biblical Studies Annual Meeting, July 25–29, 2010, Tartu (Estonia)*.

Lemche, N.P. 2013. 'Power and Social Organization: Some Misunderstandings and Some Proposals: Or, Is It All a Question of Patrons and Clients?'. In N.P. Lemche, *Biblical Studies and the Failure of History: Changing Perspectives 3* (CIS). Sheffield: Equinox: 158–68.

Lenclud, G. 2001. 'Le patronage politique: Du contexte aux raisons'. *L'anthropologie de la Méditerranée/Anthropology of the Mediterranean*, D. Albera, A. Blok and C. Bromberger (eds). Paris: Maisonneuve/Larose-MMSH: 277–306.

Lévi-Strauss, C. 1944. 'Reciprocity and Hierarchy'. *American Anthropologist* NS 46: 266–68.

Lévi-Strauss, C. 1950. 'Introduction à l'oeuvre de Marcel Mauss'. In M. Mauss, *Sociologie et anthropologie*. Paris: Presses Universitaires de France: ix–lii.

Lévi-Strauss, C. 1962. *La pensée sauvage*. Paris: Plon.

Lévi-Strauss, C. 1963. *Structural Anthropology*. New York: Basic Books [orig. French edn 1958].

Lévi-Strauss, C. 1969. *The Elementary Structures of Kinship*. Toronto: Beacon Press [orig. French edn 1949].

Levine, B. and J.-M. de Tarragon. 1984. 'Dead Kings and Rephaim: The Patrons of the Ugaritic Dynasty'. *JAOS* 104: 649–59.

Levy, T.E. (ed.). 1995. *The Archaeology of Society in the Holy Land*. New York: Facts on File.

Lichtheim, M. 1973. *Ancient Egyptian Literature. 1: The Old and Middle Kingdoms*. Berkeley: University of California Press.

Lichtheim, M. 1976. *Ancient Egyptian Literature. 2: The New Kingdom*. Berkeley: University of California Press.

Liebowitz, H. 1987. 'Late Bronze II Ivory Work in Palestine: Evidence of a Cultural Highpoint'. *BASOR* 265: 3–24.

Limet, H. 2005. 'Ethnicity'. In *A Companion to the Ancient Near East* (Blackwell Companions to the Ancient World), D.C. Snell (ed.). Oxford: Blackwell: 370–83.

Lindholm, C. 2002. *The Islamic Middle East: Tradition and Change* (2nd edn). Oxford: Blackwell.

Littlewood, P. 1974. 'Strings and Kingdoms: The Activities of a Political Mediator in Southern Italy'. *Archives Européennes de Sociologie* 15: 33–51.

Liverani, M. 1962. *Storia di Ugarit nell'età degli archivi politici* (Studi Semitici, 6). Roma: Università di Roma.

Liverani, M. 1965. 'Il fuoruscitismo nella Siria de la Tarda Etá del Bronzo'. *Rivista Storica Italiana* 77: 315–36.
Liverani, M. 1966. 'Problemi e indirizzi degli studi storici sul Vicino Oriente antico'. *Cultura e scuola* V/20: 72–9.
Liverani, M. 1967. 'Contrasti e confluenze di concezioni politiche nell'età di El-Amarna'. *RA* 61: 1–18.
Liverani, M. 1970. 'L'epica ugaritica nel suo contesto storico e letterario'. In *Atti del convegno internazionale sul tema: La poesia epica e la sua formazione* (Problemi attuali di scienza e di cultura, 19). Roma: Accademia Nazionale dei Lincei: 859–69.
Liverani, M. 1971. 'ΣΥΔΥΚ e ΜΙΣΩΡ'. In *Studi in onore di Edoardo Volterra* (Pubblicazioni della facolta di giurisprudenza dell'"università di Roma 40–45). Milano: Giuffré, VI: 55–74.
Liverani, M. 1973. 'Memorandum on the Approach to Historiographic Texts'. *Or* NS 42: 178–94.
Liverani, M. 1974. 'La royauté syrienne à l'âge du Bronze Récent'. In *Le palais et la royauté* (XIXe RAI), P. Garelli (ed.). Paris: P. Geuthner: 329–56.
Liverani, M. 1975. 'Communautés de village et palais royal dans la Syrie du IIème millénaire'. *JESHO* 18: 146–64.
Liverani, M. 1976a. 'La struttura politica'. In *L'alba della civiltà. Società, economia e pensiero nel Vicino Oriente antico*, S. Moscati (ed.). Torino: UTET, I: 275–414.
Liverani, M. 1976b. 'Il modo di produzione'. In *L'alba della civiltà. Società, economia e pensiero nel Vicino Oriente antico*, S. Moscati (ed.). Torino: UTET, II: 1–126.
Liverani, M. 1976c. 'La concezione dell'universo'. In *L'alba della civiltà. Società, economia e pensiero nel Vicino Oriente antico*, S. Moscati (ed.). Torino: UTET, III: 437–521.
Liverani, M. 1979a. 'Dono, tributo, commercio: ideologia dello scambio nella tarda età del Bronzo'. *Istituto Italiano di Numismatica. Annali* 26: 9–28.
Liverani, M. 1979b. 'Farsi Habiru'. *VO* 2: 65–77.
Liverani, M. 1979c. 'Pharaoh's Letter to Rib-Adda'. In M. Liverani, *Three Amarna Studies* (MANE, 1), M.L. Jaffe (ed.). Malibu: Undena: 3–13.
Liverani, M. 1979d. 'Social Implications in the Politics of Abdi-Ashirta of Amurru'. In M. Liverani, *Three Amarna Studies* (MANE, 1), M.L. Jaffe (ed.). Malibu: Undena: 14–20.
Liverani, M. 1979e. ''Irrational' Elements in the Amarna Trade'. In M. Liverani, *Three Amarna Studies* (MANE, 1), M.L. Jaffe (ed.). Malibu: Undena: 21–33.
Liverani, M. 1979f. 'Economia delle fattorie palatine ugaritiche'. *DdA* NS 1/2: 57–72.
Liverani, M. 1983a. 'Political Lexicon and Political Ideologies in the Amarna Letters'. *Berytus* 31: 41–56.
Liverani, M. 1983b. 'Dall'acculturazione alla deculturazione: Consideracioni sul rolo dei contatti politici ed economici nella storia siro-palestinese pre-ellenistica'. In *Forme di contatto e processi di trasformazione delle società antiche. Atti del Convegno di Cortone (24–30 Maggio 1981)* (Publications de la École Française de Rome, 67), G. Nenci (ed.). Roma: École Française de Rome: 503–20.
Liverani, M. 1983c. 'Communautés rurales dans la Syrie du II millénaire a.C.' In *Les Communautés rurales. II: Antiquité* (Recueils de la Société J. Bodin, 41). Paris: Dessain et Tolra: 147–85.
Liverani, M. 1984. 'Land Tenure and Inheritance in the Ancient Near East: The Interaction between "Palace" and "Family" Sectors'. In *Land Tenure and Social Transformation in the Middle East*, T. Khalidi (ed.). Beirut: American University of Beirut: 33–44.

Liverani, M. 1987. 'The Collapse of the Near Eastern Regional System at the End of the Bronze Age'. In *Centre and Periphery in the Ancient World*, M. Rowlands, M.T. Larsen and K. Kristiansen (eds). Cambridge: Cambridge University Press: 66–73.

Liverani, M. 1988. 'Il primo piano degli archivi di Ugarit'. *SEL* 5: 121–42.

Liverani, M. 1990a. 'Hattushili alle prese con la propaganda ramesside'. *Or* 59: 207–17.

Liverani, M. 1990b. 'A Seasonal Pattern for the Amarna Letters'. In *Lingering over Words: Studies in Ancient Near Eastern Literature in Honor of W.L. Moran*, T. Abush, J. Huehnergard and P. Steinkeller (eds). Atlanta, GA: Scholars Press: 337–48.

Liverani, M. 1990c. 'De la préhistoire à l'empire perse'. In *La Palestine: Histoire d'une terre* (Comprendre le Moyen-Orient), A. Giardina, M. Liverani and B. Scarcia Amoretti. Paris: L'Harmattan: 9–79.

Liverani, M. 1993. 'Nelle pieghe del despotismo. Organismi rappresentativi nell'antico Oriente'. *Studi Storici* 34: 7–33.

Liverani, M. 1998. *Le lettere di el-Amarna, 1. Le lettere dei 'Piccoli re'* (TVOA, 3/1). Brescia: Paideia.

Liverani, M. 1999. *Le lettere di el-Amarna, 2. Le lettere dei 'Grande re'* (TVOA, 3/2). Brescia: Paideia.

Liverani, M. 2000. 'The Great Powers' Club'. In *Amarna Diplomacy: The Beginning of International Relations*, R. Cohen and R. Westbrook (eds). Baltimore, MD: The Johns Hopkins University Press: 15–27 and 237–39.

Liverani, M. 2001. *International Relations in the Ancient Near East, 1600–1100 BC* (Studies in Diplomacy). New York: Palgrave Macmillan.

Liverani, M. 2002. 'Guerra santa e guerra giusta nel Vicino Oriente antico (1600–600 a.C.)'. *Studi Storici* 43: 639–59.

Liverani, M. 2004a. 'Telipinu, or: On Solidarity'. In M. Liverani, *Myth and Politics in Ancient Near Eastern Historiography* (BibleWorld), Intro. and ed. by Z. Bahrani and M. van de Mieroop. London: Equinox: 27–52.

Liverani, M. 2004b. 'Shunashura, or: On Reciprocity'. In M. Liverani, *Myth and Politics in Ancient Near Eastern Historiography* (BibleWorld), Intro. and ed. by Z. Bahrani and M. van de Mieroop. London: Equinox: 53–81.

Liverani, M. 2004c. 'Leaving by Chariot for the Desert'. In M. Liverani, *Myth and Politics in Ancient Near Eastern Historiography* (BibleWorld), Intro. and ed. by Z. Bahrani and M. van de Mieroop. London: Equinox: 83–96.

Liverani, M. 2004d. 'Rib-Adda, Righteous Sufferer'. In M. Liverani, *Myth and Politics in Ancient Near Eastern Historiography* (BibleWorld), Intro. and ed. by Z. Bahrani and M. van de Mieroop. London: Equinox: 97–144.

Liverani, M. 2004e. 'Aziru, Servant of Two Masters'. In M. Liverani, *Myth and Politics in Ancient Near Eastern Historiography* (BibleWorld), Intro. and ed. by Z. Bahrani and M. van de Mieroop. London: Equinox: 125–44.

Liverani, M. 2005a. 'The Near East: The Bronze Age'. In *The Ancient Economy: Evidence and Models*, J.G. Manning and I. Morris (eds). Stanford, CA: Stanford University Press: 47–57.

Liverani, M. 2005b. 'Il palazzo di Ugarit e l'economia siriana del Tardo Bronzo'. In *L'economia palaziale e la nascita della moneta: Dalla Mesopotamia all'Egeo*. Roma: Accademia dei Lincei: 121–40.

Liverani, M. 2008. 'The Late Bronze Age: Materials and Mechanisms of Trade and Cultural Exchange'. In *Beyond Babylon: Art, Trade, and Diplomacy in the Second Millennium B.C.*, J. Aruz, K. Benzel and J.M. Evans (eds). New York: The Metropolitan Museum of Art: 161–8.

Liverani, M. 2010. 'The Pharaoh's Body in the Amarna Letters'. In *ana turri gimilli: Studi dedicati al Padre Werner R. Mayer, S.J. da amici e allievi* (Quaderno di Vicino Oriente, V), M. Liverani and M.G. Biga (eds). Roma: Università degli Studi di Roma 'La Sapienza': 147–75.

Liverani, M. 2013. *The Ancient Near East: History, Society and Economy*. London: Routledge.

Llobera, J.R. 1999. *La identidad de la antropología* (2nd edn). Barcelona: Anagrama.

Loretz, O. 1984. *Habiru-Hebräer. Eine sozio-linguistische Studie über die Herkunft des Gentilismus* 'ibrî *vom Appelativum* ḫabiru (BZAW, 160). Berlin: W. de Gruyter.

Lorton, D. 1974. *The Juridical Terminology of the International Relations in Egyptian Texts through Dynasty XVIII*. Baltimore, MD: The Johns Hopkins University Press.

Lutfiyya, A.M. 1966. *Baytīn: A Jordanian Village. A Study of Social Institutions and Social Change in a Folk Community* (Studies in Social Anthropology, I). The Hague: Mouton.

Macqueen, J.G. 1995. 'The History of Anatolia and of the Hittite Empire: An Overview'. In *Civilizations of the Ancient Near East*, J.M. Sasson (ed.). New York: Scribner's Sons, II: 1085–105.

Maçzak, A. 2005. *Ungleiche Freundschaft. Klientelbeziehungen von der Antike bis zur Gegenwart* (Deutsche Historisches Institut Warschau: Klio in Polen, 7). Osnabrück: Fibre Verlag.

Magnetti, D.L. 1978. 'The Function of the Oath in the Ancient Near Eastern International Treaty'. *The American Journal of International Law* 72: 815–29.

Maidman, M.P. 1995. 'Nuzi: Portrait of an Ancient Mesopotamian Provincial Town'. In *Civilizations of the Ancient Near East*, J.M. Sasson (ed.). New York: Scribner's Sons, II: 931–47.

Maidman, M.P. 2010. *Nuzi Texts and Their Uses as Historical Evidence* (WAWSBL, 18). Atlanta, GA: Society of Biblical Literature.

Maier, J. 1995. 'The Ancient Near East in Modern Thought'. In *Civilizations of the Ancient Near East*, J.M. Sasson (ed.). New York: Scribner's Sons, I: 107–20.

Maisels, C.K. 1990. *The Emergence of Civilization: From Hunting and Gathering to Agriculture, Cities, and the State in the Near East*. London: Routledge.

Maisels, C.K. 1993. *The Near East: Archaeology in the 'Craddle of Civilization'*. London: Routledge.

Malinowski, B. 1922. *Argonauts of the Western Pacific: An Account of Native Enterprise and Adventure in the Archipelagoes of Melanesia and New Quinea*. London: Routledge.

Marcus, R. 1948. 'On the Genitive after *umma* in the Amarna Letters'. *JCS* 2: 223–4.

Marfoe, L. 1979. 'The Integrative Transformation: Patterns of Sociopolitical Organization in Southern Syria'. *BASOR* 234: 1–42.

Margueron, J.-C. 1995. 'Mari: A Portrait in Art of a Mesopotamian City-State'. In *Civilizations of the Ancient Near East*, J.M. Sasson (ed.). New York: Scribner's Sons, II: 885–99.

Margueron, J.-C. and M. Sigrist. 1997. 'Emar'. In *OxEncANE*, II: 236–39.

Marie, A. 1972. 'Parenté, échange matrimonial et réciprocité: Essai d'interprétation à partir de la société dan et de quelques autres sociétés de Côte d'Ivoire'. *L'Homme* 12/3–4: 5–46.

Marizza, M. (ed.). 2009. *Lettere ittite di re e dignatari. La corrispondenza interna del Medio Regno e dell'Età imperiale* (TVOA, 4/3). Brescia: Paideia.

Marques, A.C.D.R. 1999. 'Algumas faces de outros eus. Honra e patronagem na antropologia do Mediterrâneo'. *Mana. Estudos de antropologia social* 5: 131–47.

Márquez Rowe, I. 2002. 'The King's Men in Ugarit and Society in Late Bronze Age Syria'. *JESHO* 45: 1–19.
Márquez Rowe, I. 2003a. 'Anatolia and the Levant: Alalakh'. In *A History of Ancient Near Eastern Law* (HdO, 72), R. Westbrook (ed.). Leiden: E.J. Brill, I: 693–717.
Márquez Rowe, I. 2003b. 'Anatolia and the Levant: Ugarit'. In *A History of Ancient Near Eastern Law* (HdO, 72), R. Westbrook (ed.). Leiden: E.J. Brill, I: 719–35.
Marx, K. 1965. *Pre-Capitalist Economic Formations*. New York: International Publishers [orig. German edn 1857–58].
Matthiae, P. 2010. *Ebla, la città del trono: storia e archeologia* (Piccola Biblioteca Einaudi, 492). Torino: Einaudi.
Mauss, M. 1967. *Manuel d'ethnographie: Méthodes d'observation. Morphologie sociale. Technologie. Phénomènes artistiques. Phénomènes économiques. Phénomènes juridiques. Phénomènes moraux. Phénomènes religieux.* Paris: Payot [orig. edn 1926].
Mauss, M. 1990. *The Gift: The Form and Reason for Exchange in Archaic Society*. London: Routledge [orig. French edn 1950].
Mazar, A. 1990. *Archaeology of the Land of the Bible 10,000–586 B.C.E.* (ABRL). New York: Doubleday.
Mazzoni, S. 2003. 'Ebla: Crafts and Power in an Emergent State of Third Millennium BC Syria'. *Journal of Mediterranean Archaeology* 16: 173–91.
McCarthy, D.J. 1963. *Treaty and Covenant: A Study in Form in the Ancient Oriental Documents and in the Old Testament* (AnBib, 21): Roma: Pontifical Biblical Institute.
McGeough, K.M. 2007. *Exchange Relationships at Ugarit* (ANES – Sup, 26). Leuven: Peeters.
Médard, H. 1998. 'Postface'. In *Le clientélisme politique dans les sociétés contemporaines*, J.-L. Briquet and F. Sawicki (eds). Paris: Presses Universitaires de France: 307–16.
Meier, S.A. 1988. *The Messenger in the Ancient Semitic World* (HSM, 45). Atlanta, GA: Scholars Press.
Meier, S.A. 2000. 'Diplomacy and International Marriages'. In *Amarna Diplomacy: The Beginning of International Relations*, R. Cohen and R. Westbrook (eds). Baltimore, MD: The Johns Hopkins University Press: 165–73, 259–62.
Meillassoux, C. 1975. *Femmes, greniers et capitaux*. Paris: Maspero.
Meisel, J. 1974. 'Political Culture and the Politics of Culture'. *Canadian Journal of Political Science/Revue Canadienne de Science Politique* 7: 601–15.
Melville, S.C. 2005. 'Royal Women and the Exercise of Power in the Ancient Near East'. In *A Companion to the Ancient Near East* (Blackwell Companions to the Ancient World), D.C. Snell (ed.). Oxford: Blackwell: 219–28.
Mendelsohn. I. 1941. 'The Canaanite Term for "Free Proletarian"'. *BASOR* 83: 36–39.
Mendelsohn, I. 1955. 'New Light on the Ḫupšu'. *BASOR* 139: 9–11.
Mendelsohn, I. 1962. 'On Corvée Labor in Ancient Canaan and Israel'. *BASOR* 167: 31–5.
Michel, C. 2005. 'Le commerce privé des Assyriens en Anatolie: Un modéle du commerce archaïque selon K. Polanyi'. In *Autour de Polanyi: Vocabulaires, théories et modalités des échanges*, P. Clancier, F. Joannès, P. Rouillard and A. Tenu (eds). Paris: De Boccard: 121–33.
Milano, L. 1995. 'Ebla: A Third Millennium City-State in Ancient Syria'. In *Civilizations of the Ancient Near East*, J.M. Sasson (ed.). New York: Scribner's Sons, II: 1219–30.
Miller, J. 2013. *Royal Hittite Instructions and Related Administrative Texts* (SBLWAW, 31). Atlanta, GA: Society of Biblical Literature.

Momrak, K. 2013. 'Popular Power in Ancient Near Eastern and Archaic Greek Polities: A Reappraisal of Western and Eastern Political Cultures'. Unpublished Ph.D. Thesis, Bergen, University of Bergen.

Moorey, P.R.S. 2001. 'The Mobility of Artisans and Opportunities for Technology Transfer between Western Asia and Egypt in the Late Bronze Age'. In *The Social Context of Technological Change: Egypt and the Near East, 1650–1550 BC*, A.J. Shortland (ed.). Oxford: Oxbow Books: 1–14.

Moran, W.L. 1963. 'The Ancient Near Eastern Background of the Love of God in Deuteronomy'. *CBQ* 25: 77–87.

Moran, W.L. 1975. 'The Syrian Scribe of the Jerusalem Amarna Letters'. In *Unity and Diversity: Essays on the History, Literature, and Religion of the Ancient Near East*, H. Goedicke and J.J.M. Roberts (eds). Baltimore, MD: The Johns Hopkins University Press: 146–68.

Moran, W.L. 1992. *The Amarna Letters*. Baltimore, MD: The Johns Hopkins University Press.

Moran, W.L. 1995. 'Some Reflections on Amarna Politics'. In *Solving Riddles and Untying Knots. Biblical, Epigraphic and Semitic Studies in Honor of Jonas C. Greenfield*, Z. Zevit, S. Gitin and M. Sokoloff (eds). Winona Lake, IN: Eisenbrauns: 559–72.

Moreno García, J.M. 2014. 'Penser l'économie pharaonique'. *Annales: Histoire, Sciences Sociales* janvier–mars: 7–38.

Morris, E.F. 2005. *The Architecture of Imperialism: Military Bases and the Evolution of Foreign Policy in Egypt's New Kingdom* (Probleme der Ägyptologie, 22). Leiden: E.J. Brill.

Morris, E.F. 2006. 'Bowing and Scraping in the Ancient Near East: An Investigation into Obsequiousness in the Amarna Letters'. *JNES* 65: 179–96.

Morris, E.F. 2010. 'Opportunism in Contested Lands, B.C. and A.D. Or How Abdi-Ashirta, Aziru, and Padsha Khan Zadran Got Away with Murder'. In *Millions of Jubilees: Studies in Honor of David Silverman. Vol. 1*, Z. Hawass and J. Houser Wegner (eds). Cairo: Supreme Council of Antiquities Press: 413–38.

Morris, I. and J.G. Manning. 2005. 'Introduction'. In *The Ancient Economy: Evidence and Models*, J.G. Manning and I. Morris (eds). Stanford, CA: Stanford University Press: 1–44.

Morschauser, S. 1988. 'The End of the *Sḏf(3)–Tr(yt)* "Oath"'. *JARCE* 25: 93–103.

Moscati, S. (ed.). 1976a. *L'alba della civiltà. Societá, economia e pensiero. I: La società. II: L'economia. III: Il pensiero*. Torino: UTET.

Moscati, S. 1976b. 'Introduzione'. In *L'alba della civiltà. Societá, economia e pensiero*, S. Moscati (ed.). Torino: UTET, I: 1–17.

Muhly, J.D. 1995. 'Mining and Metalwork in Ancient Western Asia'. In *Civilizations of the Ancient Near East*, J.M. Sasson (ed.). New York: Scribner's Sons, III: 1501–21.

Müller, M. 2011. 'A View to Kill: Egypt's Grand Strategy in her Northern Empire'. In *Egypt, Canaan and Israel: History, Imperialism, Ideology and Literature* (CHANE, 52), S. Bar, D. Kahn and J.J. Shirley (eds). Leiden: E.J. Brill: 236–51.

Munn-Rankin, J.M. 1956. 'Diplomacy in Western Asia in the Early Second Millennium B.C.E.'. *Iraq* 18: 68–110.

Murnane, W.J. 1990. *The Road to Kadesh: A Historical Interpretation of the Battle Reliefs of King Seti I at Karnak* (SAOS, 42; 2nd edn). Chicago, IL: The Oriental Institute of the University of Chicago.

Murnane, W.J. 1995a. *Texts from the Amarna Period in Egypt* (WAWSBL, 5). Atlanta, GA: Scholars Press.

Murnane, W.J. 1995b. 'The Kingship of the Nineteenth Dynasty: A Study in the Resilience of an Institution'. In *Ancient Egyptian Kingship* (Probleme der Ägyptologie, 9), D. O'Connor and D. Silverman (eds). Leiden: E.J. Brill: 185–217.

Murnane, W.J. 2000. 'Imperial Egypt and the Limits of Power'. In *Amarna Diplomacy: The Beginning of International Relations*, R. Cohen and R. Westbrook (eds). Baltimore, MD: The Johns Hopkins University Press: 101–11, 247–52.

Mynářová, J. 2005. 'A Comment on the Opening Passages of the Amarna Letters – Its Structure and Its Address'. *Archiv Orientální* 73: 397–406.

Mynářová, J. 2006. 'Ugarit: "International" or "Vassal" Correspondence?'. In *L'État, le pouvoir, les prestations et leurs formes en Mésopotamie ancienne. Actes du Colloque assyriologique franco-tchèque. Paris, 7–8 novembre 2002*, P. Charvát, B. Lafont, J. Mynářová and L. Pecha (eds). Prague: Univerzita Karlova v Praze, 119–28.

Mynářová, J. 2007. *Language of Amarna – Language of Diplomacy: Perspectives on the Amarna Letters*. Prague: Czech Institute of Egyptology – Faculty of Arts, Charles University in Prague.

Mynářová, J. 2009. 'From Amarna to Ḫattušaš: Epistolary Traditions in the Amarna and Ramesside Correspondence'. In *My Things Changed Things: Social Development and Cultural Exchange in Prehistory, Antiquity, and the Middle Ages*, P. Mařikova Vlčkova, J. Mynářová and M. Tomašek (eds). Prague: Institute of Archaeology of the Academy of Sciences of the Czech Republic – Faculty of Arts, Charles University in Prague: 111–17.

Mynářová, Jana. 2014. 'Egyptian State Correspondence of the New Kingdom: The Letters of the Levantine Client Kings in the Amarna Correspondece and Contemporary Evidence'. In *State Correspondence in the Ancient World* (Oxford Studies in Ancient Empires), K. Radner (ed.). Oxford: Oxford University Press: 10–31.

Na'aman, N. 1981. 'Economic Aspects of the Egyptian Occupation of Canaan'. *IEJ* 31: 172–85.

Na'aman, N. 1988. 'Pharaonic Lands in the Jezreel Valley in the Late Bronze Age'. *Society and Economy in the Eastern Mediterranean* (OLA, 23), M. Heltzer and E. Lipiński (eds). Leuven: Peeters: 177–85.

Na'aman, N. 1990. 'Praises to the Pharaoh in Response to His Plans for a Campaign in Canaan'. In *Lingering over Words: Studies in Ancient Near Eastern Literature in Honor of W.L. Moran*, T. Abush, J. Huehnergard and P. Steinkeller (eds). Atlanta, GA: Scholars Press: 397–405.

Na'aman, N. 1997. 'The Network of Canaanite Late Bronze Kingdoms and the City of Ashdod'. *UF* 29: 599–626.

Na'aman, N. 2000. 'The Egyptian-Canaanite Correspondence'. In *Amarna Diplomacy: The Beginning of International Relations*, R. Cohen and R. Westbrook (eds). Baltimore, MD: The Johns Hopkins University Press: 125–38, 252–3.

Naderi, N. 1990. 'Max Weber and the Study of the Middle East: A Critical Analysis'. *Berkeley Journal of Sociology* 35: 71–88.

Nakhleh, K. 1975. 'The Direction of Local-Level Conflict in Two Arab Villages in Israel'. *American Ethnologist* 2: 497–516.

Newbury, C. 2000. 'Patrons, Clients, and Empire: The Subordination of Indigenous Hierarchies in Asia and Africa'. *Journal of World History* 11: 227–63.

Niehr, H. 1997. 'The Constitutive Principles for Establishing Justice and Order in Northwest Semitic Societies with Special Reference to Ancient Israel and Judah'. *ZABR* 3: 112–30.

Niehr, H. 1998. *Religionen in Israels Umwelt* (Die neue Echter Bibel – Ergänzungsband, 5). Würzburg: Echter Verlag.

Nigro, L. 1995. *Ricerche sull'architettura palaziale della Palestina nelle età del Bronzo e del Ferro: Contesto archeologico e sviluppo storico* (CMAO, 5). Roma: Università degli Studi di Roma 'La Sapienza'.

Nougayrol, J. 1963. 'Guerre et paix à Ugarit'. *Iraq* 25: 110–23.

O'Leary, B. 1989. *The Asiatic Mode of Production: Oriental Despotism, Historical Materialism and Indian History*. Oxford: Blackwell.

Oliva, J. (ed.). 2008. *Textos para una historia política de Siria-Palestina, I. El Bronce Antiguo y Medio* (Akal/Oriente, 11). Madrid: Akal.

Oller, G.H. 1995. 'Messengers and Ambassadors in Ancient Western Asia'. In *Civilizations of the Ancient Near East*, J.M. Sasson (ed.). New York: Scribner's Sons, III: 1465–73.

Oppenheim, A.L. 1960. 'Assyriology – Why and How?'. *CA* 1: 409–23.

Oren, E.D. 1984. ''Governors' Residences' in Canaan during the New Kingdom: A Case Study of Egyptian Administration'. *JSSEA* 14: 37–56.

Oren, E.D. 1997. 'The Hyksos Enigma – Introductory Overview'. In *The Hyksos: New Historical and Archaeological Perspectives* (University Museum Monograph, 96/ University Museum Symposium Series, 8), E.D. Oren (ed.). Philadelphia, PA: The University Museum – University of Pennsylvania: xix–xxvi.

Orenstein, H. 1980. 'Asymmetrical Reciprocity: A Contribution to the Theory of Political Legitimacy'. *CA* 21: 69–91.

Otto, A. 2012. 'Archaeological Evidence for Collective Governance along the Upper Syrian Euphrates during the Late and Middle Bronze Age'. In *Organization, Representation, and Symbols of Power in the Ancient Near East: Proceedings of the 54th Rencontre Assyriologique Internationale at Würzburg, 20–25 July 2008*, G. Wilhelm (ed.). Winona Lake, IN: Eisenbrauns: 87–99.

Pardee, D. 1997. 'Ugarit Inscriptions'. In *OxEncANE*, V: 264–6.

Pardee, D. 2002. *Ritual and Cult at Ugarit* (WAWSBL, 10). Atlanta, GA: Scholars Press.

Parker, S.B. (ed.). 1997. *Ugaritic Narrative Poetry* (WAWSBL, 9). Atlanta, GA: Scholars Press.

Parry, J. and M. Bloch (eds). 1989. *Money and the Morality of Exchange*. Cambridge: Cambridge University Press.

Patai, R. 1952. 'The Middle East as a Culture Area'. *Middle East Journal* 6: 1–21.

Paulus, S. 2013. 'Beziehungen zweier Großmächte – Elam und Babylonien in der 2. Hälfte des 2. Jt. v. Chr. Ein Beitrag zur Internen Chronologie'. In *Susa and Elam: Archaeological, Philological, Historical and Geographical Perspectives*, K. de Graef and J. Tavernier (eds). Leiden: E.J. Brill: 429–49.

Paulus, S. 2014. 'Babylonien in der 2. Hälfte des 2. Jts. v. Chr. – (K)ein Imperium? Ein Überblick über Geschichte und Struktur des mittelbabylonischen Reiches (ca. 1500–1000 B.C.)'. In *Imperien und Reiche in der Weltgeschichte: Epochenübergreifende und globalhistorische Vergleiche. Teil 1: Imperien des Altertums, Mittelalterliche und frühneuzeitliche Imperien*, M. Gehler and R. Rollinger (eds). Wiesbaden: Harrassowitz: 65–100.

Pébarthe, C. 2007. 'La question de la clientèle en Grèce Ancienne: Cimon versus Périclès, patronage privé contre patronage communitaire?'. In *Clientèle guerrière, clientèle foncière et clientèle électorale: Histoire et anthropologie*, V. Lécrivain (ed.). Dijon: Éditions Universitaires de Dijon: 173–97.

Peristiany, J. (ed.). 1965. *Honour and Shame: The Values of Mediterranean Societies*. Chicago, IL: University of Chicago Press.

Peristiany, J. (ed.). 1968. *Contributions to Mediterranean Sociology: Mediterranean Rural Communities and Social Change*. Paris: Mouton.

Peristiany, J. (ed.). 1976. *Mediterranean Family Structures* (Cambridge Studies in Social and Cultural Anthropology). Cambridge: Cambridge University Press.

Peristiany, J. and J. Pitt-Rivers (eds). 1992. *Honor and Grace in Anthropology* (Cambridge Studies in Social and Cultural Anthropology). Cambridge: Cambridge University Press.

Pernigotti, S. 2010. *L'Egitto di Ramesse II tra guerra e pace* (TVOA, I/7). Brescia: Paideia.

Petersen, A.R. 1998. *The Royal God: Enthronement Festivals in Ancient Israel and Ugarit?*, (JSOTSup, 259/CIS, 5). Sheffield: Sheffield Academic Press.

Petrie, W.M.F. 1898. *Syria and Egypt from the Tell el Amarna Letters*. London: Methuen.

Peyronel, L. 2008. *Storia e archeologia del commercio nell'Oriente antico* (Studi Superiori-Archeologia, 559). Roma: Carocci.

Peyronel, L. 2014. 'Between Archaic Market and Gift Exchange: The Role of Silver in the Embedded Economies of the Ancient Near East during the Bronze Age'. In *Gift Giving and the 'Embedded' Economies in the Ancient World*, F. Carlà and M. Gori (eds). Heidelberg: Universitätsverlag Winter: 355–76.

Pfälzner, P. 2007. 'Das System des 'kommerzialisierten Geschenkaustausches' im 2. Jahrtausend v. Chr. in Syrien'. In *Geschenke und Steuern, Zölle und Tribute: Antike Abgabenformen in Anspruch und Wirklichtkeit* (CHANE, 29), H. Klinkott, S. Kubisch and R. Müller-Wollermann (eds). Leiden: E.J. Brill: 109–23.

Pfälzner, P. 2012. 'Levantine Kingdoms of the Late Bronze Age'. In *A Companion to the Archaeology of the Ancient Near East*, D. Potts (ed.). Oxford: Wiley-Blackwell, II: 770–96.

Pfoh, E. 2004. 'De patrones y clientes: Sobre la continuidad de las prácticas sociopolíticas en la antigua Palestina'. *Antiguo Oriente* 2: 51–74.

Pfoh, E. 2011. 'De la relevancia de los conceptos de "sociedad estatal", "ciudad-estado" y "Estado tribal" en Siria-Palestina'. In *El Estado en el Mediterráneo Antiguo* (Estudios del Mediterráneo Antiguo – PEFSCEA, 7), M. Campagno, J. Gallego and C. García Mac Gaw (eds). Buenos Aires: Miño y Dávila: 81–104.

Pfoh, E. 2013. 'Loyal Servants of the King: A Political Anthropology of Subordination in Syria-Palestine (ca. 1600–600 BCE)'. *Palamedes: A Journal of Ancient History* 8: 25–41.

Pfoh, E. 2014. 'La política desde abajo en la Siria–Palestina de la Edad del Bronce Tardío'. *Antiguo Oriente* 12: 105–21.

Philipp, T. 2001. *Acre: The Rise and Fall of a Palestinian City, 1730–1831*. New York: Columbia University Press.

Pina-Cabral, J. de. 1989. 'The Mediterranean as a Category of Regional Comparison: A Critical View'. *CA* 30: 399–406.

Pinch, G. 1995. 'Private Life in Ancient Egypt'. In *Civilizations of the Ancient Near East*, J.M. Sasson (ed.). New York: Scribner's Sons, I: 363–81.

Pinnock, F. 2001. 'The Urban Landscape of Old Syrian Ebla'. *JCS* 53: 13–33.

Pintore, F. 1972. 'Transiti di truppe e schemi epistolare nella Siria egiziana dell'età di el-Amarna'. *OA* 11: 101–31.

Pintore, F. 1973. 'La prassi della marcia armata nella Siria egiziana dell'età di el-Amarna'. *OA* 12: 299–318.

Pintore, F. 1976. 'La struttura giuridica'. In *L'alba della civiltà. Società, economia e pensiero nel Vicino Oriente antico*, S. Moscati (ed.). Torino: UTET, I: 415–511.

Pintore, F. 1978. *Il matrimonio interdinastico nel Vicino Oriente durante i Secoli XV–XIII* (OAC, 14). Roma: Istituto per l'Oriente – Centro per le Antichità e la Storia dell'Arte del Vicino Oriente.

Pitt-Rivers, J. 1954. *The People of the Sierra*. London: Weidenfeld & Nicolson.

Pitt-Rivers, J. (ed.). 1963a. *Mediterranan Countrymen: Essays in the Social Anthropology of the Mediterranean*. The Hage: Mouton.

Pitt-Rivers, J. 1963b. 'Introduction'. In *Mediterranean Countrymen: Essays in the Social Anthropology of the Mediterranean*, J. Pitt-Rivers (ed.). Paris: Mouton: 9–25.

Pitt-Rivers, J. 1968. 'Pseudo-Kinship'. In *International Encyclopedia of Social Sciences*, D.L. Sills (ed.). New York: Macmillan/The Free Press, VIII: 408–13.

Pitt-Rivers, J. 1977. *The Fate of Shechem or the Politics of Sex: Essays on Mediterranean Anthropology* (Cambridge Studies in Social and Cultural Anthropology). Cambridge: Cambridge University Press.

Pitt-Rivers, J. 1997. 'Honour'. *Proceedings of the British Academy* 94: 229–51.

Pitt-Rivers, J. 2000. 'Las culturas del Mediterráneo'. In *Nueva antropología de las sociedades mediterráneas. Viejas culturas, nuevas visiones* (Antrazyt, 165), M.-À. Roqué (ed.). Barcelona: Icaria: 23–36.

Pitt-Rivers, J. 2012. 'The Law of Hospitality'. *HAU: Journal of Ethnographic Theory* 2: 501–17.

Podany, A.H. 2010. *Brotherhood of Kings: How International Relations Shaped the Ancient Near East*. Oxford: Oxford University Press.

Polanyi, K. 1957. 'The Economy as Instituted Process'. In *Trade and Market in the Early Empires: Economies in History and Theory*, K. Polanyi, C.M. Arensberg and H.W. Pearson (eds). Glencoe, Il.: The Free Press, 143–270.

Polanyi, K. 1960. 'On the Comparative Treatment of Economic Institutions in Antiquity, with Illustrations from Athens, Mycenae, and Alalakh'. In *City Invincible: A Symposium on Urbanization and Cultural Development in the Ancient Near East held at the Oriental Institute of the University of Chicago, December 4–7 1958*, C.H. Kraeling and R.M. Adams (eds). Chicago, IL: The University of Chicago Press: 329–50.

Polanyi, K. 1977. *The Livelihood of Man*. New York: Academic Press.

Polanyi, K., C.M. Arensberg and H.W. Pearson (eds). 1957. *Trade and Market in the Early Empires: Economies in History and Theory*. Glencoe, Il.: The Free Press.

Posener, G. 1940. *Princes et pays d'Asie et de Nubie. Textes hiératiques, sur des figurines d'envoûtement du Moyen Empire*. Bruxelles: Fondation Égyptologique Reine Élisabeth.

Possehl, G.L. 1998. 'Sociocultural Complexity Without the State: The Indus Civilization'. In *Archaic States*, G.M. Feinman and J. Marcus (eds). Santa Fe, NM: School of American Research Press: 261–91.

Potts, D.T. 1999. *The Archaeology of Elam: Formation and Transformation of an Ancient Iranian State*. Cambridge: Cambridge University Press.

Price, B.J. 1978. 'Secondary State Formation: An Explanatory Model'. In *Origins of the State: The Anthropology of Political Evolution*, R. Cohen and R. Service (eds). Philadelphia, PA: Institute for the Study of Human Issues: 161–86.

Prosser, M.C. 2010. *Bunušu in Ugaritian Society*, PhD Dissertation. Chicago, IL: Department of Near Eastern Languages and Civilizations – University of Chicago.

Pryke, L.M. 2011. 'The Many Complaints to Pharaoh of Rib-Addi of Byblos'. *JAOS* 131: 411–22.

Rabinowitz, Dan. 1997. *Overlooking Nazareth: The Ethnography of Exclusion in Galilee* (Cambridge Studies in Social and Cultural Anthropology). Cambridge: Cambridge University Press.

Rainey, A.F. 1962. *The Social Stratification of Ugarit*, Ph.D. dissertation. Ann Arbor, MI: Brandeis University, University Microfilms.

Rainey, A.F. 1978. *El-Amarna Tablets 359–378. Supplement to J.A. Knudtzon, Die El-Amarna-Tafeln* (AOAT, 8; 2nd edn). Kevelaer: Butzon & Bercker.

Rainey, A.F. 1996. *Canaanite in the Amarna Tablets: A Linguistic Analysis of the Mixed Dialect Used by Scribes from Canaan* (4 vols.; HdO, 1/25). Leiden: E.J. Brill.

Rainey, A.F. 2003. 'Amarna and Later: Aspects of Social History'. In *Symbiosis, Symbolism, and the Power of the Past: Canaan, Ancient Israel, and Their Neighbors from the Late Bronze Age through Roman Palaestina*, W.G. Dever and S. Gitin (eds). Winona Lake, IN: Eisenbrauns: 169–87.

Rainey, A.F. 2014. *The El-Amarna Correspondence: A New Edition of the Cuneiform Letters from the Site of El-Amarna based on Collations of all Extant Texts* (2 vols; ed. by W. Schniedewind and Z. Cochavi-Rainey; HdO, 110). Leiden: E.J. Brill.

Rede, M. 2005. 'Le "commerce sans marché à l'époque de Hammu-rabi": Réévaluation d'une thése polanyienne à partir d'une étude de cas'. In *Autour de Polanyi: Vocabulaires, théories et modalités des échanges*, P. Clancier, F. Joannès, P. Rouillard and A. Tenu (eds). Paris: De Boccard: 135–53.

Redford, D.B. 1984. *Akhenaten, The Heretic King*. Princeton, NJ: Princeton University Press.

Redford, D.B. 1992. *Egypt, Canaan, and Israel in Ancient Times*. Princeton, NJ: Princeton University Press.

Redford, D.B. 1995. 'The Concept of Kingship during the Eighteenth Dynasty'. In *Ancient Egyptian Kingship* (Probleme der Ägyptologie, 9), D. O'Connor and D. Silverman (eds). Leiden: E.J. Brill: 157–84.

Redford, D.B. 1997. 'Textual Sources for the Hyksos Period'. In *The Hyksos: New Historical and Archaeological Perspectives* (University Museum Monograph, 96/ University Museum Symposium Series, 8), E.D. Oren (ed.). Philadelphia, PA: The University Museum – University of Pennsylvania: 1–44.

Redford, D.B. 2003. *The Wars in Syria and Palestine of Tuthmose III* (CHANE, 16). Leiden: E.J. Brill.

Redford, D.B. 2006. 'The Northern Wars of Tuthmose III'. In *Tuthmose III: A New Biography*, E.H. Cline and D. O'Connor (eds). Ann Arbor, MI: The University of Michigan Press: 325–43.

Redman, C.L. 1978. *The Rise of Civilization: From Early Farmers to Urban Society in the Ancient Near East*. San Francisco: W.H. Freeman.

Renfrew, C. 1986. 'Introduction: Peer Polity Interaction and Socio-Political Change'. In *Peer Polity Interaction and Socio-Political Change*, C. Renfrew and J. Cherry (eds). Cambridge: Cambridge University Press: 1–18.

Reviv, H. 1969. 'On Urban Representative Institutions and Self–Government in Syria Palestine in the Second Half of the Second Millennium B.C.'. *JESHO* 12: 283–97.

Rodríguez López, A. and R. Pastor. 2000. 'Reciprocidades, intercambio y jerarquías en las sociedades medievales'. *Hispania* LX/1, núm. 204: 63–101.

Roque, M.-À. (ed.). 2000. *Nueva antropología de las sociedades mediterráneas: Viejas culturas, nuevas visiones* (Antrazyt, 165). Barcelona: Icaria.

Roque, M.-À. 2005. *Antropología mediterránea: prácticas compartidas* (Enciclopedia del Mediterráneo, 23). Barcelona: Icaria.

Rosenfeld, H. 1974. 'Non-Hierarchical, Hierarchical and Masked Reciprocity in an Arab Village'. *Anthropological Quarterly* 47: 139–66.

Rössler, M. 2007. 'Von der Gabe zur Abgabe: Transaktionen im politischen Kontext'. In *Geschenke und Steuern, Zölle und Tribute: Antike Abgabenformen in Anspruch und Wirklichtkeit* (CHANE, 29), H. Klinkott, S. Kubisch and R. Müller-Wollermann (eds). Leiden: E.J. Brill: 3–27.

Roth, M. (ed.). 1997. *Law Collections from Mesopotamia and Asia Minor* (WAWSBL, 6; 2nd edn). Atlanta, GA: Society of Biblical Literature.

Rowton, M. 1959. 'The Background of the Treaty between Ramesses II and Ḫattušiliš III'. *JCS* 13: 1–11.

Rowton, M. 1965. 'The Topological Factor in the *ḫapiru* Problem'. In *Studies in Honor of Benno Landsberger on His Seventy-Fifth Birthday, April 21, 1963* (The Oriental Institute of the University of Chicago – Assyriological Studies, 16), H.G. Güterborg and T. Jakobsen (eds). Chicago, IL: The University of Chicago Press: 375–87.

Rowton, M. 1967. 'The Woodlands of Ancient Western Asia'. *JNES* 26: 261–77.

Rowton, M. 1973a. 'Autonomy and Nomadism in Western Asia'. *Or* NS 42: 247–58.

Rowton, M. 1973b. 'Urban Autonomy in a Nomadic Environment'. *JNES* 32: 201–15.

Rowton, M. 1974. 'Enclosed Nomadism'. *JESHO* 17: 1–30.

Rowton, M. 1976. 'Dimorphic Structure and the Problem of the 'apirû-'ibrîm'. *JNES* 35: 13–20.

Rowton, M. 1977. 'Dimorphic Structure and the Parasocial Element'. *JNES* 36: 181–98.

Roy, O. 1989. 'Afghanistan: Back to Tribalism or on to Lebanon?'. *Third World Quarterly* 11: 70–82.

Sacchi, P. and P.P. Viazzo. 2014. 'Family and Household'. In *A Companion to Mediterranean History*, P. Horden and S. Kinoshita (eds). Oxford: Wiley Blackwell: 234–49.

Sahlins, M.D. 1963. 'Poor Man, Rich Man, Big-Man, Chief: Political Types in Melanesia and Polynesia'. *CSSH* 5: 285–303.

Sahlins, M.D. 1972. *Stone Age Economics*. Chicago, IL: Aldine.

Sahlins, M.D. 1985. *Islands of History*. Chicago, IL: The University of Chicago Press.

Said, E.W. 1978. *Orientalism*. London: Penguin Books.

Salzman, P.C. 1974. 'Tribal Chiefs as Middlemen: The Politics of Encapsulation in the Middle East'. *Anthropological Quarterly* 47: 203–10.

Salzman, P.C. 1978. 'The Study of "Complex Society" in the Middle East: A Review Essay'. *International Journal of Middle East Studies* 9: 539–57.

Sapin, J. 1981. 'La géographie humaine de la Syrie-Palestine au deuxième millénaire avant J.-C. comme voie de recherche historique, I'. *JESHO* 24: 1–62.

Sapin, J. 1982. 'La géographie humaine de la Syrie-Palestine au deuxième millénaire avant J.-C. comme voie de recherche historique, II–III'. *JESHO* 25: 1–49, 113–86.

Sapin, J. 1983. 'Quelques systemes socio-politiques en Syrie au 2e millénaire avant J.-C. et leur evólution historique d'après des documents religieux (Légendes, rituels, sanctuaires)'. *UF* 15: 157–90.

Sasson, J.M. 1968. 'Instances of Mobility among Mari Artisans'. *BASOR* 190: 46–54.

Savage, S.H. and S.E. Falconer. 2003. 'Spatial and Statistical Inference of Late Bronze Age Polities in the Southern Levant'. *BASOR* 330: 31–45.

Saville-Troike, M. 2003. *The Ethnography of Communication: An Introduction* (3rd edn). Oxford: Blackwell.

Scarcia Amoretti, B. 1990. 'La Palestine musulmane'. In A. Giardina, M. Liverani and B. Scarcia Amoretti, *La Palestine: Histoire d'une terre* (Comprendre le Moyen-Orient). Paris: L'Harmattan: 117–208.

Scheffler, T. 2003. '"Fertile Crescent", "Orient", "Middle East": The Changing Mental Maps of Southwest Asia'. *European Review of History* 10: 253–72.

Schemeil, Y. 1999. *La politique dans l'Ancien Orient*. Paris: Presses de Sciences Po.

Schloen, J.D. 2001. *The House of the Father as Fact and Symbol: Patrimonialism in Ugarit and the Ancient Near East* (SAHL, 2). Winona Lake, IN: Eisenbrauns.

Schneider, P. 1969. 'Honor and Conflict in a Sicilian Town'. *Anthropological Quarterly* 42: 130–54.

Schulman, A.R. 1964. 'Some Observations on the Military Background of the Amarna Period'. *JARCE* 3: 51–69.

Schulman, A.R. 1979. 'Diplomatic Marriage in the Egyptian New Kingdom'. *JNES* 38: 177–93.

Scott, J. 1977. 'Patronage or Exploitation?'. In *Patrons and Clients in Mediterranean Societies*, E. Gellner and J. Waterbury (eds). London: Duckworth: 21–39.

Service, E.R. 1978. 'Classical and Modern Theories of the Origins of Government'. In *Origins of the State: The Anthropology of Political Evolution*, R. Cohen and E.R. Service (eds). Philadelphia, PA: Institute for the Study of Human Issues: 21–34.

Sethe, K. 1926. *Die Ächtung feindlicher Fürsten, Völker und Dinge auf altägyptischen Tongefäßscherben des Mittleren Reiches*. Berlin: APAW.

Several, M.W. 1972. 'Reconsidering the Egyptian Empire in Palestine during the Amarna Period'. *PEQ* 104: 123–33.

Sherrat, A. and S. Sherrat. 2001. 'Technological Change in the East Mediterranean Bronze Age: Capital, Resources and Marketing'. In *The Social Context of Technological Change: Egypt and the Near East, 1650–1550 BC*, A.J. Shortland (ed.). Oxford: Oxbow Books: 15–38.

Sherrat, S. 2003. 'The Mediterranean Economy: "Globalization" at the End of the Second Millennium B.C.E.'. In *Symbiosis, Symbolism, and the Power of the Past. Canaan, Ancient Israel, and Their Neighbors from the Late Bronze Age through Roman Palaestina*, W.G. Dever and S. Gitin (eds). Winona Lake, IN: Eisenbrauns: 37–62.

Shunnaq, M. 1997. 'Political and Economic Conflict within Extended Kin Groups and Its Effects on the Household in a North Jordanian Village'. *Journal of Comparative Family Studies* 28: 136–50.

Silva Castillo, J. 2005. 'Nomadism Through the Ages'. In *A Companion to the Ancient Near East* (Blackwell Companions to the Ancient World), D.C. Snell (ed.). Oxford: Blackwell: 126–40.

Silverman, S. 1968. 'Agricultural Organization, Social Structure, and Values in Italy: Amoral Familism Reconsidered'. *American Anthropologist* NS 70: 1–20.

Silverman, S. 1977. 'Patronage as Myth'. In *Patrons and Clients in Mediterranean Societies*, E. Gellner and J. Waterbury (eds). London: Duckworth: 7–19.

Silverman, S. 2001. 'Defining the Anthropological Mediterranean: Before Aix 1966'. In *L'anthropologie de la Méditerranée/Anthropology of the Mediterranean*, D. Albera, A. Blok and C. Bromberger (eds). Paris: Maisonneuve/Larose–MMSH: 43–57.

Simmel, G. 1950. 'Superordination and Subordination'. In *The Sociology of Georg Simmel*, trans. and ed. by K.H. Wolff. Glencoe, IL: The Free Press: 181–306 [orig. German edn 1908].

Singer, A. 1994. *Palestinian Peasants and Ottoman Officials: Rural Administration around Sixteenth-Century Jerusalem* (Cambridge Studies in Islamic Civilization). Cambridge: Cambridge University Press.

Singer, I. 1991. 'A Concise History of Amurru'. In *Amurru Akkadian: A Linguistic Study* (HSS, 41), S. Izre'el (ed.). Atlanta, GA: Scholars Press: 134–95.

Singer, I. 1999. 'A Political History of Ugarit'. In *A Handbook of Ugaritic Studies* (HdO; Abt. 1, Der Nahe und Mittelere Osten: Bd. 39), W.G.E. Watson and N. Wyatt (eds). Leiden: E.J. Brill: 603–733.

Smith, M.G. 1968. 'Political Organization'. In *International Encyclopedia of the Social Sciences*, D.L. Sills (ed.). New York: The Macmillan Company and The Free Press, XII: 193–202.

Smith, M.L. 2005. 'Networks, Territories, and the Cartography of Ancient States'. *Annals of the Association of American Geographers* 95: 832–49.

Smith, M.S. and W.T. Pitard. 2009. *The Ugaritic Baal Cycle, Volume II. Introduction wih Text, Translation and Commentary of KTU/CAT 1.3–1.4* (VTSup, 114). Leiden: E.J. Brill.

Smith. S. 1949. *The Statue of Idrimi* (Occasional Publications of the British Institute of Archaeology at Ankara, 1). London: The British Institute of Archaeology at Ankara.

Smith, S.T. 1991. 'A Model for Egyptian Imperialism in Nubia'. *GM* 122: 77–102.

Smith, S.T. 2003. *Wretched Kush: Ethnic Identities and Boundaries in Egypt's Nubian Empire*. London: Routledge.

Sofri, G. 1969. *Il modo di produzione asiatico: Storia di una controversia marxista*. Torino: Einaudi.

Solans, B.E. 2011. *Poderes colectivos en la Siria del Bronce Final*, PhD Dissertation. Zaragoza: Universidad de Zaragoza.

Solvang, E.K. 2006. 'Another Look "Inside": Harems and the Interpretation of Women'. In *Orientalism, Assyriology and the Bible* (HBM, 10), S.W. Holloway (ed.). Sheffield: Sheffield Phoenix Press: 374–98.

Sommerfeld, W. 1995. 'The Kassites of Ancient Mesopotamia: Origins, Politics, and Culture'. In *Civilizations of the Ancient Near East*, J.M. Sasson (ed.). New York: Scribner's Sons, II: 917–30.

Southall, A. 1988. 'The Segmentary State in Africa and Asia'. *CSSH* 30: 52–82.

Spalinger, A.J. 1981. 'Considerations on the Hittite Treaty between Egypt and Hatti'. *SAK* 9: 299–358.

Spalinger, A.J. 1996. 'From Local to Global: The Extension of an Egyptian Bureaucratic Term to the Empire'. *SAK* 23: 353–76.

Spalinger, A.J. 2005. *War in Ancient Egypt: The New Kingdom*. Oxford: Blackwell.

Stager, L.E. 1985. 'The Archaeology of the Family in Ancient Israel'. *BASOR* 260: 1–35.

Starke, F. 2005–6. 'Los hititas y su imperio. Constitución, federalismo y pensamiento político'. *RIHAO* 12–13: 189–303.

Stol, M. 1995. 'Private Life in Ancient Mesopotamia'. In *Civilizations of the Ancient Near East*, J.M. Sasson (ed.). New York: Scribner's Sons, I: 485–501.

Strange, J. 2000. 'The Palestinian City-States of the Bronze Age'. In *A Comparative Study of Thirty City-State Cultures* (Historisk-filosofiske Skrifter, 21/Det Kongelige Danske Videnskabernes Selskab), M.H. Hansen (ed.). Copenhagen: C.A. Reitzels Forlag: 67–76.

Struve, V.V. 1969. 'The Problem of the Genesis, Development and Disintegration of the Slave Societies in the Ancient Orient'. In *Ancient Mesopotamia: Socio-Economic History*, I.M. Diakonoff (ed.). Moscow: Nauka: 17–69 [orig. in Russian 1933].

Sugerman, M. 2000. 'Trade and Power in Late Bronze Age Canaan'. In *Exploring the Longue Durée: Essays in Honor of Lawrence E. Stager*, in J.D. Schloen (ed.). Winona Lake, IN: Eisenbrauns: 439–48.

Sweet, L.E. and T.J. O'Leary (eds). 1969. *Circum-Mediterranean Peasantry: Introductory Bibliographies*. New Haven, CT: Human Relations Area Files Press.

Tadmor, H. 1982. 'Treaty and Oath in the Ancient Near East: A Historian's Approach'. In *Humanizing America's Iconic Book*, G.M. Tucker and D.A. Knight (eds). Chico, CA: Scholars Press: 127–52.

Testart, A. 2005. 'Les royautés archaïques sont–elles marquées par la redistribution? (critique de la trilogie: réciprocité, redistribution, échange)'. In *Autour de Polanyi: Vocabulaires, théories et modalités des échanges*, P. Clancier, F. Joannès, P. Rouillard and A. Tenu (eds). Paris: De Boccard: 67–81.

Testart, A. 2006. *Des don et des dieux: Anthropologie religieuse et sociologie comparative* (2nd rev. edn). Paris: Errance.

Testart, A. 2007. 'Clientèle, clientélisme, évergétisme et liturgie'. In *Clientèle guerrière, clientèle foncière et clientèle électorale: Histoire et anthropologie*, V. Lécrivain (ed.). Dijon: Éditions Universitaires de Dijon: 219–39.

Testart, A., V. Lécrivain, D. Karadimas and N. Govoroff. 2001. 'Prix de la fiancée et esclavage pour dettes. Un example de loi sociologique'. *Études rurales* 159–60: 9–33.

Testart, A., N. Govoroff and V. Lécrivain. 2002. 'Les prestations matrimoniales'. *L'Homme* 161: 165–96.

Thiesse, A.M. 1999. *La creation des identités nationales: Europe XVIIIe siècle–XXe siècle*. Paris: Éditions du Seuil.

Thomas, K. 1963. 'History and Anthropology'. *Past & Present* 24: 3–24.

Thompson, E.P. 1971. 'The Moral Economy of the English Crowd in the Eighteenth Century'. *Past & Present* 50: 76–136.

Thompson, J.A. 1974. 'The Significance of the Verb *Love* in the David-Jonathan Narratives in 1 Samuel'. *VT* 24: 334–8.

Thompson, J.A. 1977. 'Israel's 'Lovers''. *VT* 27: 475–81

Thompson, T.L. 1974. *The Historicity of the Patriarchal Narratives: The Quest for the Historical Abraham* (BZAW, 134). Berlin: W. de Gruyter.

Thompson, T.L. 1992. *Early History of the Israelite People: From the Written and Archaeological Sources* (SHANE, 4). Leiden: E.J. Brill.

Thompson, T.L. 1999. *The Bible in History: How Writers Create the Past*. London: Jonathan Cape.

Thompson, T.L. 2005. *The Messiah Myth: The Near Eastern Roots of Jesus and David*. New York: Basic Books.

Thompson, T.L. 2007. 'A Testimony of the Good King: Reading the Mesha Stele'. In *Ahab Agonistes: The Rise and Fall of the Omri Dynasty* (LHB/OTS, 421/ESHM, 6), L.L. Grabbe (ed.). London: T & T Clark: 236–97.

Thuesen, I. 2000. 'The City-State in Ancient Western Syria'. In *A Comparative Study of Thirty City-State Cultures* (Historisk-filosofiske Skrifter, 21/Det Kongelige Danske Videnskabernes Selskab), M.H. Hansen (ed.). Copenhagen: C.A. Reitzels Forlag: 55–65.

Tomes, R. 2005. *'I Have Written to the King, My Lord': Secular Analogies for the Psalms* (HBM, 1). Sheffield: Sheffield Phoenix Press.

Tönnies, F. 1887. *Gemeinschaft und Gesellschaft. Grundbegriffe der reinen Soziologie*. Leipzig: Fues's Verlag.

Tugendhaft, A. 2012. 'How to Become a Brother in the Bronze Age: An Inquiry into the Representations of Politics in Ugaritic Myth'. *Fragments* 2: 89–104.

Valensi, L. 1974. 'Anthropologie économique et Histoire: L'oeuvre de Karl Polanyi'. *Annales. Histoire, Sciences Sociales* 29: 1311–19.

Vallogia, M. 1976. *Recherche sur les 'messagers' (wpwtjw) dans les sources égyptiennes profanes* (Centre de Recherches d'Histoire et de Philologie de la IVème section de l'Ecole practique des Hautes Etudes, II/Hautes Etudes Orientales, 6). Genève: Droz.

Van de Mieroop, M. 2007. *The Eastern Mediterranean in the Age of Ramesses II*. Oxford: Blackwell.

Van der Steen, E. 2013. *Near Eastern Tribal Societies during the Nineteenth Century: Economy, Society and Politics between Tent and Town* (Approaches to Anthropological Archaeology). Sheffield: Equinox.

Van der Toorn, K. 2000. 'Cuneiform Documents from Syria-Palestine. Texts, Scribes, and Schools'. *ZDPV* 116: 97–113.

Vandersleyen, C. 1995. *L'Egypte et la vallée du Nil. Tome 2: De la fin de l'Ancien Empire à la fin du Novel Empire* (Nouvelle Clio). Paris: Presses Universitaires de France.

Van Dijk, J. 2003. 'The Amarna Period and the Later New Kingdom (c. 1352–1069 BC)'. In *The Oxford History of Ancient Egypt*, I. Shaw (ed.). Oxford: Oxford University Press: 265–85.

Van Soldt, W.H. 1995. 'Ugarit: A Second Millennium Kingdom on the Mediterranean Coast'. In *Civilizations of the Ancient Near East*, J.M. Sasson (ed.). New York: Scribners' Sons, II: 1255–66.

Van Soldt, W.H. 2010. 'The City-Administration of Ugarit'. In *City-Administration in the Ancient Near East: Proceedings of the 53e Rencontre Assyriologique Internationale. Vol. 2* (Babel und Bibel, 6), L. Kogan, N. Koslova, S. Loesov and S. Tishchenko (eds). Winona Lake, IN: Eisenbrauns: 247–61.

Van Soldt, W.H. 2013. 'The Extent of Literacy in Syria and Palestine during the Second Millennium B.C.E.'. In *Time and History in the Ancient Near East: Proceedings of the 56th Rencontre Assyriologique Internationale at Barcelona, 26–30 July 2010*, L. Feliu, J. Llop, A. Millet Albà and J. Sanmartín (eds). Winona Lake, IN: Eisenbrauns: 19–31.

Vargyas, P. 1988. 'Stratification Sociale à Ugarit'. In *Society and Economy in the Eastern Mediterranean* (OLA, 23), M. Heltzer and E. Lipiński (eds). Leuven: Peeters: 111–23.

Vernus, P. 2011. 'Los barbechos del demiurgo y la soberanía del faraón. El concepto de 'imperio' y las latencias de la creación'. In *El Estado en el Mediterráneo antiguo. Egipto, Grecia, Roma* (Estudios del Mediterráneo Antiguo – PEFSCEA, 7), M. Campagno, J. Gallego y C.G. García Mac Gaw (eds). Buenos Aires: Miño y Dávila: 13–43.

Viazzo, P.P. 2009. *Introduzione all'antropologia storica* (4th edn). Bari: Laterza.

Vidal, J. 2006a. *Las aldeas de Ugarit según los archivos del Bronce Reciente (siglos XIV–XII a.n.e)* (AULAOS, 21). Barcelona: AUSA.

Vidal, J. 2006b. 'Ugarit at War (1)'. *UF* 37: 653–72.

Vidal, J. 2010. 'Sutean Warfare in the Amarna Letters'. In *Studies on War in the Ancient Near East: Collected Essays on Military History* (Alter Orient und Altes Testament, 372), J. Vidal (ed.). Münster: Ugarit-Verlag: 95–103.

Vidal, J. 2015a. 'Reflexiones historiográficas sobre el Orientalismo Antiguo'. In *Descubriendo el Antiguo Oriente: Pioneros y arqueólogos de Mesopotamia y Egipto a finales del s. XIX y principios del s. XX* (Bellaterra Arqueología), R. Da Riva and J. Vidal (eds). Barcelona: Bellaterra: 25–36.

Vidal, J. 2015b. 'El descubrimiento arqueológico de la antigua Ugarit. Análisis de un relato eurocéntrico'. In *Descubriendo el Antiguo Oriente: Pioneros y arqueólogos de Mesopotamia y Egipto a finales del s. XIX y principios del s. XX* (Bellaterra Arqueología), R. Da Riva and J. Vidal (eds). Barcelona: Bellaterra: 197–213.

Vidal-Naquet, P. 1964. 'Histoire et idéologie: Karl Wittfogel et le concept de "mode de production asiatique"'. *Annales: Économies, sociétés, civilisations* 19: 531–49.

Vita, J.-P. 1995. *El ejército de Ugarit* (Banco de Datos Filológicos Semíticos Noroccidentales – Monografías, 1). Madrid–Zaragoza: Consejo Superior de Investigaciones Científicas.

Vita, J.-P. 2010. 'Scribes and Dialects in Late Bronze Age Canaan'. In *City-Administration in the Ancient Near East: Proceedings of the 53e Rencontre Assyriologique Internationale. Vol. 1 Part 2* (Babel und Bibel, 6), L. Kogan, N. Koslova, S. Loesov and S. Tishchenko (eds). Winona Lake, IN: Eisenbrauns: 863–94.

Von Dassow, E. 2004. 'Canaanite in Cuneiform'. *JAOS* 124: 641–74.

Von Dassow, E. 2008. *State and Society in the Late Bronze Age: Alalaḫ under the Mittani Empire* (Studies on the Civilization and Culture of Nuzi and the Hurrians, 17). Bethesda, MD: CDL Press.

Von Dassow, E. 2014. 'Levantine Polities under Mittanian Hegemony'. In *Constituent, Confederate, and Conquered Space: The Emergence of the Mittani State* (Topoi – Berlin Studies of the Ancient World, 17), E. Cancik-Kirschbaum, N. Brisch and J. Eidem (eds). Berlin: W. de Gruyter: 11–32.

Von Schuler, E. 1969. 'Beziehungen zwischen Syrien und Anatolien in der Späten Bronzezeit'. In *La Siria nel Tardo Bronzo* (Orientis Antiqvi Collectio, IX), M. Liverani (ed.). Roma: Centro per la Antichità e la Storia dell'Arte del Vicino Oriente: 97–116.

Wachtel, N. 1971. *La vision des vaincus: Les indiens du Pérou devant la conquête espagnole (1530–1570)*. Paris: Gallimard.

Wachtel, N. 1974. 'L'acculturation'. In *Faire de l'histoire, I: Nouveaux problèmes* (Bibliothèque des histoires), J. Le Goff and P. Nora (eds). Paris: Gallimard: 124–46.

Wallace-Hadrill, A. (ed.). 1989. *Patronage in Ancient Society*. London: Routledge.

Warburton, D. 2003. 'Love and War in the Late Bronze Age: Egypt and Hatti'. In *Ancient Perspectives on Egypt* (Encounters with Ancient Egypt), R. Matthews y C. Roemer (eds). London: UCL Press: 75–100.

Weber, M. 1978. *Economy and Society: An Outline of Interpretive Sociology*. Berkeley: University of California Press [orig. German edn 1922].

Weiner, A.B. 1992. *Inalienable Possessions: The Paradox of Keeping-While-Giving*. Berkeley: University of California Press.

Weinfeld, M. 1976. 'The Loyalty Oath in the Ancient Near East'. *UF* 8: 379–414.

Weinfeld, M. 1995. *Social Justice in Ancient Israel and in the Ancient Near East*. Jerusalem: The Magness Press.

Weingrod, A. 1968. 'Patrons, Patronage, and Political Parties'. *CHHS* 10: 377–400.

Weingrod, A. 1977. 'Patronage and Power'. In *Patrons and Clients in Mediterranean Societies*, E. Gellner and J. Waterbury (eds). London: Duckworth: 41–51.

Weinstein, J.M. 1981. 'The Egyptian Empire in Palestine: A Reassessment'. *BASOR* 241: 1–28.

Weippert, H. 1988. *Palästina in vorhellenistischer Zeit* (Handbuch der Archäeologie/Vorderasien II, Band I). München: C.H. Beck.

Wengrow, D. 1996. 'Egyptian Taskmasters and Heavy Burdens: Highland Exploitation and the Collared–Rim Pithos of the Bronze/Iron Age Levant'. *OJA* 16: 307–26.

Wente, E.F. 1967. *Late Ramesside Letters* (SAOC, 33). Chicago, IL: The University of Chicago Press.

Westbrook, R. 2000. 'International Law in the Amarna Age'. In *Amarna Diplomacy: The Beginning of International Relations*, R. Cohen and R. Westbrook (eds). Baltimore, MD: The Johns Hopkins University Press: 28–41, 239–42.

Westbrook, R. (ed.). 2003a. *A History of Ancient Near Eastern Law* (2 vols.; HdO, 72), Leiden, E.J. Brill.

Westbrook, R. 2003b. 'Anatolia and the Levant: Emar and Vicinity'. In *A History of Ancient Near Eastern Law* (HdO, 72), R. Westbrook (ed.). Leiden: E.J. Brill, I: 657–91.

Westbrook, R. 2005a. 'Penelope's Dowry and Odysseus' Kingship'. In *Symposion 2001: Vorträge zur griechischen und hellenistischen Rechtsgeschichte (Evanston, Illinois, September 5–8, 2001)*, R.W. Wallace and M. Gagarin (eds). Wien: Verlag der Österreichischen Akademie der Wissenschaften: 3–23.

Westbrook, R. 2005b. 'Patronage in the Ancient Near East'. *JESHO* 48: 210–33.

Whitelam, K.W. 1979. *The Just King: Monarchical Judicial Authority in Ancient Israel* (JSOTSup, 12). Sheffield: JSOT Press.

Whiting, R.M. 1995. 'Amorite Tribes and Nations of Second-Millennium Western Asia'. In *Civilizations of the Ancient Near East*, J.M. Sasson (ed.). New York: Scribner's Sons, II: 1231–42.

Wikan, U. 1984. 'Shame and Honour: A Contestable Pair'. *Man* NS 19: 635–52.

Wilhelm, G. 1995. 'The Kingdom of Mitanni in Second-Millennium Upper Mesopotamia'. In *Civilizations of the Ancient Near East*, J.M. Sasson (ed.). New York: Scribner's Sons, II: 1243–54.

Wilson, J.A. 1948. 'The Oath in Ancient Egypt'. *JNES* 7: 129–56.

Wilson, J.A. 1951. *The Burden of Egypt: An Interpretation of Ancient Egyptian Culture*. Chicago, IL: The University of Chicago.

Wilson, S. 1988. *Feuding, Conflict and Banditry in Nineteenth-Century Corsica*. Cambridge: Cambridge University Press.

Wiseman, D.J. 1953. *The Alalakh Tablets* (Occasional Publications of the British Institute of Archaeology at Ankara, 2). London: The British Institute of Archaeology at Ankara.

Wiseman, D.J. 1954. 'Supplementary Copies of the Alalakh Tablets'. *JCS* 8: 1–30.

Wiseman, D.J. 1982. '"Is It Peace?": Covenant and Diplomacy'. *VT* 32: 311–26.

Wissler, C. 1927. 'The Culture-Area Concept in Social Anthropology'. *The American Journal of Sociology* 32: 881–91.

Wissler, C. 1928. 'The Culture-Area Concept as a Research Lead'. *The American Journal of Sociology* 33: 894–900.

Wittfogel, K.A. 1957. *Oriental Despotism: A Comparative Study of Total Power*. New Haven, CT: Yale University Press.

Wolf, E.R. 1966. 'Kinship, Friendship, and Patron-Client Relations in Complex Societies'. In *The Social Anthropology of Complex Societies* (Association of Social Anthropologists Monograph 4), M. Banton (ed.). London: Routledge: 1–22.

Wolf, E.R. 1982. *Europe and the People without History*. Berkeley: University of California Press.

Woolley, L. 1955. *Alalakh: An Account of the Excavations at Tell Achtana in the Hatay, 1937–1949* (Reports of the Research Committee of the Society of Antiquaries of London, 18). London: The Society of Antiquaries.

Wyatt, N. 1999. 'Degress of Divinity: Some Mythical and Ritual Aspects of West Semitic Kingship'. *UF* 31: 853–87.

Wyatt, N. 2005. 'Epic in Ugaritic Literature'. In *A Companion to Ancient Epic* (Blackwell Companions to the Ancient World), J.M. Foley (ed.). Oxford: Blackwell: 246–54.

Wyatt, N. 2007. 'The Religious Role of the King of Ugarit'. In *Ugarit at Seventy-Five*, K.L.Younger, Jr. (ed.). Winona Lake, IN: Eisenbrauns: 41–74.

Xella, P. 2002. 'Aspects du 'sacerdoce' en Syrie ancienne: Remarques methodologiques et examen d'un cas particulier'. *Numen* 49: 406–26.

Yasur-Landau, A., J.R. Ebeling and L.B. Mazow (eds). 2011. *Household Archaeology in Ancient Israel and Beyond* (CHANE, 50). Leiden: E.J. Brill.

Yoffee, N. 1993. 'Too Many Chiefs? (or, Safe Texts for the '90s)'. In *Archaeological Theory: Who Sets the Agenda?*, N. Yoffee and A. Sherrat (eds). Cambridge: Cambridge University Press: 60–78.

Yon, M. 1997. 'Ugarit'. In *OxEncANE*, V: 255–62.

Yon, M. 2006. *The City of Ugarit at Tell Ras Shamra*. Winona Lake, IN: Eisenbrauns.

Zaccagnini, C. 1973. *Lo scambio dei doni nel Vicino Oriente durante i secoli XV–XIII* (OAC, XI). Roma: Centro per le Antichità e la Storia dell'Arte del Vicino Oriente.

Zaccagnini, C. 1976a. 'Le tecniche e le scienze'. In *L'alba della civiltà. Società, economia e pensiero nel Vicino Oriente antico*, S. Moscati (ed.). Torino: UTET, II: 291–421.

Zaccagnini, C. 1976b. 'La circolazione dei beni'. In *L'alba della civiltà. Società, economia e pensiero nel Vicino Oriente antico*, S. Moscati (ed.). Torino: UTET, II: 423–582.

Zaccagnini, C. 1981. 'Modo di produzione asiatico e Vicino Oriente antico: Appunti per una discussione'. *DdA* 3: 3–65.

Zaccagnini, C. 1983. 'Patterns of Mobility among Ancient Near Eastern Craftsmen'. *JNES* 42: 245–64.

Zaccagnini, C. 1987. 'Aspects of Ceremonial Exchange in the Near East during the Late Second Millennium B.C.'. In *Centre and Periphery in the Ancient World*, M. Rowlands, M.T. Larsen and K. Kristiansen (eds). Cambridge: Cambridge University Press: 57–65.

Zaccagnini, C. 1989–90. 'Dono e tributo come modelli istituzionali di scambio: echi e persistenze nella documentazione amministrativa vicino–orientale del Tardo Bronzo'. *Scienze dell'antichità: storia, archeologia, antropologia* 3–4: 105–10.

Zaccagnini, C. 1990. 'The Forms of Alliance and Subjugation in the Near East of the Late Bronze Age'. In *I trattati nel mondo antico: Forma, ideologia, funzione*, L. Canfora, M. Liverani and C. Zaccagnini (eds). Roma: L'Erma di Bretschneider: 37–79.

Zaccagnini, C. 1999. 'Aspetti della diplomazia nell Vicino Oriente antico (XIV–XIII secolo a.C.)'. *Studi Storici* 40: 181–217.

Zamora, J.-A. 1997. *Sobre 'El modo de producción asiático' en Ugarit* (Banco de Datos Filológicos Semíticos Noroccidentales – Monografías, 2). Madrid-Zaragoza: Consejo Superior de Investigaciones Científicas.

Zamora López, J.-A. 2006. 'El sacerdocio en el Levante próximo-oriental (Siria, Fenicia y el mundo púnico): las relaciones entre el culto y el poder y la continuidad con el cambio'. In *Entre Dios y los hombres: El sacerdocio en la Antigüedad* (SPAL Monografías, VII), J.L. Escacena Carrasco and E. Ferrer Albelda (eds). Sevilla: Universidad de Sevilla: 57–82.

Zwickel, W. 2012. 'The Change from Egyptian to Philistine Hegemony in South–Western Palestine during the Time of Ramesses III or IV'. In *The Ancient Near East in the 12th–10th Centuries BCE: Culture and History. Proceedings of the International Conference held at the University of Haifa, 2–5 May 2010* (AOAT, 392), G. Galil, A. Gilboa, A.M. Maeir and D. Kahn (eds). Münster: Ugarit Verlag: 595–601.

# INDEX OF TEXTUAL REFERENCES


Ancient Near East

*ANET*$^3$

18–22 56 n. 14, 107 n. 13
25–9 56 n. 14, 69
199–203 55 n. 4
201–6 15
230–34 27 n. 3
233–63 56 n. 14
234–45 27 n. 4
245–8 14
253–8 14
328–9 56 n. 14, 107 n. 13
395 76
416 24
433 81

*ARE*

II §§ 252–95 68
II §§ 391–540 69
II §§ 391–574 27 n. 4
II §§ 412–43 18
II § 447 87 n. 43
II §§ 455–75 18
II § 467 87 n. 46
II §§ 477–83 18
II § 491 18
II §§ 498–501 18
II § 509 18
II §§ 517–19 18
II §§ 525 18
II §§ 529–34 18
II §§ 563–91 69
II §§ 780–90 14
III §§ 305–51 14

*ARM*

I 7:32–45 87 n. 56
I 24 86 n. 40
I 44 87 n. 56
I 46 86 n. 40
I 68 87 n. 56
I 77 86 n. 40
I 99 87 n. 56
I 115 87 n. 56
II 15:1–29 87 n. 56
II 40 86 n. 40
II 101:8–31 87 n. 56
II 127:1–13 87 n. 56
IV 65 87 n. 56
IV 79 87 n. 56
V 5:18–19 85 n. 9
V 54 87 n. 56
VI 26:Rv 5′-7′
XIII 16:11′-15′ 87 n. 56
XIII 21:rev 1′-2′ 87 n. 56
XIII 44 87 n. 56
XIII 139:rev 4′-20′ 87 n. 56
XIII 142:37–42 87 n. 56
XIII 147:27–33 87 n. 56
XIV 3 87 n. 56
XIV 5 87 n. 56
XIV 6 87 n. 56
XIV 15 87 n. 56
XIV 16 87 n. 56

*AT*

2:27 110, 148 n. 16
3:38 110, 148 n. 16
15 139

*Code of Ḫammurabi*

§§ 137–8 86 n. 41
§§ 138–9 86 n. 41
§ 142 86 n. 41
§ 149 86 n. 41
§§ 159–61 86 n. 41
§§ 162–4 86 n. 41
§§ 163–4 86 n. 41
§ 166 86 n. 41
§ 167 86 n. 41
§§ 171–2 86 n. 41
§§ 171–4 86 n. 41
§ 176 86 n. 41
§§ 178–84 86 n. 41

*CTH*

26 149 n. 22
41 165 n. 8
42 76
47 165 n. 7
49 165 n. 8
51–2 76
54 119 n. 16
66 115
76 148 n. 20
91 55 n. 4
92 58 n. 33, 76
93 139
94 149 n. 21
110 148 n. 19

*EA*

1–15 16
1–39 85 n. 11
1:1–9 164 n. 1
1:10–17 72
1:12 76
1:61–2 68
2:1–5 164 n. 2
2:3–5 61 n. 55
3:7–8 76
3:9–22 88 n. 61
3:13–14 82
4 76
4:4–9 58 n. 34
4:6–7, 7–14 76
4:15–18 85 n. 10
4:21–2 76
4:41–3, 44–50
5:16–17 88 n. 60
6:13–16
7:1–7 58 n. 37
7:33–6, 37–9, 59–61 84 n. 9
7:37–9 85 n. 10
7:49–50 82
9:16–18 84 n. 9
10:8–9 16
10:11, 23 85 n. 10
10:12–27 84 n. 9
11 16
11:7–9 88 n. 60
11:16–18 rev 15 77
11:22–4 16
11 Vs 7–8 76
11 Rv:11–22 74
11 Rv:22–3 85 n. 10
13 16, 70, 84 n. 7
14 16, 71, 84 n. 7
15 164 n. 3
16:1–2 17
16:1–5 58 n. 37
16:9–18 86 n. 35
16:32–3 85 n. 10
16:32–4 84 n. 9
17 71
17:19–30 27 n. 9
17:21–9 165 n. 4
17:36–54 165 n. 4
17:26–7 87 n. 48
17:51–4 85 n. 10
19:1–8 58 n. 37
19:5–8 61 n. 55
19:17–23 88 n. 60
19:66–70 84 n. 9
19:74–9 85 n. 10

20–22 87 n. 48
20:71–6 84 n. 9
20:72 85 n. 10
21:1–12 58 n. 37
22 84 n. 7
23:13–25 80
24 87 n. 48
24:I 74–7, 79–82 85 n. 10
24:III 5–7 84 n. 9
24:III 22–3 88 n. 59
24:III 35–6 87 n. 48
24:III 37–8 76
25 84 n. 7
25–9 87 n. 48
26:45 85 n. 10
27:1–6 58 n. 37
27:10–11, 64–5 85 n. 10
27:16–28 84 n. 9
28:16–22 82
29 82
29:1–5 58 n. 37
29:16–18 76
29:18–20 87 n. 48
29:65, 125, 132 85 n. 10
29:156–60, 168–70, 172 84 n. 9
30 81
31–2 76
31:11–14 77
32–4 86 n. 35
35 84 n. 7
35:19–20 85 n. 10
35:19–22, 40–42, 43–8 84 n. 9
35:26 80
35:27–9 148 n. 11
37 84 n. 7
37:13–17 84 n. 9
40 70, 85 n. 13
40:18–23 84 n. 9
41 84 n. 7
41:1–6 58 n. 37
41:16–22 165 n. 5
41:36–8 84 n. 9
41–2 85 n. 11
42:15–26 166 n. 19
44 85 n. 19
44:20–28 84 n. 9
47:21 167 n. 34
48 85 nn. 11–12
49 85 n. 12
49:22–6 80
51 29 n. 34
51 rev.:1–6 144
51 rev.:12 167 n. 34
53:11–16 144
53:40–44 77
59 140, 148 n. 13, 159
59:13–14 82
65 61 n. 61
68:1–3 60 n. 48
68:11 167 n. 34
70:1–3 60 n. 48
71 166 n. 23
73 85 n. 21, 141, 166 n. 23
73:23–33 118 n. 7
73:26–9 148 n. 12
73:42 167 n. 34
74 159
74:1–2 60 n. 48
74:7, 11 167 n. 34
74:25–9 148 n. 12
74:35 118 n. 7
74:53–5 52
74:55–9 57 n. 24
75:1–2 60 n. 48
75:25ff 148 n. 14
76 166 n. 23
76:1–3 60 n. 48
76:17 166 n. 30
77:37 107 n. 7
78:1–3 60 n. 48
79:1–3 60 n. 48
81 53
81:1–2 60 n. 48
81:11–13 148 n. 12
81:33 107 n. 7
82 85 n. 21, 141
83:1–3 60 n. 48
83:7–11 166 n. 22
83:14–16 166 n. 22
85:33–8 52
86 85 n. 21
87 85 n. 21
88 53
88:1–2 60 n. 48
88:28–34 52
88:42–5 165 n. 17

89:1–2 60 n. 48
89:39–43 148 n. 11
90–92 53
90:1–9, 22–3, 63–4 58 n. 35
91:1–2 60 n. 48
91:1–5, 36–8 58 n. 36
91:27–30 52
92:1–2 60 n. 48
92:30–4 59 n. 40
93 166 n. 23
94:1–2 60 n. 48
96 85 n. 21
99 61 n. 59, 85 n. 12
99:6–9 29 n. 34
99:10–20 87 n. 43
100 140, 148 n. 13, 159
101:38 167 n. 34
105:83 167 n. 34
106:4 167 n. 34
107:9 167 n. 34
107:45–6 147 n. 3
108:13–17 147 n. 3
108:22 167 n. 34
109:42 167 n. 34
112:7–18 166 n. 20
114:31 22
114:54, 67 167 n. 34
116:29, 55 167 n. 34
117:79 22
118:56 167 n. 34
119:15–16 29 n. 34
119:25, 45 167 n. 34
121:11–17 52
126:7–42 61 n. 62
127:25 167 n. 34
129:35–8 166 n. 21
132:9 167 n. 34
132:19–21 166 n. 30
136–8 148 n. 13, 157
136 159
136:8–13 148 n. 11
137:46–8 148 n. 13
138:35–47 148 n. 11
138:71–3 148 n. 11
138:87 167 n. 34
139 148 n. 13
139:1 58–9 n. 39
141–2 61 n. 59
141:1–2 57 n. 22
142:1 57 n. 22
143:1–2 57 n. 22
144:1–2 57 n. 22
146:14 59 n. 41
147:66 59 n. 40
148:25 59 n. 40
149:17–27 166 n. 27
149:30 59 n. 42
149:57–60 148 n. 13
149:83 88 n. 59
150:4–21 166 n. 28
150:14–19 52
151:59 59 n. 42
155:17–23 52
155:48 167 n. 34
155:67–8 59 n. 41
157 158
158 85 n. 21, 141, 165 n. 18
158:1 57 n. 20
161:51–3 29 n. 34
164 85 n. 21, 141
169:7–8 52
180:18 167 n. 34
185:71 167 n. 34
189:9–12 118 n. 8
189:15 167 n. 34
190:1–5 52
192:4 167 n. 34
195:24–32 59 n. 45, 166 n. 30
198:10 167 n. 34
201:11–23 166 n. 29
202:7–18 166 n. 29
203:9–19 166 n. 29
204:9–20 166 n. 29
205:9–18 166 n. 29
206:9–17 166 n. 29
215:16–17 52
216 61 n. 61, n. 71
218 61 n. 71
220–1 61 n. 71
226 61 n. 59
228:15–16 118 n. 8
229:12–14 81
230:1–8 58 n. 38
238 52
234:1–9 60 n. 50
241:19 167 n. 34

242:5 167 n. 34
243:4 167 n. 34
246:4 167 n. 34
246:rev 5–10 166 n. 30
252 61 n. 59
257:7–19 165 n. 13
267 61 n. 61, n. 71
271:9–21 61 n. 63, 107 n. 7
272:10–17 118 n. 7
285:5–6 29 n. 34
286:9–13 165 n. 15
286:12 29 n. 34
286:51–2 118 n. 7
288:11–15 165 n. 16
288:9–15 29 n. 34
296:23–9 22
302–3 61 n. 59
302 :11–18 81
303 61 n. 61, n. 71
316 165 n. 14
319 61 n. 61, n. 71, 165 n. 14
320:16–25 61 n. 60, n. 71, 165 n. 14
321–2 61 n. 61, 165 n. 14
329:13–20 81
330 61 n. 59
367:1–21 61 n. 59
367:6–21 52
369 61 n. 59, 85 n. 12
370 61 n. 59

*KUB*

III, 70 85 n. 19
XXI, 33 76
XXI, 38 Vs 47′-49′ 75
XXI, 38 Vs 54′-5′ 75

*KTU*

1.14 166 n. 32
2.11 45
2.12 45
2.13 45
2.14 45
2.16 45
2.24 45
2.30 45
2.33 45
2.34 45
2.38 45
2.40 45
2.42 45
2.44 45
2.45 45
2.47 45
2.51 45
2.61 45
2.63 45
2.64 45
2.64 45
2.68 45
2.70 45
5.10 45
200 107
267 107
268 107
282 107
350–1 107
421 107

*PRU*

II 9 (RS 15.111) 107 n. 9
II 12 147 n. 3
II 24 (RS 15.022) 107 n. 9
II 25 (RS 15.032) 107 n. 9
II 106 (RS 15.115) 107 n. 9
III 10 (RS 10.046) 85 n. 23
III 12–13 (RS 11.730) 85 n. 23
III 13–14 (RS 16.111) 85 n. 22
III 18 (RS 15.24 + 50:12–21) 84 n. 9, 85 n. 17
III 80 (RS 16.239) 148 nn. 5–6
III 81 (RS 16.239) 148 n. 7
III 82 (RS 16.143) 148 n. 6
III 84 (RS 16.157) 148 nn. 6–7
III 85 (RS 16.250) 148 n. 6
III 86 (RS 16.250) 148 n. 7
III 114 (RS 16.353) 148 n. 6
III 135 (RS 15.137) 148 nn. 6–7
III 140 (RS 16.132) 148 n. 5
III 140–41 (RS 16.132) 147 n. 3, 148 n. 7
III 162 (RS 16.348) 148 n. 6
III 166 (RS 16.386) 148 n. 6
IV 4 85 n. 17
IV 6 85 n. 17

IV 7B 85 n. 17
IV 18 85 n. 17
IV 35–6 (RS 17.132) 165 n. 6
IV 40–43 (RS 17.227) 165 n. 7
IV 68 (RS 16.269) 148 n. 8
IV 80–81 (RS 17.382) 118 n. 8
IV 102–5 (= *CTH* 93) 139
IV 107–8 (RS 17.238) 149 n. 21
IV 119 (RS 17.133) 110
IV 121–22 (RS 17.352) 148 n. 9
IV 126–7 (RS 17.159) 75
IV 133–4 (RS 17.116) 165 n. 11
IV 191 (RS 17.247) 85 n. 20, 148 n. 19
IV 196–7 (RS 17.78) 85 n. 24
IV 132–4, 228–9 85 n. 15
IV 133–4 (RS 17.116) 84 n. 9, 85 n. 10
IV 126–7 (RS 17.159) 75
IV 180 (RS 17.286) 85 n. 22
IV 214 (RS 17.152) 85 n. 22
IV 218 (RS17.425) 45
IV 221 (RS 17.383) 45
IV 222–3 85 n. 16
IV 223 (RS 17.422) 45
IV 226 (RS 17.391) 45
IV 229 (RS 18.54 A:17′-20′) 84–5 n. 9
IV 284–6 (RS 19.68) 75
IV 294 57 n. 19
V 11 (RS 19.116
V 66 (RS 18.076) 107 n. 9
V 67 (RS 18.079) 107 n. 9
VI 4:7–9 85 n. 9
VI 7A 85 n. 25
VI 16 85 n. 9

*Ug*

V 20–80 58 n. 33
V 69–76 147 n. 3
V 80–82 85 n. 22
V 80–83 84 n. 7
V 92 (RS 20.03:10–13) 85 nn. 9–10
V 97 85 n. 14
V 98 85 n. 12
V 100 85 n. 14
V 101–2 85 n. 12, n. 21
V 117–119 85 n. 16
V 118 (RS 20.16) 45
V 120–21 85 n. 15
V 122–3 85 n. 17
V 135 85 n. 16
V 138 (RS 20.151) 45, 85 n. 16
V 139 (RS 20.219) 45
V 142–3 (RS 20.239) 110
V 152 85 n. 16
V 585 (RS 24.271) 166 n. 32

*Urk.*

IV, 662, 8–12 57 n. 23
IV, 759, 8–15 57 n. 22
IV, 896, 15–17 57 n. 26
IV, 1738 87 n. 48

Old Testament

*Deuteronomy*

32:39 52

*1 Samuel*

2:6 52

*Psalms*

33:5 166 n. 32
72:1 166 n. 32
99:4 166 n. 32

# INDEX OF AUTHORS


Abdul-Kader, M. 9 n. 2
Abel, F.M. 28 n. 17, 42
Abrahamian, E. 118 n. 2
Abulafia, D. 135 n. 5
Ackerman, S. 149 n. 12
Aharoni, Y. 127
Aḥituv, S. 10 n. 5, 22, 27, 29 n. 30
Ahlström, G.W. 9 n. 3, 10 n. 4, 20, 23, 27 n. 4, 119 n. 17, 165 n. 17
Akkermans, M.M.G. 97
Albera, D. 5, 124–5, 135 n. 3
Albright, W.F. 2, 28 n. 20, 61 n. 56
Aldred, C. 9 n. 2, 20, 28 n. 18
Almond, G. 149 n. 24
Alt, A. 10 n. 9, 28 n. 22, 108, 118 n. 2, 149 n. 28
Altman, A. 39, 56 n. 11, 114–15
Álvarez-Pedrosa, J.A. 55 n. 6
Anbar, M. 107 n. 13
Anderson, B. 35
Antoun, R. 103
Appadurai, A. 71
Archi, A. 10 n. 8, 113
Arensberg, C.M. 65
Arnaud, D. 33, 61 n. 54, 165 n. 6
Artzi, P. 27 n. 9, 148 n. 13, 159
Aruz, J. 84 n. 8
Asad, T. 61 n. 57
Assmann, J. 165 n. 10
Astour, M.C. 29 n. 30, 32, 127
Aubet, M.E. 65–6, 84 nn. 3–4, n. 7, 85 n. 27
Auffarth, C. 88 n. 64
Avruch, K. 71
Axtell, J. 106 n. 1
Bahrani, Z. 106 n. 3
Bailey, F.G. 7
Balandier, G. 10 n. 15, 128
Balazote, A. 65
Balza, M.E. 119 n. 13
Banfield, E.C. 135 n. 1
Barreyra, D. 148 n. 12
Barthes, R. 62 n. 77, 84 n. 2
Beal, R.H. 10 n. 9
Beckman, G. 3, 10 n. 9, 15, 44, 55 n. 4, n. 6, 57 n. 19, 58 nn. 32–3, 61 nn. 52–3, 76, 80, 88 n. 62, 114–15, 119 nn. 13–14, 148 n. 20, 149 n. 22, 165 n. 8, n. 12
Befu, H. 136 n. 10, n. 18
Belmonte Marín, J.A. 54 n. 3, 55 n. 7
Bender, D.R. 119 n. 11
Bernabé, A. 55 n. 6
Berridge, G. 35,
Bienkowski, P. 84 n. 6
Bittel, K. 55 n. 5
Black[-Michaud], J. 136 n. 14, n. 17
Bleiberg, E.L. 21, 28 n. 18, 57 n. 26, 85 nn. 29–30, 86 n. 31
Bloch, Marc. 91, 106 n. 2, 112
Bloch, Maurice. 84 n. 4
Blok, A., 5, 124–5, 131, 135 n. 3, n. 7, 136 n. 9
Bohannan, P. 92
Boissevain, J. 5, 135 n. 3, 136 n. 9, 162
Bolin, T.M. 163
Boltanski, A. 135 n. 9
Bonte, P. 10 n. 13, 129
Bordreuil, P. 61 n. 55, 118 n. 5
Bottéro, J. 3
Boudou, B. 88 n. 63

Bourdieu, P. 8, 63, 71, 86 n. 37, 88 n. 57, 96, 115, 136 n. 16
Bournazel, E. 118 n. 3
Boutruche, R. 112
Boyer, G. 108, 118 n. 2
Braudel, F. 13, 135 n. 2, 148 n. 18
Bresson, A. 135 n. 5
Briant, P. 118 n. 4
Briend, J. 15, 56 n. 14, 107 n. 13, 119 n. 14
Briquet, J.-L. 136 n. 9
Bromberger, C. 5, 135 n. 3
Bryan, B. 27 n. 3, 27 n. 9
Bryce, T. 10 n. 9, 13, 14, 17, 27 n. 7, n. 14, 55 n. 5, 56 n. 16, 75, 88 n. 59, 137 n. 19, 148 n. 18
Buchholz, H.-G. 87 n. 53
Buccellati, G. 10 n. 15, 94, 106 n. 5, 149 n. 27
Buckley, T. 135 n. 2
Bunimovitz, S. 28 n. 19, 92, 95, 107 n. 7
Bunnens, G. 148 n. 14
Burguière, A. 93
Burke, A.A. 19, 100
Burke, P. 106 n. 2
Burkert, W. 79
Burling, R. 65

Caisson, M. 162–3
Campagno, M. 29 n. 32, 107 n. 12, 95–7, 137 n. 19, 165 n. 10
Campbell, E.F. 10 n. 4, 54 n. 2
Campbell, J.K. 128, 131, 136 n. 9
Caquot, A. 61 n. 55
Carneiro, R. 95, 107 n. 12
Caro Baroja, J. 135 n. 7
Cassar, C. 5, 131
Cassin, E. 118 n. 5
Cathcart, A. 136 n. 13
Chamboredon, J.C. 63
Chaney, M.L. 9 n. 3
Charpin, D. 87 n. 52, 118 n. 4
Chesson, M.S. 149 n. 28
Childe, V.G. 95
Chilton, S. 149 n. 24
Christiansen, B. 162
Claessen, H. 96
Clastres, P. 10 n. 15, 97, 107 n. 12
Clifford, J. 84 n. 1, 94
Cline, E.H. 27 n. 7
Clines, D.J.A. 62 n. 67, n. 78
Cochavi-Rainey, Z. 84 n. 8, 165 n. 15
Cohen, Abner. 10 n. 15, 149 n. 28
Cohen, Amnon. 127
Cohen, R. 3, 13, 42, 56 n. 15, 57 n. 18
Cohn, B.S. 91
Comaroff, J. and J. 106 n. 1
Conte, É. 10 n. 13, 129
Cooper, J. 56 n. 15
Coote, R.B. 27 n. 7, 127
Couto-Ferreira, E. 87 n. 52
Coy, P. 149 n. 29
Crown, A.D. 88 n. 59
Cunchillos [Ilarri], J.-L. 45, 54, 55 n. 7, 60 n. 46
Curtis, M. 109, 118 n. 4, 119 n. 10

Dalton, G. 65
David, S.R. 21, 166 n. 24
Davis, J. 5, 123, 125, 131
Davis, N.Z. 91
Dawod, H. 10 n. 13, 136 n. 13
De Geus, C.H.J. 96
de Tarragón, J. 161
del Olmo Lete, G. 110, 118 n. 4, 147 n. 4
Deliège, R. 73, 86 n. 37, 137 n. 20
Deniaux, É. 135 n.9
Detienne, M. 106 n. 1
Devecchi, E. 119 n. 13, n. 18, 162
Diakonoff, I.M. 109, 119 n. 12
Di Bella, M.P. 136 n. 9
Diego Espinel, A. 68
Dion, P.-E. 96
Dittmer, L. 149 n. 24
Dossin, G. 55 n. 10
Dothan, T. 27 n. 7
Doumani, B. 127
Dresch, P. 10 n. 13, 129, 136 n. 11
Drower, M. 23, 28 n. 21, 147 n. 3
Druckman, D. 71–2
Dube, S. 106 n. 1
Duma, J. 135 n. 9
Dupuy, F. 65–6
Durand, J.-M. 43, 55 n. 11, 60 n. 51, 85 n. 9, 87 n. 55, 118 n. 4, 164 n. 1
Durkheim, É. 6, 167 n. 35
Dussaud, R. 56 n. 14

Ebeling, E. 112, 119 n. 2
Ebeling, J.R. 149 n. 28
Eco, U. 61 n. 56, 62 n. 68, n. 77, 63, 84 n. 2
Edel, E. 77–8, 80
Edgerton, W.F. 57 n. 23, 58 n. 30
Edzard, D.O. 84 n. 8
Eickelman, D.F. 135 nn. 7–8
Eidem, J. 56 n. 15, 57 n. 19
Eisenbeis, W. 86 n. 32
Eisenstadt, S.N. 135 n. 9
Eliade, M. 87 n. 44
Eriksen, T.M. 35
Evans-Pritchard, E.E. 7, 91, 136 n. 11
Eychenne, M. 119 n. 11
Eyre, C.J. 86 n. 31, 165 n. 10

Fabian, J. 93
Fafchamps, M. 136 n. 9
Falconer, S.E. 149 n. 28
Fales, F.M. 29 n. 30, 134, 137 n. 19, nn. 20–1
Farriss, N. 91–2
Faulkner, R.O. 10 n. 6, 38, 57 nn. 25–7, 58 n. 28, 62 n. 66, n. 73, n. 78
Faust, A. 19
Feely-Harnik, G. 106 n. 1
Feleppa, R. 56 n. 17
Fensham, F.C. 43, 113, 142, 148 n. 11
Finkelstein, I. 27 n. 7, 54 n. 1, 92, 100, 107 n. 7
Finley, M.I. 82, 88 n. 63, 135 n. 9
Flammini, R. 165 n. 17
Fleming, D.E. 3, 55 n. 11, 99, 139
Foster, G.M. 131, 136 n. 17
Frandsen, P.J. 21, 28 nn. 21–2, n. 27, n. 29, 29 n. 30, n. 33
Frankfort, H. 58 n. 31
Freu, J. 14, 15, 20, 27 n. 8, 114, 119 n. 16

Gaál, E. 118 n. 9
Gadot, Y. 28 n. 28
Galán, J.M. 27 n. 14, 41, 56 n. 14, 69
Gardiner, A.H. 40, 55 n. 4
Garnsey, P. 136 n. 9
Geertz, C. 166 n. 26
Gelb, I. 106 n. 3
Gellner, E. 5, 129, 136 n. 9
Gesenius, W. 62 n. 78
Gestoso [Singer], G.N. 10 n. 4, 28 n. 15, 29 n. 34, 84 n. 6
Gevirtz, S. 61 n. 56
Giardina, A. 171 n. 3
Gilmore, D.D. 123, 131, 135 n. 3
Gilsenan, M. 140
Giry-Deloison, C. 135 n. 9
Giveon, R. 28 n. 22
Glassner, J.-J. 94
Gledhill, J. 10 n. 15
Godelier, M. 65–6, 136 n. 12
Goedicke, H. 38, 57 n. 27
Goetze, A. 10 n. 8
Gofman, A. 10 n. 16
Goldstone, J.A. 94
Gonen, R. 19
González Alcantud, J.A. 136 n. 17
Goodell, G.E. 130
Goody, J. 125, 148 n. 17
Goren, Y. 54 n. 1
Gouldner, A.V. 6, 128–9, 136 n. 10
Govoroff, N. 86 nn. 38–9
Graeber, D. 71, 84 n. 4
Gray, J. 108, 118 n. 2
Greenberg, M. 3
Greengus, S. 86 n. 40
Greensfield, H.J. 119 n. 11
Greenstein, E.L. 55 n. 8
Gregoire, J.-P. 87 n. 51
Gregory, C.A. 84 n. 4
Gregory, J.M. 136 n. 17
Grimal, N.-C. 37–8, 57 n. 21, n. 25, 59 n. 43
Groll, S.I. 28 n. 21, 107 n. 11
Grottanelli, C. 88 n. 64
Gunter, A.C. 87 n. 51
Güner, S. 71–2
Güterbock, H.G. 76

Hachmann, R. 28 n. 26
Hage, P. 74
Haldon, J. 94
Halpern, B. 22
Handy, L.K. 104, 161, 164
Hannig, R. 10 n. 6, 58 n. 28, 62 n. 66
Hansen, M.H. 94, 97

Harary, F. 74
Hardin, J.W. 149 n. 28
Harris, M. 56 n. 17
Harris, W.V. 5, 135 n. 3
Hartog, F. 63
Hasel, M.G. 10 n. 5, 22
Hathaway, J. 119 n. 11
Hawley, R. 55 n. 7
Helck, W. 9 n. 2, 10 n. 4, n. 7, 21, 28 n. 18, 57 n. 27, 84 n. 8
Heltzer, M. 42, 110, 118 n. 4, 149 n. 27
Herman, A.L., Jr. 166 n. 24
Herr, L.G. 106 n. 5
Herrenschmidt, O. 147 n. 3
Herzfeld, M. 88 n. 64, 106 n. 1, 125
Herzog, Z. 19
Hess, R.S. 165 nn. 15–16
Higginbotham, C. 163
Hill, G.W. 135 n. 2
Hitchcock, L. 87 n. 53, 135 n. 5
Hobsbawm, E.J. 35
Hoffmeier, J.K. 28 n. 21, 165 n. 15
Hoffner, H.A., Jr. 3, 10 n. 9, 15, 55 n. 6, 76
Holder, G. 118 n. 6
Holladay, W.L. 62 n. 67, n. 78
Holmes, Y.L. 88 nn. 59–60
Horden, P. 5, 124, 126, 128, 131, 135 n. 3, n. 5
Horowitz, W. 142
Hourani, A. 132
Huehnergard, J. 57 n. 20
Humphreys, S.C. 84 n. 3

Ibn Khaldun. 128–9
Ilan, D. 100
Imparati, F. 10 n. 9, 113, 119 n. 13, n. 15, 137 n. 19
Ingham, J.M. 149 n. 29
Izre'el, S. 46–7, 54 n. 1, 165 n. 15

Jabar, F.A. 10 n. 13, 136 n. 13
Jabbra, J.G. 133
Jabbra, N.W. 133
Jacobsen, T. 148 n. 13
Jackson, M. 171 n. 2
James, A. 10 n. 5, 100, 107 n. 7
Jankowska, N.B. 148 n. 13
Janssen, J.J. 21, 86 n. 31
Jasmin, M. 95, 101
Joffe, A.H. 106 n. 5
Johnson, A. 167 n. 36
Jones, P. 58 n. 31
Jongsma, T. 119 n. 11
Jönsson, C. 166 n. 24
Julliard, J. 10 n. 15
Jursa, M. 106 n. 3

Kalluveettil, P. 113, 162
Karadimas, D. 86 n. 39
Kemp, B.J. 23, 28 n. 21, 56 n. 16
Kempinski, A. 100
Kestemont, G. 56 n. 15, 86 n. 34, 143
Kettering, S. 132, 135 n. 9, 136 n. 18
Khazanov, I.M. 10 n. 13
Khoury, P.S. 10 n. 13, 104, 127, 129, 132
Kitchen, K.A. 54 n. 2
Klengel, H. 14, 27 n. 2, n. 7, n. 14, 42, 85 n. 18, 102, 107 n. 5
Knapp, A.B. 84 n. 6, 135 n. 5
Knauf, E.A. 171 n. 3
Knudtzon, J.A. 30, 42, 167 n. 34
Korošec, V. 10 n. 8, 55 n. 11, 57 n. 19, 113, 119 nn. 13–15
Kostiner, J. 10 n. 13, 104, 129
Kramer, S.N. 106 n. 3
Krämer, G. 132
Krauss, R. 30
Kristiansen, K. 80, 85 n. 27
Kühne, C. 54 n. 2
Kupper, J.-R. 42, 55 n. 10

Labat, R. 27 n. 12, 32, 46
LaBianca, Ø.S. 171 n. 2
Laburthe-Tolra, P. 56 n. 17
Lackenbacher, S. 55 n. 7, 107 n. 10, 115, 119 n. 16
Lafont, B. 56 n. 15, 106 n. 3
Lafont, S. 118 n. 3
Landsberger, B. 148 n. 15
Langdon, S. 40, 55 n. 4
Langgut, D. 27 n. 7
Lapidus, I.M. 98, 136 n. 12
Larsson, T.B. 80, 85 n. 27
Lebrun, R. 15, 119 nn. 14–15
Leca, J. 129, 136 n. 9
Leclair, E.E., Jr. 65

Lécrivain, V. 86 nn. 38–9, 135 n. 9
Lehman, E.W. 149 n. 24
Lehmann, G. 92
Lehner, M. 142, 165 n. 10
Lemche, N.P. 5, 6, 10 n. 13, 18, 27 n. 2, 28 n. 23, 93, 118 n. 7, n. 9, 119 n. 17, 129, 135 n. 8, 144, 149 n. 23, n. 26, 160
Lenclud, G. 167 n. 36
Lévi-Strauss, C. 7,8, 10 n. 6, 56 n. 17, 63–4, 73, 130
Levine, B. 161
Levy, T.E. 92
Lichtheim, M. 56 n. 14, 69, 107 n. 13
Liebowitz, H. 28 n. 22
Limet, H. 29 n. 32
Lindholm, C. 135 n. 8
Litt, T. 27 n. 7
Littlewood, P. 136 n. 18
Liverani, M. 3, 4, 9 n. 4,10 n. 4, 13, 19, 22, 27 n. 2, n. 7, 28 n. 26, 27 nn. 11–14, 28 n. 27, 29 n. 33, 29 n. 34, 30, 31, 36, 39, 41–3, 48–53, 54 n.1, n. 3, 55 n. 7, n. 9, 56 n. 15, 57 n. 19, n. 21, 58 n. 36, n. 38, 59 nn. 43–4, 60 nn. 48–9, 61 n. 56, n. 58, nn. 61–2, n. 64, 62 n. 72, 64, 66–72, 74–5, 77, 84 n. 5, n. 7, 86 n. 34, 87 n. 44, n. 51, n. 53, 93, 106 n. 5, 107 n. 6, n. 10, 110, 117, 118 nn. 4–5, 119 n. 12, nn. 16–17, 126, 135 n. 6, 138–9, 143, 147 n. 1, n. 3, 148 n. 11, n. 13, n. 18, n. 20, 149 n. 27, 147 n. 1, n. 3, 158, 162, 165 n. 10, 166 n. 25, n. 32, 167 n. 32, n. 34, 170, 171 n. 1, n. 3
Llobera, J.R. 84 n. 1, 125
Loretz, O. 3
Lorton, D. 38, 41, 57 nn. 21–3, nn. 26–7, 58 n. 29, 116
Lutfiyya, A.M. 103

Macqueen, J.G. 14, 27 n. 7
Maçzak, A. 135 n. 9
Magnetti, D.L. 162
Maidman, M.P. 55 nn. 12–13
Maier, J. 171 n. 1
Maisels, C.K. 95, 99
Malinowski, B. 5, 84 n. 4
Manning, J.G. 65
Marcus, G.E. 84 n. 4, 94
Marcus, R. 61 n. 56
Marfoe, L. 145–6, 149 n. 28
Margueron, J.-C. 33, 55 n. 10
Marie, A. 73
Marizza, M. 55 n. 6, 61 n. 53
Marques, A.C.D.R. 5
Márquez Rowe, I. 107 n. 10, 118 n.5, n. 9, 147 n. 2
Marx, K. 66, 109, 117
Matthiae, P. 61 n. 51, 98
Mauss, M. 5, 10 n. 16, 84 n. 4
Mazar, A. 22, 25, 28 n. 19, 100
Mazow, L.B. 149 n. 28
Mazoyer, M. 14, 114
Mazzoni, S. 98–9
McCarthy, D.J. 113, 119 n. 13, n. 16, 162
McGeough, K.M. 84 n. 6, 118 nn. 2–3
Médard, H. 130
Meier, S.A. 75, 77
Meillassoux, C. 65–6
Meisel, J. 149 n. 24
Melville, S.C. 87 n. 45
Mendelsohn, I. 118 n. 9
Mettam, R. 135 n. 9
Michel, C. 106 n. 3
Milano, L. 98
Miller, J. 114, 119 n. 13
Momrak, K. 148 nn. 14–15
Moorey, P.R.S. 79, 87 n. 52
Moran, W.L. 28 n. 27, 30, 42, 54 n. 1, 56 n. 16, 61 n. 64, n. 71, 85 n. 11, 148 n. 17, 149 n. 22, n. 25
Moreno García, J.C. 86 n. 31
Morris, E.F. 22, 24, 28 n. 21, 29 n. 31, 60 n. 49, 148 n. 18
Morris, I. 65
Morschauser, S. 57 n. 27
Moscati, S. 10 n. 16, 54, 94, 106 nn. 3–4
Muhly, J.D. 87 n. 53
Müller, M. 22, 24, 100
Munn-Rankin, J.M. 39, 44, 55 n. 11, 57 n. 19, 60 n. 51, 86 n. 41
Murnane, W.J. 3, 10 n. 4, 14, 56 n. 14, 57 n. 21
Mynářová, J. 30, 42, 54 n. 1, n. 3, 56 n. 16, 60 n. 47, 62 n. 67, 148 n. 17

Na'aman, N. 10 n. 5, 23, 28 n. 24, n. 28, 54 n. 1, 61 n. 58, 100, 107 n. 7
Naderi, N. 119 n. 10
Nakhleh, K. 103
Newbury, C. 136 n. 18
Niehr, H. 147 n. 2, n. 4, 161, 167 n. 32
Nigro, L. 28 n. 25, 100
Nougayrol, J. 139, 148 n. 16

O'Leary, B. 84 n. 5, 109
O'Leary, T.J. 124
Oliva, J. 55 n. 11
Oller, G.H. 81,
Oppenheim, A.L. 106 n. 3
Oren, E.D. 22, 27 n. 3
Orenstein, H. 130
Oshima, T. 142
Otto, A. 148 n. 14

Pardee, D. 55 n. 7, 162
Parker, S.B. 162
Parry, J. 84 n. 4
Passeron, J.-C. 63
Pastor, R. 128
Patai, R. 135 n. 4
Paulus, S. 27 n. 10, n. 12
Pearson, H.W. 65
Peatrik, A.-M. 118 n. 6
Pébarthe, C. 135 n. 9
Peristiany, J. 5, 124, 131
Pernigotti, S. 59 n. 44
Petersen, A.R. 147 n. 4, 167 n. 33
Petrie, W.M.F. 1, 12
Peyronel, L. 17, 66, 68, 84 n. 7
Pfälzner, P. 86 n. 36, 105
Pfoh, E. 18, 106 n. 5, 127, 148 n. 11
Philipp, T. 127
Pina Cabral, J. de. 125
Pinch, G. 137 n. 19
Pinnock, F. 98
Pintore, F. 22, 28 n. 28, 61 n. 58, 75–6, 78, 87 n. 47, nn. 49–50, 147 n. 2
Pitard, W.T. 162
Pitt-Rivers, J. 5, 73, 82–3, 87 n. 47, 88 n. 61, 124–5, 127, 129–31, 149 n. 29
Podany, A.H. 39, 56 n. 15, 61 n. 51, 75, 86 n. 40
Polanyi, K. 65, 84 nn. 3–4, 106 n. 3
Poly, J.-P. 118 n. 3
Posener, G. 56 n. 14
Possehl, G.L. 104
Potts, D.T. 27 n. 12
Price, B.J. 106 n. 5
Prosser, M.C. 107 n. 10
Pryke, L.M. 166 n. 21
Puech, É. 15, 119 n. 14
Purcell, N. 5, 124, 126, 128, 131, 135 n. 3, n. 5

Rabinowitz, D. 127
Rainey, A.F. 30, 31, 46, 54 n. 2, 108, 118 n. 2, 147 n. 3, 166 n. 31
Rede, M. 106 n. 3
Redford, D.B. 2, 9 n. 2, 10 n. 4, n. 7, 22, 27 n. 3, 28 n. 15, n. 26, 38, 57 n. 21
Redman, C.L. 95
Renfrew, C. 100
Reviv, H. 148 n. 13
Rodríguez López, A. 128
Roniger, L. 135 n. 9
Roque, M.-À. 5, 135 n. 1, n. 3
Rosenfeld, H. 130
Rössler, M. 65, 84 n. 4
Roth, M. 86 n. 41
Rowton, M. 3, 8, 42, 58 n. 32, 106 n. 4, 149 n. 23, 166 n. 31
Roy, O. 132

Sacchi, P. 119 n. 11
Sahlins, M.D. 6, 56 n. 17, 63, 65–6, 128–30
Said, E.W. 10 n. 4
Sanmartín, J. 110
Salzman, P.C. 6, 133
Sapin, J. 25, 29 n. 30, 42, 105, 107 n. 13, 135 n. 6, 149 n. 27, 161
Sasson, J.M. 87 n. 55
Savage, S.H. 149 n. 28
Saville-Troike, M. 61 n. 57
Sawicki, F. 136 n. 9
Scarcia Amoretti, B. 102, 171 n. 3
Scheffler, T. 9 n. 1
Schemeil, Y. 10 n. 15, 129, 136 n. 9

Schloen, J.D. 9, 36, 99, 106 n. 3, 108–9, 111, 113, 118 n. 1, 119 nn. 10–11, 138, 140–3, 146, 149 n. 20, nn. 22–3, n. 28, 161, 165 n. 10
Schneider, P. 136 n. 9
Schulman, A.R. 10 n. 4, 75
Schwartz, G.M. 97
Scott, J. 136 n. 14
Service, E.R. 95
Sethe, K. 56 n. 14
Seux, M.-J. 56 n. 14, 107 n. 13
Several, M.W. 10 n. 4
Sherrat, A. 75
Sherrat, S. 75, 87 n. 53
Shunnaq, M. 103
Sigrist, M. 33
Silva Castillo, J. 149 n. 23
Silverman, S. 123, 130, 135 n. 1, 136 n. 9
Simmel, G. 158
Singer, A. 102
Singer, I. 119 nn. 16–17
Skalník, P. 96
Smith, M.G. 10 n. 15
Smith, M.L. 28 n. 24
Smith, M.S. 162
Smith. S. 55 n. 9
Smith, S.T. 21, 24, 28 n. 21, n. 29, 29 n. 32
Sofri, G. 84 n. 5, 118 n. 4
Solans, B.E. 139, 148 nn. 15–16
Solvang, E.K. 85 n. 26
Sommerfeld, W. 27 n. 10
Southall, A. 136 n. 11
Spalinger, A.J. 19, 40, 55 n. 4, 57 n. 21, 61 n. 58, 86 nn. 31–2
Stager, L.E. 92
Starke, F. 10 n. 9, 14, 15, 27 nn. 5–6, 119 n. 13, n. 15, n. 17
Stein, D.L.
Stol, M. 137 n. 19
Strange, J. 100
Struve, V.V. 109
Sugerman, M. 84 n. 6
Sweet, L.E. 124

Tadmor, H. 162
Testart, A. 73, 84 n. 3, n. 5, 86 nn. 38–9, 163, 165 n. 9
Thiesse, A.M. 35
Thomas, K. 91
Thompson, E.P. 136 n. 9
Thompson, J.A. 149 n. 22
Thompson, T.L. 19, 27 n. 7, 53, 55 n. 13, 102, 113, 119 n. 11, 135 n. 6, 161
Thuesen, I. 100
Tomes, R. 52
Tozy, M. 5, 135 n. 3
Tönnies, F. 6
Tugendhaft, A. 57 n. 18

Valensi, L. 84 n. 3
Vallogia, M. 88 n. 59
Van de Mieroop, M. 14, 58 n. 32, 59 n. 44
Van de Velde, P. 96
Van der Steen, E. 10 n. 13, 88 n. 64
Van der Toorn, K. 48
Vandersleyen, C. 9 n. 2, 30
Van Dijk, J. 9 n. 2, 27 n. 3
Van Soldt, W.H. 32, 110, 118 n. 5, 141, 148 n. 17, 149 n. 27
Vargyas, P. 149 n. 21
Vernus, P. 29 n. 31
Viazzo, P.P. 84 n. 1, 106 n. 1, 119 n. 11
Vidal, J. 32, 93, 118 n. 1, n. 4, 141, 147 n. 3, 166 n. 31
Vidal-Naquet, P. 118 n. 4
Vita, J.-P. 47, 54, 139, 147 n. 3
Von Dassow, E. 15, 27 n. 8, 32, 47, 55 nn. 8–9, 110, 118 n. 6
Von Schuler, E. 14, 119 n. 13

Wachtel, N. 21, 91
Wallace-Hadrill, A. 135 n. 9
Warburton, D. 55 n. 4
Warnier, J.-P. 56 n. 17
Waterbury, J. 5, 136 n. 9
Weber, M. 96, 119 n. 10
Weiner, A.B. 84 n. 4
Weinfeld, M. 162, 166 n. 32
Weingrod, A. 136 n. 9, 160, 165 n. 9
Weinstein, J.M. 10 n. 4, 22, 28 n. 22
Weippert, H. 28 n. 25, 100
Wengrow, D. 28 n. 28
Wente, E.F. 62 n. 72
Westbrook, R. 13, 42, 56 n. 15, 57 n. 18, 86 n. 41, 118 n. 5, 149 n. 22
Whitelam, K.W. 27 n. 7, 127, 147 n. 2

Whiting, R. 55 n. 10
Wikan, U. 125
Wilhelm, G. 27 n. 8
Wilson, J.A. 9 n. 2, 38, 57 n. 23, n. 27
Wilson, S. 136 n. 14
Wiseman, D.J. 55 n. 8, 139, 148 n. 16, 162
Wissler, C. 135 n. 2
Wittfogel, K.A. 118 n. 4
Wolf, E.R. 91, 136 n. 14
Woolf, G. 136 n. 9
Woolley, L. 32
Wyatt, N. 147 n. 4, 162, 167 n. 33

Xella, P. 139

Yasur-Landau, A. 149 n. 28
Yoffee, N. 107 n. 12
Yon, M. 32, 107 n. 6

Zaccagnini, C. 38–9, 57 n. 19, 66–7, 79, 84 n. 5, nn. 7–8, 85 nn. 9–10, 86 n. 32, n. 34, 86 n. 36, n. 41, 87 n. 51, nn. 54–5, 88 nn. 57–8, 106 n. 3, 118 n. 4
Zamora [López], J.-A. 84 n. 5, 118 n. 1, n. 4, 147 n. 4, 149 n. 21, 161
Zwickel, W. 18

# INDEX OF SUBJECTS


Abdi-Aširta 40, 50, 140, 157
Abdi-Ḫeba 155
Abi-Milku 159–60
Addad-nirari I 17
Aḫenaten 1, 9 n. 2, 14, 30–1, 37
*aḫḫūtu* 35, 36, 39, 57 n. 18, 81
Akkadian 3–4, 30–4, 36, 39, 46–8, 50–3, 55 n. 7, 57 nn. 19–20, 77, 162, 165 n. 15, 166 n. 32, 167 n. 34
Alalaḫ (site, archives) 15, 30, 32–3, 55 n. 8, 60 n. 51, 86 n. 40, 105, 110, 118 n. 5, 139, 147 n. 3, 148 nn. 14, 16
Alašiya 13, 31, 42, 70, 80, 85 nn. 13, 22
alliance (symmetrical, asymmetrical) 8, 9, 13–14, 16–17, 20, 32, 36, 39, 40, 42, 55 n. 6, 63–84, 98–9, 104, 114 n. 4, 116, 119 n. 16, 128, 136 n. 12, 144, 146–7, 150–4, 157, 162, 169
Amarna (period, age, letters) 1–4, 6, 8, 13, 16, 18–20, 22, 25–6, 28 n. 24, 30, 32–5, 37, 40, 42–53, 54 n. 1, 56 nn. 14, 16, 57 n. 22, 58 n. 36, 60 n. 51, 61 nn. 55–6, 64, 62 n. 72, 64, 66, 68, 71–2, 74, 76–7, 80, 82–3, 86 n. 37, 96, 103–4, 141, 144, 146, 148 nn. 17–18, 150, 154–5, 159, 163, 169–71
Amenḥotep I 14/II 14, 16, 18, 20, 38/ III 14, 16, 20, 23, 31, 40, 76, 87 n. 48, 151/IV 14, 16–17, 31, 76, 87 n. 48, 152
Amurru 2, 15, 18, 21, 32, 36, 40–1, 49, 54, 75–6, 85 nn. 21–2, 114, 119 n. 16, 140–1, 148 n. 18, 154, 156–7
Arrapḫa 16, 34, 108
Arzawa 13, 15, 31, 42, 47, 76–7
Asiatic Mode of Production 9, 66, 84 n. 5, 108–9, 113, 116, 118 nn. 1, 4
Assyria 13, 15–17, 31, 34, 41, 42, 67, 71, 75, 108, 151
Aššur-uballit 17
authority 3, 8, 53, 56 n. 14, 77, 80, 101, 103–4, 106, 109, 111, 113, 115, 133–4, 140, 142, 148 n. 15, 159–61, 165 n. 10, 170
Aziru 1, 36, 49, 85 n. 21, 140–1, 156–9, 166 n. 24

Babylon, Babylonia 13–14, 16–17, 27 n. 12, 31, 33, 40–4, 46–8, 60 n. 51, 61 n. 52, 67–8, 71–2, 74–7, 80–1, 96, 108, 150–1, 160–2
*balāṭu* 37, 51–2, 166 n. 28
Bentešina 40, 75–6
Beqa‘ 18, 21, 145
Beth-šean 22
Biryawaza 118 n. 8, 160
broker, brokerage 4, 132–3, 136 n. 18, 139–40, 142, 144, 146, 156, 162
Byblos 18, 23, 29 n. 34, 37, 40, 49, 54 n. 3, 56 n. 14, 60 n. 48, 69, 85 n. 21, 96, 103, 139–41, 155, 157–8, 165 n. 17

Canaan, Canaanite (language) 2, 19, 21–2, 25, 27, 28 n. 23, 29 n. 30, 46–9, 51, 53, 61 n. 56, 62 n. 78, 81, 101
chiefdom 8, 104, 107 n. 12, 128–9, 147, 170

city-state 9, 19, 25, 94–8, 100–2, 104–5, 124, 141, 145, 148 n. 15
client, clientelism 5, 9, 98, 107 n. 11, 110, 129–34, 136 nn. 9, 13, 17–18, 137 n. 2, 144, 153–64, 165 n. 9, 166 n. 24, 169–71

diplomacy 34–7, 39, 41, 54, 56 n. 15, 60 n. 51, 64, 77, 79, 82, 152, 169

Ebla (site, archives) 61 n. 51, 74, 96, 98–9
Egypt, Egyptian 1–4, 6, 8, 10 nn. 5, 7, 13–27, 27 nn. 3, 9, 28 nn. 17–18, 21–2, 27–9, 29 nn. 30–2, 34, 30–2, 34–5, 36–43, 45–53, 54 n. 3, 55 nn. 4, 14, 56 nn. 14, 16, 57 nn. 21, 25, 58 nn. 30–1, 38, 59 nn. 43–4, 60 nn. 48–9, 51, 61 nn. 58, 64, 62 nn. 72, 78, 67–72, 74–8, 80–1, 85 nn. 11, 13, 21, 29, 86 n. 31, 87 nn. 46, 49–50, 88 nn. 59–60, 95, 98, 101–2, 104, 119 n. 11, 124, 134, 137 n. 19, 139–42, 144, 146–7, 147 n. 4, 150–1, 154–63, 165 nn. 10, 15, 17, 168–71
elite emulation 163
Emar (site, archives) 15, 33, 118 nn. 5, 9, 139, 165 n. 6
exchange (symmetrical, asymmetrical) 5–6, 8, 16, 17, 31, 37, 39, 42, 45–6, 50–1, 52–4, 56 n. 17, 63–88, 102, 130–3, 139, 141, 147 n. 3, 149 n. 25, 151–4, 163, 169

feudal, feudalism 2–3, 9, 27, 28 n. 20, 108–9, 111–13, 117, 118 nn. 1–3, 133, 158, 162

gift 5, 31, 57 n. 26, 64, 67–72, 74, 76, 80–2, 85 n. 11, 86 n. 31, 88 nn. 57, 60, 151, 154

*ḫabiru* 3, 19, 41–2, 50, 52, 58 n. 36, 59 n. 45, 140, 142, 153, 160, 166 n. 31
*habitus* 131, 136 n. 16
historical anthropology 63, 91–2, 94, 106 n. 1
honour 5, 36, 83, 88 n. 64, 123–4, 129–34, 157, 161
hospitality 71, 79, 81–3, 88 nn. 61, 63–4, 104, 124, 137 n. 21, 166 n. 28, 170
household 61 n. 55, 82, 84 n. 3, 111, 113, 118 n. 1, 119 n. 11, 134, 138, 141–3, 146, 148 n. 15, 148 n. 20, 149 nn. 22, 28, 150–4, 161
Ḥatšepsut 68
Ḫalab 15, 18
Ḫammurabi, Code of 74, 86 n. 41
Ḫana 15
Ḫanigalbat 15–16, 85 n. 18
Ḫatti 3, 10 n. 9, 13–18, 25, 31, 39, 40–2, 44–5, 55 n. 4, 58 n. 33, 59 n. 44, 60 n. 49, 61 n. 52, 75–8, 80, 85 nn. 18–19, 101, 112–17, 119 n. 16, 134, 137 n. 19, 139, 142–5, 147, 150–4, 162, 168–70
Ḫattušili II 16/III 15, 31, 39–41, 61 n. 52, 75–6, 80, 85 n. 18, 139, 142
*ḫazannu* 49, 107 n. 11, 110, 117, 155, 164
Ḫurri 15, 153

*ilku* 34, 139
international (relations, diplomacy) 4, 13, 25, 27 n. 1, 34–42, 64, 71, 77, 81, 116, 143, 169
*inw* 19, 38, 57 n. 26, 68–70, 74, 78, 85 nn. 28–30, 86 n. 31, 87 n. 43

Jerusalem 47, 54 n. 3, 95, 102, 148 n. 17, 155, 165 n. 15

Kadašman-Enlil I 16, 40, 61 n. 52, 76, 81, 150/II 80
Karkemiš 15, 18, 85 n. 24, 142
king, kingship 2–4, 8–9, 13, 36–42, 94, 98–106, 108–19, 138–67
kinship (relation, structure) 5–6, 8, 36, 43–5, 61 n. 53, 65–6, 73, 77, 83, 95, 97–9, 103–4, 109, 111, 123, 125, 128–30, 133, 134, 136 nn. 11, 13–14, 137 n. 20, 145–6, 148 nn. 18, 20, 149 n. 29, 161, 169–70
Kizzuwatna 15, 119 n. 16
Kumidi 21, 54 n. 3
Kurizalzu I 76

*longue durée* 13, 92, 96
loyalty 3–4, 14, 22, 28 n. 27, 36, 38, 57 n. 27, 58 n. 38, 61 n. 64, 101, 112–15, 131–2, 139, 144, 149 n. 25, 150, 152–6, 161–2, 166 n. 24, 167 n. 34, 169–70

Mari (site, archives) 33, 44–5, 55 nn. 10–11, 60 n. 51, 74, 80, 86 n. 40, 87 n. 55, 99, 107 n. 13, 164 n. 1
*maryannu* 108, 110, 117, 139, 147 n. 3, 162
Megiddo 18, 22, 37, 54 n. 3
Mediterranean (anthropology of the, Eastern) 4–6, 9 n. 1, 10 n. 14, 15, 21, 28 n. 17, 32, 79, 87 n. 47, 99, 117, 123–8, 131, 135 nn. 2, 5, 7, 136 n. 9, 162–3
Mittani 1, 13–18, 20, 25, 31–2, 34, 42, 67, 76, 80–1, 87 n. 48, 101, 151, 168
Mukiš 18, 152
Muršili II 15, 114, 143, 153
Muwatalli 18, 76, 142

*naṣāru* 36, 49, 51–2
Niqmadu 152–3
Niya 15, 18
Nubia 14, 19, 21–5, 28 nn. 21, 27, 29, 29 n. 32, 56 n. 14, 67, 87 n. 50
Nuḫašše 15, 18, 54 n. 3, 114
Nuzi (site, archives) 15, 33–4, 55 n. 12, 108, 118 n. 5

ontology (native political) 9, 164, 169–70

patrimonial, patrimonialism 9, 109, 111, 113, 116–17, 118 n. 1, 119 n. 10, 129, 134, 138–47, 150, 152, 154–6, 161–3, 164 n. 1, 165 n. 10, 169–70
patron–client (relation) 5–6, 8–9, 107 n. 10, 117, 123–4, 126–34, 136 nn. 17–18, 138, 142, 147, 152, 154–5, 160, 162–4, 169–71
patronage 5–6, 9, 123, 127–34, 135–6 n. 9, 136 nn. 13–15, 18, 138, 143, 144–7, 150, 152–6, 160–4, 165 nn. 9–10, 17, 167 n. 36, 169, 171
peer polity interaction 100
political culture 7, 144, 149 n. 24, 164, 169
politics 2, 4–5, 7–9, 10 n. 16, 138–67
prestige 4, 8, 17, 40, 42, 56 n. 14, 59 n. 43, 65, 67–9, 71–2, 74–5, 80, 83, 84 n. 7, 85 n. 27, 86 n. 37, 88 nn. 57–8, 103, 105, 123, 128–33, 140, 144, 146, 159–60, 162, 166 n. 26
propaganda 41, 59 n. 43

Qadeš (site, battle) 2, 14–15, 18, 23, 54 n. 3, 114, 118 n. 8, 158

*rābiṣu* 3, 21, 70, 85 n. 13, 102, 158
Ramesses II 14, 18, 31, 39, 41, 59 n. 44, 76–7, 80, 85 n. 19/III 14
reciprocity (relation, symmetrical, asymmetrical) 4, 6, 16, 29 n. 34, 36, 48, 51–3, 58 n. 37, 65–73, 75–6, 79, 80–1, 83–4, 86 n. 37, 88 n. 63, 97, 101–2, 114–15, 128–30, 133–4, 136 n. 10, 143–4, 146–7, 150–2, 154–7, 163, 169–70
redistribution 21, 65–6, 79, 80, 84 n. 3
Rib-Hadda 29, 37, 40–1, 43, 49, 53, 60 n. 48, 85 n. 21, 103, 141–2, 155, 157, 160, 165 n. 17, 166 n. 21, 169

shame 5, 124, 129, 163
Sinuhe 29 n. 32, 56, 104
social magic 115
state (primary, secondary), statehood 2, 5–6, 8–9, 20–1, 23, 95–105, 106 n. 5, 107 n. 12
subordination (political) 3, 9, 18, 32–3, 36, 40–1, 44, 51–2, 55 n. 6, 66, 73, 103, 112–13, 115–17, 119 nn. 13, 16, 125, 129, 144–5, 150, 153–5, 158–63, 165 n. 6, 169
symbolic capital 8, 80, 88 n. 57, 97
Ṣumura 21, 158
Šalmanasar I 17
*šulmānu* 70, 82
Šuppiluliuma I 15–18, 76, 142, 152, 156, 158/II 15

Thutmose I 14/III 14, 16, 18–19, 21, 28 n. 15, 37, 38, 69, 86 n. 32/IV 14, 20, 76
tribe, tribal (organisation, state, kingdom) 5–6, 8, 34, 36, 56, 98–100, 103–5, 107

n. 13, 126, 129, 133, 136 n. 12, 137 n. 20, 141, 144, 147, 148 n. 18, 170
tribute 19–20, 23–4, 28 n. 18, 48, 51, 57 n. 26, 67–70, 72, 74, 87 n. 43, 110, 114, 119 n. 14, 153, 155
Tudḫaliya I 15–16/IV 15, 75, 85
Tukulti-ninurta I 17
Tunip 15, 18, 54 n. 3, 140, 151, 158
Tutu 36, 57 n. 20, 85 n. 21, 141, 156
Tyre 45, 54 n. 3, 159–60, 165 n. 15

Ube/Upe 21
Ugarit (site, archives) 9, 15, 18, 30–3, 36, 44–5, 54 n. 3, 55 n. 7, 57 n. 19, 58 n. 33, 60 nn. 46, 49, 75, 80, 85 nn. 11, 20–5, 99, 102, 105, 107 n. 6, 108–11, 113–14, 117, 118 nn. 1–5, 9, 119 n. 16, 138–45, 147, 147 nn. 3–4, 148 nn. 14, 16, 152–4, 158, 160–2, 164, 166 n. 32, 170

vassal, vassalage 3–4, 10 n. 8, 15, 18, 20, 22–3, 25, 28 n. 27, 29 n. 34, 38, 42, 44–6, 48, 50, 61 n. 64, 75–6, 88 n. 60, 109, 112–17, 119 n. 14, 142, 158, 163

Wenamun 56, 69

Yarimuta 22

Zakar-Baal 69